IVY WHEN YOUNG:
The early life of I. Compton-Burnett
1884–1919

DATE DUE FOR RETURN

XXXXXXXX		

This book may be recalled
before the above date

90014

IVY WHEN YOUNG

The early life of I. Compton-Burnett

1884–1919

by

HILARY SPURLING

LONDON
VICTOR GOLLANCZ LTD
1974

ISBN 0 575 01768 6

Printed in Great Britain by
The Camelot Press Ltd, London and Southampton

CONTENTS

ILLUSTRATIONS

Following page 64

Alderman Rees and his family at Dover (*photo. Grossman, Dover*)

James Compton Burnett

Katharine Rees (*photo. Lambert and Weston, Dover and Folkestone*)

Ivy at Chesilbank (*photo. Gunn and Stewart, Richmond*)

Guy at Chesilbank (*photo. Gunn and Stewart, Richmond*)

Noel at Chesilbank (*photo. Gunn and Stewart, Richmond*)

Nellie Smith (Minnie) at Hove (*photo. Mayall and Co., King's Road, Brighton*)

Vera at Hove (*photo. Edmund Wheeler, 43 Western Road, Brighton*)

Judy at Hove (*photo. Edmund Wheeler*)

Dr Compton Burnett with Topsy (*photo. Edmund Wheeler*)

The drawing room, Addiscombe College, for the Daughters of Gentlemen, Hove

Following page 176

Ivy with friends at Royal Holloway College, from a college photograph, autumn term 1902 (*courtesy of R.H.C.*)

Mrs John Compton Burnett with her pupils at Howard College, Bedford, in the 1890s

Members of staff at Royal Holloway College who supplied models for *Dolores*, from college photograph 1902 (*courtesy of R.H.C.*)

Noel at King's, from a drawing by Kennard Bliss in the *Basileon*, June 1914 (*courtesy of the Librarian, King's College, Cambridge*)

Following page 240

Compton-Burnett family group, 1912

'The Family' from Ivy's copy of *The Note-Books of Samuel Butler*, p. 31

Jack Beresford, from a painting by Lucy Graham Smith, 1913

Tertia Beresford at Easton Grey

Ivy

Dorothy Beresford before her marriage

First page of Noel's last letter to Ivy, written from the Somme on Saturday, 1 July 1916

Note in Ivy's hand, from her copy of *The Note-Books of Samuel Butler*, p. 22

FOREWORD

THE LIFE OF Ivy Compton-Burnett falls into two parts, sharply divided by the first world war. She was thirty when the war began; when it ended, her settled background, her home and occupation had all gone, and the last of the people who had mattered most to her was dead. After 1918 she drew a line beneath everything that had gone before, and drew it with a finality and force which had drastic repercussions on her life—'Ivy Compton-Burnett embodied in herself a quite unmodified pre-1914 personality', wrote Anthony Powell, describing his first meeting with her in the 1950s—as on her work. This book is an attempt to show what lay behind the split; and to suggest some of the uses to which she put the experiences of her first thirty-five years in the nineteen novels written during the next fifty.

No diaries or other papers and practically no letters written by Dame Ivy before 1919 survive, so by far the greater part of my material reached me by word of mouth. I owe more than I can say to her sisters, Miss Vera and Miss Juliet Compton-Burnett, for their generosity, patience and perseverance in reconstructing for me things that happened in the Compton-Burnett household before 1915. Without them this book could not have been written, and I have relied so heavily on their recollections that it would have been impossible to annotate each separate instance. Any quotations about their family not specifically attributed come from them; otherwise I have put references to sources and other material of small general interest in numbered notes to each chapter, listed at the back of the book. It seemed important to give these in full because so much of my information came privately, and also for the sake of anyone who may wish to check on the many factual discrepancies between this and the various other accounts of Dame Ivy's life published since her death. But curious or directly useful information is given in footnotes on the relevant page, so I hope that people who find the numbers irritating will feel that the notes to which they refer may safely be ignored throughout.

My principal unpublished sources have been Noel Compton-Burnett's letters to Oscar Browning (whose correspondence, in the possession of Hove Public Library, includes one letter apiece from Ivy and her mother), Jack Beresford, Elliott Felkin (these belong respectively to Mrs J. B. Beresford and Mrs Basil Marsden-Smedley), and Sir Charles Webster (among Webster's papers at the London School of Economics); and a number of letters from Ivy herself, kindly shown me by her cousin Katie (who prefers not to be identified more closely than this). I am much indebted to Mr Anthony Compton-Burnett for permission to quote from Dame Ivy's books and from the manuscript of *The Last and the First*, and to five people who took great pains to put their special knowledge at my disposal: Professor S. T. Bindoff for access to Webster's papers, for a survey of activities among historians at King's College, Cambridge, before the first war, and for reading and assessing Noel Compton-Burnett's fellowship thesis for me; Dr Frank Bodman for answering my queries about homoeopathic history in general, and about the career of Dr James Compton Burnett in particular, and for reading my first chapter; Mr L. R. Conisbee for investigating Ivy's schooldays in Bedford; Mrs Hilda Stowell for an exhaustive search of Hampshire records in pursuit of Richard Burnett and his son Charles Compton; and the Clacton historian, Mr Kenneth Walker, for countless details about Dame Ivy's family in north-east Essex, for examining the topographical references in *Dolores*, and for a guided tour of the sites which provided the setting for that novel.

Among Ivy's contemporaries at school and college, I am especially grateful to Mrs Marjorie E. T. Andrewes, Miss Isabel M. Bremner, Miss Mabel Eastaugh, Mrs J. A. Elliott, Miss Grace J. Fothergill and Mrs A. E. Rampal; and, among her brother's friends at King's, to Mr Leigh Farnell, Mr W. H. Haslam, Mr Raisley Moorsom and the Rt Hon. Philip Noel-Baker.

My next heavy debt is to Ivy's many friends who spared neither time nor trouble to help me, particularly to members of the Beresford, Kidd and Felkin families—Mrs J. B. Beresford, Mrs Alan Kidd, Mrs Elliott Felkin, Miss Rosemary Beresford, Mr and Mrs Benedict Beresford, Mrs Penelope Douglas, Mr and Mrs Roger Kidd; Mrs Basil Marsden-Smedley for making available Ivy's books and letters; Walter and Barbara Robinson for showing me their letters, and their invaluable 'Notes of Conversations Between Ourselves and Ivy'; Elizabeth Taylor for allowing me to see the letters which she wrote to Robert Liddell describing what had passed each time she took lunch or tea with Ivy; and to Mr Liddell himself for suggesting that I see these letters, for showing me his own, and for his guidance when I first began this book.

This is not the place to thank all the people who knew Ivy after 1919, but I should like to thank all those who cast light on her early life: Lady Ashton, Mr Simon Blow, Mr Rex Britcher, Miss Eva Fox, Dr George Furlong, Miss Cicely Greig, Mr Soame Jenyns, Mr Francis King, Mrs Viva King, Miss Olivia Manning, Mr Julian Mitchell, Mrs George Orwell, Mrs Graham Rawson, Miss Elizabeth Sprigge, Mrs Arthur Waley and Mr Francis Wyndham.

I am also grateful to the following for advice, information and permission to reproduce or quote from material in their possession: Mrs Margaret Aldridge, Mr C. G. Allen of the London School of Economics, Messrs Edward Arnold, Mr T. A. Baker of the Clacton branch of Essex County Library, the Rev. A. J. W. Barker Vicar of Dent, Miss Patricia Bell Bedfordshire County Archivist, Professor Ian A. Boyd, Mrs Violet Bower, Dr Peter Burnett, Mr Richard Burton of Royal Holloway College, Mr Christopher Carter ('Touchstone' of the *Bedfordshire Times*), Mr Michael Clapham, Mr and Mrs Percy Compton-Burnett, Mr Raymond A. Cook, Mr Arthur Cook Editor of the *Times Literary Supplement*, Miss Kay Dick and Messrs. Duckworth, Mr C. Dobson Headmaster of King Edward VI School Southampton, Mr Jack Dove Librarian of Hove Central Library, Miss Elizabeth Ellem of King's College Library, Dr Ulick R. Evans, Mr David Fletcher of William Blackwood and Sons, Professor John Fletcher, Mr P. N. Furbank, Dr A. C. Gordon Ross, Mr I. W. Green, Mr Lionel Hale General Secretary of the British Homoeopathic Association, Mr John B. Hall of Dover Harbour Board, Mrs Norah Harvey-Lloyd, Miss Gwenda Haynes-Thomas, the Rev. Edward Hayward, the House Governor of the Hospital for Sick Children Great Ormond Street, Miss J. L. Hurn Registrar of Royal Holloway College, Miss Enid Johnson, Colonel Johnson, Mr M. Jolliffe Librarian of Royal Holloway College, Mrs Leonard Humphreys, Mr W. R. Mowll, Dr A. N. L. Munby Librarian of King's College, Mrs L. D. O'Nions Librarian of Hastings Public Library, Miss Derryan Paul Archivist of Royal Holloway College, Mr Eric J. B. Pearson, Mr Anthony Powell, Mrs Margaret Powell, the Rev. J. Pringle Vicar of Owslebury, Sir Dennis Proctor, Mr Maurice G. Rathbone Wiltshire County Archivist, Professor O. L. Richmond, Mr A. J. Ricketts Dover Borough Librarian, Miss Lucy Robertson of Edinburgh University Library, Mr Neil Robertson of Glasgow University, Miss Seeley M. Sherbrooke, Miss L. I. Smith, Mrs Stoll of the Faculty Library Royal London Homoeopathic Hospital, Mr Storey of the Historical Manuscripts Commission, Mr R. J.

Thomas of Mowll and Mowll, Mrs Geoffrey Toulmin, Mr Stephen Toulmin, the Rev. Canon C. Wells Rural Dean of Winchester, Mr N. C. Wilde of Bedford Central Library, Mr A. C. Young of the Royal London Homoeopathic Hospital Management Committee.

Lastly, I should like to thank Sybille Bedford for reading my manuscript and D. H. Smith for designing my book jacket.

I did not know Dame Ivy, and it is with considerable misgiving that I write of her on first-name terms, but I could see no alternative which, repeated too often, would not sound either clumsy or longwinded.

HILARY SPURLING

IVY WHEN YOUNG:

The early life of I. Compton-Burnett

1884–1919

CHAPTER ONE

Parents and Grandparents

I

'The pinch of poverty and the weirdness of want'

THE BURNETTS OF HAMPSHIRE lived, at the turn of the eighteenth century, in a place called Gavelacre on the banks of the River Test, some eleven miles from Winchester along the old Roman road to the east of Salisbury plain. There are records of fishing and farming Burnetts in the county for hundreds of years before that, many of them as humble and no doubt as difficult to trace as the Gavelacre Burnetts who seem to have lived in the parish at least since 1737, and who remained there until well into the nineteenth century as labourers or small tenant farmers. Gavelacre Farm was not large enough to support more than one tenant so that younger sons like Richard and William Burnett, born in 1779 and 1790, had to seek their fortunes elsewhere. Both described themselves as yeomen, though neither was strictly entitled to the claim, since their family owned no land. Judging by gaps in the registers at their own and the half-dozen neighbouring parishes, these Burnetts were probably nonconformist; but all that can be said with certainty is that both left home in their early twenties, and both married sisters called Compton.

The Comptons of Winchester were well-to-do tradesmen: John Compton (who was born in 1749) was a blacksmith, his only son was a watchmaker and, by way of a dowry for his two daughters, he lent each of his sons-in-law £300. Richard Burnett married Catherine Maria Compton at St Maurice's, Winchester, on 29 October 1803. Eight years later his younger brother William married her sister Anne. The younger couple had six children, the elder seven who were nearly all baptized in their mother's name of Compton, so that in the early years of the nineteenth century there were two young families of Compton Burnetts growing up on small, rented farms close to Winchester. By the middle of the century several of the more ambitious sons of the first marriage had moved to the large coastal towns, Southampton or Portsmouth, where they became shopkeepers, coal merchants, corn dealers, while the abler of their sons in turn entered the professions.

Within three generations at least one branch of the family had abandoned farming, left Hampshire and severed all connection with trade.
Richard Burnett's grandson James was an eminently successful doctor,
with a large London practice and a country villa at Pinner, by the time
that the seventh of his thirteen children, Ivy Compton-Burnett, was
born on 5 June 1884.

How much Ivy knew of this family history is doubtful. Intermarriage
between pairs of brothers and sisters, a recurrent theme in her books,
was a common enough pattern among cousins and uncles and aunts on
both sides of the family in her own and her parents' generations, producing sometimes rather more complex relationships than the fairly
straightforward union of the Compton sisters with the Burnett brothers
some eighty years before she was born. Family tradition seems to have
been vague on the matter, asserting only that the Burnetts descended
originally from the seventeenth-century historian Bishop Burnet; this
belief is repeated in a biography of Ivy's father by his friend Dr Clarke,*
who probably had it at first hand from Dr or Mrs Compton Burnett.
Dr Clarke's description of more immediate ancestors is short but suggestive: 'The name Compton was taken about the year 1770, on the
marriage of James' grandfather with a Miss Compton of Hampshire, a
lady of large fortune, at whose desire the addition was made.' The
summary is accurate (except for the date), and interesting because it
seems likely that none of her great-grandchildren knew that this Miss
Compton was a blacksmith's daughter, and her fortune a loan of £300.
Ivy herself, when asked where her family came from, gave much the
same account as her father's biographer: 'James Compton Burnett
descended from an old Scotch family, the younger branch of which
came south. A notable member of this branch was Gilbert Burnet,
Bishop of Salisbury . . . who flourished from 1643 to 1715. From him
James Compton directly descended.'[1]

Gilbert Burnet (the younger son of an Aberdeen advocate, and
nephew to the ancient Scottish family of baronets called Burnet or
Burnett whose line still continues) left Scotland round about 1675 for
London where, being a Whig of stern moral principles and fond of

* *Life and Work of James Compton Burnett, M.D.*, by J. H. Clarke. This is a strictly
professional life (the few facts in Dr Clarke's brief biographical section evidently
reached him on hearsay and are often misleading), written shortly after Dr Burnett's
death and intended as at once a valediction and a vindication of the homoeopathic
faction to which both Clarke and Burnett belonged. Though somewhat sketchy at
times, for reasons of professional discretion (see chapter six), it provides a sympathetic
portrait by a close friend and colleague.

speaking his mind on both counts, he pursued a fairly tricky course at court. He reformed the Earl of Rochester in a spectacular deathbed conversion, but failed signally to do the same for Charles II. Withdrawing to The Hague he was outlawed under James for high treason, and returned at the abdication in high favour with William and Mary. He had three wives, three sons and two daughters (one of whom was mother to the poet Gray's friend Richard West, who died young, believing that his mother had murdered his father); his fame rests chiefly on his skill as a brilliantly racy though by no means impartial historian of his own times. Dr Clarke detected in this ancestry 'the source whence Dr Burnett's mental vigour was derived' and, even allowing for a gap of two centuries, the resemblance between the two men is sufficiently striking. The Bishop's robust prose style is informed by vast knowledge and an equally prodigious memory; his nature was fiery and furiously inquisitive; his contemporaries were divided between those who marvelled at his extraordinary personal magnetism and those who, like Swift, smarted under his reforming zeal, his vituperative pamphlets and 'a boisterous vehement manner of expressing himself'[2] peculiarly exasperating to his enemies. On all these counts, and perhaps especially the last, one might well argue a close affinity between Bishop Burnet and his supposed descendant, James Compton Burnett; and one might even extend the likeness to some of the formidable fathers depicted in James' daughter's books.

But, appropriate though the Bishop may seem as an ancestor for I. Compton-Burnett, he must unfortunately be discarded for at least two reasons. In the first place, there were Burnetts living in the Test valley near Winchester long before the Bishop left Scotland; and even supposing that one of his sons or grandsons had happened to settle in Hampshire, among a whole tribe of completely unconnected English Burnetts, it is barely conceivable that the descendants of so prominent a statesman, diplomat and churchman should have sunk, in so short a time, to become obscure nonconformist tenant farmers, marrying the daughters of a Winchester tradesman and showing no sign whatever of patronage from anyone more important than their local squire.* In the

* See Appendix i for a fuller account of Ivy's ancestry. Anthony Powell, in a letter to the author, confirms that the extraordinary number of mariners, seafaring characters and husbandmen named Burnett recorded in the Winchester and Southampton areas before and during the eighteenth century 'clearly indicates that the Hampshire Burnetts were modestly placed over a long period. . . . If one accepts this, the conclusion is that there was *not enough time* for the Bishop's family to have emigrated to Hampshire and gone down hill on quite such a steep and numerous scale. . . .'

second place, the Bishop's male line ended with a single great-grandson, born in 1740, who was a surgeon at Chigwell in Essex and died there, leaving one unmarried daughter.[3]

It is not hard to see how the claim to the Bishop arose in a family as energetically determined to rise in the world as the Compton Burnetts seem to have been. Little is known of Ivy's great-grandfather, the Richard Burnett of Gavelacre who had left home to be married in 1803, save that he obtained enough money from his father-in-law to take a tenancy from the lord of the manor of Wherwell (the next hamlet, a mile or so downstream from Gavelacre Farm) where he impressed the vicar sufficiently to become in the next ten years his church warden and parish overseer. Charles Compton Burnett, Ivy's grandfather and the youngest of Richard's four sons, was born at Wherwell in 1811. He was married on 5 June 1834 to Sarah Wilson, the daughter of a small farmer some thirty miles south at Alverstoke. His sister, Martha Compton Burnett, had married Sarah's brother Jesse one month before. Two years later Charles' eldest brother, Richard, married Agnes Wilson and, when Martha died in her twenties, Jesse Wilson took as his second wife Ann Compton Burnett, youngest sister to Charles and Richard and Martha (an illegal match, since it was not until 1907 that a man was permitted by act of parliament to marry his deceased wife's sister). Ivy's ancestors might well have agreed with the girl who said in one of her books: 'I think we are overdoing this intermarrying.'*

Ivy's father, James, the youngest child of the second of these four marriages, was born on 21 July 1840, 'at Redlynch near Salisbury, his father being', according to Dr Clarke, 'a considerable landowner in the neighbourhood'.[4] But Charles Compton Burnett had moved just over the Wiltshire border to Redlynch less than a year before James was born. He described himself (like his father before him, and with no better claim) as a yeoman but, since he does not appear on the local Tithe Apportionment or on the electoral register, he can hardly have owned any land in the district. He moved about and switched jobs all his life, and he seems to have been a farm labourer in the early part of James' boyhood. James himself acquired in these years an abiding love of the country which he later shared with his daughter Ivy. His own

---

* *Elders and Betters*, p.222. The *Cambridge Review* for 29 October 1907 reported a telling speech by Ivy's brother Noel in his first debate at the Union against the motion, 'That this House regrets the Deceased Wife's Sister's Act'; but there is no means of knowing whether Noel's support of the new bill had anything to do with the marriages of his great aunts, Martha and Ann Compton Burnett.

recollections of birds nesting and fishing, of collecting tips from woodmen on the cure of snake-bite or how to charm warts, are invariably
happy (save that once, 'with the help of a village apothecary and half-a-
hogshead of mixture', he had nearly died of pleurisy). Otherwise he
was a dreamy child, tall and sturdy, dark-eyed, dark-haired and clear-
skinned, fond of exploring the woods alone and 'always thoughtful
beyond his years'. He had an elder brother Charles and a sister Sarah,
aged five and three when he was born, but he seems to have been
closest to his brother John who was one year older; and he was especially devoted to his mother, often recalling her later to his own children,
and writing always with the utmost respect and enthusiasm of mothers
in general.

When James was ten or eleven his father moved to Southampton
and set up shop at 74 French Street, in what was then one of the poorer
parts of the city. James' uncle, Richard Compton Burnett, had been
living for some time in West Street where he worked as a labourer and
his wife, Agnes, as a dress- and straw-bonnet-maker. Another uncle,
William, was a general dealer in Gosport. Charles himself a few years
later started a small coal-and-corn-dealing business which (with help
from his brother Richard) he ran for the next ten years from the same
address. Southampton possessed already several families of rather more
prosperous Burnetts, among them an accountant named John James
Burnett who, though evidently unrelated to the Compton Burnetts, is
interesting because of his ancestry. John James claimed descent from the
naval physician-general Sir William Burnett, a surgeon in Nelson's
fleet who was decorated as a young man at Trafalgar and knighted a
quarter of a century later for medical reforms in the navy. What is
interesting is that John James' ancestor was a Scotsman who came south
to make his career in England like the seventeenth-century Bishop
Burnet; and perhaps it was this which suggested a similarly illustrious
pedigree to John James' neighbour, the coal dealer, Charles Compton
Burnett. The claim was unquestioningly accepted by Charles' descendants, and the whole affair passed so rapidly into family legend that by
the time Ivy grew up her father even had an engraving of Sir William
Burnett hanging on his walls for good measure.*

---

* Listed in the estate agent's brochure when the contents of Dr Burnett's house were
sold in 1915.

Sir William (1779–1861) came from much the same part of Scotland as Bishop
Burnet's family, but there seems to have been no more connection between the
Stuart bishop and the Victorian surgeon than between the two Southampton families

Times must often have been hard for James and his brothers in the days when their father was attempting to establish a footing for himself in Southampton. All hands were needed in the family business and, though the three boys were no doubt already destined by their parents for the professional classes, they may well have been required to help alongside their uncle and various cousins in the shop, or with the numerous sidelines started by their father in the 1850s. Charles and John both eventually became Congregationalist ministers, harking back perhaps to the original Gavelacre Burnetts who had probably attended the Congregationalist chapel at Andover. James himself had always wanted to be a doctor. He afterwards held strong views on a sound education, and proved a liberal parent in this respect to his daughter Ivy; but, though he seems to have attended the village school as a small boy at Redlynch, there are no records of James or his brothers at King Edward's grammar school in Southampton. His biographer is vague at this point, saying only that he left school at sixteen, finished his education in France and 'travelled for several years, principally on the continent' before he arrived round about 1865 at the medical school in Vienna. Tuition at Vienna was free, a subject on which James later felt keenly: 'It is right to explain that this has been a common thing in German universities from time immemorial, and it is not there thought by any means an undignified thing to receive gratuitous instruction, as it is the *right* of poor students, especially such as matriculate with honour. . . .'* James' father can have been in no position to support him at this time for, though he seems to have flourished in the 'fifties and early 'sixties as a dealer and carrier of corn and coal (operating at one point, jointly with his brother Richard, from three different addresses), he had abandoned the business by 1865, becoming instead a dairyman at Millbrook, two miles outside Southampton. Four years later, just before his son left Vienna to take an M.B. at Glasgow, Charles had moved again to Pinks Farm at Dibden, where he leased three fields (one arable, two pasture, just enough to keep a horse) and remained for

* *Ecce Medicus*, p.17. According to Kay Dick (*Ivy and Stevie*, p.27), Ivy said that her father had studied under Freud in Vienna, but Freud was nine years old at the time.

named Burnett who severally laid claim to these ancestors. A fanciful turn of mind in the Compton Burnetts is borne out by a later and even wilder claim, on the part of Ivy's cousins, to be related to the romantic authoress Frances Hodgson Burnett (*née* Hodgson in 1849 at Manchester, emigrated as a child to America where she married and later divorced a citizen of Knoxville, Tennessee, named Swan Moses Burnett).

the next decade. One may perhaps detect fellow feeling in Dr Compton Burnett's word, delivered years later, on another brilliant medical student: 'he knew but too well the pinch of poverty and the weirdness of want'.[5]

Ivy never knew her paternal grandfather, who died the year before she was born. Her father, who was fond of recalling in middle age the woods and fields of his boyhood, seldom spoke of his early struggles or indeed of anything that had happened in the fifteen years between his leaving Redlynch and reaching Vienna. Ivy's own friends in later life generally assumed that she came, as the families do in her books, of a long line of country squires settled for hundreds of years in the same place.* In fact she had moved with her family four times before she was fourteen, living on housing estates or in brand new suburban developments and hearing practically nothing about her Compton Burnett relations. The setting she later chose for her novels was the traditional one, hallowed by literary precedent, providing ample scope and a stable background for the tyrannical passions which chiefly absorbed her attention. She herself had always known comfort and material security in a provincial society where class distinctions seemed paramount and immutable; the family history remained in her childhood largely unknown save for what might be built on a few Wilson teaspoons, the engraving of Sir William Burnett and a photograph of Compton village church in Wiltshire which hung in one of the bedrooms. In so far as she cared about her ancestors at all, Ivy accepted the story that her great-grandfather had married a Miss Compton who brought him a fortune. This fortune was said to have been recklessly squandered by her great-uncles, 'all of whom died on the hunting field save one, and he was kicked to death by his horse in the stable'.[6] But the second part of this story had mellowed with time as much as the first since, of Ivy's three Compton Burnett great-uncles, one was in middle age a labourer whose wife sold straw bonnets in Southampton; and another was a grocer who died at seventy-six of bronchitis, leaving £46 14s. 2d, when Ivy was one year old.

---

* 'Originally, she [Ivy] told me, her family came from Wiltshire, the village of Compton; she was a descendant of a Bishop Burnett [sic] who married a Miss Compton. The family, to use her word, was "raised" on an estate, and one appreciated the truth of this in her fiction.' (Ivy and Stevie, p.27.) Miss Dick's account may conveniently serve to typify the muddled impression Ivy contrived to leave on her friends; whether or not she actively put it about that she was raised on an estate, the assumption was certainly one she did nothing to contradict.

Her father by this time had long since lost sight of his Hampshire connections. But the break with his family was probably not as decisive, and certainly not as dramatic, as the break he had also made at the very start of his career with the medical profession. As a young man in the medical school at Vienna James Compton Burnett seems to have been in his element, charmed by his studies, by the place itself and by the German language. For the rest of his life his conversation and writings were peppered with anecdotes of his student days on the continent, with Viennese proverbs, quotations from Schiller and practical cures picked up on his travels. He is said to have spent an extra two years studying anatomy for pleasure at Vienna—'my own dear old alma mater', as he afterwards called it—and acquitted himself so well that, when he finally returned to enrol at the Glasgow medical school, he was permitted to take his M.B. in one year instead of the usual three or four. But, on graduating in 1872 amid the congratulations of his professors, he took a post at the Barnhill Parochial Hospital and Asylum in Glasgow where he was promptly converted to homoeopathy, a step which in those days meant professional death.

Dr Burnett had left university with strictly orthodox medical views, 'having been taught by good men and true that Homoeopathy was therapeutic Nihilism'.[7] This was the current view at the time, often expressed with a great deal more virulence. Homoeopathy in Britain was confined to a more or less persecuted sect, actively ridiculed in the universities and widely despised outside them. Its followers were looked upon as quacks or cranks, its practice had narrowly escaped being declared illegal in the 1850s and the British Medical Association pro- hibited homoeopaths from joining its ranks. The professor of anatomy at Glasgow in 1873 had begged his most promising pupil not to throw his life away, for it was true that, as Dr Burnett himself afterwards bitterly put it, 'the social value of [surgery] is—a baronetcy. The social value of [homoeopathic remedies] is—slander and contempt.'* When urged not to abandon orthodox medicine, Dr Burnett had declared that 'he could not buy worldly honours at the cost of his conscience',[8] but one may readily detect behind his conscientious objection an equally keen resentment of received authority. Perhaps because of his

* *Tumours of the Breast*, p.15. One cannot help suspecting that the source of this par- ticular outburst was Sir James Paget (George Eliot's physician and serjeant-surgeon to Queen Victoria, created a baronet in 1871) whose consulting rooms were across the road from Burnett's, and who regularly figures in the doctor's writings as a notorious enemy.

early hardships, there was something about social ostracism which suited him. The aggressive and dictatorial impulses which play such a large part in the novels of I. Compton-Burnett were by no means unknown to her father. He remained all his life uncompromisingly independent and furiously scornful of nervous hesitation or compromise in other people. His immediate reaction, on resolving to try a first experiment in homoeopathy, suggests already the belligerent streak in his character which was later to be fully developed: 'I would try the thing at the bedside, prove it to be a lying sham, and expose it to an admiring profession'.

He was thirty-two years old. He had reached without help against substantial odds a point at which a brilliant career was confidently predicted ahead of him. But he had been increasingly discouraged for some time and, considering the wretched conditions under which poor medical students and inexperienced young doctors then worked in the ill-ventilated, overcrowded, smallpox- and cholera-ridden tenements of Glasgow, it is scarcely surprising that Dr Burnett, in his first post at Barnhill, had half determined to throw up medicine altogether and emigrate as a farmer to America. His own account of what happened next admirably conveys both the extreme vehemence of his nature, whether in passive despair or energetic reaction, and the tender, even shrinking sensibility which is evident in all his clinical writings and which—together with his passionate regard for truth and his considerable gifts as a storyteller—he later passed on to his daughter Ivy:

A number of years ago, on a dull dreary afternoon, which I had partly occupied at B— Hospital with writing death certificates, I suddenly rose and felt something come over me, for the fiftieth time at that period. I hardly knew what, but it grew essentially out of my unsatisfactory clinical results. I had been an enthusiastic student of medicine originally, but an arrantly sceptic professor quite knocked the bottom out of all my faith in physic, and overmuch hospital work and responsibilities, grave beyond my age and experience, had squeezed a good deal of the enthusiasm out of me. After pacing up and down the surgery, I threw myself back into my chair and dreamily thought myself back to the green fields and the early bird's-nesting and fishing days of my childhood. Just then a corpse was carried by the surgery window, and I turned to the old dispenser, and enquired in a petulant tone, 'Tim, who's that dead now?' 'Little Georgie, sir.'

Now little Georgie was a waif who belonged to nobody, and we had liked him and had kept him about in odd beds, as one might keep a pet animal. Everybody liked little Georgie; the most hardened old pauper would do him a good turn, and no one was ever more truly regretted than he.

It all came about in this way: One day I wanted a bed for an acute case, and I ordered little Georgie out of his bed in a warm, snug corner, to another that was in front of a cold window; he went to it, caught cold, had pleurisy, and Tim's reply gives the result.

Said I to myself: If I could only have stopped the initial fever that followed the chill by the window, Georgie had probably lived. But three medical men besides myself had treated Georgie—all in unison —and all hospital men; still pleurisy followed the febricula, dropsy followed the pleurisy, and poor little Georgie died. Old Tim was a hardened man, and I never saw him shew any feeling or sentiment of any kind, or regret at anybody's death, but I verily believe he was very near dropping just one wee tear over Georgie's memory, for I noticed that his attention was needlessly and unwontedly fixed on the surface of the bottles he was washing. Be that as it may, Georgie was no more, and I FELT SURE HE NEED NOT HAVE DIED, and this consciousness nearly pressed me down into the earth.[9]

Confiding his despondency that night to his friend Alfred Hawkes at the Royal Infirmary, who recommended homoeopathy, Dr Burnett furtively purchased—'very much as if I were contemplating a crime'— Richard Hughes' two manuals, on pharmacodynamics and therapeutics, which at that time provided the standard introduction in English to this dangerous ground:

I mastered their main points in a week or two, and came from a consideration of these to the conclusion either that Homoeopathy was a very grand thing indeed, or this Dr Hughes must be a very big ——. No, the word is unparliamentary. You don't like the word ——? Well, I do, it expresses my meaning to a T; on such an important subject there is for me no middle way, it must be either good clear God's truth, or black lying.

One hundred years later, the sequel is still remembered with awe in homoeopathic circles. Hughes had suggested aconite as a remedy for simple fever and Dr Burnett determined to test the advice on his children's fever ward, dosing all the patients down one side with Fleming's Tincture of Aconite and treating the others as usual. Within twenty-four hours all the aconite children were cured (save one who had measles) and smartly discharged, while the rest still languished in hospital. The experiment was repeated with the same startling results until a truculent nurse, impatient of the doctor's hard heart, dosed all the patients indiscriminately from 'Dr Burnett's Fever Bottle' and emptied the ward.

The doctor was 'simply dumbfounded', spent his nights reading homoeopathic literature and, having suffered a conversion which he afterwards compared to St Paul's on the road to Damascus, instantly resolved 'to fight the good fight of homoeopathy with all the power I possess: were I to do less I should be afraid to die'.[10] His M.D. thesis, submitted when his year's term at Barnhill elapsed, was rejected for heretical, homoeopathic tendencies (a second thesis was accepted in 1876). But early in 1874 Dr Burnett had found an opening in Chester, attracted no doubt by its nearness to Liverpool which rivalled London as a centre of homoeopathic activity. Liverpool was the seat of Dr John Drysdale, founding editor of the *British Journal of Homoeopathy*, who very soon became 'Burnett's chief hero among his contemporaries'. Drysdale was then in his late fifties, had qualified at Edinburgh and spent several years in the great continental medical schools before settling in Liverpool, where his successes in the cholera epidemic of 1849 had so 'roused the envy of his allopathic colleagues' that he was forthwith 'expelled from the Liverpool Medical Institute'. Eight years later the Liverpool Homoeopathic Society was founded, and it was largely because of Drysdale's perseverance that there grew up around him a group of ambitious young homoeopaths (including Burnett's future biographer, John Clarke, and his Glasgow friend Alfred Hawkes), among whom Dr Burnett evidently found himself in congenial company.

He does not seem to have had consulting rooms of his own in Chester, though he afterwards described treating patients at the Chester dispensary which operated from Pepper Street in rooms given free by a homoeopathic chemist named Edward Thomas.[11] Edward Thomas' son John later became a homoeopathic physician, and so did his brother Henry who lived in Whitefriars where Dr Burnett also had lodgings. Homoeopaths in those days had no choice but to hang together in cliques which perhaps explains why, almost as soon as he arrived in Chester, Dr Burnett began paying court to Edward Thomas' daughter

Agnes. She was twenty-one when she met him, presumably through her father or uncle, and they were married shortly afterwards on 6 July 1874. It was a bold move for a newly qualified young doctor without means of his own, especially since Agnes (who was the eldest of ten) cannot have brought him much of a dowry. Her father had inherited a printing business (later producing, among other homoeopathic works, several of his son-in-law's books) in Bridge Street Row next door to his chemist's shop (which stocked 'Homoeopathic Cocoa, Tooth Powder, Pomade etc. etc.' as well as homoeopathic medicines and literature); he was also a practising homoeopathic vet, much in demand among local farmers to look over their diseased pigs, cattle and horses. Within a few months of his marriage Dr Burnett had moved to Liverpool, setting up his plate in what were probably rented premises at 51 Hamilton Square, Birkenhead, where his first child, Olive, was born in 1875. He had a son, James, two years later and another daughter, Margaret (called Daisy), in 1878, by which time he could afford to move his family and consulting rooms a few doors down the square to a house of his own at number seventeen.[12]

He had prospered from the start in Liverpool where he was house surgeon at the homoeopathic dispensary in Hardman Street, pursued a stiff programme of scientific research, read papers to the Homoeopathic Society, became a voluminous contributor to medical journals and built up for himself a practice so thriving that, years later, devoted patients still travelled down from the north to consult him in London. He seems to have drawn this practice chiefly from the local gentry, regularly visiting the country seats of neighbouring squires (where he noted that the horses sent to fetch him in a trap from the station were impressively faster and smarter, in cases of grave illness, than the ambling grass-fed ponies considered quite adequate for routine calls) and growing exceedingly familiar with what he called 'your thoroughly gouty individual' (for whom, in spite of his local reputation as a fierce teetotaller, Dr Burnett prescribed Scotch whisky as often as not). His fame spread fast. Dr Clarke, who was himself no mean physician, considered Dr Burnett 'one of the most remarkable Healers of modern times';[13] and certainly the doctor's own clinical records contain several instances of what must have seemed to his patients little short of miraculous cures.

As 'a struggling young doctor'[14] he had against all expectation speedily cured one important lady in the north of hepatalgia, earning both her gratitude and a notable access of patients. He rescued two maniacal ladies—one of them so violent that it took three or four people to fetch her away in a reinforced carriage—in the nick of time from imprisonment in lunatic asylums for life, being stoutly resisted in both cases by sceptical friends and relations. He was called in May 1875 to examine a case of acute ophthalmia which, being 'specially anxious to make a hit', he cured right away to his patient's amazement; whereupon he treated her cataract so dramatically that, hearing a commotion in his hall one day, he found his door burst open as she stormed his consulting room crying aloud that she had recovered her sight. The case 'made a considerable stir', all the more so because the lady had been distinctly ashamed (as his patients commonly were) of having any truck with a homoeopath in the first place: one testy squire, suffering horribly from eczema, made the dire mistake of consulting in 1874 an eminent skin specialist who 'used such language about me professionally that my patient would not allow my name to be mentioned in his house for nearly three years'. Repenting too late, the luckless old gentleman returned to Dr Burnett only to die of an ossified heart brought on by the ministrations of the malevolent skin doctor.

This cautionary tale, narrated with marked relish, is typical of Dr Burnett's many subsequent encounters with orthodox practitioners—'our friends, the enemy' as he habitually called them—in a lifelong campaign which reached major proportions when, in August 1879, he was appointed editor of the *Homoeopathic World*. This mild and comparatively obscure monthly paper became an offensive weapon in the hands of its new editor, who devoted his very first leader that September to rallying the homoeopathic troops behind him against the medical establishment: 'We are free men, and we refuse to allow our rights to free thought and free action to be trampled under foot by any earthly powers whatsoever. It is useless to prate about peace, there is no peace but the peace of the manacled and the fettered.'

For the next five years Dr Burnett breathed flame, waging a regular feud with the *Lancet* ('The Egyptians worshipped their leeks and onions, in fact grew their gods in their own gardens, and British surgeons worship their *Lancet*, and of course are bound by their religious vows. . . .')[15] which that paper returned with interest. It was common practice in his day for both doctors and eminent patients to disclaim publicly any connection with homoeopathy. Professional medical bodies forbade their members to consult with, or even to meet, their homoeopathic colleagues: 'We shall not condescend to treat such vulgar trade-unionists and ratteners other than with contempt,' wrote Dr

Burnett when the Royal College of Surgeons of Ireland passed a resolution to this effect. 'They must feel their position insecure, and so it is,
or they would not so far forget themselves. THEY MERELY WANT THE
MONOPOLY, and no means seems too bad to get it.' Orthodox chemists
refused to stock, and orthodox medical journals to advertise, homoeopathic medicines or literature. The medical journals would not willingly
print contributions which so much as mentioned the name of homoeopathy or its founder: 'Now we will not only not omit them, but WE
WILL have them WRIT LARGE,' wrote Dr Burnett excitedly in his own
journal.

As a freedom fighter, a furious polemicist, an outstanding diagnos-
tician and a scientific researcher whose name had penetrated even
orthodox medical circles, he rapidly became one of the acknowledged
leaders of homoeopathy. He had left Liverpool for London a few
months before he took over the *Homoeopathic World*, moving his family
to Lewisham, where his son James died of concussion in May 1879,[16]
and where his second son, Richard, was born the following October.
Iris was born at 4 Harley Place sixteen months later, by which time Dr
Burnett must already have been looking for a larger place with a garden
in the more salubrious air outside London. By 1881 he had reached a
position sufficiently solid to do so. He had published the first six of his
twenty-six medical books, had a seat on the medical committee of the
London Homoeopathic Hospital and two years later a lectureship at the
hospital's medical school. He had begun treating patients at the
homoeopathic headquarters in Finsbury Circus but very soon moved
to a better address near Harley Street, retaining both practices to the
end of his life. He started at much the same time to invest in speculative
property development and, in September 1881, acquired a house deep
in the country—No. 2 Onslow Villas, Woodridings, Pinner—in which
to install his wife and children while he himself travelled daily to
London.

Agnes presumably welcomed this arrangement. Relations between
Dr Burnett and the Thomases seem to have been cordial, judging at
any rate by the fact that Agnes' father began contributing veterinary
notes to the *Homoeopathic World* soon after his son-in-law became
editor, starting with a case of Red Mange in a dog named Percy in
January 1882. Shortly afterwards Agnes' uncle was writing on gall-
stones from Llandudno (where he had opened a hydro); and one may
perhaps deduce from an energetic defence by the editor of homoeopathic chemists in general ('A special training is absolutely needful, and

also capacity, and above all *conscientiousness*. . . .'),[17] printed immediately below Edward Thomas' first article, that Dr Burnett thoroughly approved of his father-in-law. Agnes had spent all her life in the north, surrounded by a large and affectionate family from whom she had scarcely been parted for, even when she moved to a home of her own, it was still no great distance to her father's house in Pepper Street, Chester. She was greatly attached to her nine younger brothers and sisters who, according to one of her nieces, were all 'deeply fond of her' in return. In Birkenhead she had lived above the consulting rooms but, considering the vast amount of work her husband accomplished in their first seven years of marriage, she can never have been used to spending much time in his company. She bore him six children and died, survived by the last, in childbirth at Pinner on 8 September 1882. Twelve months and three days later Dr Burnett was married again to Katharine Rees, the beautiful daughter of Alderman Rowland Rees, J.P., civil engineer, architect and prospective Mayor of Dover.

Fools, imbeciles, idiots and donkeys'

KATHARINE REES WAS twenty-seven when she married and had long
been accustomed to admiration. Her father, the Alderman, was a
prominent citizen of Dover, a prime mover in local controversy and a
pillar of the Methodist chapel. She herself had 'the high, arched nose
and high, arched brow, the full blue eye and short but finished build'[18]
which, nearly half a century later, her daughter Ivy passed on to Sophia
Stace in *Brothers and Sisters*. Her long golden hair was famous in her
family and so was the story that, when Queen Victoria came to Dover,
Katie joined the procession and rode round the town with her sister
Lizzie acknowledging applause and bowing to the populace from an
open carriage. Years later she liked to tell over to her daughters the long
list of suitors rejected in her youth, among them a future judge whom
she had seriously considered but turned down for his pompous address;
whereupon her stepmother said, 'My dear, be careful. You may do this
once too often.'

She fell ill not long afterwards and is said to have been convalescing
with her married sister Lizzie when she met her husband by chance in
the winter of 1882. The Reeses were already homoeopathic enthusiasts
and they had relations in Liverpool named Thomas who, whether or
not they belonged to the same family as Dr Burnett's first wife, were
probably the indirect means of introducing him to his second.[19]
Whatever the connection, rumours from Liverpool had so impressed
Katharine's brother-in-law that he took her up to town to consult Dr
Burnett, who instantly fell in love with her. Five years after their
marriage her husband gave, as the twenty-sixth of his *Fifty Reasons for
Being a Homoeopath*, his own account of this meeting:

It may be half a dozen years ago that an unusually beautiful, sweet
girl, a good way in her twenties, residing in an important provincial
town, was noticed to fade and get weak, with peculiar ill-defined
throat symptoms, weakness in her back, rectal and uterine irritation,
weakness and emaciation. People could not think what had come over
her. She is one of those human high-breds who will not cave in, but,

if duty calls, will go on till they drop: till then, existing on their 'go' rather than on their physique.

In life they are commonly misunderstood, and because they can put on a spurt or clear a very high-fenced difficulty *au besoin*, the un-knowing and non-observant think they are really strong, but are lazy or sham.

'Oh! she nursed her nieces for weeks and never had her clothes off, but did not seem to mind it a bit, and now she would have you believe she is so delicate; she shams, it's all put on.' But it is not put on at all; if you will examine their heads you will find the animal sphere almost entirely absent. . . .

The lady in question has the most exquisitely intellectual development, a wonderful arch of cerebrum, but no occipital power worth while.

Well, the patient in question had been through a domestic trial and had *bent*; some thought she had *broken*.[20].

Dr Burnett's attitude to his wife's nervous temperament is revealing in the light of what happened later, and so is his report of uncharitable comments passed by her friends and relations in whom family pride, family possessiveness and the family temper were all apt to run high. The passage goes on to describe how the local physician diagnosed Bright's Disease, recommended that the patient wear flannel all over and predicted that, though she might last for some time with care, she could never get well: 'Much family council was held together, and the outlook being dark and hopeless, the young lady was brought to me.' Dr Burnett cured her in eight months with *Mercurius vivus*,* where-upon she got married, had 'several bouncing children' and afterwards remained in excellent health. Mrs Compton Burnett was naturally charmed with this public tribute to her beauty and goodness and, since her conduct as mother and stepmother exposed her to criticism and 'misunderstanding' after her marriage quite as much as before, her husband's enthusiastic defence of her character must have been a particular satisfaction. The date puts their first meeting not later than January 1883. They were married on 11 September by Katharine's elder brother, the Rev. Allen Rees, at the Wesleyan Centenary Chapel

---

* 'In Bright's disease a past grandmaster in therapeutics has all his work cut out, and he will need all his knowledge, however great, of climate, diet, raiment and thera-peutics,' wrote Dr Burnett seven years later (*Gout and Its Cure*, p.155) when he found tincture of cloves a great help, though *Mercurius* remained his chief standby.

in Dover, spent their honeymoon in Paris and returned in October to Pinner where, nine months later, Ivy was born.

Dr Burnett ever after maintained that his second wife was 'the love of his life'. But she was also gay, imperious, exacting, fond of town life and 'not at all maternal' when she married a widower fifteen years older than herself, becoming stepmother to his five small children, and went to live in the country. By 1883, her five brothers and three elder sisters had nearly all long since left home. Elizabeth, who was two years older and remained all their lives Katie's closest sister, had been married at twenty-two in 1875. Their mother died in 1877, whereupon Katie kept house for her father until in his sixties he suddenly married again. Her stepmother was not unkind but, as the only unmarried daughter at home, Katie must have been glad four years later of the chance to become mistress of her own establishment. She seems to have taken much the same view as the second Mrs Hutton (who is similarly placed in Ivy's first novel): 'The father, whose home she ordered, had himself taken a second wife; and though her late esteem of stepmothers had not been flattering to the class, she found that their sway appeared less repellant regarded as wielded than obeyed.'[21]

Dealings between a stepmother and her stepchildren are scrutinized with minute, even reckless, attention in the works of I. Compton-Burnett. 'A family is itself. And of course there are things hidden in it. They could hardly be exposed,' says Hugo Middleton in *The Mighty and Their Fall*, while watching the first meeting between a second wife and an eldest daughter supplanted, as Dr Compton Burnett's eldest daughter had been, by her father's new marriage. The second Mrs Middleton had hoped for a life without constraint or concealment, and had been by no means prepared by her future husband for the shock of meeting his family:

'He simply said he was a widower with a mother and five children.'
   'Simply!' said Hugo. 'And you thought you could live a life that was what it seemed!'[22]

Ivy's mother never cared greatly for small children, her own or anyone else's. When she married Dr Burnett she took on his first wife's two sons and three daughters—all under eight years old, and the eldest at least fiercely hostile towards their new mother—and had seven more of her own. She disliked living in the country, and her new home was not even in Pinner itself but a few miles outside on a recently built housing estate reached by a muddy lane from the village. She was passionately devoted to her husband, as he was to her, but for most of their married life Dr Burnett lived at an hotel in London, joining his family at weekends, seldom taking more than five days' holiday together, and only towards the end of his life allowing himself one day at home in the middle of the week, which he allotted to writing. Katharine possessed in abundance the magnetism that goes with decided views and a forceful personality. But she had also intense nervous energy for which she can have found little outlet, living in isolation with the children's nurse, increasing numbers of nursery maids, governesses and household servants, moving in the next fourteen years to a series of steadily larger houses, making few friends and no intimate companions outside her own family, always without her husband, and surrounded always by more and more children.

Dr Burnett's eldest daughter, Olive, had her eighth birthday in October 1883, when her father brought home a new wife almost the same age as her own mother had been when she died. In the interval before his second marriage Olive had come to think of herself as her father's especial companion, allowed downstairs after her brothers and sisters were in bed to dine with him alone on the nights when he came back from London. What must have been particularly bewildering for a small child—and made her dismissal even harder to bear, when she was abruptly banished to the nursery again—was the fact that her father was so evidently in love with the newcomer. Courtship and marriage had occupied rather less than a year in an affair which, as both parties later declared, had begun with love at first sight; and by all accounts Ivy's mother took few pains to conceal the feelings that had lain behind her precipitate romance, and afterwards came to dominate her life. Olive, who remembered her own mother clearly, never forgave this usurpation and always bitterly resented her stepmother's presence. Her sister Daisy, who was five, may also have remembered their mother but the others were probably too young: Richard had been three, Iris eighteen months and Charlie a few days old at her death. They never spoke of her afterwards, or not at any rate in front of their half-brothers and -sisters. They called their father's second wife Mother, except for Olive who spoke of her always as 'Mrs Burnett'; her own children called her Mummy or Mum. In a few years Olive was old enough to be sent away to boarding school (which was not then usually considered, as it was to be later, the proper place for young girls from

respectable families) where Daisy and Iris soon followed her. Ivy and
her four younger sisters were educated at home.

There seems to have been a break with the Thomas family much as
there was with Dr Burnett's own Hampshire relations round about the
time of his second marriage. His father, Charles Compton Burnett,
had died on 21 August 1883, three weeks before the wedding. His
father-in-law, Edward Thomas, who had been a regular contributor
to the *Homoeopathic World* in Agnes Burnett's lifetime, sent in his last
paper in October 1883, the month in which the editor returned from
his second honeymoon. After that contributions from Edward and
Henry Thomas abruptly ceased, and the Thomases never came south
to visit Agnes' children, though Olive and Daisy were several times
sent on their own to stay with their grandparents and their four maiden
aunts in Chester. They had five Thomas uncles only one of whom had
children, all born long after the little Compton Burnetts, who apparently
said nothing on their visits to the north about their own difficulties at
home.[23] This loss of contact must have contributed to the stepchildren's loneliness in a home where their background counted for nothing,
their father was seldom available and their own concerns were increasingly overshadowed by the arrival of Ivy and, after her, of six more
half-brothers and -sisters.

It is perhaps small wonder that earlier ties should have receded in Dr
Burnett's household before the claims of his second wife's numerous
Rees connections. Katharine Compton Burnett took no small pride in
her own side of the family. 'We are descended from Ap Rees ap Rees
ap Madoc' was one of her favourite sayings, and her children often
teased her about this vague but princely ancient Welshman thought to
to have bequeathed royal blood to later, more humdrum nineteenth-
century Reeses. Katharine's father, from whom she had inherited a strong
partiality for her own relations as well as much else in her character,
became Mayor of Dover less than two months after her marriage. James
Compton Burnett inscribed his next book, published just before Ivy
was born, 'To that Eminent Christian Citizen and Ardent Champion
of Liberty Rowland Rees J.P. Mayor of Dover the following pages are
admiringly dedicated by their author'.[24] The admiration was mutual,
for after his retirement, the Mayor moved to be near his son-in-law's
family and spent the next eleven years a few streets away from the house
where Ivy grew up. She was eighteen when he died, and must have
heard a great deal in her childhood about his exploits in public and
private life. His first wife, Ivy's grandmother, was christened Sophia

Sabine; his second wife's surname was Stace; all three names were borrowed by his granddaughter when she came to choose names for her fearsome domestic tyrants and, in so far as one can trace any of her material back to a single source, her grandfather himself may be said to live on in the novels of I. Compton-Burnett.

Rowland Rees was the 'peremptory man'[25] whom, towards the end of her life, Ivy described to Julian Mitchell. He himself boasted that the notorious temper, for which he was famed and feared in Dover, had descended to him from another 'ardent champion of liberty', Ap Rice ap Howell ap Rowland ap Rees. But all that is known for sure is that Rowland's father was a John Rees from Wales who arrived, probably round about 1808, at Great Clacton in Essex where he built the eleven Martello towers on the east coast, put up to withstand Napoleon after the French invasion scare at the start of the century. Seven of John Rees' towers still stand,[26] though they proved useless after the peace of 1815 and were never even garrisoned. Rowland, who was the second of John's eight children, was born and baptized in 1816 at Great Clacton, and grew up in a house within the curtilege of one of the towers on a desolate site (now Butlins' holiday camp) overlooking the North Sea at Clacton Wash.

Ivy and her Rees cousins later maintained that both Rowland and his father had been army officers but, since neither appears on the army lists, family memories on the Rees side seem to have been no more dependable than they were on the Burnetts'. John Rees had come to Clacton as Clerk of Works to the Royal Engineers; he was remembered long afterwards by an ancient inhabitant who said that old Mr Rees carried on a business as coal merchant at the Wash (which was then a popular landing place for smugglers, as well as for legitimate cargoes) when the Napoleonic wars were over; what is certain is that, some time after 1825 when his eighth child was baptized at Great Clacton, John Rees moved with his family to Dover where enormous defensive works were under construction on the Western Heights. He had married in 1813 Nancy Sadler, one of the sixteen children of George Sadler of 'Three Chimneys' who belonged to solid, East Anglian farming stock. Ivy said that her great-grandmother 'had the misfortune to stand too close to a cannon one day when it went off and deafened her'. This was why, when Nancy Rees later lived as a widow with her son Rowland, his children were all obliged to learn sign language, being forbidden to speak in her presence: 'Ivy's mother and her brothers and sisters could all talk on their hands'.[27]

Rowland had followed his father at nineteen as a clerk to the Royal Engineers, and had married at twenty-one Sophia Sabine Broad,[28] daughter of Charles Broad, a carver and gilder of Bench Street. The Broads had attended St Mary's, Dover, for generations but Rowland, who was posted as a young married man to Gibraltar and there converted by the local Methodist missionary, brought up his children as staunch Wesleyans. Piety combined with a marked inclination to power made him at various times circuit steward, class leader, six times lay representative at Methodist conferences and a celebrated local preacher. He was active in the cause of total abstinence, a leading member of the Dover Temperance Reformers and a fervent supporter in the 'seventies and 'eighties of the Social Purity Movement, resembling in this as in much else the elder Andrew Stace in *Brothers and Sisters*: 'One of the religious movements had swept him away in his youth; and a stern and simple Protestantism had mingled with his pride of race, had leavened his mind and his outlook, had given him a passionate zest for purity of life, and an eager satisfaction in the acknowledged rectitude of his own.'[29]

The force which had swept Rowland Rees away in his youth was embodied in William Rule, the formidable Methodist minister who had chosen Catholic Gibraltar of all places to become the chief Wesleyan missionary outpost in the British army. Dr Rule, whose ambition was no less than the wholesale conversion of Spain, had been persecuted on, and twice expelled from, the mainland. His activities in Gibraltar itself had meanwhile so exasperated the commander of the British garrison that soldiers were permitted to attend the Wesleyan chapel only after direct intervention from Whitehall; and he had simultaneously caused such perturbation among the Roman Catholic clergy that Pope Gregory VI was moved to issue a specific warning against him. Matters came to a head in 1839, the year of Wesley's centenary and also of Rowland Rees' conversion, when a new Bishop and Vicar Apostolic—'once an Inquisitor in Seville, in the last days of the Horrible Tribunal'[30]—was dispatched to the Rock expressly to crush Dr Rule. The intrepid missionary merely redoubled his efforts to enlighten the priest-ridden papists, ably assisted in his six mission schools as in his more daring evangelical exploits by Rowland Rees, who delighted long afterwards to relate to his grandchildren how he had smuggled satchels full of Bibles over the border to Spain* (a feat which would have

---

* Dr Rule (who had personally visited the spot where the last Spanish Quaker was hanged by the Inquisition in 1821) describes how, round about 1839, he ventured over

gladdened the heart of the lay preacher in Ivy's first novel who, though he shuddered perfunctorily at agnosticism and atheism, thought Roman Catholicism far more pernicious than either). After two years at Gibraltar and a brief spell at Portsmouth, Rowland Rees was posted next to Hong Kong where he won fame as the first man to organize Methodist class meetings in China; and, before he left, had extracted recognition of the Lord's Day observance from the government of 'that densely populated and thoroughly idolatrous empire'.

After ten years or so in the ordnance civil service, he retired in the mid-1840s to Dover where he set up in private practice as an architect and surveyor, embarking simultaneously on a strenuous career of public appointments. Many of the best houses built in the town between 1850 and 1860 were his, and so was the National Provincial Bank. As Surveyor to the Paving Commissioners, he had charge from 1849 of lighting, maintaining, draining and paving the streets of Dover. As Engineer and Surveyor to the corporation (when the Paving Board was dismantled in 1850), he reformed the town's sewage, initiating a vast new arterial system of drainage and water supply which cost £70,000 and took thirty years to pay off (the citizens of Dover groaning the while under an unprecedented rate of three shillings in the pound). Resigning this post not without acrimony in 1861, he became Engineer, Architect and Receiver of Rents to the Harbour Board and stayed there for practically a quarter of a century; his plan for extending Dover harbour was turned down in 1882 (as were all the other plans submitted at that time). He had been elected town councillor in 1862, an alderman three years later, and remained Alderman Rees with barely a gap until on 9 November 1883—at an election so tense that the police were flung aside and the great burnished bar of the Council Chamber torn down 'by the rush of the outside burgesses to be present'[31]—he became Mayor by the chairman's single casting vote.

The following Sunday the Mayor, 'being a Wesleyan and a much stauncher political nonconformist than Wesleyans usually are', broke the established mayoral custom of attending church in state: a shrewd

---

the border again 'with a young man then acting as assistant missionary' in a 'carriage well packed with New Testaments', distributed them free to a grateful crowd, narrowly outwitted the constable sent to arrest him, whipped up his horse, galloped back to Gibraltar and 'did not slacken speed till we were beyond the possibility of being overtaken'. (*Recollections*, p.160.) Contemporary accounts of Rowland Rees' career in the Methodist press confirm his prowess as a Bible smuggler, so I see no reason why this young assistant should not have been Ivy's grandfather.

conclusion to a singularly intransigent career devoted, on at least two
major and innumerable minor occasions in the past thirty-four years,
to vigorous agitation for local reform. Wesleyan Methodism remained
for most of the nineteenth century a stoutly conservative body, Tory
by inclination though officially non-political, and distinctly timid,
when not positively repressive, in its attitude to the comparatively few
but conspicuous radical agitators whom the movement was nonetheless
bound to produce: laymen trained to manipulate the democratic
processes of church government, accustomed to public speaking and
anxious to command a wider audience than their own humble chapel-
going congregations. Rowland Rees was 'in his element', as a contemporary account nicely said, 'in putting his shoulder to the wheel,
helping to get the car of public business out of the ancient ruts'.
Inefficiency annoyed him; but, though his principles were libertarian,
his temperament was autocratic, obstinate, overbearing, quick to take
umbrage and mortally offensive when crossed.

Throughout his career the Dover papers regularly record Rowland
Rees taking part amid 'uproar' in the exchange of 'smart blows',
reporting the first and one of the fiercest of these turbulent scenes
barely six months after his début, on 14 June 1849, as a newly appointed
young officer to the Paving Board. Complaints were constantly laid
that summer against the lamentable ineptitude, parsimony and pro-
crastination of the Paving Commissioners who, in spite of rising cholera
and the repeated remonstrances of their Surveyor, could by no means be
brought to approve the newfangled notion of paving and sewaging the
town. They were moreover implacably, and not unnaturally, opposed
to the Public Health Act of 1848 (a measure in their own words 'fraught
with mischief, pregnant with litigation, tyrannical in its machinery and
tending most materially to interfere with constitutional rights, and
to the subversion of the liberty of the subject'),[32] one of the great
reforming bills of the nineteenth century whereby the Board itself
would inevitably be abolished. Accusations of lying, forgery, fraud
and threats of libel were freely bandied at the Board's meetings between
the conservative majority and the Surveyor's small radical faction. In
Christmas week 1849, the Commissioners flatly rejected the Act's
adoption; four days later, at a specially convened and 'densely crowded
Common Hall', Rowland Rees' counter motion was carried by two
to one over the heads of his employers, who were shortly afterwards
obliged to assist at their own dissolution.

At its first meeting on 3 August 1850, the corporation unanimously

invited Mr Rees to continue in his old post under the newly constituted
Board of Health. But the Surveyor's path ran no more smoothly than
before and, by October, he had already detected 'dishonourable and
unprincipled' plotting against him, protesting that he 'would rather
resign his office and go out of every public thing'[33] than tolerate interference from his new employers. In the next ten years he was frequently
accused of petty offences (charging too much in fees, appropriating
too many perquisites and percentages, neglecting public for private
business) and angrily retaliated, expostulating against the 'malignity' of
his enemies, observing that 'those who had attacked him had mistaken
their man', denouncing their complaints as 'calumnious', 'incapable of
proof', 'abusive, low and contemptible'. In November 1858, the Board
of Health proposed to reduce his salary, a resolution instantly repudiated
by the Surveyor who declined thereafter to draw so much as a penny;
matters were still unresolved two years later, when he submitted
simultaneous plans for a new reservoir and for doubling his pay. His
supporters declared him 'the worst paid man in town'. His opponents
argued that, since the Surveyor had 'frequently insulted the Board',
'had never performed his duties to their satisfaction, and had invariably
set them completely at defiance', he was entitled neither to his salary
nor to his post as their officer.

In May 1861, at a sensational meeting which several times threatened
to turn into a riot to the vast amusement of a packed public gallery,
the Surveyor was finally dismissed by a manœuvre which one of his
only three supporters pronounced 'unmanly, un-English and un-
parallelled in the history of public bodies'.[34] Freely distributing threats,
abuse, charges of conspiracy and promises to sue on all hands, the
victim himself declared that 'of all the scandalous doings that had come
to his knowledge this was the most cowardly, the most unjust attack
that had ever been made upon him in his lifetime'. But Mr Rees had
put in much time that summer campaigning against the commissioners
of Dover harbour—'dragging those gentlemen through their own
harbour mud' as a friend loyally said—till in June they resigned in a
body. Whereupon, the ancient authority being declared obsolete under
the 1861 Harbour Act, the first move of the new Harbour Board which
replaced it was to employ Rowland Rees at twice his old salary.

What had maddened his previous employers was the suspicion that
the Surveyor was 'too strong for them, too long-headed and would
over-ride them, as many believed he had over-ridden them for a long
time'. Precisely the same suspicion maddened his colleagues on the

town council for the next twenty years and more: 'If Rees had been "at it", men read the papers to see what Rees had been "at".'[35] More often than not his agitations promoted the noblest causes—liberty of the citizen, religious tolerance, freedom of speech—privileges he seldom cared to extend to any persuasion except his own. Views with which he disagreed were dismissed as moonshine or claptrap, aldermen stout enough to oppose him were grievously badgered and bullied although, as one of them plaintively said, 'the Council was not composed wholly of fools, imbeciles, idiots and donkeys, as he had heard Alderman Rees call the members'.[36]

If Ivy's grandfather was as gruff with his family as he was with his colleagues in public, he could also on occasion be excellent company. A pleasant account of evenings at the Reeses' is given by the Rev. Hugh Price Hughes, another belligerent Welshman who had begun his career in 1869 as a Methodist minister in Dover and afterwards gratefully remembered his welcome by the Alderman's family. Old Mrs Rees, for whose sake the Alderman had forbidden his children to speak save in sign language, died at the age of eighty-one in 1868. Nine years later his wife died, 'respected and beloved by all who knew her' according to the *Methodist Recorder*, on 6 July 1877, when she was sixty-three. In the eighteen months before he re-married, his household was run by his daughters Katie and Lucy (who had been widowed young, and returned to her parents' house with slender means and two small children). According to a family tradition which Ivy later put to memorable use in *A House and Its Head* and *The Mighty and Their Fall*, her grandfather had spoken no word of his intentions until shortly before the wedding when, summoning his family about him, he formally announced that he meant to marry again, had made due provision for Lucy and desired his children to meet his betrothed.

Teresa Miriam Stace was then in her mid-fifties, the daughter of a surgeon in Southampton who had recently died, leaving her with a house of her own and a comfortable income to run it.[37] She was married by licence on 21 January 1879, at a Presbyterian church in Southampton; how or when she had first met her husband his family never discovered. She was handsome, intelligent, humorous, and seems to have got on well with her stepchildren though there are indications that she could not wholly approve Katharine's behaviour when she in turn acquired stepchildren. Katharine herself liked and perhaps admired her stepmother for, however irascible Rowland Rees may have been, his second wife had a will as strong. Nearly ninety years later, Ivy told

Julian Mitchell that her grandfather 'disapproved very strongly indeed of the Married Women's Property Act. He spent all his first wife's money—"not unvirtuously, but on setting up sons in foolish businesses and so on". When she died, "he lamented her", then married again. But he was quite unable to get control, as he wished, of his second wife's fortune, and when she died, she left it back to her own family "as she had every right to do". He was furious, being a tyrannical as well as a peremptory man.'[38] Rowland Rees' first wife had not been a rich woman but he certainly disinherited three of his sons because, as he said in his will, they had 'already had more than their share of my property'; and it was true that, when his second wife died without children of her own many years later, she left what remained of her marriage portion—£6,726—back to her Stace nephews and nieces.

Her husband's employees at the Harbour Board had been so moved by the marriage that they drew up a congratulatory address to their chief 'when he took upon himself sweet bondage for the second time'.[39] He was elected Mayor four years later; and his term of office was marked not so much by any outstanding civic achievement as by the tremendous scenes regularly enacted within the mayor's parlour, scenes so disreputable and sometimes so hilarious that the local reporters took to recording them under the headline BAITING THE MAYOR. Minor points of procedure ostensibly prompted these brisk bouts of name-calling but what was at issue was clearly the Mayor's own domineering personality. A skilled heckler himself, he now found his victims uniting against him, the timid egging on the brave to open revolt, so that the Mayor—protesting that his mutinous council had perpetrated 'the greatest breach of order that has ever been offered to any Mayor in England'—came on at least one occasion perilously close to deposition. It is a situation by no means uncommon, in a domestic setting, in the novels of I. Compton-Burnett; and readers accustomed to the sophistries of arbitrary parents and grandparents in her fiction may well find something oddly familiar in, for instance, the accents of mingled grief, rage and mortification with which, having signally failed to impose his will on a recalcitrant watch committee, her grandfather in fact promptly proclaimed himself the injured party:

Public objects, public duty and public convenience alone influenced me. . . . To suggest that I am setting up my will in opposition to that of the Committee is perfectly absurd. I hate assumptions of personal power. There is no man in Dover who is more opposed to the assumption of personal power than I am, particularly in corporation affairs, therefore the idea that I should set up my arbitrary power in opposition to the wish of the Committee is perfectly absurd. I never assumed anything of the kind. That resolution was passed, I said: 'Pass your resolution, it will be inconvenient for me, and I shall not be able to attend, but pray do not consider me in the matter.' . . . I am the Mayor and you having chosen to elect me to that office, although I attach very little importance to these attacks personally, I do not wish indignity to be done to the office of Mayor by an insult offered to me. . . . Pass your resolution by all means, but for the reasons I have given I could not attend those meetings, and I am sure my fellow townsmen would not ask me to allow myself to be shut up in a private room to be insulted and called all sorts of names, behind the back of the public.[40]

But, if Alderman Rees was widely detested in Dover, he was also greatly esteemed. He had been 'loved and reverenced'[41] by Hugh Price Hughes, who never forgot the debt incurred as a young man in his first ministry at Dover. Hughes later became (after Wesley himself and the conservative Jabez Bunting who dominated the movement in the first half of the nineteenth century) the third major influence on Wesleyan Methodism. A tireless enemy to social and moral corruption in the 'eighties and 'nineties, founding editor of the *Methodist Times*, keeper of the nonconformist conscience (a cliché he had himself coined) and pioneer of the Forward Movement in Methodism, he was also largely responsible for rallying the nonconformist vote behind Gladstone. By his savage denunciations at the height of the Parnell scandal, Hughes precipitated Gladstone's ultimatum and subsequent disaster for the Liberal Government, a feat for which we may thank Ivy's grandfather. It was Alderman Rees who, as a 'red-hot Radical', had first turned the young Hughes into a Liberal, introduced him to Josephine Butler (promoter of Social Purity and an early exponent of women's liberation), encouraged him to take up his lifelong crusade as a public saviour and generally pointed him in the direction of what, some thirty years later, the *Spectator* called 'his noble advocacy of social righteousness'.

On a humbler level the men of the Harbour Board seem to have been especially fond of their chief. They had waited on him in a body at the time of his second marriage; they waited again when his daughter Katharine left home, and on his election as Mayor two months later;

and some thirty or forty of them crowded into the dining room of his house on the Esplanade to console and salute him, and to give him a barometer when, in February 1885, he retired after 'a difference of opinion at the Harbour Board'.[42] This one arose, as differences commonly did throughout his career, from a dispute over money; and it is perhaps not altogether surprising to find that, on leaving the post he had held for twenty-four turbulent years, Alderman Rees also left Dover for good three months later. 'In bidding goodbye to the Alderman, with whom we have often differed but oftener agreed,' wrote the *Dover Express* in guarded farewell, 'we cannot help feeling that taking him for all in all, we ne'er may see his like again.'

The Alderman moved with his wife to Great Clacton, where he built himself a capacious, pink-and-white house in the decorative seaside style of the period, and moved again seven years later to a house in Hove round the corner from his son-in-law, James Compton Burnett. These two, who had presumbly met for the first time in 1883, had each instantly recognized in the other a kindred spirit. What seems to have drawn them together was their common support for the campaign against compulsory vaccination which was at its height in the year of their meeting. 'Every right-minded man knows that compulsory vaccination is a criminal act against the sacredness of the person and an infamous outrage on human nature. . . . For the love of God and man, for love of home and country, the people should resist this horribly wicked law,' wrote the Mayor of Dover in a letter dated December 1883, which was widely publicized in the press, cruelly derided in the *Lancet*, and which went on to demand 'the infliction of condign punishment on the wretch who should dare to perpetrate such an act as compulsory vaccination'.[43] In his book *Vaccinosis* (dedicated to the wrathful Mayor) Dr Burnett had argued much the same case, in terms no less heated, on medical grounds. Both were men of far-sighted, radical views which both were apt to forget in the delight of confounding their enemies. 'They have their just reward—the spittle of contempt,' wrote James Compton Burnett in one of the many fighting editorials whose language equals, and often surpasses, the vigour of his father-in-law's political invective.

Dr Burnett had abandoned allopathy because he was convinced that the future of scientific medicine lay with the homoeopaths; but his propagation of this new creed was undertaken more often than not for the sheer pleasure of war, as he himself was well aware—'I do it just to . . . slap the jeering ignorance of orthodoxy in the face.' This was all his life a favourite pastime of Alderman Rees, and indeed the atmosphere of schoolboy ragging and baiting which pervaded the mayor's parlour at Dover in 1884 is not a thousand miles away from the piratical exuberance with which the Editor of the *Homoeopathic World* hands out the Black Spot to orthodox medicine: 'We wish to say that we mean *war*, and not peace; we know allopathy, root and branch, and we condemn it as *bad*, altogether *bad*, and pernicious. We will have nothing but war to the bitter end with allopathy *because it is bad, false in principle and pernicious in practice*, and we know whereof we write. We ask nothing better from the allopaths than *war*, and the fiercest fighting till they or we kiss the dust.'[44]

This intransigent, ambitious, independent, progressive and radical background is not perhaps what might have been expected for I. Compton-Burnett. One might legitimately have supposed her the daughter of an impoverished country squire, living in a house inhabited by generations of her forbears on a dwindling income from its ancestral lands, such as provides the setting for practically all her twenty novels. But nonconformity—whether medical, political or religious—was the characteristic expression of iron wills on both sides of her family. Her Burnett ancestors, who had almost certainly been nonconformist as far back as the eighteenth century, had risen in three generations from farm labourers to the prosperous middle classes; the same stubborn energy is evident throughout her maternal grandfather's career; both Burnetts and Reeses might have taken as their guiding rule the rousing words with which her father concluded his New Year editorial for 1881: 'Let our motto be—Forward! We have dangled our legs on the banks of the river of expectancy long enough.'

CHAPTER TWO

1884–1896

I

'I was a child of passion'

ON 13 JUNE 1885, eight days after Ivy's first birthday, her brother Guy was born. The two were inseparable as small children, 'like twins' as she said long afterwards;[1] their next brother, Noel, who was three and a half years younger than Ivy, tagged on after his elders or, as they all three passed into the schoolroom, sometimes repaired to the nursery to play with the four younger sisters who arrived at intervals over the next decade. Already Ivy's family background has become recognizably the world of her novels (which practically all take place in the 1890s, or the early years of the next century, roughly the period between her tenth and twentieth birthdays): a large and sequestered Victorian household permitting small contact with people outside it, staffed by domestics who all slept under its roof, and running to a rigid timetable which sharply divided parents and children, masters and servants, nursery, schoolroom and drawing room parties.

Except perhaps for the unusually large number of strong wills shut up together inside it, the Compton Burnetts' seems to have been a perfectly conventional establishment. It followed what must then have been a commonplace pattern whereby those families who had only comparatively lately, and at the expense of considerable effort, attained middle class status were also those who had most to lose by any relaxation of the social code, and therefore those who most stringently enforced and perpetuated the crushing load of respectability which bore down on so many Victorian childhoods. Ivy herself said that the society which allowed later generations to live and mix more freely produced people less dangerous but duller:

Isolation and leisure put nothing into people. But they give what is there, full play. They allow it to grow according to itself, and this may be strongly in certain directions.

I am sure that the people who were middle-aged and elderly when

I was young, were more individualized than are now my own
contemporaries. The effect of wider intercourse and self-adaptation
seems to go below the surface, and the result is that the essence of
people is controlled and modified. . . .

Imagine a Winston Churchill, untaught and untrained and
unadapted in the sense we mean, and then immured in an isolated life
in a narrow community, and think what might have happened to
his power, what would have happened to it.[2]

Already one may begin to suspect how deeply she drew later on
things she had seen as a child. Her grandfather's unrestrained appetite
for power; her mother's similarly imperious temperament aggravated
by 'isolation and leisure', and the effect of so much pent-up, frustrated
energy on her own children as much as on her stepchildren; the strain
under which the first family grew up; Ivy's absorption from infancy
in the lives of her two brothers, both of whom died young: all these
provided dimly outlines which were to take shape in the novels of I.
Compton-Burnett, and so did her father's partial withdrawal from
family life. Arthur Waley, who was one of the very few visitors
admitted to stay with the Compton Burnetts before the first war,
maintained that the doctors in her books—for the most part gentle and
perceptive, but invariably peripheral characters—were taken from Ivy's
father. She lived at home according to an outward routine which
scarcely changed, though it grew harsher towards the end under the
shadow of sudden death and perpetual mourning, until the household
dissolved in 1915. This dissolution, the deaths of her father and mother
and her two brothers, together with the war itself, broke for ever the
world in which she had lived for thirty-one years and on which her
mature imagination drew for the rest of her life.

'I was a child of passion,' said Ivy looking back, and described how
when Guy was given a ball while she was presented with a useful
pinafore, she was so maddened by the injustice that she stamped and
roared 'till my family feared for my life'.[3] One might have expected
a passionate nature from the violent undercurrents as much as from the
fearful explosions in her books but, outside the immediate circle
bounded by her nurse and her brothers, Ivy seems to have been a
resolutely reticent small girl, learning early that principle of concealment which was afterwards invariably central to her theory of
survival:

'Our true selves should not be anything to be ashamed of,' said Faith.

'I don't think it would be nice not to be ashamed of them,' said Hope. 'I am ashamed and terrified of mine, and even more of other people's.'[4]

Ivy's sisters Vera and Juliet, who were six and eight years younger, could barely remember even once seeing her lose her temper, though their nurse often said she had been a difficult baby, much given to tantrums. This was 'before she had learnt to hide herself', and both agreed that the hiding began very soon. Throughout the time when they lived together at home, including a period when Ivy taught them herself in the schoolroom, they had never known her break those habits of reserve and watchfulness—'eyes that roved and suddenly withdrew as if their owner were informed'[5]—well known to her friends in later life. Probably she had herself and her family under close observation by the time she was three years old, the age at which Freud held that the essential foundations of character have already been laid down. It is also the age of the youngest (and some of the most idiosyncratic as well as the most enchanting) characters in her books who—since Ivy shared her mother's lack of maternal feeling and, once she had left the nursery herself, never again voluntarily had anything to do with small children —must have been drawn from her own recollections of desire and grati-fication and the struggle for power at that age. Few other novelists have caught so sharply the desperate emotions of very small children, or noted how quickly they acquire wordly wisdom—something sadly familiar to Nevill Sullivan, in *Parents and Children*, who at three years old is sufficiently shrewd to have grave misgivings when his mother promises him a present for tomorrow:

'No, today,' said Nevill, with rising feeling. 'Today.'
'Tomorrow will soon be here,' said Luce.
'It won't,' said Nevill, in a tone of experience.[6]

Nevill, who was the first of her three-year-olds, veers as rapidly between resignation and rage as the last, Henry Egerton in *A God and His Gifts*, whose days are darkened by the prodigious virtues of a small relation named Maud (' "Come and let us tell you about Maud," said Merton. "Very good girl. Not at all spoilt. Not stamp and cry," said Henry, openly forestalling information.') The clash of wills may be less ruinous in infancy but it is no less bitter than in middle or old age, and not to be soothed by a chorus of interfering adults when Maud's arrival interrupts Henry, who is making a drawing:

[Maud] entered, glanced at Henry and stood in silence. Henry returned the glance and looked away.

'Say good-morning to Great-Grandma,' said Merton.

Maud remained silent.

'Come, surely you can say a word.'

'Pencil,' said Maud, looking at Henry's occupation.

The latter did not raise his eyes, and Maud's also maintained their direction.

'Let her have the pencil, Henry,' said Ada. 'She is younger than you, and she is your guest.'

Henry put it smoothly behind his back.

'Come, the house must be full of pencils,' said Hereward, glancing at his son.

Maud looked round for signs of this, and seeing none, made an advance on the pencil and acquired it.

Her host broke down.

'Come, what a way to behave!' said Ada.

'Paper,' said Maud.[7]

But it was not until she was nearly sixty that small children began to play any great part in the novels of I. Compton-Burnett. Her first eight books dealt almost entirely with relations inside much older families, and one may perhaps gauge how hard this particular knot had been to untie by the fact that, for ten years after her own family broke up, she wrote nothing at all though the bulk of her material had lain ready to hand, almost from birth, in the years before she left home. Samuel Butler, whose *Note-Books* came as a crucial formative influence at the start of her career as a novelist, describes what must have been a familiar precaution of Ivy's in his note, 'On Wild Animals and one's Relations': 'If one would watch them and know what they are driving at, one must keep perfectly still.'[8]

Not that her early childhood was by any means unhappy. Ivy's mother, always inclined to prefer her sons, was nonetheless fond of this eldest child who had inherited her own colouring—dark blue eyes and golden hair—combined with her husband's sturdy build, his clear complexion, broad brow and the curious set of his eyes, what Ivy called 'the cut of the face'.⁹ She was a delicate baby and remained to the end of her life peculiarly prone to colds on the chest. All her brothers and sisters, except Noel, 'were more or less puny at birth', and all but Noel 'were oiled daily during the first year of their lives' with excellent results, on their father's instructions. For all his pugnacity in public, Dr Burnett at home was a tender and thoughtful parent, recommending that cod liver oil be discarded in favour of salad oil 'which is much less nasty', and leaving a charming description of his scheme for the Compton Burnett nursery:

> The mother, or nurse, in charge of the child to have a large pinafore of flannel. . . . She is to be seated in front of a good fire, an ample screen at her back to keep off the draughts. A large soup-plate full of fine salad oil to be slightly warmed and standing near at hand. The babe to be held naked in the lap and the whole of the oil very gently and very slowly and *playfully* rubbed into its entire body, excepting its face and hands, and then the babe to be dressed for the night.¹⁰

By far the most important person in the children's lives was their nurse, Ellen Smith—Ivy's beloved Minnie—who had come at the age of twenty-three to keep house for their father and take charge of the nursery when his first wife Agnes died, and who remained with the family for the rest of her life, bringing up all twelve children in turn. For most of their lives she was the only mother the stepchildren had known, and they loved her as dearly as the second family did. '"You love Mummy and you love Daddy," said Mrs Compton Burnett, to which Ivy replied: "But I love Minnie best."'¹¹ Ivy's sisters remembered Minnie as imperturbable and selflessly kind: she had 'very large eyes— very dark, almost green, a wonderful colour—a long nose, soft hair, large capable hands. Nothing put her out of her stride, she could put up with anything—and she had a lot to put up with, too.' She gave up her own independent existence without regret or the least trace of sanctimoniousness because 'it was her pleasure to do so', and she became, as successive catastrophes darkened their childhood, 'prop and mainstay' to the whole household. Much the same might be said of Miss Patmore who was nurse to Sophia Stace's unfortunate children in *Brothers and Sisters* and who bears, in character as much as in looks, an unmistakable likeness to Minnie: 'Miss Patmore was a spare young woman of Sophia's age with a thin, sallow face, a narrow, long nose, and large, kind eyes. Her chief qualities, almost her only ones, for she was built on simple lines, were a great faithfulness, a great kindness and a great curiosity.'[12]

Miss Smith, like Miss Patmore, was a haberdasher's daughter, a fact which set her well above most nurses since it meant that she had a home of her own and was not obliged to earn a living. Her father, Joseph Smith, kept a large and prosperous draper's shop in St Matthews Street, Ipswich, had sent his daughter to boarding school, and subsequently left her a competence in his will.[13] Minnie might have lived at home if she chose but she disliked her stepmother and returned only on occasional visits, causing consternation in the Compton Burnett nursery. 'Well, if this goes on I shall go for a holiday,' she would say when the children became obstreperous, a threat which they parried with the constant refrain: '*Promise* you won't go away for a holiday this year'. Guy had named her on one of these visits to her sisters in Ipswich when, as a baby of two, he had cried himself sick till consoled with her dressing gown which he made into a doll and called 'Minnie', so that the name was waiting for her when she got back.

Minnie's disposition may have been exceptionally sweet, but selflessness was the price then automatically exacted from nannies in return for their charges' devotion. Nineteenth-century autobiographies commonly describe children who lived in terror of their nurses' departure, who would have thought it gravely improper to be bathed or dressed or even to have had their hair brushed by their mothers and indeed, except when sent for downstairs or on formal rounds of the nursery and schoolroom, seldom encountered their mothers at all. ' "She loved us but she didn't like us very much," Ivy said. . . . "Well, she showed great interest when we were ill and so on, you know. We knew she cared. But we really loved Minnie." '[14] It was Minnie who took Ivy for the first time to the seaside to visit her grandfather at Clacton and said, when Ivy asked uneasily if the water would come any nearer, 'Not if you're a good girl, Miss Ivy';* and it was Minnie who first introduced her to 'Puss in Boots and Jack the Giant Killer at an age when it is right that giants should be killed, and even bearable that Red Riding Hood should be eaten by the wolf in the bed'[15] (though Minnie had a milder version in which the heroine

---

* Or was this perhaps the 'under-nurse', who made Ivy feel guilty and 'always said, when it thundered, "That is God, angry with you," because she, Ivy, had hit one of her brothers or stolen a chocolate'? (*Ivy and Stevie* by Kay Dick, p.29; Ivy's first sight of the sea is described by Julian Mitchell in the *New Statesman*, 5 September 1969.)

escaped). It is evidently Minnie who stands behind a long line of
capable, inquisitive, absolutely dependable nurses who provide a
secure retreat in the disasters of infancy—the death of a hen or a surfeit
of Ring-a-ring-o'-roses—as from the treacherous, veiled brutalities of
the adult world: a line which begins with Miss Patmore in *Brothers and
Sisters* and runs through Hatton in *Parents and Children*, Fanshawe in
Darkness and Day, Bennet in *The Present and the Past*:

> Bennet was a small, spare woman of forty-five, with a thin, sallow
> face marked by simple lines of benevolence, long, narrow features
> and large, full eyes of the colour that is called grey because it is no
> other. She took little interest in herself, and so much in other people
> that it tended to absorb her being. When the children recalled her
> to their world, she would return as if from another. They loved her
> not as themselves, but as the person who served their love of them-
> selves, and greater love has no child than this.[16]

Minnie took great pleasure in the country round Pinner and often
talked afterwards of its woods and paddocks and orchards, and the
beautiful garden at No. 2 Onslow Villas. Ivy had inherited from her
father an abiding love of 'the real country, where I can pick primroses',
but her mother still hankered after town life so, early in 1887, the family
moved nearer London to a house called Chesilbank at Twickenham
where Noel and Vera were born. Ivy remembered, from well before
her third birthday, a miniature dustpan and brush with which she used
to sweep the step of the house at Pinner; and she told Julian Mitchell a
story about herself and Guy at Chesilbank which illustrates the inad-
vertent harshness of advanced Victorian parents who, like Dr Burnett,
did not believe in coddling children: 'One day . . . she and her brother
were out in the garden. It was so cold that they cried to be let in.
Their mother appeared at a window and promised them each a penny
booklet with a bright cover if they would stay outside for another
half hour. Cold was thought good for children.'[17]

So was simple living and plain food. The children's rooms had bare
cork linoleum fitted throughout; convention decreed a 'miserable
fire' in the nursery and no fires at all in the bedrooms ('if you saw the
girl coming in with the kindling, you knew you were ill and the doctor
was coming'). The bedsteads were iron, the basket chairs decrepit
and the nursery table top had a ledge underneath on which the children
were accustomed to deposit layers of unwanted food. Thrift

collaborated with accepted medical opinion on nursery diets: meat was considered too rich, sugar unwholesome, jam morally unwise and sponge cakes were only for visitors, which perhaps explains why, when Ivy later did her own housekeeping, she paid particular attention to copious helpings of roast meat, boiled hams, substantial puddings and sumptuous teas with three courses, hot, savoury and sweet. Dr Burnett, progressive in this as in much else, believed that fruit and vegetables led to longevity and brought up his children as vegetarians for the sake of their health (though meat and drink were allowed downstairs which suggests that he had somewhat relaxed his earlier teetotalism). His attitude to infant malpractices like masturbation or bed-wetting—generally held to be vicious, and often punished with astonishing violence—was invariably liberal, and so were his views on dress at a time when girls were regularly put into stays at thirteen, and when respectable children wore for playing, even in the height of summer, thick, black, woollen stockings, laced boots and high-necked, long-sleeved overalls. 'If Daddy had had his will,' said Mrs Compton Burnett, 'you'd all have gone barefoot.'

Sea air was a tonic of which he approved, and probably the reason why, at the beginning of December 1891, he moved his wife and nine children—three of whom at least were already delicate and dangerously susceptible to the pneumonia which in the end killed Guy and nearly killed Ivy—to Hove, then just beginning to become a fashionable adjunct to Brighton. 'From August to the end of December the climate of Brighton is probably the best in England, but the spring is boisterous, windy and often very cold,' advised the *Homoeopathic Directory* and Dr Burnett had devised his own mysterious system for rating in order of precedence the coastal resorts which he prescribed for ailing small children: 'a few years' residence at the seaside, preferably the first year or so at Worthing, the second at Brighton, and then a year or two at Eastbourne or Folkestone'.[18]

It is a curious thing that, whereas the people in her books live mostly on their family estates in manor houses built by their ancestors, Ivy herself had known only brand-new houses of the kind put up in suburban developments all over the Home Counties in the late nineteenth century to cope with the demands of the rising business and professional classes. It is doubtful whether, before she was thirty, she has so much as visited what is generally meant by an English country house. The nearest approach to a 'place' in her family was probably the original home of her great-grandfather Burnett at Gavelacre (a pleasant compact farmhouse which still stands), but Ivy can scarcely have known of its existence. Otherwise there was Valley Farm, a farm-house not much bigger than a fair-sized cottage with a pretty, pillared porch at Great Clacton, which several times changed hands among her mother's relations and which she remembered from her first visit to the seaside before she was six. Her grandfather's new house, Hillside in Burr's Road, could be seen at Clacton until quite recently; and one of her uncles built himself in 1886 a solid, roomy, red-brick residence, called Soetrana or Clay Hall, which may still be seen nearby. From the time of his second marriage, her father had begun to invest systemati-cally in speculative property development, buying land and putting up houses on the Woodridings Estate at Pinner; at Great Clacton, on the Greens round about where his wife's relations owned property, and at Clacton-on-Sea (then a seaside settlement barely ten years old and developing swiftly on rather humbler lines than the middle-class suburbs of Brighton); and on the outer fringes of Hove.

The houses he built were nearly all small shops or semi-detached cottages, two rooms up and two down, designed for the working classes. The houses he lived in were considerably grander, and grew more so as his family increased: No. 2 Onslow Villas was one of a pair (Dr Burnett soon bought the other half) of handsome, plain but substan-tial, red-brick, three-storied dwellings which stood in their own grounds at Woodridings. The estate itself, the very first in a district since smoth-ered by housing estates, had been built for wealthy London commuters (Mrs Beeton had lived at Woodridings, and so had Nelson's daughter by Lady Hamilton) after the railway reached Pinner in 1844. It was three minutes' walk from Hatch End railway station, and a mile or so across fields from Pinner itself along a footpath 'impassable for mud for five months out of twelve'.[19] Chesilbank at Twickenham stood in Cambridge Park on the banks of the Thames, a suburb much like Woodridings and built for much the same purpose. When Ivy was seven and a half, and the family moved to Hove, they lived at 30 First Avenue which, as its name implies, was one of the original avenues running down to the sea when the town was laid out in the 'sixties and 'seventies.

Hove at the beginning of the last century had been a decayed fishing village with barely a hundred inhabitants. The coming of the railway and the westward expansion of Brighton meant that, by the time the Compton Burnetts arrived, it was a wilderness of raw red brick with a population of 26,097 which has continued to grow ever since. In 1891 there were five churches, all newly built or still under construction in styles running from Early Decorated to Romanesque and Italian Gothic. Waterhouse's town hall was finished in 1882, and the public library in 1891; the school to which Ivy was sent at fourteen was new, as was her brothers' prep school and Brighton College itself which they later attended. The family moved for the last time, in 1897, a few streets westward to The Drive 'in the midst of fashionable Hove', a spot where, as a contemporary directory proudly records, the stranger 'cannot help being struck with the air of wealth and refinement'[20] and where the Compton Burnetts settled at number twenty: a thirteen-bedroomed slab in red brick with white facings known ever after among Dr Burnett's children as 'that hideous house'.

Carriages, waiting while their owners paid calls, filled the road outside the new house two or three deep every afternoon (though the first motor car had already caused a commotion in The Drive two years before the Compton Burnetts arrived). Opposite lived a General Basden who, taking umbrage as most people did at having a homoeopath for a neighbour, refused to permit his wife to call which was a great grief to Mrs Compton Burnett. 'He was a thorn in my mother's flesh for many a long year,' said her daughter Vera. Margaret Powell gives a startling account of libertinism, alcoholism, even outright violence practised behind closed doors by the master or mistress in two highly respectable establishments on The Drive when her mother (who was four years older than Ivy) worked there in the 1890s, first as a fourteen-year-old kitchen maid to a family named Benson and later to another family as a plain cook. The Bensons had 'kept a satisfactory staff as mum puts it. A butler, footman, housemaid and under-housemaid, a lady's-maid and a valet, a gardener, a coachman and a stable-boy.'* The Compton Burnetts had roughly the same number of servants, except that they kept no carriage, their footman was replaced by a boy and their butlers doubled as valets (one made a habit of filching the fees

* *My Mother and I* by Margaret Powell, p.40. This book gives a fascinating account of life both above and below stairs in fashionable Hove when Ivy was young (for the occasion on which the Bensons' servants were roused one night by their mistress's curses as she attempted to split her husband's bedroom door with an axe, see p.43; for further lecherous exploits among the Compton Burnetts' neighbours, see p.68); and I am grateful to Mrs Powell for asking her mother if she had any recollection of Dr Burnett: 'although she vaguely remembers the name I'm afraid that she cannot recall any incidents of that period. As Mother explained, she was always in the kitchen, these being basements naturally the view was somewhat restricted.'

from Dr Burnett's coat pockets and later absconded with the family silver).

Under-servants, known in the family as 'squalors', had no claim in those days to names or clothes of their own: the page's suit was handed down whatever the shape or size of each new boy and a nursemaid called Leeney passed on her name to two more, the three being distinguished for their mistress's convenience as Fat, Thin and Dignified Leeney. But the cook, a Plymouth Brother with a repertoire of Temperance hymns, held her own even with Mrs Compton Burnett who loved cooking though she entered the kitchen at some risk to herself: 'My mother was a woman who feared neither God nor man, but she did fear that cook,' said Ivy.[21] Next in order of consequence was the manservant Ager, an imposing person, 'fond of long, important words' and so lordly that the whole family trembled when Ager was asked to help the nursemaid lift the perambulator up the front steps. Ager had succeeded George Harvey, whom Mrs Compton Burnett had once been obliged to reprove for drowning the cook's voice when she sang. Vera Compton-Burnett has a curious memory of Harvey performing before her one day when she was a baby and he found her alone in her high chair at First Avenue: 'I can see him now, making faces and dancing in front of me'. None of the children was allowed in the kitchen and, according to her sisters, Ivy even as a small girl had scarcely set foot below stairs. But it must have been from things seen and heard in these years that she drew the sad procession of page boys hopelessly aspiring to higher things in her books, the sardonic and self-assured cooks, the butlers whose vocabulary is so much more ambitious than their masters' and the manservants who pull furtive faces or mimic their betters behind their backs to an audience of conspiratorial children.

Ivy detested Hove to the end of her life and steadfastly refused to visit friends who lived in Brighton. 'It's a horrid, horrid place,' she said with unaccustomed venom to one[22] who had happened to mention it shortly before she died. Throughout the twenty-four years that the family lived there, Hove was rapidly rising and sprawling around them, 'showing an activity on the part of the speculative builder almost more remarkable than one could have believed', as the *Hove Gazette* noted when the census figures were published for 1901. But much of the land later sold for building was still wild fields and there were open downs at the back of the town. The Drive was a piecemeal extension of Grand Avenue, a grandiose thoroughfare running from Church Street to the sea front and bordered by what was then a rough meadow full of buttercups and daisies, wild rose and apple trees. The little Compton Burnetts on their walks picked clover and sea pinks and took sugar to feed the donkey who lived in a field beside the town hall. Thrift grew on the marshes westward towards Portslade (where Dr Burnett later bought building plots to erect small villas in rows), and Ivy told Sonia Orwell long afterwards that her pleasantest memory was of great swathes of wild flowers growing between the downs and the sea.

She had small, delicate hands and always loved small things—single flowers better than double ones, wild flowers better than either and harebells best of all. Long after she had left off playing dolls' houses, she kept a collection of minute dolls in an old dress box and, when she was sixteen or so, she would make dolls for her sisters out of petals and twigs, fastened with thorns and exquisitely dressed. Some sixty years years later, Elizabeth Taylor lunched with her just before Christmas: ' "My mother", Ivy said, "told me that, when I was a child, she spent all the year looking out for small things to put in my stocking. I remember those more than all the dolls I had—especially a little box of glass beads." '[23] Once she was taken by Minnie to stand against the railings and watch the Prince of Wales drive by. On a visit to London designed as a treat, she had been thoroughly bored by the Tower; what she liked best was to be put in a cab with Guy by their father, and driven about the streets.

Dr Burnett, having settled his family at Hove, had taken to staying in London at the Holborn Viaduct Hotel, returning twice a week to spend Wednesdays and weekends at home. He arrived by cab from the station late at night and would visit the children at breakfast next morning to make sure they had swallowed their compulsory porridge —'It's no good having a big brain box if you don't put anything in it' was a regular saying of his—before taking the five eldest, from Ivy down to Juliet (called Judy), along the street to a fruit shop where each might choose whatever he or she pleased. The party then proceeded a few minutes' walk to the sea where he would throw down his small change and, in the early morning before anyone much was about, the children would scramble for pennies on the front (the money was not to spend but to fill money boxes). On Sunday evenings there were sweets and games when their father played bear, crouching under the furniture and growling 'Hinaus' and 'Herein'; the smallest children would dip in his pockets for coins, or he would tell stories from the fire. This was after family prayers with a procession of manservant and maids, hymns and readings from the Family Bible. On ordinary nights one may suppose that Ivy and Guy economized with something more like the prayer— 'May I be forgiven and saved'[24]—invented by Rose Lovat, aged ten, for her younger sister Viola in *Darkness and Day*: a formula which, as Rose explains, avoids time and effort being wasted on 'a long prayer and a hymn', while neatly covering all the salient points.

'We came of a booky family'

ROSE AND VIOLA share a world of their own, secure from the disturbing vagaries of grown-ups and sheltered even from their nurse's intrusion, a withdrawal common enough in the novels of I. Compton-Burnett though the relationship is generally between an elder or dominant girl and a boy, a year or so apart in age. The theme of brother and sister runs through every single one of her books, from the six to thirteen year olds—Honor and Gavin Sullivan in *Parents and Children*, Julius and Dora Calderon in *Elders and Betters*, Clemence and Sefton Shelley in *Two Worlds and their Ways*, Henry and Megan Clare in *The Present and the Past*, Claud and Emma Challoner in *A Heritage and its History*, Leah and Hengist Middleton in *The Mighty and their Fall*—to Emily and Nicholas Herrick (who is seventy) in *Pastors and Masters*. It is first elaborated in *Brothers and Sisters* where—apart from the central incestuous pair—there are no less than five sets of brother and sister, all living in the same village, all in their middle or late twenties, all contemplating, and several of them actually attempting without success, intermarriage with one another. The relationship itself, beginning for mutual comfort and protection in the nursery, strengthening on contact with harsh or intemperate adults into a deeper protective bond, ripening often in middle age when fear no longer obtains, provides an intimacy more satisfactory and closer—or at any rate examined in greater depth—than even the happiest marriages in her books. Honor Sullivan, aged ten, expounds the practical aspects to her younger brothers:

> 'Why can't brothers and sisters marry?' said Gavin.
> 'Because they have to start a family,' said his sister. 'If they married people in the same one, there would never be any new ones. But they can live together.'
> 'Do they have any children then?'
> 'I don't think they do so often. But they can adopt some.'

'He will be your little boy,' promised Nevill in full comprehension.[25]

The relationship between Honor and Gavin Sullivan was the one which Ivy's sisters thought came closest to Ivy's with Guy. Gavin is his mother's favourite, a slow, shy child, the younger by 'a year all but two days' and dependent on Honor for leadership whether in tormenting the governess, misleading their mother or simply in construing the mysterious undercurrents of adult conversation which Honor can follow and he can't. Guy Compton-Burnett was also his mother's favourite. Ivy had been 'quicker than Guy as a little girl' but, as he grew older, 'even Ivy looked up to Guy' who developed into a brilliant as well as an uncommonly sweet-tempered boy with a strength of character which, in times of crisis, was recognized by the whole family. He had dark curly hair, grey eyes and 'a steadfast face'.* Minnie loved him especially, his younger sisters adored him and there can be small doubt that, as Honor loved Gavin, so Ivy loved Guy more than anyone else in the world.

Noel, who shared the schoolroom with Ivy and Guy, was a backward child, often left out by his elders and obliged to fall back on his sister Vera who was three years younger. He seems to have been one of those solitary children isolated in a large family between older and younger pairs, like the twelve-year-old James Sullivan in *Parents and Children*:

The two sisters lived for each other, as did Honor and Gavin; and James lived to himself like Nevill, but with less support, so that his life had a certain pathos. He would remedy matters by repairing to the nursery, where Hatton's welcome and Honor's inclination to a senior brought Nevill to open, and Gavin to secret despair. The suffering of his brothers was pleasant to James, not because he was malicious or hostile, but because the evidence of sadness in other lives made him feel a being less apart. He showed no aptitude for books, and this in his sex was condemned; and he carried a sense of guilt which it did not occur to him was unmerited. It was a time when

* Guy and Noel Compton-Burnett are described in the persons of Fabian and Guy Clare on p.14 of *The Present and the Past*: 'Fabian at thirteen had a broad face and brow, broad, clear features and pure grey eyes that recalled his sister's. Guy was two years younger and unlike him, with a childish, pretty face, dark eyes that might have recalled [his baby brother's], but for their lack of independence and purpose, and a habit of looking at his brother in trust and emulation.' (Ivy's sisters confirm that this is an exact likeness of their own brothers.)

endeavour in children was rated below success, an error which in later years has hardly yet been corrected, so that childhood was a more accurate foretaste of life than it is now.[26]

Often, in the novels, the gap between an elder pair and a tiresome younger brother narrows with time so that—as happened with Ivy and Guy and Noel when they reached their teens—the pair becomes a trio. But as a small boy Noel, who was handsome and dreamy like his father in childhood, had been young for his age and 'imaginative but not clever'; his sisters remembered him still at nine or ten years old galloping up and down the street alone, pretending to be a horse with invisible reins at the corners of his mouth. He was a secret poet, like James Sullivan ('James could not refer to . . . the poems which to himself were proof of [his cleverness], as he had revealed them to no one, and was postponing publication until his maturity')[27] and several of the other lonely children in his sister's books ('"People can't be very open about poems," said Guy, with a flush. "Anyone who is a poet knows that."'). All the Compton Burnett children were dab hands at composing limericks and verses in competition to see who was fastest; and they all wrote poems, encouraged by their father who would reward them with pennies—'so much for a poem, so much less for a hymn, because hymns were easier'. But only Noel retained his childhood facility as a grown-up ambition to the point at which, in 1914 just after he had been elected a Fellow at Cambridge, he proposed abandoning scholarship and turning poet instead.

None of his early verses survive, but there is a fragment written by Ivy (with Guy's help) about their governess, a Miss Mills commonly known as 'Miss Smills' to her pupils:

> There once was a lady, Miss Mills was her name,
> She wrote a bad novel and thought to get fame.
> But when she found no one would publish her book
> To gambling she very wickedly took.
> And worse than all her troubles yet
> She very soon got into debt. . . .

This was only the beginning of a long and fearsome saga, remorselessly chanted aloud in the Compton Burnett household, which followed the lady as she took to stealing to pay off her gambling debts, was imprisoned for theft and sank steadily through a great many stanzas to touch the bottom of crime and ignominy. There was not a word of truth in it: if Miss Mills had written a novel, it was unknown to her pupils whose gloomy notion of a literary career was prompted as much by their own literary ambitions as by their naturally dim view of authority.

Ivy and Guy were ringleaders in the nursery, experts at dressing up and make-believe, pressing the others into service as pall bearers or corpses when they staged a funeral, as the Clare children and the Middletons do in her books. They invented an octopus, which lived behind a grating in the garden and terrorized their brothers and sisters, and when Ivy was ten or eleven they organized a Royal Academy to which all the children contributed paintings. A few years later the two boys would come up to the nursery to amuse the younger ones on Sunday mornings ('All the heathen practices we had were on a Sunday morning,' because there were lessons the rest of the week) with 'horrific games which terrified us out of our lives'. The most impressive of these took place behind locked doors with the blinds drawn when Guy, wearing a mask with lighted candles at the eye holes, became an idol known as 'The Holy Beckle'. The Beckle would issue pronouncements as to what had to be done (generally the decapitation of one of the dolls) whereupon their mother, hearing agitated screams from above, would call from downstairs: 'Which one of you's hurt?'

Ivy by this time was too old to take part any longer in idolatrous rites. But as small children she and Guy had their own gods, named Polio and Elephantas, enshrined on two little ornamental stucco pillars in the back garden. All the children were obliged to kneel and pray to these gods, and to make sacrifices ordained by Ivy and Guy as high priests: 'The gardener was furious when Polio ordained that all young leaves be picked as a sacrifice,' said Juliet Compton-Burnett. Similar offerings ('Flowers and grasses and acorns and things') are made by Dora and Julius Calderon, aged ten and eleven in *Elders and Betters*, in the hope of propitiating their god and averting disasters which loom when a family of unknown relations settle in the neighbourhood:

'O great and good and powerful god, Chung,' said Theodora Calderon, on her knees before a rock in the garden, 'protect us, we beseech thee, in the new life that is upon us. For strangers threaten our peace, and the hordes of the alien draw nigh. Keep us in thy sight, and save us from the dangers that beset our path. For Sung Li's sake, amen.'

'For Sung Li's sake, amen,' said her brother.

'Guard us from the boldness of their eyes and the lewdness of their tongues,' went on Theodora. 'For their strength is great, and the barbarian heart is within them. Their eyes may be cold on the young, and harsh words may issue from their lips. Therefore have us in thy keeping. For Sung Li's sake, amen.'

'Sung Li is a good name,' said Julius as they rose from their knees. 'Enough like Son and yet not too much like it. It would not do to have them the same.'

'Blasphemy is no help in establishing a deity,' said his sister, in a tone of supporting him. 'And the power of Chung is real, though it is only used for those who believe in him. And he would always help people's unbelief.'[28]

'I do not claim that the children in my books, any more than their elders, resemble the actual creatures of real life,'[29] said Miss Compton-Burnett just after *Elders and Betters* was published. What is extraordinary about these particular children is not so much their habit of serving strange gods, nor the liturgical language reserved for this purpose, but rather their power of articulating the miseries generally endured by actual children with a dumb sense of injustice and falsehood. Dora and Julius are past masters at dissimulation: 'It was held that their amusement was their own affair, and confidence on the point was not misplaced, as their pastimes included not only pleasure, but religion, literature and crime. They wrote moral poems that deeply moved them, pilfered coins for the purchase of forbidden goods, and prayed in good faith to the accepted god and their own, perhaps with a feeling that a double share of absolution would not come amiss.'[30] They keep a strict confessional account of daily transgressions like fibbing and fighting ('"O great and good and powerful god, Chung," prayed Dora, "forgive us, we beseech thee, the lie that has passed our lips. For we have uttered to thy handmaid, our governess, the thing that is false, yea and even to our mother. . . ."') but they also intercede to be rid of the subtler duplicities commonly visited on children by even the most well-meaning adults.

Worst of these is the obligation, imposed involuntarily to their mutual embarrassment, to simulate the frank, winning ways considered by their parents proper to childhood: shifty, shame-faced caperings performed with a wholly fraudulent artlessness which makes them considerably more wretched than the comparatively straightforward predicaments evaded by the lie direct. Other novelists have written without sentimentality about children but few have portrayed them on such absolutely equal terms as beings no less intelligent than grown-ups but powerless and hopelessly vulnerable, dwarfed in an alien world whose customs they must obey without understanding. Conversely, the grown-ups in this book are reflected from below as fickle, careless, remote and incalculable giants whose casual actions rebound ominously on the children, whose motives can only be dimly grasped and pieced together with difficulty, whose slipperiness has to be met as best one may with nervous prevarication. These things make for a life of constraint and oppression, further shadowed by the children's guilt at their own double dealing. Small wonder that Dora prays to the god for a ripe old age: 'For it would not be worth while to suffer the trials of childhood, if they were not to lead to fullness of days'.

The trials of childhood naturally foster, at first by instinct, later from hard experience, the growth of reticence and caution. Absolute loyalty requires that the children present a united front to their father when he comes to enquire into a fight which—though it leaves Julius bitten and scratched, Dora with hair torn out and her ribbon undone—both stoutly and promptly deny ('"You did not hit your sister, did you, my boy?" said Thomas, struck by something battered in his daughter's aspect, but assuming that his son would not transgress a certain limit.') Ivy's sisters remembered her being driven, on at least one occasion, to retaliate with tooth and nail on Guy. But such matters, like religion and poetry, were covered by the code of concealment and mutual support between brother and sister which (in youth and middle age as much as in childhood) is violated only by hypocrites or fools in her books.

There were, in any case, other distractions in the Compton Burnett schoolroom. Miss Mills, who was homely and kind but not what her pupils called clever, was fair game to Ivy and Guy who 'played her up a good deal'. She had come to take over the education of the elder trio from Minnie when Ivy was six or seven years old, and she remained until superceded by the daily tutor who taught them Latin and Greek. She was reluctant to leave and tried unsuccessfully, many years later, to persuade Mrs Compton Burnett to take her back for the two youngest of Ivy's four sisters. But her position, like that of so many dependents in Victorian households, cannot have been easy. She lived with the family, took meals in the schoolroom where her word was supposedly law, and remained in her free time awkwardly placed between the servants' hall and the downstairs drawing room, neither welcomed in nor officially excluded from either. A governess's lot was seldom happy, as one of them points out in *Daughters and Sons* to a visitor who had tried to defend it:

> 'What is a little impatience, hastiness—tyranny if it must be said, compared with a real isolation and loneliness?'
> 'I am afraid it must be said, and they are a great deal worse.'[31]

Ivy, who early acquired a reputation for wit and had never been backward at passing remarks, often 'got the better of Miss Mills'. One may suppose that, like Honor in *Parents and Children* (who had already had two governesses when she grimly prepared to do battle with a third), she knew 'the tricks of the trade' and 'the nature of the beasts'. Probably no one now will ever know what passed between Ivy and Guy and Miss Mills in the schoolroom but it is perhaps not entirely unfair to detect some faint reflection of past personal triumphs in the fiendish ingenuity with which Honor Sullivan and Rose Lovat, each ably abetted by her younger brother or sister, persecute their respective governesses. Governesses in the novels fall roughly into two categories: on the one hand those who, possessing like Miss Lacy in *Elders and Betters* an understanding of children not often shared by their parents, are involuntarily respected and occasionally feared by both parents and pupils; and on the other those who, like the Sullivans' Miss Pilbeam or the Lovats' Miss Hallam, have neither the learning nor the moral ascendancy required to keep order. Greed in a governess is always a prime cause for mirth in her pupils, and so are dowdy or insecure clothes—hats which come off in a wind, skirts which unravel at the back or get torn in scuffles with a schoolroom chair. The Compton Burnetts' Miss Mills belonged more or less to the second division, a class well represented by Mildred Hallam in *Darkness and Day* whose first lesson ends in outright defeat by her pupils, and whose second lesson drives her almost to tears:

> 'You think you are patient,' said Viola, wiping her brush. 'But I can tell from your voice that you are not.'
> 'Well, people's patience does not last for ever. It is as well to learn that.'
> 'Yours did not last even for half-an-hour,' said Rose, looking at the clock. 'We have never had anyone with so little.'
> 'I have any amount if there is a reasonable demand on it.'
> 'Well, then you would not want it.'

Alderman Rees and his family at Dover in the 1860s. *Left to right*: Mr and Mrs Rowland Rees, Allen, Katharine, George, Elizabeth, Charles, Rowland, Lucy, John, Sophia

James Compton Burnett at the start of his career

Katharine Rees before her marriage

Ivy at Chesilbank *c.*1887

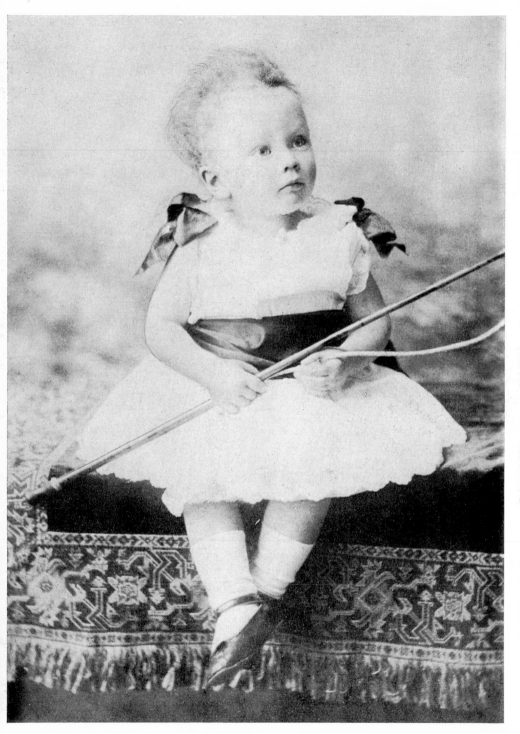

Guy at Chesilbank *c.*1887

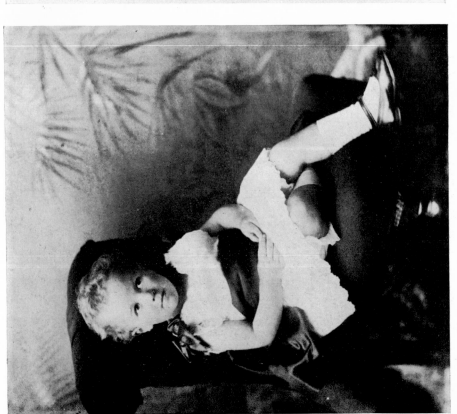

Noel at Chesilbank c.1890

Nellie Smith (Minnie) in her mid-thirties at Hove

Vera and Judy at Hove c.1898

Dr Compton Burnett with Topsy *c.*1898

The drawing room, Addiscombe College, for the Daughters of Gentlemen,
Hove

'And you have less even than you pretend to have,' said Viola.

'And so I suppose you expect me to lose it?'

'Well, we were waiting for that,' said Viola, in an almost engaging tone.

'And then what is to happen?' said Mildred.

'You will say you can't teach us, and stop coming, and we shall go back to learning with Fanshawe. But I daresay you will have your pay for the month. The last governess did.'[32]

But, however poorly the Compton Burnetts may have thought of their governess, she had given them at least one cause for gratitude. It seems to have been Miss Mills who first set Ivy on the track of losing her religion, something she had always mistrusted, gradually ceased to credit and finally discarded as easily as she had earlier relinquished Polio and Elephantas. As a small child she had accepted without question what her elders taught her: 'But I never liked the religion. I never liked it,' she said in a tape-recorded conversation with Kay Dick in 1963. 'I didn't like all the atonement and all that, you know. I didn't like it at all. I thought it was a disagreeable and humiliating religion ... I questioned it because, of course, science came into the air, you see, and Darwin came, and I remember when I was very tiny, about seven, the governess told us that men—I suppose she was modern—descended from monkeys. I remember telling my nurse that she said that, and she said it was very wicked to say that men were not created by the Almighty.'[33] Ten years before this conversation with Miss Dick took place, Ivy had put the identical scene into *The Present and the Past*, where the nursemaid Eliza takes much the same dubious view as Minnie had done when Megan and Henry Clare, aged seven and eight, are launched on modern thought by their governess:

'Are animals of the same nature as we are?' said Henry. 'Monkeys look as if they were.'

'Yes, that is the line of the truth. A scientist called Darwin has told us about it. Of course we have developed much further.'

'Then weren't we made all at once as we are?' said Megan. 'Eliza says that would mean the Bible was not true.'

'It has its essential truth, and that is what matters.'

'I suppose any untrue thing might have that. I daresay a good many have. So there is no such thing as truth. It is different in different minds.'

'Why, you will be a philosopher one day, Megan.'[34]

Mr Salt, the tutor who taught Ivy and her brothers, inspired confidence, unlike Miss Mills, and found unusual aptitude in at least his
two elder pupils. All three of them liked him and, long after the boys
had been dispatched on various, more or less disastrous forays to prep
and public schools, Ivy continued to take Latin and Greek lessons alone
with Mr Salt, who prepared her for the entrance examination when she
finally left home to read classics at college. Such a thing, for a nicely
brought-up girl who had no need to earn her living, was almost
unheard of: history and literature, a little French, music lessons and
sums were as much as was generally considered advisable, or even
decent. Clever daughters of liberal parents might be permitted to share
lessons with their brothers at first but to insist on continuing was worse
than eccentric, and almost bound to end in tears—as it did in Charlotte
M. Yonge's *The Daisy Chain* when, for the sake of 'all the little common
lady-like things' prized by her dear mamma, Ethel May was reluctantly
forced at fifteen to give up learning Latin and Greek with her brother.

The Daisy Chain was a book much beloved by the younger Compton
Burnetts, partly no doubt because its account of nursery and schoolroom life in a doctor's household so closely resembled their own. The
eleven May children divide up by age and sex as the Compton Burnetts
did, the boys preparing for Oxford, the church or the navy, the girls in
fee to dull and crotchety governesses. Worst of Ethel's troubles is her
beloved brother's heartless condescension, when she confides the cause
of her misery to him: 'I assure you, Ethel, it is really time for you to
stop, or you would get into a regular learned lady, and be good for
nothing'.[35] What had been accepted as a matter of course in the 1850s,
when *The Daisy Chain* was published, had become an issue hotly
debated by the time Ivy reached the schoolroom. Alarming examples
of the New Woman—'Not bold or bad she had yet lost that ineffable
something which gives womanhood its essential charm, endows it with
its special power, and throws over it, as it were, a veil of mystic beauty'
—are depicted in Mrs Lynn Linton's *The One Too Many* (1894), a novel
devoted to exposing in dreadful detail the dire effect on a Girton girl of
'that boasted Higher Education which had ruined her nervous system,
prematurely initiated her into the darker secrets of life, and by these two
things destroyed the very well-springs of her health and happiness'.
That Dr Burnett agreed with the general opinion is evident from a
passage in his *Delicate, Backward, Puny and Stunted Children* (published
when Ivy was eleven years old, and presumably nearing the stage at

which Guy would begin to outstrip her) on the relative powers of boys
and girls:

... most of what is commonly said on this point is nothing but weak
twaddle. Only the Almighty can make a New Woman. Put broadly,
up to the age of puberty, the girl, all other things being equal, beats
the boy; with puberty the damsel throws away every month a vast
amount of fluid power in the order of Nature. Let us call this *pelvic
power*. Assuming the girl to be the superior of the boy up to the
pelvic power stage,—which, indeed, anyone can observe for himself,
in his own sphere,—but once arrived at the stage of pelvic power, and
the girl is left behind in her lessons by her brother in the natural order
of things, or else the girl's brain saps the pelvis of its power, when she
will also lose in the race with the boy, because he will be physically
well, while she, with disordered pelvic life, must necessarily be in ill-
health, more or less. The whole thing is a question of energy. . . .

The New Woman is only possible in a novel, not in nature . . . I
have very many times watched the career of exceedingly studious
girls who spent the greater mass of their power in mental work, and
in every case the pelvic powers decreased in even pace with the expenditure of mental power. Not one exception to this have I ever seen . . .
I have sat at the feet of Nature a good many years, and I give it as my
opinion that to be a mother in its best sense is the biggest thing on
earth, and comes nearer the Creator's work than anything else under
heaven; to be a learned girl or woman graduate is a very good and
respectable thing enough, and twelve of them make a dozen.

At the same time, genius has no gender; it can be in a female or in a
male, as the case may be.[36]

Dr Burnett can have had small grounds at this stage for detecting
genius under his roof, but he was by no means an autocrat, or not at
least in his family circle; and his wife, who had herself acquired the
usual accomplishments including embroidery and the singing of
drawing-room ballads at a Miss Hadden's academy in Dover, shared his
respect for intelligence and a sound education. 'We came of a booky
family,' said Ivy[37] and, however heartily her father may have deplored
the New Woman, there seems to have been no question but that his
daughter should learn Latin and Greek like her brothers.

But it was only the middle three who were booky. The four youngest
daughters were musical, an interest which absorbed them almost from

the nursery onwards; and the five stepchildren, having no pretentions to learning, were separately educated. Although the youngest, Charlie, was only eighteen months older than Ivy and considerably closer to her than Noel in age, it was apparently never contemplated that he or any of the others should share a governess, let alone a tutor, with his half-brothers and -sister. Relations between the two families were on the whole cool. Olive, Daisy and Iris had been sent as soon as they were old enough to a boarding school kept by their aunt, Mrs John Compton Burnett, in Bedford, and so were out of the house for most of Ivy's time in the schoolroom. Dick and Charlie attended a day school in Hove and when they left, at the age of fifteen or so, were both articled to solicitors in London. This suited Dick, who was stolid and competent, but not Charlie who was always a daredevil, never cared for the law and had been the kind of boy who could take to the sea and swim without being taught, or jump on a bicycle for the first time at seven years old and ride it away. Of Dr Burnett's four sons, he was the wildest and by far the best-looking, with classical features and blazing blue eyes. The neighbours would send over in a high wind, when Charlie was little, to ask did his mother know there was a small boy flying a kite on the roof?

Charlie can have had little in common with the three immediately below him, who were none of them fond of outdoor pursuits. Olive and Dick were too old to impinge much on the schoolroom party and Iris, being practical and good with her hands, interested them as little as Charlie. Daisy, however, liked children: she was pious, domesticated, 'a home bird', and when she left school would preside over nursery meals at one end of the table with Minnie at the other and the little ones, from Ivy down to the baby in its high chair, ranged in between. Only Daisy got on with their stepmother, and only Olive bore her an open grudge. The others kept whatever they felt to themselves, and none of them was on particularly easy or intimate terms with the rest of the family. Their father being mostly away, their stepmother resenting his absence and never in any case markedly well-disposed towards her stepchildren, their lives had always been hard: Olive and the two boys took the earliest possible chance to leave home, an escape which cost Olive at least a prolonged and desperate struggle.

Ivy and her brothers must have seen enough as small children to grasp the causes of unhappiness and tension, and they saw a great deal more later. But the three lived to themselves, constrained in the company of grown-ups, wholly at ease only with each other and Minnie, impervious to their elder brothers and sisters, ignoring the younger ones and scarcely meeting the outside world except for occasional cousins. It was a conventionally sheltered upbringing, and Ivy took from it things of which she can have been barely aware at the time—except in so far as she was an attentive and thoughtful child, like Fabian Clare in *The Present and the Past*, who at thirteen years old is rebuked by his governess for saying that a good many people can't think:

'And you are one of the fortunate ones who can?' said Miss Ridley, using a dry tone.

'I am one of the unfortunate ones who do. That is how I should put it.'[38]

CHAPTER THREE

1897–1901

I

'No good can come of it'

THE COMPTON BURNETTS had a family pew at St John's Church, Hove, a few minutes' walk from First Avenue and not much further on foot or by carriage from The Drive. In so far as one may judge from his habit of unselfconsciously proclaiming God's truth, calling down God's blessing and committing himself to God's will in his books, Dr Burnett seems to have held the accepted beliefs of his day without qualms, and perhaps without attaching any special importance to them. Religion, or the lack of it, plays no great part in his daughter's books except as a convenient indication of social and intellectual standing. An active faith is generally a sign of mental or moral obtuseness, a passive faith the outcome of a civilized tolerance towards the ways of the world; and since (after the first one) the novels deal exclusively with the educated classes and more particularly with the landed gentry, religion as a matter of course means allegiance to the established church. Vicars (apart from the excellent Rev. Oscar Jekyll in *A House and Its Head* whose Christmas sermon 'was to earn a parishioner's comment, that faith as deep as his would hardly appear on the surface. In fact, his concern with his faith was limited to this level, as it was years since it had existed on any other. . . . He hoped his duties would be less well done by a stupider man, as a believer would probably be; and his views, though of some inconvenience to himself, were of none to his congregation, as they were beyond the range of its suspicions')[1] are usually odious, fools and toadies or worse. Dissent is relegated more or less to the servants' hall, or to occasional minor characters like the schoolmaster Mr Bigwell in *Two Worlds and Their Ways*—an early, high Victorian example of a type which in both life and literature was becoming increasingly familiar and fashionable by 1947, when the novel was published—who came of a working-class, chapel-going family in the north and lost no opportunity of proclaiming in public that he was not ashamed of the fact.

Dr Burnett's first wife's family, the Thomases, had been church people and her children, unlike their half-brothers and -sisters, maintained a strong religious bias. Daisy, who in her twenties twice underwent nervous breakdowns which took the form of a mild religious mania, eventually 'gave herself to Jesus' and set out, to Ivy's amusement, as a missionary for Northern Nigeria; Iris, who became a nurse before the first war at the Temperance Hospital in London, remained like her elder sister an ardent and active churchwoman to the end of her life. Katharine Compton Burnett's position was more equivocal. There was still in the late nineteenth century a gulf fixed between church and chapel whose adherents, ranking low in the social hierarchy, kept themselves to themselves, confined their evangelical attentions as a rule to the labouring classes and had indeed only reluctantly and after long altercation been admitted to such elementary privileges as attendance at the older universities or entry to the learned professions. Methodists in particular traditionally looked with suspicion on any but the most limited education, and mistrusted all reading matter (John Wesley's own annotated Shakespeare had been burnt shortly after his death by a zealous disciple, on the ground that it was 'useless lumber') save the Bible and the Methodist Hymn Book, supplemented on occasion by tracts and sermons. Rowland Rees himself had been converted during a campaign directed almost entirely at the lowest ranks of the army; and the social limitations involved in his choice of religion afterwards inevitably proved a sore point with later generations of Reeses.

It cannot have been pleasant for anyone as sensitive as Ivy's mother to find herself exposed, when she left home, to the kind of slights for which nothing in her background could have prepared her. Family pride was her delight, as it had been her father's, and perhaps also a consolation, even a form of self-defence, in the peculiarly difficult and lonely position imposed by her marriage. Certainly she always considered that, in the choice of his first wife, her husband had married beneath him and, though she took her place at his side without question in public, in private she deplored the unorthodoxy which blocked his professional career. James Compton Burnett would do anything to please her short of changing his medical faith: she had to be content with extolling his achievements, despising a profession which ostracized him, and inserting a hyphen into his name to make it look better. But it must have been a further blow to discover that her father's prominence in Wesleyan circles, which had been a source of rejoicing at Dover, was likely to prove a grave disadvantage in fashionable Hove; and, having

suffered much from the handicap of being a homoeopath's wife, she saw
no reason why she should suffer for being a Methodist's daughter as well.

But her transfer of allegiance was made discreetly, and never wholly
completed. Rowland Rees was not a man easily flouted, though what
later became a widespread retreat from chapel to church among his
descendants had already begun in his lifetime when his youngest son
George became an Anglican priest ('a spanking parson' was Ivy's
phrase for her Uncle George, who had impressed her as a child by con-
suming a whole haddock for breakfast besides quantities of bacon and
eggs). It was Rowland Rees' elder son Allen, however, who regularly
officiated at the marriages of his brothers and sisters. One of Ivy's
cousins was a Methodist missionary in China while her mother's
favourite sister, Elizabeth, and Elizabeth's husband, Robert Blackie,
continued the family tradition as strong chapel people. Of all their
relations the Compton Burnetts saw most of their Aunt Lizzie, Uncle
Robert and the ten Blackie cousins who overlapped them in age down-
wards from Olive to the four youngest daughters. The two families
exchanged visits, spent holidays together and, in Ivy's early childhood,
several times foregathered at Clacton where her grandfather had settled
in 1885 and the Blackies a few years before. Nearly eighty years after
that summer at Clacton when she first saw the sea, Ivy 'remembered
driving in the governess cart, pulled by a donkey, with her brother, the
governess and the nurse. "They are all gone now," she said, "the village
has gone, the donkey has gone, the governess cart has gone, and certainly the governess and the nurse have gone."'[2]

Robert Blackie, who looked forward to a substantial inheritance
from his father's engineering business in Liverpool, had moved to
Essex round about 1880, established his family at Valley Farm a mile or
so over fields to the sands of Clacton-on-Sea, promptly built himself a
handsome and much larger mansion on the site of what had once been
a thatched cottage called Clay Hall, and generally set up in some style
as a gentleman farmer.* He was elected Sea Defence Commissioner

---

* Robert Blackie and his father, who had come south to marry one of Rowland Rees'
Pudney cousins at Clacton, between them bought up all the small properties (Valley
Farm, the Pudneys' Coppins Hall and Coppins Wick, the Sadlers' Clay Hall) associated with their wives' families; several of these (Coppins Wick, parts of Valley Farm
and Clay Hall Farm, sites at Magdalen Green) later passed to their still more prosperous relation, James Compton Burnett, who also acquired the Clacton Mansion House,
Foots Farm at Little Clacton and High Birch Farm at St Osyth. Terrace houses put up
on these building plots would have been the nearest thing to an ancestral estate in the
Compton Burnett family.

shortly after he arrived, besides sitting on the Board of Guardians and the parochial committee for Clacton-on-Sea. As a keen local preacher, an impassioned teetotaller and steward of the Clacton Methodist circuit from 1882 to 1887, he took no small pleasure in supervising local religious affairs. He was known as 'the Squire' to his Compton Burnett nephews and nieces on account of his lavish notions of the state due to a gentleman, resembling at any rate in this respect Sir Godfrey Haslam in *Men and Wives* who also came of dissenting stock, had inherited an industrial fortune from his 'dear old parents', purchased a country house in which to install his family and his newly acquired family portraits, and lived comfortably thereafter on an income which, though a source of considerable discomfort to his butler Buttermere, caused none to himself. ('Nothing to be ashamed of in my heritage, Buttermere, in a useful little fortune and title earned by providing people with things they need, by putting at their hand what sufficed unto them. I should blush for myself if I blushed for it.')³ Like Sir Godfrey, Robert Blackie was fond of delivering long extempore prayers to his family in private.

Together with his father-in-law, Rowland Rees (many of whose strong views he shared), Mr Blackie was frequently at the centre of local controversy in what proved a comparatively short but stormy career at Clacton. Always an enthusiastic speaker on behalf of the Liberal party, he was convicted in 1885 of assault at a Clacton election meeting; he was brought before the magistrates again in 1886 for failing to pay sea defence and general rates, and yet again the same year for refusing to vaccinate his children (whereupon, with support from Rowland Rees, he organized an anti-vaccination meeting as part of a campaign which culminated in the local doctor's resigning his seat on the Sanitary Committee, of which Robert Blackie was then chairman); and he was so vehemently in favour of signing the pledge that, in 1888, he notified the local press that he 'desired henceforward to work his farm on total abstinence principles'.⁴

For the past few years he had managed the farm at Coppins Hall for his two maiden aunts, Miss Eliza and Miss Mary Grace Pudney, the last of a line which had owned Coppins Hall Farm for nearly two hundred years. The Misses Pudney were renowned in their lifetimes, and remembered locally for another quarter of a century, as outstanding—whether for piety, good works or missionary zeal—among the 'elect ladies' of Clacton. They organized charity bazaars in the 'eighties, held weekly prayer meetings in their farm kitchen and drove out on

Sundays in an old-fashioned carriage to Trinity Methodist Church at
Great Clacton. They also dominated the Trinity Ladies' Sewing Meeting, an 'ever-green and ever-fruitful organization' which was perhaps
the precursor of Lady Haslam's ineffable working parties in *Men and
Wives*, where the sterner business of scandal, gossip and long-standing
feuds leaves the ladies scant time for the manufacture of flannel petti-
coats for orphans:

> 'Really this is not fit for the poor. I don't see how any unfortunate
> person could wear it, not anyone already unfortunate.'
> 'It is plain and strong,' said Mellicent.
> 'I hardly liked to put it into words, but it is, isn't it?'[5]

Missionary work among the neighbouring hamlets was vigorously
prosecuted by local evangelists 'eager for more conquests in Christ',
and nowhere more so than at Coppins Hall where the labouring population was 'greatly blessed' and 'soundly converted' at first in open air
services, later in a barn owned by the Misses Pudney, and finally in a
brand-new chapel built on land given 'in answer to prayer'[6] by Dr
Compton Burnett. Since the doctor all his life could refuse his wife
nothing, the prayers were presumably hers for Mrs Compton Burnett,
though she had preferred church to chapel for herself and her children,
seems always to have retained some misgivings about the exchange.

Ivy had probably been taken as a small child to visit, and would
certainly have heard stories about, the Misses Pudney and their
widowed sister Georgiana Blackie (mother to her Uncle Robert), who
all three lived to a great age, Miss Eliza dying in 1892 at eighty years
old, Mrs Blackie at eighty-four in 1901, and Miss Mary Grace at ninety-
one on 29 January 1911, a month before I. Compton-Burnett's first
novel was published. They were first cousins to her grandfather Rowland Rees (his mother and theirs had been sisters, Nancy and Lucy
Sadler) as well as connections twice over by the simultaneous marriages
in 1875 of their nephew and niece, Robert and Esther Blackie, to Mrs
Compton Burnett's sister and brother, Elizabeth and Charles Rees.
Ivy's uncle and grandfather had both left Clacton by the time she was
eight years old (Robert Blackie moving to Norfolk, Rowland Rees to a
house in St John's Road, Hove) but when she began work in her early
twenties on a novel startlingly different in both kind and quality from
any of her later work, she drew copiously on material supplied by her
Methodist connections. The complicated family tree linking Pudneys,

Reeses, Blackies and Burnetts is reproduced almost branch for branch in *Dolores*, and the atmosphere of pious ferment at Clacton in the 'eighties and 'nineties is as faithfully drawn in the Wesleyan background to that novel. The Coppins Hall barn, the public conversions, the local preachers patronizing a chapel congregation composed of small shop-keepers and cottagers all reappear in *Dolores*, and so does the evangelical fervour prevalent for at least two generations on the Rees side of the family: '"No, I don't agree with you there, Mrs Cassell," said Mr Blackwood loudly; "I don't agree with you. I remain a staunch up-holder of *Temperance* myself. We Wesleyans don't shrink from showing our colours for a cause we honestly have at heart; and I shall never shrink from showing mine for Temperance. Ah, yes; there are Wes-leyans in every part of the world, showing their colours for what they believe in their hearts to be right."'[7]

On Ivy's father's side of the family colours were less strident, and not so insistently shown. Generations of Burnetts seem to have switched back and forth as a regular thing between nonconformity and the established church, but the Congregational movement belonged to an older, staider and rather more cultivated tradition of dissent than John Wesley's society. James Compton Burnett's brother John, when Ivy first knew him, was a Congregational minister without a congregation of his own, occupied in preaching and teaching at Bedford. He had begun his career with churches at Burnham in Essex and Saxmundham in Suffolk but, being obliged by poor health to retire from the ministry in his late thirties, had moved to Bedford in 1877 where he joined first Howard Congregational Church (named for the philanthropist and prison reformer John Howard, who was a founder member in 1772) and later Bunyan Meeting (named for John Bunyan who became its minister shortly after the meeting began in 1650). Both these churches organized classes, lectures, Sunday schools and a well-established net-work of lesser churches, for Bedford had been since Cromwell's time a centre of religious independence. Bunyan Meeting especially—which had connections with Whitbreads, Wilberforces, Kingsleys and is several times depicted in the novels of Mark Rutherford, whose father was superintendent of Sunday schools in the 'forties—flourished in the second half of the nineteenth century under the Rev. John Brown, a man of considerable energy, charm and resource, ecclesiastical historian, author of the standard life of John Bunyan, and grandfather to Maynard and Geoffrey Keynes. The Rev. John Compton Burnett was a friend of Dr Brown, and his active supporter at Bunyan Meeting. Ivy's uncle took services, gave lectures, preached in its five village churches and was for ten years an able and unusually popular secretary of the Bedford Union of Christians.[8] His wife's school for girls, Howard College (where Ivy herself was sent for a couple of terms at the age of seventeen), had a reputation for 'careful Christian training, high class teaching, physical training'[9] and was one of the more select establishments in a town noted for its private schools.

Ivy's Uncle Jack and Aunt Sarah (their four children were older even than Dr Burnett's first family) paid fairly frequent visits to Hove. Sarah Compton Burnett was an imposing figure, stout and stately, dressed generally in black, with a black satin reticule and a manner calculated to inspire awe rather than affection in her nephews and nieces, as in her pupils. Her husband was more approachable; he took Scripture lessons at Howard College where the girls both liked and looked up to him. The two brothers seem to have shared much the same disposition. Both were by inclination gentle and genial and, both having married formidable wives, they remained so fond of one another that, whether fairly or not, one cannot help recalling the two mild and amiable middle-aged brothers, Edgar and Dudley Gaveston in *A Family and a Fortune*, whose devotion was grounded in a 'friendship which dated from their infancy'.[10] Dr. Burnett was a huge man, tall and so broad that the desk in his library at The Drive had had to be specially built for him; his brother was as tall but slighter, less robust, with a stoop imposed by a delicate constitution; and it is at least possible that the characteristic image of the Gavestons—'two tall figures', the one bending towards the other, strolling arm in arm on the terrace and watched from the windows by Edgar's children—may have been suggested by a memory of Jack and Jim Compton Burnett walking and talking together at Hove.

Other members of the family were less in evidence, Dr Burnett's eldest brother and sister (another Aunt Sarah) being both for similar reasons disgraced. Ivy's Uncle Charles, who was a Congregational minister at Sheerness and Newmarket in the 'sixties, had emigrated in 1873 to America and shortly afterwards died there; he was said to have married his cook, a scandal mentioned only with bated breath in the Compton Burnett household. His sister had married a policeman in Bournemouth and, for all the good it did her in the family, 'might as well have married a convict and gone to Botany Bay'. Both were effectively erased from the family annals, along with the fact that their father had been a shopkeeper, coal merchant and dairyman. It is difficult to overestimate the importance of such social considerations in middle-

class, high Victorian England: one of the things which had disgusted
Ivy, and presumably shaped her attitude to the church, was her memory
of 'our parson in Hove telling my mother he wanted a curate to
call on the trades people'.[11] This parson was occasionally invited to dine
but the Compton Burnetts were not over strict about church attendance: they went sometimes to St John's, sometimes to the parish
church of All Saints which was nearer The Drive, and only on special
occasions (when the girls had new frocks) to church parade on the
front which was then the high spot of the week for fashionable Hove.
Mrs Compton Burnett liked driving out with Ivy or another of her
daughters to hear the Rev. A. D. Spong (namesake of the unspeakable
Dominic Spong in *Men and Wives*) of Cliftonville Congregational
Church, whose sermons were much admired and regularly reported in
the local press; but though she publicly attended the Anglican service
with her family in the morning, she would often slip out privately at
night with her stepdaughter Daisy for evening worship at the Methodist
chapel.

Ivy was duly baptized, confirmed and sent at fourteen to a High
Church school. She herself on different occasions and to different
people later set the date of her own disillusionment at various ages,
ranging from ten to seventeen: 'I was brought up perfectly ordinarily
in the Church of England but when I was sixteen or seventeen my
reason naturally rejected such nonsense. No good can come of it. Its
foundations are laid in fostering guilt in people—well, that obviously
makes it easier for our Pastors and Masters when we are young,' she
told Elizabeth Taylor in 1957. In the same decade she told Barbara and
Walter Robinson that 'My brother gave up believing in God at the
same time as Father Christmas, he realized they couldn't both be true.
And it was a terrible shock.' The brother in question was almost certainly the ten-year-old Guy at Christmas 1895, when Ivy was eleven
years old. Probably their scepticism grew gradually, encouraged by a
series of shocks like this one (or Miss Mills' revelation when Ivy was
seven) and sharpened in reaction to the kind of treatment meted out by
his grandmother to Hengist Middleton, who with his sister had played
a shabby trick on their governess: '"Hengist, you thought we did not
know. But there was Someone Who knew. Can you tell me Who saw
what you did, and saw into your hearts as you did it?" Selina had no
religion herself, but feared to let her grandchildren do without it.'[12]

It is not now easy to gauge the misery and resentment inflicted on
small children taught to believe literally in hell fire or (as Ivy remem-

bered being told by the under-nurse) that thunder was a sign of God's anger, in retaliation for some nursery crime, and would shortly be fol-lowed by His punishment. Ivy and her brothers seem to have reached their position of humorous incredulity easily and early, without assist-ance and apparently without any of the torments suffered by an older generation of conscientious Victorians who, like Henry Sidgwick in fact and Robert Elsmere in fiction, lost their faith as adults and whose lives were blighted, even broken, by agonizing problems of conscience. But appearances may be deceptive. Religious guilt was a part of that oppressive burden cast off with such an immense sense of relief at the turn of the century by Ivy's generation, and from which she herself had not escaped entirely unscathed. Dolores' prolonged career of self-sacrifice, in I. Compton-Burnett's first novel, recalls in its frantic, un-relieved gloom the conflicts commonly endured by Victorian heroes and heroines in the throes of religious doubt, a struggle at its most tortuous in Edmund Gosse's *Father and Son*, at its most hectic in Mrs Humphrey Ward (whose heroine's doctrine of self-sacrifice, in *Robert Elsmere*, repays comparison with Dolores'), and which casts a shadow even over the cheerful domesticity of Charlotte M. Yonge (when Norman May's faith is sorely tried in *The Daisy Chain*). Religious pressure varied from the simpler nursery forms of emotional blackmail to the curdled cruelty systematically practised by the Rev. Theodore Pontifex on his son in Samuel Butler's *The Way of All Flesh*. In her late thirties, Ivy still felt strongly enough on the subject to mark with a pencil line this passage in her copy of Butler's *Note-Books*:

Religion.
Is there any religion whose followers can be pointed to as distinctly more amiable and trustworthy than those of any other? If so, this should be enough. I find the nicest and best people generally profess no religion at all, but are ready to like the best men of all religions.[13]

Butler's view coincides exactly with what later became Ivy's own characteristic position, given sombre expression by France Ponsonby discussing her Aunt Hetta in *Daughters and Sons*:

'She goes to church,' said Muriel. 'And she does not have to go, does she?'
'If she were religious, she would not go,' said France. 'She would have thought about her religion and lost it.'[14]

We know something of what this relaxed and rational attitude had cost Samuel Butler, from his letters and his father's and from his own scarifying account of an upbringing which left him in some ways at least emotionally crippled for the rest of his life. Ivy's childhood, at any rate on this count, bears no comparison with Butler's; but long afterwards she would sometimes speak with a vehemence that suggests an abiding grudge against religion, all trace of which is expunged from her books where the customary attitude among the astute, young or old, is the kind of amused scepticism she had once shared with her brother. Her bitterness in later life may be seen perhaps as a measure of her pain at their loss, strengthened possibly by the fact that Guy and Noel—who both naturally possessed, in their sister's phase, 'a religious temper and no beliefs'[15]—had each severally turned at the end to the Bible for consolation in face of death.

However that may be, religious difficulties apparently caused no particular friction in the Compton Burnett household. It was accepted as a matter of course that Ivy and Guy and Noel (known as Jim to his family and friends because he disliked his baptismal name, or Noll to his younger sisters) should attend church 'under duress at times', and it later became a question as to which one should accompany their mother if she were going. 'My mother, I think, rather lost her beliefs because we did, or sort of half lost them,' Ivy said to Kay Dick. By this time Dr Burnett had died, and his wife seems to have made no bones about her children's rationalism—tolerating it perhaps as a sign of intelligence, and so a source for pride, as she had earlier tolerated Ivy's learning Greek with her brothers.

'Thirteen . . . is a suffering age'

THE CONCEIT OF parts, which Boswell discerned and Dr Johnson approved in Mrs Thrale, was rife in the Compton Burnett schoolroom as it will be among clever and competitive children brought up, as these were, to furnish their brain boxes with nourishing porridge in a family whose other members were duller, and despised on that account. Ivy had inherited from her father his studious temperament and respect for learning, from her mother that 'exquisitely intellectual development' which had inspired such detached, professional pleasure in Dr Burnett when they first met. Her children's intelligence was a keen satisfaction to Mrs Compton Burnett, as it is to other strongminded mothers in her daughter's books. Anxiety on this score comes naturally to Eleanor Sullivan who, in spite of evidence daily supplied to the contrary by her son James, still cannot entertain 'the possibility of an absolutely ordinary child'; or to Sophia Stace whose habit of comparing her own children favourably with their humbler cousins, the Latimers, sustains her rare moods of complacency: 'My family could hardly escape intelligence, with their parents what they are.'[16] Ivy's achievements and Guy's were a congenial topic whenever the Blackies came to stay at Hove, and a cause of some asperity between the two sisters: 'Well, my dear, your children may have all the brains,' said Aunt Lizzie, 'but mine have the looks.'

Intelligence was evidently a weapon in Ivy's childhood, as it is in her books. It is also the moral principle which underlies all her work, the source of perception (without which there can be no self-knowledge) and so of all generosity. Conversely, ignorance is the pretext which enables the insensitive safely and with a good conscience to practise all forms of meanness:

'I can do no more for you, Mortimer. The truth is the kindest thing.'
'Is that so? I wonder what would be the unkindest.'[17]

The same code is advanced in book after book, by shrewd and experienced adults like Mortimer Lamb in *Manservant and Maidservant* or
Rachel Hardistie in *Men and Wives* ('Being cruel to be kind is such
dreadful cruelty. Being cruel to be cruel is better'), as by inexperienced
and unhappy children like Clemence Shelley in *Two Worlds and Their
Ways*. It is curious to note the clumsiness with which Clemence (whose
schoolmistresses, having convicted her of cheating at school, casually
smash her security at home by sending a full account to her mother)
painfully works out for herself the doctrine unobtrusively practised,
and so much more gracefully expressed, by sophisticates like Rachel or
Mortimer: 'I don't think they were kind. No kind person would have
told about it. They knew what that meant, or knew part of it. I could
see they did. They were too stupid to know all of it, but stupidity is not
kindness. I don't think a really kind person would ever be stupid.'[18]
   Clemence Shelley at thirteen bears much the same relation to Ivy
herself in childhood as the ten-year-old Honor Sullivan in *Parents and
Children*. Both Clemence and Honor are bright little girls, both inclined
to disparage their governesses, both naturally adopting an attitude at
once encouraging and protective towards a timid younger brother who
is his mother's favourite. Both excel at arithmetic, Honor ostentatiously
outstripping her maladroit governess at sums, Clemence doing hers so
much faster than the rest of the form that she has to be checked by her
maths mistress: 'Clemence has done it in her head! So I will ask her not
to answer the next one. We must all be given a chance, and mere
quickness is not everything.' In 1965, Elizabeth Taylor encountered
much the same situation when, on being asked if she could do a tricky
income tax calculation in her head, Ivy replied: 'I have done so. I am very
good at arithmetic. When I was at school, I was so good that I wasn't
allowed to answer the questions, but had to give the other girls a chance'.
   Like Ivy, Clemence (who had already begun Latin and Greek at home
with her brother's tutor) has specially arranged private Greek lessons at
school, proudly refuting 'the theory that classical and mathematical
ability do not meet'. Clemence has her fourteenth birthday in her first
term at school, Ivy was just turned fourteen when she was sent in the
autumn of 1898 to Addiscombe College for the Daughters of Gentlemen in Hove. The two establishments have so much in common that it
is unreasonable not to suspect some admixture of personal experience
underlying Clemence's dreadful first day at school, and her first
encounter with that surreptitious, sly brutality cultivated with such

expertise by hardened schoolgirls—a brutality barely concealed when, having subjected the newcomer to a ruthless interrogation on her cleverness, age, future prospects, her parents, home and family circumstances, the other girls crowd into the dormitory while matron unpacks to inspect Clemence's clothes, and pass biting remarks on her lack of a party frock:

> 'What are those things?' said Esther, indicating some linen in Miss Tuke's hands. 'Underclothes?'
> 'Now what do you think they would be?' said Miss Tuke, shaking them out.
> 'I don't know,' said Verity, in a low tone, as though good manners deterred her from going further.[19]

Clemence's hair is another incentive to wit among her companions who tirelessly draw each other's, the matron's and their form mistress's attention to what strikes them as an odd and conspicuous hair style. Ivy had been proud of her long curly hair which she wore loose, tied back with a ribbon when she was fifteen or so, till she had it put up in a roll at the back of her head. Both her clothes and her hair had given rise to comment when, at eighteen, she went away to college: 'No one could deny her brains and probably her coaches had a better opinion of her than we did, but she did not really fit into ordinary academic life,' wrote a contemporary who wishes to remain anonymous. 'My chief recollection of her is as a rather badly dressed—but most of us were— girl with an incredible head of peroxide golden hair dressed in defiance of any fashion in a top-knot.'

Five different schools are examined in the novels of I. Compton-Burnett, but the only other small girl at school is Amy Grimstone in *The Last and the First* (the novel on which Dame Ivy was still at work when she died, published posthumously in 1971). Amy suffers under all the same heads as Clemence: painfully shy and self-conscious, agonized at school functions, going in mortal shame of her shabby clothes, her embarrassing relations and of not having a new dress for the school play. When her school is threatened with extinction, Amy is philosophical:

> 'How will you feel if the school is given up, and you have to go to another?'
> 'I am not sure, Grannie,' said Amy, seeing no prospect of real change unless all schools met this fate.[20]

That the system is unfair, inevitable and 'part of a great wrong' is also the view of Oliver Shelley, Clemence's older stepbrother in *Two Worlds and Their Ways*, who retains a vivid memory of his own school: 'It taught me to trust no one and to expect nothing. . . . To keep everything from everyone, especially from my nearest friends. That familiarity breeds contempt, and ought to breed it. It is through familiarity that we get to know each other.' The same point is put later in the same book from the opposite side, in a discussion between the matron and the headmaster's wife on the cruelty of older boys:

'The new boys do not meet that here.'
'Might they not be asked the number of their sisters and their fathers' Christian names? The rumours cannot be quite without foundation.'
'That would not hurt them.'
'I never know why it hurts them so much. But it seems to be recognized.'[21]

Clemence and her younger brother Sefton are rightly apprehensive when the time comes for them to move on from governess and tutor. Ivy and her brothers had also made scenes when all three were dispatched simultaneously to school, Ivy to Addiscombe College, the boys to a prep school in Cromwell Road near The Drive kept by a Mr Charles Holland. Noel, who at eleven years old was already an accomplished mimic, privately regaled his sisters with imitations of Mr Holland extolling the merits of his 'little fellows' to their parents: 'But when the little fellows were in class, it was quite another story,' said Noel darkly. He and Guy later became weekly boarders, coming home on Friday evenings after school tea. When they were asked by their headmaster what was the first thing they did on reaching home, both replied with one voice: 'Have tea'. But neither was the kind of small boy likely to cause a moment's uneasiness to nervous adults like Terence Calderon, who has doubts of his cousin Reuben in *Elders and Betters*: 'I hope he is not a great hearty creature. If he is, I have been misled. I know he is thirteen, and that is a suffering age.'[22]

The Compton-Burnetts were not hearty creatures. Guy's chest had always been weak, and his health so frail that, when he was sent on to Tonbridge at fourteen, he was brought home desperately ill after two terms and nearly died of pneumonia. Noel who, according to his father, had been 'so strong and robust at birth that it was thought needless to bother' about oiling him, had fallen back by the time he was eight years old to become 'by far the least fine and strong'[23] of them all. At thirteen or fourteen he strained his back while running downhill with Vera and Judy, was laid up for weeks and could never again play strenuous games. Guy was similarly forbidden on account of his chest. Addiscombe College had its own sports ground on The Drive where in the afternoons there were games of hockey in winter, tennis and cricket in summer, in which neither Ivy nor her sisters took part.

Vera had been sent to school in 1899, in hopes of avoiding a fresh outbreak of the fuss and tears which had afflicted her elders the year before. Judy joined her in 1901 and so did their next sister, Katharine (called Topsy), a particularly bright and self-possessed child of five. Topsy was once caught and reproved by the headmistress, Miss Cadwallader, for laughing at another small girl in the kindergarten: 'But, Topsy, you don't know everything yourself, do you?' 'No,' replied Topsy firmly. 'And neither do you, Miss Cadwallader, do you?' The Compton Burnett girls were remembered by their contemporaries at school as shy, hesitant, withdrawn and shabbily dressed. They took no extras save elocution, attended no dances, plays or painting exhibitions, didn't mix, made few friends and never asked anyone home to play—'When school was over they packed their satchels and spoke to no one, they came straight down, took their hats from their pegs and went home to work.' But they were undeniably clever. Vera, coming downstairs one day as Miss Cadwallader was interviewing the anxious parent of a prospective pupil in the hall below, overheard her say with emphasis: 'There goes one (we have them all) of a very gifted family.'

There were three Misses Cadwallader: the two eldest—Miss Catherine who was the nominal headmistress, taught poetry and scripture, took prayers and received the parents, and Miss Laura who took the top classes and was widely feared by her duller pupils—ran the school in partnership with Miss Katherine Marsland, a mathematician from Newnham. The youngest sister, Miss Frances (known as 'Fussy Frances' to her charges), did the housekeeping together with the Matron, Miss Lane, who looked after the boarders' clothes. Addiscombe College occupied two adjoining houses, numbers 39 and 41 Tisbury Road (which runs directly behind The Drive), and prided itself on its excellent tone, drawing its pupils mainly from the professional classes, among them a good many doctors' daughters, holding cricket matches in the summer with Roedean, and boasting a dancing mistress who had once taught the Prince of Wales and his brother. It was also devoutly

High Church—'rather too high for comfort', as one of its pupils recalled. Ivy herself remembered with distaste interminable lessons on 'history of the prayer book, history of Collects and all kinds of such things'. The Misses Cadwallader wore black in Lent ('And I can remember Miss Laura coming into prayers on Ash Wednesday with the most dismal countenance you can imagine'),[24] celebrated Ascension Day with a school picnic on the downs and on Sundays conducted a crocodile of the twenty-five boarders, dressed in the school uniform of green skirts, white blouses and white hats with a Welsh dragon badge (the Cadwalladers, like the Reeses, claimed descent from a royal Welsh line), to St Barnabas church.

But their views on education for girls were considered distinctly advanced. They were unusually particular about their staff and its qualifications, retaining a resident mademoiselle (though the standard of compulsory French speaking remained fairly elementary: '*Donnez-moi un bun*'), a visiting German Fräulein, and visiting masters for music, elocution and riding. Miss Laura and Miss Marsland had read English and mathematics at London and Cambridge respectively, a great thing in those days as Ivy confirmed in *The Present and the Past* ('Miss Ridley had obtained a degree, a step whose mystic significance for a woman was accepted at that date even by those who had taken it').[25] Their pupils learnt Latin but no Greek, overstepping even in this the bounds of Mrs Lynn Linton's ideal (a maiden 'not attuned to aught but the tender things of everyday life—innocent, unsuspicious, affectionate—just the good, dear girl of a quiet English home'), but conforming to the conditions exacted from poor Ethel May in *The Daisy Chain*, who had been induced to give up her dearest wish on the grounds that she could not both learn Greek and remain 'a useful, steady daughter and sister at home . . . The sort of woman that dear mamma wished to make you, and a comfort to papa.'[26] Ivy, however, remained adamant, neither innocent nor unsuspicious, unattuned to the tender, everyday things ('Which finger do I put the thimble on?' she asked once to tease in a needlework class), and content to study Greek alone in private coaching sessions at school with Mr Salt. Any girl not positively incapable at Addiscombe College was expected to sit the Cambridge Local Board examinations, but Ivy was again unique in proposing to go on to university.

Vera Compton-Burnett remembered Miss Laura Cadwallader as 'rather the New Woman, very shirty' (that is, she wore a shirt and tie and was 'as like a man as it is possible to be, without actually being one'). She was grave, stern, highly esteemed for her awesome B.A., and took small part in the everyday affairs of the school. One may suspect that, of all the mistresses, Miss Laura was the one most likely to appeal to Ivy who recounted with the respect of one wit for another her remark, on handing back the form's work, to one Florence who was not much of a hand at writing essays: 'Mean little handwriting, Florrie, and mean little ideas.' Miss Laura's particular friend was Miss Marsland (the two had been colleagues at Portsmouth High School before taking over Addiscombe College in 1896), who had 'a high, shiny forehead, long hair oiled and coiled like a great Chelsea bun', and whose geometry lessons are still remembered with pleasure by several of her pupils: 'Miss Marsland was *quite different* from the Cadwalladers. She was gentle and kind and, if you were naughty, she dissolved into tears.'[27] By all accounts the pair closely resembled two of the three partners at Clemence's school in *Two Worlds and Their Ways*:

Miss Marathon's upright figure, pronounced nose and prominent, expressionless eyes gave her a somewhat forbidding aspect, that was hardly borne out by her pupils' demeanour towards her. She sat among them and supervised their needs in a manner at once precise and kindly, critical and tolerant. Miss Laurence was recognized as too intellectual for tangible affairs, and remained aloof and did nothing, thereby both creating and fulfilling a part. Her pupils regarded her with affection and fear, or merely with the latter. Miss Marathon they regarded with neither, and with no other particular feeling.[28]

Miss Catherine Cadwallader, who cultivated a winning manner and a penchant for pastel shades, pale fawn, grey lace, floating draperies, was 'the opposite of her sister', though equally formidable in a different way. An associate of Cheltenham Ladies' College, her function was to cajole, reassure and entertain the parents—a part she played as expertly as Amy Grimstone's headmistress or Mr Merry in *Pastors and Masters*, both insinuating, equivocal, even sinister creatures, both strangely relaxed among the various forms of uneasiness which inevitably exist in a school, both adept at making capital out of a natural vagueness as to the identity and achievements of any particular pupil:

'Well, Mr Merry,' said a father, 'so you haven't put my boy among the prize-winners? Of course, I don't mean that. But he doesn't go in for taking prizes, does he?'

'Ah, your boy,' said Mr Merry, who knew the ill policy of honesty with parents; 'and a nice boy too! No, he doesn't go in for taking prizes. No, not yet. But I tell you what.' Mr Merry's voice became intimate. 'If I had a boy, I should like him to be your boy. I will tell you that.'[29]

Like Mr Merry, Miss Cadwallader was in her element at the school prize-giving for which Hove Town Hall was taken every year, and for which the staff and parents (Dr Burnett only after stiff protest) wore evening dress, the children their party frocks.

Ivy took her matriculation when she had just passed her seventeenth birthday in the summer of 1901, and was then sent for a couple of terms to Howard College at Bedford so that she might grow accustomed to life away from home. Bedford in those days was in its late Victorian heyday, a centre for private boarding schools and a favourite retreat of the army and navy (a local directory for 1902 lists among the town's residents a retired vice-admiral, a paymaster-in-chief, a deputy inspector-general R.N., two naval captains, a commander and two lieutenants, four generals, one lieutenant-general, two major-generals, thirty-five colonels, sixteen majors and twenty-two captains). The countryside came right up to the rim of the town, nightjars sang in the outskirts and the corncrake could still be heard within half a mile of Howard College at 77 Bromham Road; 'old gentlemen on tricycles, riding three abreast, in authoritative measured tones would discuss their afternoon's golf or the iniquities of the latest budget, as they returned home along Bromham Road'; the town's peace was broken only by 'furiously driving butcher boys' or, on market days, by sheep which 'ran down any available turning and through garden gates left open (those of Howard College among others)'.[30] The school itself was another enlightened establishment, run on much the same lines as Addiscombe College and pluming itself, according to the Rev. John Compton Burnett, on moral guidance, physical training and mental work in that order.* It took some thirty or forty boarders, half a dozen

---

* Ivy's uncle died before he knew that she would amply fulfil a prophecy he had made in an address to the school in 1899: 'He found it difficult to give any adequate report of the real work they were doing. Theirs was largely a sowing of seed which would produce its harvest in the characters and lives of their pupils in after years. . . . They aimed first of all at the true physical training of their pupils. They were careful not only about diet and light, about ventilation and drill. They went further; they were specially considerate of means for the expansion of the chest, which was not only of such prime importance in the child's development, but enriched the blood and told

day girls, and drew special attention in advertisements and prospectus
to its site on gravel soil, its lighting, ventilation, sanitary arrangements
and the exertions of its drill sergeant.

Ivy's Aunt Sarah ran it, though she did no teaching herself, ruling her
staff, her pupils and her husband—who was 'a little retiring as he was
very much dominated by his wife'[31]—with a despot's authority. Ivy's
uncle had in fact died a few months before she reached Howard College
but, so far as the school was concerned, his departure meant only that
his widow became its nominal as well as its actual head. A contemporary of Ivy well remembered saying to another girl, 'Oh, we are making a row,' and being overheard, called back and curtly rebuked by
Mrs Compton Burnett: 'Never say "row", say "hubbub".' Ivy herself
long afterwards described her cousin Maude, who helped in the school
and was then nearly thirty, being treated before company as tersely as
if she were still in the nursery: 'Maude, leave the room'. The family
lived in the school buildings (which had been specially built in 1878,
now converted into flats), and left a vivid memory with Ivy's contemporary: 'I enjoyed the Rev. Compton Burnett's scripture lessons
immensely, he was a very good teacher . . . Maude Compton Burnett
was just like her mother. I was afraid of her. Not a bit like her father.'

It is difficult to avoid the conclusion that memories of both Howard
College and the day school at Hove contributed later to the school in
Two Worlds and Their Ways whose headmistress is also a connection by
marriage and Clemence's courtesy aunt, the redoubtable Lesbia Firebrace. 'This place is a nest of professional eavesdroppers,' complains
one of her discomfited pupils, unwisely goaded by Miss Firebrace's
habit of being neither seen nor heard:

> 'It is true that I have a profession, Esther, but it is not that of
> eavesdropper. I have a right to walk where I will in my own house,
> and I shall continue to use it. And it is a pity you so often say things
> that you do not wish to be heard, that is, that you are a little ashamed
> of. If you broke yourself of the habit, you would not need to be con-
> cerned about what you choose to call eavesdropping.'

---

powerfully on the whole physical life. In their mental work they tried really to educate,
to guide and strengthen the mind for gaining and assimilating knowledge in the future
of the pupil's life. The higher moral results they valued most of all. They remembered
that true refinement is of the heart—"'Tis only noble to be good".' (Report in the local
press, supplied by the Bedfordshire County Archivist.)

There was a silence over this choice of Esther's, and Lesbia continued in an even, distinct tone.

'I do not take a harsh or narrow view of the intercourse amongst you. No, I do not, Esther. You are allowed more latitude than is often the case. You would not meet it everywhere. I know that young people must talk, and that it is idle to look for much weight or worth in what they say—or to listen for it, if you will.' Miss Marathon just raised her eyes at this open appraisement. 'But things must be kept within certain bounds, and within those bounds they will be kept. Do you understand me, Esther?'[32]

Miss Firebrace is one of those demanding, implacable, by no means unintelligent but disingenuous women, common enough in the novels of I. Compton-Burnett, devoured by an urge to power whose full implications are hidden even from herself. It was the force of her will, dreaded as much by Clemence's parents as by the school's staff and pupils, which brought her niece to the school in the first place. It seems at least possible that Ivy, too, had been sent like her stepsisters to boarding school at her aunt's insistence, and certainly the reasons for which she was sent were much the same as those Lesbia exploits for bullying Clemence's parents. One cannot build much on a novel written nearly fifty years later, and which has its own independent existence; but it is perhaps worth noting that when the other girls—driven to retaliate by dominating someone even younger and weaker than themselves—close in on Clemence, one of their favourite needling points is her relation to the headmistress. It is a subject expressly forbidden by Miss Firebrace, and one to which Clemence's tormentors are irresistibly drawn:

'Is it anything to be ashamed of?' said Gwendolen, again. 'I don't see so much disgrace in keeping a school. Perhaps there isn't any.'

'I should say there is no occupation that carries less disgrace, Gwendolen. Miss Firebrace merely meant that no difference was to be made.'

'Does it make any other difference to come to a school kept by a relation, by a connection?' said Esther, in a tone at once blunt and innocent.

'I suppose not, if it is to be forgotten,' said Clemence.

'I meant any difference of any kind.'

'Does Miss Firebrace do you charity, or do you do her charity?' said Gwendolen, laughing at her own openness.

'Oh, I expect we do her charity,' said Clemence, finding the situation taken in hand by something outside herself, and surprised at her ease in it. 'That is how it would be.'[33]

This is the beginning of a career of inexperienced lies and evasions which lead inevitably to humiliating public exposure. The cause of Clemence's final undoing is her mother's ambition: Maria Shelley, being like Sophia Stace and Eleanor Sullivan inordinately proud of her children's intelligence and anxious for them to excel, conveys her anxiety to her daughter who, coming head of her class effortlessly at first, later with increasing difficulty, desperate to win and maintain her mother's approval, embarks on a course of systematic cheating which is detected as easily as her earlier, wretchedly inept attempts at duplicity had been, and punished the more cruelly in proportion as the mistresses' power exceeds the girls'. Whether or not Ivy herself had come similarly to grief is immaterial. What matters is that it is at school that Clemence first learns by necessity ('. . . necessity is the mother of invention. The hard mother of a sad and sorry thing') the harsh lessons formulated again and again in the novels of I. Compton-Burnett.

Ivy at school had been aloof and self-contained, discouraging intimacy with the other girls—'she had her tongue in her cheek with most of them'—and no doubt as vulnerable as other intelligent, sensitive children dispatched alone from the seclusion of family life to an alien world mined with traps for the unwary. Precisely this experience is described in the autobiography of Charles Darwin's granddaughter, Gwen Raverat, who was a year younger than Ivy and who, after a happy Oxford childhood spent at home with her family, her nurse and her brother's tutor, was sent at sixteen to a boarding school where, 'with all the bewildered avidity of an anthropologist trying to understand the minds of the natives', she attempted to fathom unintelligible and hitherto unknown schoolgirl customs like games and gossip and hat-pin-knobbing: '. . . the chief thing I learnt at school was how to tell lies. Or rather, how to try to tell them; for, of course, I did it very badly. Still, I did my best to pretend that I liked what I didn't and that I didn't like what I did. But it was no good; they knew perfectly well that there was something wrong about me, so that I always felt inferior and out of it, just as I did at a party. . . .'[34] Five years before Gwen Raverat's autobiography was published in 1952, I. Compton-Burnett,

looking back over the same distance of half a century, had given the
same dispassionate insight to her fourteen-year-old heroine in a scene
where Clemence sums up for her younger brother her own experience
at school: '... there is not much that I don't know now. I know such a lot
of unexpected things. Things that are said and not thought, and things
that are thought and not said. And there are so many of both. I should
never have known, if I had stayed at home, or never have known that I
knew. That is another thing you learn, to know what you know.'[35]

We know that school had come as a severe emotional shock to Ivy, a
shock doubly painful because it meant that she was for the first time
detached from her brothers and from the mutual security, protection
and imaginative sympathy that had enclosed her from infancy—something which consoles even the solitary Amy Grimstone, questioned by
her elder brother and sister after a school concert has taxed her powers
of endurance beyond breaking point:

> 'It is nothing,' said Amy ... 'Or nothing you would understand.'
> 'Was it everything?' said Erica, in a tone that denoted under-
> standing.
> 'Yes it was,' said Amy, in one that accepted it.[36]

We may perhaps suspect that Ivy had suffered at public functions, as
Amy and Clemence do in her books, from the strain of mediating
between the two incompatible worlds of home and school. We know
that her classical learning set her apart from the other girls; that she
never willingly took part in games, clubs, debates or organized social
activity of any kind at school or college; that she made no particular
friends at her first school, and only one at her second—a certain Daisy
Harvey, also a boarder at Howard College, who went on with Ivy to
Royal Holloway College and remained there her only close companion.
We know that, at two at least of these establishments, she was considered odd and unapproachable by girls who inclined more readily to
the atmosphere of boisterous juvenile domesticity combined with
moral earnestness which obtained at all three. And we know that round
about the time when she went to school—the age at which her younger
sisters first clearly remember her—she was already beginning to assume
at will a mask impenetrable outside the family circle, and penetrated
within it only by her two brothers.

What is curious about *Two Worlds and Their Ways* is that its author
here examines the process whereby Clemence acquires a similar mask;
and what is perhaps even more curious is to compare Clemence at

fourteen with a long line of older heroines in whom one may divine
the same vulnerability, though age and experience conceal it rather
more successfully than Clemence's miserably frail defences. It is
precisely this mask of frivolous indifference, assumed with such gaiety
and grace in face of catastrophe, which has caused so much difficulty to
readers who find in I. Compton-Burnett a disconcerting heartlessness.
The misunderstanding is natural enough, since it means that the delicate
veneer of wit maintained by her characters has concealed, as its ingenious inventors mean it to do, the turbulent emotions beneath. But it is
nonetheless interesting to find that in *Two Worlds and Their Ways*—
published in 1947, mid-way through her career as a novelist—I.
Compton-Burnett explicitly acknowledges the underlying perturbation and fear so often elaborately disguised elsewhere in her books. The
source of courage is made transparently clear when Clemence, exposed
as a cheat before a tribunal of schoolmistresses who remain unmoved by
her painful, blurted explanations as by her agonizingly controlled pleas
for mercy, is saved from abject collapse (though not from despair) by
the cold eye of Miss Firebrace: 'what Clemence saw as relentless and
shallow penetration, struck her pride and gave her a calm front'.
Clemence dreads above all that her parents should learn of her downfall, the school report threatening destruction of her world at home as
well as at school. She moves with a sense of unreality through the end-
of-term party, her first indication that outsiders may remain perfectly
unruffled even by another's unendurable distress—'The lack of imagination staggered her and wrought in her a lasting change'—and
through the farewells when school breaks up next morning: 'She
followed her companions to the cab and the train with no sign of her
inner tumult.'[37]

'A calm front', 'inner tumult', and a staggering lack of imagination
on the part of those who accept the one without discerning the other
beneath it, are constant themes throughout the work of I. Compton-
Burnett. It is pride which gives Clemence courage, pride which sustains
her and lends her a sense of superiority, even in her utmost unhappiness,
towards those blind or indifferent to the suffering they cause. Greater
sufferings than Clemence's are endured by older heroines with incomparably greater sang-froid; but it is not perhaps too much to suggest
that Clemence's very rawness and immaturity may shed some light on
how and why Ivy herself acquired in childhood the beginnings of that
stoical composure which enabled her afterwards to endure pain and loss
with a calm front.

CHAPTER FOUR

James Compton Burnett

JAMES COMPTON BURNETT died suddenly of heart failure at his hotel in London during the night of Monday, 1 April 1901, two months before Ivy's seventeenth birthday. He had travelled up to town as usual that morning and spent the day visiting patients. Almost the only warning noticed by his family beforehand had been that, while taking his customary walk on Sunday, he turned back half way because of a pain at the chest which he attributed to indigestion, ' "though", he added in a casual way, half speaking to himself, "it's rather like angina pectoris" '.[1] Ivy had never seen a great deal of her father. In what little time he spent at home she had been one among twelve although, as the eldest child of his beloved second wife, she had no doubt a special claim on his affections. 'In human life we have our favourites; we have them in our families,'[2] he said and, in a family with one parent as openly partial as the second Mrs Compton Burnett, it must have been hard to avoid attempts to redress the balance. But the self-contained trio in the schoolroom can have had no more than their fair share of his attention when so much of it was devoted to amusing the younger ones and, with the older ones, to easing the tensions which tended to spring up around his wife. His death marked the end of what had hitherto been, at any rate for the second family, a secure and cheerful childhood. 'It had been so joyous till then,' said Vera Compton-Burnett. 'The sun suddenly went out.'

Their father's death brings a similar eclipse on the Stace children in *Brothers and Sisters* which, of all the novels of I. Compton-Burnett (except for the early *Dolores*, an indiscretion in several senses and so immature that it can scarcely be seen as belonging to the main body of her work), is the one most intimately connected with her own life. *Brothers and Sisters*—published in 1929, when Ivy was in her mid-forties—was her third book and the only one in which she directly retraces the period between the last year of her father's life and her mother's death ten years later. Other books may contain characters and incidents drawn, more or less distinctly, at greater or less distance, from memories of her childhood and adolescence; but *Brothers and Sisters* contains recognizable portraits of Ivy and her brothers, her parents, her grandfather Rowland Rees and her nurse Minnie. They are of course well disguised: transposed to an ancestral manor house in the country, stripped of extraneous trappings, accompanied by a charming attendant cast of wholly imaginary characters and subjected to an eventful plot involving family skeletons, missing documents, long-lost parents and a steady flow of marriage proposals. But the central situation—the death of Christian Stace, his wife's tyrannical grief and his children's subsequent suffering—reflects all the more soberly for its extravagantly fictional setting events in the Compton Burnett household.

Christian Stace is the first of Ivy's doctors (again, apart from Dr Cassell in *Dolores* who was taken from quite another model), and the one who most closely resembles her father: 'He had a slow, strong brain and a personality felt as a support, a religious temper and no beliefs, a gentle opinion of others and a high one of himself. As a physician and a man, he was becoming much beloved, a fact that called for no surprise, and from him had none.'³ Dr Stace, like Dr Burnett, travels up to town to attend to a large London practice which keeps him away from home by day and consequently aloof from family affairs; he, too, diagnoses in himself the signs of impending heart failure which shortly afterwards kills him; and his conversation (as, for instance, when his wife asks if there is any chance of a cure: '"All the chances," said Christian . . . "I am as busy as can be with my precious self. So are one or two others of the trade. We all think I shan't be got out of the way so easily."') reproduces both the tone and the turns of phrase characteristic of Ivy's father. 'Simple goodness' is the phrase most readily applied by his family and friends to Christian, as it commonly was to Dr Burnett: 'He was a remarkably strong character of a rugged, massive type, straightforward and direct to a degree,' wrote the *Monthly Homoeopathic Review* when he died. 'He was simply a grand man, a lover of his kind, a faithful physician, the impersonation of kindness and sweetness . . .' wrote Dr Frank Kraft in the *American Homoeopathist*. His biographer and friends abound in tributes to the 'merry twinkle in his eye', his 'uncommonly potent personality', 'that magnetism, that witchery, that individuality which held his auditor from the first moment'; and indeed one may still sense from his books, nearly a hundred years after they were written, something of the forcefulness

and charm of a bonhomous nature revealed with perfect unselfcon-
sciousness for, unlike Sir Roderick Shelley in *Two Worlds and Their
Ways*, Dr Burnett was accustomed to 'write the word he spoke'.
Reading him is much like being subjected to his bluff handshake which
'left a feeling of heartiness and good will'.[4]

Simplicity, heartiness and good will are generally ominous signs in
his daughter's books, indicating an alarming lack of self-knowledge
which allows the ostensibly simple and hearty to vent their underlying
ill will unmolested and with undiminished, often greatly enhanced,
self-esteem. But Dr Burnett's straightforwardness was genuine, the
outcome of that furious appetite for work typical of so many professional men in the second half of the nineteenth century, which left
neither time nor taste for introspection. His practice was vast—'one of
the largest consulting practices in London' according to his obituary in
the *Westminster Gazette*—and, judging by the patients singled out in his
case histories, select: 'a lady of rank', 'a gentleman of position and
means', 'an author of eminence', 'the little son of a distinguished clergyman' are typical of a clientèle drawn occasionally from the nobility and
soundly based on the country squires who journeyed to consult him
from Cheshire and from the Home Counties, on London merchants,
professional men, staff officers and their dependents. In all his voluminous writings, I find reference among his patients to one seaman in
Liverpool, one Kentish servant and one charwoman with a bad heart
whom he cured free of charge on her mistress's recommendation, and
who thereafter became a legend to his children:

> ... I saw no more of her for some time until one day she was ushered
> into my consulting room. She came up to where I was sitting, told
> me she was perfectly well, could do any work with ease, and—then
> occurred one of the sweetest incidents of my professional life—the
> old lady (and *what a lady*!) put a tiny packet on my desk, tried to say
> something, burst into tears and rushed out!
>
> I never saw her again, and have often since wished I had kept that
> particular sovereign and had it set in diamonds.[5]

But there was another side to his character not seen by his family and
friends, the bellicose and litigious side uninhibitedly expressed throughout his career at the expense of 'our friends, the enemy', his orthodox
professional colleagues. Religious imagery was frequently necessary to
convey the fury of his feelings on this point: having compared his own

conversion to St Paul's, he liked later to see himself as marshalling the
forces of homoeopathy 'in the obscurity of schism' against the medical
establishment, the soi-disant 'true *Ecclesia medica catholica*'. 'Though one
rose from the dead they would not believe' was a favourite slogan in
his battle against a profession which he habitually characterized as dishonest, dense-minded, insolent, imbecilic and afflicted by 'the traditional dementia of all who are doomed to extinction'.[6] The *Homoeopathic World* under his editorship became a convenient campaign
ground for goading his enemies, confounding their politics, frustrating
their knavish tricks and rallying support in turn for the gallant fighting
homoeopaths of Norwich, Halifax (the editor's jubilation in December
1880 at the downfall of 'the dapper allopaths of Halifax' is pleasant to
see), Bath and Liverpool. His *Fifty Reasons for Being a Homoeopath* was
provoked in 1888 by a young doctor who called him a braggart and a
quack and who was in return chastised by Dr Burnett as a liar for whose
ignorance 'I have the most absolutely unspeakable contempt'. Quackery
was a sore point with homoeopaths, being a charge constantly laid
against them and one which Dr Burnett returned with energy, calling
down vengeance in his pages on all quacks, gulls (among them Sir
William Jenner who regularly earned his displeasure as President of the
Royal College of Physicians) and 'eye-carpenters' (or ophthalmic
surgeons), on 'Mrs Dr Grundy' and all those led astray by 'the apron-
strings of Mrs Lancet', and, with especial venom, on all pseudo- and
crypto-homoeopaths ('the mean men that have crawled into professional chairs with the aid of purloined portions of the homoeopathic
Materia Medica and simultaneous abjurations thereof. These creeping
things inspire disgust').[7]

His wrath scarcely abated when in April 1885 he resigned his editorship because of pressure of work. He was still liable to harry those of his
patients rash enough to object to the time he took to effect a cure (long,
slow healing was a crucial point in his treatment) or, blackest of crimes,
to suggest recourse to another branch of the profession. His satirical
outbursts on these occasions recall the tirades of his daughter's domestic
tyrants who, like Dr Burnett, are apt to complain of people 'banding
together and baiting me as if I were just a person to be put right about
everything!'[8] Something very like their characteristically self-righteous
assumption of divine right is evident in, for instance, his aggrieved
account of a country clergyman's wife with a tumour at the breast
whose husband, after two years' apparently ineffectual treatment,
requested a second opinion from the distinguished surgeon, Sir James

Paget (whose consulting rooms were opposite Burnett's, and a perpetual mortification to him):

> To this I declined to assent. . . . Truth to tell, I am sick and weary of the lying statements that the knife is even any, and least of all the only cure for tumours. . . .
> But to return to my patient and her choleric husband, I absolutely declined any second opinion.
> Why?
> Simply because a very considerable number of people with tumours literally die of doctors' opinions, and then what is the use or value of the opinion of never so eminent a pathologist on a therapeutic point? Just none.
> Of course, I know it is said to be very unprofessional to decline an eminent colleague's opinion in a given case. But I did it for my patient's good, *not* for my own; and, moreover, they do the same to me when people want my opinion.[9]

One may readily detect in this and similar passages a resemblance to the many intemperate fathers who, like Ninian Middleton in *The Mighty and Their Fall*, are commonly compared to God ('There are the anger, jealousy, vaingloriousness, vengefulness, love, compassion, infinite power. The matter is in no doubt')[10] in the novels of I. Compton-Burnett. But what drives Ninian and his like to excess is their lack of occupation, the fatal sense of mighty powers unfulfilled in a life with no outlet beyond the immediate domestic circle. Dr Burnett was fully occupied by a professional round which afforded more than sufficient outlet for his considerable energies; and we have his younger daughters' evidence that his character at home revealed nothing more intimidating than the soothing mildness of Christian Stace. The most one can say is that, like his fourth daughter, Dr Burnett well understood the urge to intolerance and tyranny and that—also like her, though for wholly different ends—he exploited to the full its dramatic possibilities. He clearly derived the greatest enjoyment from hurling his thunderbolts like Jove; from the biblical precedent which he selected for the crypto-homoeopaths who betrayed his creed ('Well, they serve a purpose. So did Judas'); and from the god-like vantage point whence he contentedly surveyed the trail of humiliation and havoc left in his wake: 'The frankness and honesty of one's allopathic colleagues are wonderful articles. However, they have, as usual, had to munch the leek.'[11]

D

Many of his harshest judgements come from *Tumours of the Breast*, a peculiarly fiery work published in 1888 and full of that long rankling bitterness which invariably consumed Dr Burnett when he contemplated the ravages inflicted by contemporary surgery. But it should be remembered that, if homoeopathy in the 'eighties and 'nineties was under constant fire from without, it was torn simultaneously by civil war within. Dr Burnett had to contend not simply with crypto-homoeopaths like Joseph Kidd, who had attended Disraeli in his last illness, publicly renounced his homoeopathic allegiance and became the object of a blistering, often libellous onslaught in the *Homoeopathic World* for eight months thereafter; or allopaths like Robert Koch who, as the first to isolate the drug tuberculin which ultimately eradicated consumption, won a renown in the early 'nineties which Burnett (who claimed to have pioneered the same methods five years before Koch) held to be rightfully his. Homoeopathy itself was meanwhile split into two warring factions, the one led by Burnett and a group of his friends (among them his future biographer, John Clarke), the other by the immensely influential Richard Hughes. It was Hughes' *Manual of Pharmacodynamics*, the first authoritative homoeopathic textbook published in English, which had recruited Burnett himself and practically the whole of Burnett's generation of rising young homoeopaths in Britain. But Hughes was severely puritanical by temperament, a fundamentalist and a purist, resenting on the one hand all attempts to tamper with his own interpretations of what he regarded as revealed truth laid down by the movement's founder, Samuel Hahnemann, and detesting, on the other, an *ad hoc*, empirical or individual approach to clinical symptoms. Both views are vigorously repudiated in Burnett's opening manifesto in the *Homoeopathic World* for September 1879. Hughes' ambition was to convert the allopathic world by presenting scientific evidence so codified and purged of extraneous detail as to be irrefutable on any objective reading, a dream which Burnett denounced as timid, conventional and dangerously restrictive.

The battle was at its fiercest in the last fifteen years or so of Burnett's life. Hughes, who was considerably older, finally achieved supreme authority in the homoeopathic world and managed thereafter to block all roads to power as long as he lived. In 1883 he had selected John Clarke, one of his own most promising medical students, as his assistant editor on the *British Journal of Homoeopathy*; the appointment lasted two years before Hughes realized his mistake, and it was the first and last office Clarke ever held. In 1890 Clarke 'let his hair down and bared his teeth'[12] in a paper, 'The Two Paths in Homoeopathy', intended as an outright challenge to Hughes. Burnett meanwhile had been obliged, whether by overwork or by hostile pressure from above, to resign his own official appointments and to concentrate, as Clarke was forced to do for the rest of his life, on private practice. The two combined with Robert Cooper, another outstanding practitioner and Burnett's closest friend, and Thomas Skinner (a celebrated renegade, once notorious as a 'persecuting allopath' in Liverpool, who had recanted dramatically in the early 'seventies and became a leading homoeopathic authority on the use of drugs at high potency) in a dining club, later known as the Cooper Club, which met regularly on weekday evenings in London to discuss problems of therapeutics and, no doubt, of medical politics.

Clarke later described the other leading members of the Cooper Club as 'the three most potent influences on the evolution of British Homoeopathy today',[13] and wrote in 1901: 'It is not too much to say that during the last twenty years Burnett has been the most powerful, the most fruitful, the most original force in homoeopathy'. Clarke was himself a physician to be reckoned with, and in time the author of a medical encyclopaedia which rivalled Hughes'. But it is possible that partisan feeling affected his judgement of his contemporaries and that he was a trifle hampered, in his enthusiastic life of his friend, by the professional discretion which forbade any but the vaguest reference to Hughes or to what he called 'the littlenesses and paltry jealousies that not infrequently arise'. Many of Burnett's works (including the *Cure of Consumption* which, according to Clarke, 'establishes beyond question his claim to immortality and the eternal homage of his kind')* have inevitably been superceded by twentieth-century developments. Recent opinion would argue that his single most important contribution to medical history was his first book, *Natrum Muriaticum* (1878), which demonstrated Hahnemann's cardinal theory of drug dynamization at a time when the point was hotly disputed by allopaths, and which was noticed with

---

* Burnett's book was published in November 1890 (shortly after Koch's discovery of tuberculin) with a preface furiously denouncing the persecution of homoeopaths by 'the very men who now lie prone at Dr Koch's feet in abject adoration. . . . True, we work in the obscurity of schism, but we work nevertheless; and although to him all the honour, and to us ridicule, misrepresentation and hateful slander, still we pray we may never be weary in well-doing.' I am grateful to Dr Frank Bodman for the information that Burnett's 'bacillinum' (which was considered superior to Koch's rival preparation by its inventor) was in fact 'a much cruder agent prepared from tuberculous sputum and probably contaminated with secondary germs'.

respect—a rare accolade for a homoeopath—even in the strictly orthodox *British Medical Journal*.

But, apart from this one closely reasoned argument, Burnett's twenty-six books and pamphlets consist for the most part of strings of case histories, jotted down 'in odd scraps of time, sometimes in carriages or at railway stations, and not infrequently when tired',[14] and interspersed with more or less random reflections, proverbs, rhyming jingles, quotations from Schiller and Goethe, snatches of conversation and anecdote, anything which happened to take his fancy as he wrote. He undeniably used medicines to cure cataracts and tumours, both then commonly subject to the surgeon's knife; and his caution on the use of the drug tuberculin, or on the dire effects of vaccination, was salutary in an age when dangerously, even murderously large doses were regularly prescribed by orthodox practitioners. But his brilliance lay not so much in his books—which are in any case so unspecific as to be virtually useless from the point of view of passing on scientific information—as in the originality of his individual diagnoses. He was an intuitive and deductive practitioner. His essential requirements were time, patience and 'the ladder of remedies', a series of different medicines prescribed at different potencies and subtly adjusted to the needs of a particular case. The trickiest problems pleased him most, and the quirkier the solution the better it suited him ('Now the homoeopathic treatment of the shingles after-pains is one of the prettiest bits of therapeutic sharpshooting imaginable . . .'). Many of his remedies were known, as he frequently noted with engaging complacency, only to himself; and his pride was not easily mollified when patients made what he called 'tedious recoveries', thereby cheating him of a radical cure.

He was, as a great many early homoeopaths had to be, largely self-educated: an omnivorous reader not only of his contemporaries in German, French and English but of their predecessors who, long before Hahnemann first formulated the homoeopathic law of similars,* had speculated on the subject in the sixteenth and seventeenth centuries. His library at Hove contained volumes on mediaeval alchemy, obscure

---

* The British Homoeopathic Association's official *Guide to Homoeopathy* defines this law as follows: 'Homoeopathy is a branch of medicine based on the principle that "like cures like", namely that a substance which, in certain forms and doses, causes disease symptoms may also be used to cure illnesses showing similar symptoms. The homoeopathic physician seeks to correct the disorder which causes the symptoms. This requires a study of the individuality of every patient. The remedy, which is specially prepared, is usually given in very small doses, and acts by stimulating the natural defences and recuperative powers of the body.'

medical treatises in Latin and copies of Hahnemann's seminal translation of William Cullen's *Materia Medica*, 'two ragged old books'[15] published at Leipzig in 1790. In his own books, he is as likely to quote with approval from the sixteenth-century Johannes Fernelius or the seventeenth-century Robert Fludd, from Rademacher or Paracelsus (whom he especially revered as Hahnemann's immediate forerunner), as from the nineteenth-century experiments of Pasteur or Koch. He was, moreover, 'an intrepid prover', testing his prescriptions first on himself according to Hahnemann's teaching (often with disconcerting or disagreeably painful results), and boasting that anyone who lived in the country would find a pharmacopoeia sufficient to supply the needs of a lifetime in the plants growing within half a mile of his door.

He several times compares the practice of homoeopathy to gardening or chess, both favourite pastimes of his, both calculated to appeal to a temperament which derived particular satisfaction from protracted, crafty and crabwise manœuvres. Traces of his own country background are evident throughout his writings—in the truculent independence of mind which led him, on the one hand, to denounce received authority and, on the other, to startle conventional opinion with therapeutic tips collected from the most abstruse and arcane learned authorities; in his vigorous, unsystematic reading habits and in his simultaneous insistence on practical experiment. Something very like the countryman's contempt for book-learning emerges when, in the introduction to his *Fifty Reasons*, he loses his temper at dinner over the nuts and wine:

> My dear fellow, your mind is as full of scholastic conceit as an egg is full of meat, and you are therefore a doomed man so far as scientific medicine is concerned ... your knowledge is like those Neapolitan walnuts there, which have been dried in a kiln, and thereby rendered sterile; plant them, and they will not germinate, and it is just thus with your scholastic learnings. .... You have no living faith in living physic—so far as the really direct healing of the sick is concerned all your medicine is *dead*, as dead as a door-nail.[16]

The ten-year-old schoolboy who had wandered alone in the woods round Redlynch, learning from woodmen how to charm warts or cure snakebite with snake venom, has much in common with the erudite doctor who, in late middle age, still took a mischievous pleasure in scandalizing his staider professional colleagues by recommending nettle-tea or a poultice of ivy leaves. All his life Dr Burnett delighted to experiment with esoteric, then almost unknown drugs and at the same time to prescribe the homeliest remedies drawn from the unlikeliest sources: essence of walnuts or acorns for a pain in the spleen (from a German carpenter who advised cracked acorns in brandy), tincture of nettles for ague (from a charwoman who cured one of his patients quicker than he could), greater celandine for jaundice, bruisewort for swellings, couch grass for the bowel and the common daisy for dermatitis.[17]

Burnett's shock tactics, his chatty tone and resolutely empirical attitude to clinical symptoms were anathema to Richard Hughes, who regularly gave him curt, dismissive reviews and a distinctly ungenerous obituary in the *Journal* when he died.[18] Worse even than Burnett's lack of scientific method was his defiantly popularizing approach, which Hughes regarded as little less than sabotage of his own more discreet efforts to further their common cause. Neither, as it turned out, proved in the long run especially successful. Burnett's reputation lived on, if at all, in the writings of a lone disciple, Dr Margaret Tylor; and his name in the Compton Burnett Chair of Homoeopathy, founded through the efforts of John Clarke who had hoped that his friend might hold it in his lifetime—a scheme effectively scotched by Hughes, so that the chair (which has since been held by some of the most distinguished names in homoeopathy) was established only after both Hughes and Burnett were dead. Hughes himself had been 'virtually forgotten' by the 1930s, his books unread and his battles unsung even in homoeopathic circles.

But, however dim the mark left on posterity, reverberations of turmoil and skirmish can hardly have escaped Dr Burnett's family in his lifetime. Hughes was something of an academic snob, though his qualifications (an Edinburgh L.R.C.P. and three honorary M.D.s from American colleges whose degrees were not recognized in England) were markedly inferior to Burnett's—a fact which, one may suspect, gave considerable satisfaction in the Compton Burnett household. It is perhaps worth noting that, in Ivy's first novel, one of Dr Cassell's many disadvantages is that 'his degrees were American'; and that Dolores' father 'had once, in talking with his wife, gone so far as to observe that Cassell was an illiterate, canting fool'.[19] We have Dr Burnett's own word that his career was followed at home with keen attention, 'my wife urging me to publish my experience with Bacillinum two or three years before Koch's cure was heard of, but I hesitated, because I felt the world was not ripe for it, and a man with a very large family has no right to court ruin—so I held back'. The book's eventual publication was not well received and: 'when I showed the review to my wife, she exclaimed, "What a cruel shame!"'.[20]

It was not only Mrs Compton Burnett who took to heart her husband's setbacks and triumphs. His children were familiar from their earliest years with his characteristically independent and individualistic outlook, as with the country maxims which reinforced his demands for practical action: 'If you want roasted pigeon for dinner you must procure the pigeon and roast it; it will not fall ready roasted into your mouth.'[21] Ivy herself at the very end of her life still used in conversation or correspondence expressions she had heard from her father sixty or seventy years before; and, like her brothers and sisters, she must have imbibed in childhood something of his scorn for received opinion, his reliance on first-hand observation and analysis, his absolute regard for truth. Above all she must have noted the passion—nonetheless genuine for being expressed with such sonorous, rhetorical enjoyment—with which he held his libertarian principles:

We are not believers in authority. . . . We shall try to keep constantly before us that theories and hypotheses are the curse of our art, and the bonds and fetters that make free minds slaves. . . . Prejudice, ignorance, authority, *a priori* tall talk, we will leave as fit food for the perennial babes of the *Lancet, et hoc genus omne.* . . .

We were born free, we will live free, we will die free, and freedom shall be our children's heritage. To those who would forge fetters that they may lead us into bondage we declare war to the bitter end.[22]

'It darkened the day'

IVY HAD INHERITED her father's looks (the 'wide face' and 'deep-set eyes' shared also by Christian Stace and his daughter Dinah), his love of gardening and of the open country, and traces at least of his robust disposition. A photograph taken when she was just turned eighteen shows a plump, smiling schoolgirl with an open expression and wavy hair. Arthur Waley, who met her for the first time some six or seven years after Dr Burnett's death, remembered Ivy in her early twenties as 'a vigorous, healthy, country-bred girl, big and bouncing'.[23]

Subsequent events, and the development of her own nature, worked a change which makes his description difficult to reconcile with the shy, inconspicuous, tart-spoken woman described by her friends in the 1920s and 30s, or the formidable Miss Compton-Burnett with delicate, austere features and a delicate, austere wit who became something of a legend to literary London after the second war. But Ivy had learnt from earliest childhood to treat people with a reserve and suspicion wholly foreign to her jovial, ebullient father who remained all his life forthright to the point of naïveté in his fervent reactions to other people and their machinations. For Dr Burnett there was 'no middle way, it must be either good clear God's truth or black lying'. One can't help feeling that he would have shown small patience with the subtle reservations familiar, in his daughter's books, to circumspect characters like Mortimer Lamb or Dudley Gaveston—though he would surely have warmed to Dudley's bluff, impetuous niece, Justine, who has no hesitation in making pronouncements as emphatic as Dr Burnett's own:

'Truth is truth and a lie is a lie', . . . [said Justine] . . . 'We ought not to mind a searchlight being turned on our inner selves, if we are honest about them.'

'That is our reason,' said Mark. ' "Know thyself" is a most superfluous direction. We can't avoid it.'

'We can only hope that no one else knows,' said Dudley.[24]

But, even in her later, mature self, it is not hard to detect traits which —however modified and adapted—Ivy shared with her father. The work of both shows the same driving energy, the same urge to diagnose any given situation to its furthest limits. 'We want to know the whole thing,' says a character in *Daughters and Sons*. 'Our curiosity is neither morbid nor ordinary. It is the kind known as devouring.'[25] Ivy and her father might have said the same. Both were intensely inquisitive about human nature whose moral workings, in the novels of I. Compton-Burnett, are subjected to a scrutiny as rigorous and uncompromising as the doctor's relentless concentration on its physical symptoms. A curious incident in his *Diseases of the Spleen* well illustrates both the indifference to material surroundings so marked in his daughter, and that severely professional eye for essentials which Ivy's friends found on occasion so disconcerting:

Some time since I was casually sitting in a pretty garden with a gentleman. . . . And then in a twinkling he exclaimed—'Oh, what lovely tints, just look at the shade of the plum-tree across the path, and that green, I mean there just by the nut-tree.' Need I say he is an artist?

I had not noticed any of the pretty things to which he called my attention, but I *had* seen a small issue—a tiny aperture in his skin covering his larynx.[26]

Both Ivy and her father often drew startling conclusions from direct, practical observation, both being perfectly indifferent to the dictates of convention or fashion: it was precisely its unconventional flexibility which, according to Dr Burnett, constituted the strength of the homoeopathic system, 'rendering, however, its practice disgustingly difficult'.[27] Certainly the doctor's intuitive approach to medicine—'I let my imagination play about a case' was one of his characteristic sayings— closely resembles what little Ivy vouchsafed to her friends about her own working methods. Dr Burnett, whose constant boast was that 'Homoeopathy wins by being in harmony with the spirit of the advanced men of the times', had preached revolutionary doctrines in medicine; his daughter, though she made no overt reference to the matter, actually achieved revolution in her own sphere, drawing the novel away from the overblown naturalistic school still lingering on from the nineteenth century towards a style which more nearly approaches the concise formality of the other major arts in the twentieth century.

It is, however, hard to imagine a technique more unlike Dr Burnett's diffuse, conversational essays, dashed down in cabs or at railway stations, than his daughter's compact prose, exquisitely balanced and refined by a process which involved several drafts. One might perhaps argue a similarity between the doctor's trained habit of precision when describing his patients—'Young Lord X . . . was pale, spare, neck long and thin, and in the neck his glands visible from their very considerable enlargement and induration, and his temper most miserable'; 'they [consumptives] are mum, taciturn, sulky, snappish, fretty, irritable, morose, depressed and melancholic, even to insanity'[28]—and I. Compton-Burnett's descriptions of her own characters in terms so laconic that, at first reading, one is liable to underestimate the amount of information conveyed in the fewest possible words. But otherwise the two will bear no comparison. Dr Burnett had had in his youth a feeling for language so great that he had hesitated on the point of devoting his career to philology, 'but neither words nor the study of words could long suffice to absorb the energies of the young Burnett, and he finally decided to make medicine his profession'.[29] There remains in his books evidence of that spontaneous storyteller's gift which makes his case histories as absorbing to the layman, and often as entertaining, as Sherlock Holmes': a cab draws up at the door, from it descends a nervous clergyman, a veiled lady or an Indian army officer in distress who, on being ushered into the doctor's consulting rooms, pours out a tale of woe to which the doctor listens attentively, rapidly sifting out clues and proceeding via investigation and treatment to a more or less unexpected, almost invariably successful solution to what had hitherto frequently been, in the hands of less expert practitioners, an insoluble mystery. Conan Doyle (who wrote his first Sherlock Holmes story in April 1891, while waiting in vain for patients to arrive at his brand-new consulting rooms in Devonshire Place, just round the corner from Dr Burnett's establishment at 86 Wimpole Street) is said to have modelled Holmes' detective methods on the diagnostic system practised by Dr Joseph Bell of the Edinburgh Infirmary, so it is not perhaps surprising that Dr Burnett should have hit on the same excellent receipt for popular success.

One of the charges regularly laid against Dr Burnett by Richard Hughes was that he wrote '*ad populum*'. The same is true, in *Daughters and Sons* (1937) and *A God and his Gifts* (1963), of the two successful authors, John Ponsonby and Hereward Egerton, each of whom has a child also determined to write. John Ponsonby's daughter, France, and Hereward Egerton's son, Merton, both mean to write books which, unlike their fathers', shall not pander to popular taste, an ambition which not unnaturally causes hard feeling between parent and child. The two fathers produce quantities of what seems to be fairly run-of-the-mill Victorian popular fiction, bringing tears to their readers' eyes, a mixture of pride, social embarrassment and gratitude ('of course people do earn by it, even more than by serious books they say. . . . And we welcome the help with expenses')[30] to their families, and making their children wince at their sentimental excesses. Both write to 'serve many thousands of people', both are household words (as the name Compton Burnett had been throughout Ivy's first twenty years in homoeopathic circles), and both are uneasily aware that their reputations are unlikely to outlast their own lifetimes. It is this dark suspicion which adds jealousy to the already awkward situation brought about by their children's loftier views: 'I would rather write nothing than write as he does', says Merton Egerton, to which his shrewd brother replies: 'Well, that should offer no problem'. France Ponsonby is more tender towards her father: 'He would have written better, if he had written for fewer and earned less. And it is for us that he earns; he does not spend on himself. It is all subtle and sad, and he is very pathetic.' Apart from his pathos, all we know of John Ponsonby's career is that he began to write early, driven to eke out a precarious income for the sake of his growing family (' "He could not hold his public without his popular touch", said Victor. "And we should be badly off, if he did not hold it. . . ." '); that his books, like Dr Burnett's, have prefaces in which he proposes to thank his friends for insights received; and that he has immortalized in his books, as Dr Burnett had done in his, the disingenuous saying that 'a woman's work is the highest in the world'.[31]

All of which is by no means to suggest that John Ponsonby resembles James Compton Burnett, only that Ivy made use in both novels of knowledge derived from her father's success as a popular writer. She herself had written, or at any rate disclosed, nothing in his lifetime though both she and her brothers were already determined to write,*

* 'I think I always felt I should, and I think my brothers did too . . . I think we always assumed we should write, and talked as if we should. Our parents were interested in writing, and we grew up with the feeling.' (Ivy Compton-Burnett in *Review of Eng. Lit.*, October 1962.)

and equally determined no doubt to avoid their father's artless and emotional 'popular touch'. The elaborate figures of speech in which Dr Burnett habitually indulged—'Homoeopathy is the winning horse at the Medical Derby of the world, and will presently be hurried past the winning post by Orthodoxy itself as her rider'[32]—are suspect more often than not in the novels of I. Compton-Burnett, where an injudicious use of words tends to reflect on the speaker's part a similar coarseness of moral fibre. But there can be small doubt, from the way she talked of him afterwards, that Ivy had loved her father dearly. His death was 'a deep sorrow' to her, the first of many in the next fifteen years which she bore with the same outward composure. If there are glimpses of Dr Burnett at all in his daughter's books, it is in the tenuous but wholly amiable character of Christian Stace; or perhaps in the type most fully developed in Justine Gaveston who, like Dr Burnett, is garrulous, demonstrative, overbearing and interfering, uninhibited in manner and self-congratulatory in tone: 'I sound my bracing note and snap my fingers at the consequences'. No type is further removed from the subtle, wary, introspective characters on whom the principle of virtue generally depends in the novels of I. Compton-Burnett. But, if Justine is without the restraints imposed by self-consciousness, she is also completely unselfish, and proves in the end the one dependable source of support in an unstable household. Her stepmother's comment on Justine might serve as an epitaph on Dr Burnett: ' "I like good people," said Maria, with the simplicity which in her had its own quality, something which might have been humour if she could have been suspected of it. "I never think people realize how well they compare with the others." '[33]

Dr Burnett's death came at a time when his family could ill afford to be without his support. His wife, who had never been strong, possessed none of the placidity which might have fitted her better to contend with the fatigue of constant child-bearing, a miscarriage and the strain of his absence in London. Her father had lived for the past ten years in St John's Road near The Drive but, though she saw them often, neither he nor her stepmother was particularly interested in domestic concerns, and neither can have provided much of a substitute for the intimate companionship she craved as an outlet for a possessive and passionate nature. The 'unusually beautiful, sweet girl' with whom Dr Burnett had fallen in love eighteen years before had become a demanding, imperious woman, still beautiful but increasingly dissatisfied with the monotony of life at Hove cooped up with Minnie and growing numbers of children in 'that hideous house'. Ivy, whom she loved as her first child, and the two sons she adored, had exhausted her admittedly small stock of maternal feeling. The four youngest daughters (Stephanie Primrose, called Baby, was born at The Drive on 19 April 1899) were apparently regarded almost from birth as a burden rather than a pleasure. Her five stepchildren meanwhile had reached the stage at which they contemplated escape or at least, since escape for the three girls could not easily be reconciled with propriety, some respite from the frustrations all five had endured since infancy. Mrs Compton Burnett seems to have reacted to what must at times have been a wretched situation with uncertain temper and occasionally spectacular displays of nervous irritation; Ivy described years later how, driving out one day in a carriage, her mother lost patience with her lap-dog and flung it suddenly straight through the open window.[34]

How far Dr Burnett was aware of the underlying frictions in his household is impossible to say. We know that he had urged his wife to avoid working herself into a fury, and that long afterwards she would dispassionately repeat his warning that her fits of rage might lead to cancer (cancer of the breast, diagnosed nine years after his death, eventually killed her). He was constantly at hand 'to comfort her and smooth her path', to shield her as much as her children from the consequences of her own outbursts. But we know, too, that he took an optimistic view of her temperament: 'She is one of those human high-breds who will not cave in, but, if duty calls, will go on till they drop'. Having noted when they first met that 'in life' such high-breds 'are commonly misunderstood', he continued to the end of his life to take her part with unwavering loyalty. He himself, however, was often lonely, if one may judge by his descriptions of evenings spent dining with patients in London, with his colleagues in the Cooper Club or working alone at his hotel, and by the way in which every spare scrap of time was parcelled out between his books and his practice. His presence had always been a restraining influence, but much of what went on at home in his absence presumably escaped him. He seems to have been, like Christian Stace, 'happy that his wife should be the ruling spirit of his home. He knew her little and she knew him well, the relation between herself and her father, that seemed to her natural.'

If Christian unmistakably resembles James Compton Burnett, then Sophia Stace with her 'nerve storms' and her 'habitual fits of crying', her absorbing love of her husband and the jealous irritation she vents on her children, is in both looks and character the nearest Dame Ivy

ever came to a direct portrait of her mother: ' . . . Sophia made life easy
only for her husband. Sophia was a woman to whom one man was
her life. For her children her love demanded more than it gave.'[35]
The secluded lives of the three Stace children—the intimacy between
Dinah and Andrew, the comparative immaturity of their younger
brother Robin, the 'literary gifts' of the elder pair accepted by the family
as a natural outcome of 'the Stace fluency in words', and nurtured in
long hours spent alone together in the schoolroom made over into a
study—correspond to the Compton Burnetts' daily routine; and the
parallel was in any case confirmed by Noel's friends, Arthur Waley and
Elliott Felkin, who recognized in Sophia Stace their own memories of
Katharine Compton Burnett.[36] The Stace children discuss their mother
in private with a freedom which matches their restraint in her presence,
and one can't help suspecting that their verdict is in some sense a version
of the kind of conversation which took place in the Compton Burnett
schoolroom between Ivy and her two brothers:

> 'What passes me is, how Father has never got to know Sophia,'
> said Robin. 'Day after day, year after year it goes on under his eyes,
> and he never sees it.'
> 'Not under his eyes, just away from them,' said Dinah. 'Don't
> you see how Sophia is on her guard?'
> 'Yes. Her cunning is on the scale of the rest of her,' said Andrew.
> 'I always have doubts about Sophia's scale,' said Robin. 'I think
> she is rather a small, weak person in many ways. It is known that I
> am a little like her. Now Father is on a more considerable scale,
> though I often think his simplicity is the most appreciable thing
> about him.'[37]

The few months before Dr Burnett's death had not been particularly
easy ones. His first family were by now nearly all grown up. His
eldest son Richard had qualified by November 1900 as a solicitor but
the 'wild dog' Charlie, also articled in his teens and living in digs with
his brother in London, showed signs of turning out less satisfactorily,
and was perhaps already flirting with the kind of trouble ('spending
what he shouldn't have') which overtook him after his father's death.
Olive, who was twenty-five and 'very much the New Woman', had
also left home that autumn. Of all the stepchildren Olive had always
been the one who most stubbornly refused to acknowledge their
stepmother's authority and, at a time when young ladies were expected

to remain under their fathers' roofs till marriage or death removed them, she had paid dearly for her freedom. The ugly scenes between a stepmother and an eldest stepdaughter determined to leave home in Ivy's first and last books—separated by a gap of almost sixty years— suggest perhaps how deep an impression this upheaval made on the family. Olive, having gone to London to learn shorthand and typing, was 'regarded as somebody on the wrong path altogether'. Iris, who remained at home for another five years, was no happier than her eldest sister. Only Daisy at twenty-two seemed outwardly content with her lot, supervising the nursery, paying calls with her stepmother and cheerfully performing the domestic duties which Ivy detested. Guy, meanwhile, who had been sent alone to Tonbridge in the summer of 1900, fell ill with pneumonia at the end of the autumn term and was fetched home by his father in an ambulance. His condition had been critical, and he was still convalescent when Olive shocked her family again by coming down from London with her hair cropped short: 'I remember it was just before Christmas,' said Vera Compton-Burnett. 'It darkened the day.'

This was the last Christmas of their father's life, with all twelve children assembled at Hove from Olive to the baby who was twenty months old. Dr Burnett's last book was published that spring, and he continued to work as furiously as ever though several of his sayings, reported later, suggest that he was not unaware of approaching death. 'You can't work an old horse too long, but it will fall,' he said to a friend three or four weeks before he died and, to another, 'My only hope is that I may die in harness.' Some twenty years later Ivy marked with a pencil in her copy of Butler's *Note-Books* a passage on physical excellence as a criterion of morality, which runs in part: 'In the case of those who are not forced to over-work themselves—and there are many who work themselves to death from mere inability to restrain the passion for work, which masters them as the craving for drink masters a drunkard—over-work in these cases is as immoral as over-eating or drinking.'[38]

Dr Burnett's beloved brother Jack visited Hove for the last time in February or March and died, after a lingering illness, at Bedford on 21 March 1901; Charles Compton Burnett represented his father at the funeral, together with a wreath inscribed 'In loving memory from Jim'. On 23 March Dr Burnett made a new will and ten days later he was dead, an instance perhaps of his own theory set down twelve years before on the causes of Angina Pectoris: 'Fag is a potent factor in angina; and so is wounded pride and nerve shock. Not infrequently fag and shock combine to produce it.'[39]

He was sixty. Twelve of his thirteen children survived him. The eldest was twenty-five, the youngest not quite two when he died but, though both his wives had belonged to large families and though he himself came of a prolific and fertile line, Dr Burnett had no further descendants. Of his twelve children, one died young of pneumonia; another was killed in the first war; three committed suicide. Two of his four sons made brief, childless marriages, his eight daughters remained unmarried so that, though he himself had ardently believed that 'the true source of national greatness is large families of healthy children',[40] his only legacy to posterity lies in the novels of his fourth daughter: an astonishing and sometimes fearful monument to family life.

CHAPTER FIVE

Katharine Compton Burnett

I

'Simply the deepest mourning that is made for a widow'

FROM THE DAY of Dr Burnett's death his children found their own
world overthrown. 'It changed totally,' said Vera Compton-Burnett.
'And that was why Ivy lived so much in retrospect.' Accounts of what
followed in the next weeks and months at Hove suggest much the same
atmosphere as Ivy herself later described in the Stace household:
'Sophia's grief hung like a pall on the house, crushing its inmates with
a load as if of guilt, that their sorrow was less great than hers.'[1] The
news reached Hove on Tuesday, 2 April; Dr Burnett was thought to
have died as he prepared for bed the night before and had been found
that morning by the hotel staff when his breakfast remained untouched
and his cab drawn up at the door. His wife started out at once alone
for London, leaving the children at home in Minnie's charge with the
blinds down. The funeral took place a week later at St Leonard's
church, Aldrington, set back from the sea a mile or so from The Drive
on the western outskirts of Hove. St Leonard's had been a favourite
goal for the doctor's Sunday strolls, when the family would walk
across fields by the sea to inspect his property at Aldrington where he
had always said he would like to be buried. In the next ten years
Marjorie Andrewes, who was in the same form as Vera at school and
who lived with her parents on the road to St Leonard's, would regularly
see Mrs Compton Burnett pacing slowly past their house with one or
more of her daughters, all dressed in black, speaking to no one and
carrying flowers to lay on his tomb—a plain cross in polished pink
marble inscribed at the top *Semper Fidelis*, and at the foot: 'In tender
loving memory of my dear husband James Compton Burnett M.D.
Who passed away 2nd April, 1901, aged 60. "In secure and certain
hope."' More than seventy years later, Dr Burnett's cross, which now
bears inscriptions for his wife and four of her children, is still noticeably
taller, shinier and more imposing than any other monument in the
graveyard.

'Ivy lived rather under the shadow of death,' said her sister, 'and death in those days had its trappings. Coal black from head to foot, and my mother in deepest widow's weeds.' Mrs Compton Burnett never again went out of mourning, indeed her behaviour recalls Josephine Napier's dramatic reaction to her own widowhood in *More Women Than Men* ('"Simply the deepest mourning that is made for a widow," said Josephine, in an almost light tone. "That is all I have to say."')[2] She wore streamers and crape to the knee for two years and, though she may then have made some concessions in dress, she wore full mourning again two years later when Guy died. She had put the whole family into black, down to the baby in her pram who could not remember her father and who had a dark grey pelisse tied over her bonnet with black ribbons. Topsy, at five years old, wore unrelieved black like her six elder sisters for at least a year ('I should think it was more than a year, because the things wouldn't have worn out'). When the Queen died, seven weeks before Dr Burnett, promenaders on the Hove sea front had all worn black for the next four Sundays but, even in those days, Mrs Compton Burnett's notions of mourning were considered extravagant, at any rate for small children: one of the things about the Compton Burnett girls which had most impressed their contemporaries at school was that 'they all always wore black—and perhaps that depressed them'. Ivy was still in mourning for her father when she went up to Royal Holloway College in the autumn of 1902, and she wore black again for Guy throughout her last year at college.

The three little girls—Vera was ten and Judy seven years old—were encouraged by their mother to make doleful tableaux in the graveyard, weaving daisy chains to hang on their father's tomb. Minnie taught Topsy to kiss her father's photograph ('Daddy's picture') so that she should never forget him. All three seem to have performed these sentimental observances with the same sense of dismay and obscure distaste as Julius and Dora Calderon, who are similarly obliged in *Elders and Betters* to serve as an outlet for adult emotions which they can neither understand nor appease. One may perhaps date from this time Ivy's acute sensitivity to the bewilderment of desolate small children placed as her own sisters had been, either forgotten altogether in a house overtaken by mourning, or as arbitrarily remembered and harshly rebuked for violating the solemnity due to bereavement; one thinks of Dora's 'peaked and staring face' on the day of her mother's death, or the Humes' nervous laughter in *Mother and Son* ('"Are we supposed to be joking?" said Adrian. "No, we are supposed to be sorrowing. We are joking."'").[3] But the heaviest burden of their mother's grief fell on the older children. Mrs Compton Burnett was inconsolable and her despair took the form of open lamentation. 'My mother not being able to take the loss in an heroic way—and I'm afraid she wasn't,' she gave way to terrifying storms of crying which lasted sometimes all night and, though the younger ones would lie awake in bed and hear her, the older ones lived in her presence under what became an almost intolerable strain. 'She did grieve sincerely for her husband. But she expressed her grief vocally, and that was very hard on her children. On Guy and Ivy especially.'

Vera Compton-Burnett's description of her mother will be already familiar to readers of *Brothers and Sisters*. Sophia's self-dramatization as she sinks distraught to the ground or 'sends her cries through the house', her screams, 'her slow, solemn voice', her unsatisfactory last moments alone with her husband's body—'Sophia's lifelong exercise of her own will had led her almost to expect response from the dead'—together with the obligation to provide a less inadequate response as she kneels weeping beside his empty chair drive her two eldest children to the limits of their strength: 'Andrew and Dinah stood by, stunned and helpless. Sophia was just enough conscious of their presence to know that her laments were heard.'[4] The book was written long after both Ivy's brothers and her mother were dead, and it is no doubt fruitless to speculate as to how far the burden on Andrew and Dinah— 'Come with me, my dears. We three will go away and be together. . . . We will go apart, and try to meet together our great, great sorrow. Great for you all, but infinitely greater for me. You will have to remember that, in all your future dealings with me'—corresponds to the demands made, more than twenty years before, on Guy and Ivy at Hove; or what bitter memory may have underlain the moment when Sophia calls for Robin who, 'white and trembling' on the day of his father's death, lacks the courage to face his mother in her extremity: 'She went to the door and called, more clearly, as no answer came, unconscious that she sent a shiver through her son and daughter, that was to return to them all their lives.'

Noel Compton Burnett was thirteen when his father died, and young for his age. Robin Stace is twenty-two but, like Noel, he retains a childishness which at once protects him from his mother's deepest feeling and leaves him more pitilessly exposed in moments of crisis than his elder brother and sister. One of several traits which the two have in common is dependence on their former nurse, for the Staces'

Patty ('Miss Patmore had been their nurse and nearly their mother in childhood, and they had for her much of the feeling that might have been Sophia's'), like the Compton Burnetts' Minnie, is the sole buttress between themselves and their mother's ruthless exploitation of her position:

'Well, I have said goodbye to him,' said Sophia. 'I have said my farewell that is to last my life, my life that will never be a life to me again. Your dear father! My husband!'

She stooped her face, contorted again with weeping, over her teacup, and Robin's face showed a spasm of stricken nerves. . . .

'He must go to bed early,' said Sophia to Patty. 'He had better go directly after this. Andrew and Dinah can sit up for a little while with me.'

'Oh, I think they all ought to go to bed,' said Patty, her tone bringing a change to Sophia's face. 'Dinah looks dreadfully shaken, and Andrew is very tired. And you ought to go to bed early too. You know you ought. You will be worn out.'

'Well, I will go to bed or I will sit up,' said Sophia in an aloof monotone. 'Nothing that I do will make any difference to me now. Nothing will ever help me again. But I will go to bed, so that other people may go. So that they will not feel that they have to wait up with me, to watch with me one hour.'

A sound as of hysteria came from Robin.

'Are you laughing, my son?' said Sophia, in a simply incredulous voice.

Ivy's two younger sisters maintain emphatically that her books contain no hint of a portrait of Guy: 'The quality was the same, but never the character.' Nonetheless, if one sets their account of their father's death beside the sixth chapter of *Brothers and Sisters*, one has the curious impression of seeing the same event reflected in two different mirrors. It was Guy who, like Andrew Stace, stood next to his father in his mother's affections, and Guy who 'bore the brunt with my mother. It took too much toll.' Both sisters repeated this phrase, 'too much'. Andrew, spent and desperate in the early days of Sophia's widowhood, becomes as Guy had done chief source of support to the household, attending on his mother and protecting his sister who meets Sophia's eyes, and Sophia's exaltation of her own loss as a means of detracting from other people's, in silence. When Dinah remains at home on the day of the funeral: 'The brothers knew which was the heavier part; and Dinah, white-faced in the black that was rather too plainly poorer than her mother's, was sadder to them than Sophia.' Guy would sit alone with his mother when no one else could do it. Noel was too young, Ivy too withdrawn and Minnie (whose growing importance in the household had made for an uneasy relationship with its mistress) preoccupied with the younger children. Daughters had in any case never been much consolation to Mrs Compton Burnett: 'She gave her maternal love to Guy, but she took far more than she gave.'

Both Ivy's sisters conjure up a horrifying image of grief, settling like a black cloud on the house, blotting out the happiness of their own childhood, disfiguring their mother, draining Guy's strength which was called on and unreservedly given to sustain the whole family. A light had gone out with their father's death and never returned. Their mother remained self-absorbed, sunk in immoderate mourning, increasingly forgetful of her younger children who turned instead to their brother. For the next four years Guy, not quite sixteen when his father died, took on responsibility not only for his mother's exorbitant emotional needs but also for the comfort and security of his small sisters. 'He was so *very* kind—kindness is the wrong word. He was our ideal,' said Vera Compton-Burnett. 'Guy was a saint,' said her sister, 'I can't remember a single thing he ever said or did to hurt anyone. He brought happiness to a household that lacked it totally. *How* he tried to take the place—to fill the hollow left by my father's death—for the young children.'

One may suspect something, if not of Guy's character, at least of his quality in Terence Calderon who, in a distracted and grief-stricken household in *Elders and Betters*, is the only person prepared to give time and attention to his little brother and sister after their mother has died. Dora and Julius are wholly at ease with Terence who takes them for granted, and whose humorous, matter-of-fact gravity comes as an inexpressible relief when, after the miseries and fears and nervous exhaustion of an impossible day, they come in from the garden to find him seated with his book in the firelight at the schoolroom table. Their father's unexpected severity, alternating with an even more disconcerting, exaggeratedly sentimental view of the dead, especially disturbs them:

'He would hardly be in form at the moment,' said Terence.
This allusion to the circumstances struck Dora as so boldly humorous, that she fell almost into hysterics.

'Take care. Shrieks of mirth are not the sounds expected at this juncture,' said Terence, forgetting how easily they occurred at such a point.

His sister's sense of the ludicrous received a further spur.

'I hope we shall be able to maintain the required deportment,' said Terence. 'I cannot say I detect any signs of promise.'

Dora shook in silent helplessness.[5]

Outbursts of nervous laughter, sharply checked in the presence of adults and exploding in hysterical reaction behind their backs, come again and again in I. Compton-Burnett's accounts of children subjected to emotional pressure beyond their bearing. It was a form of release familiar enough in her own family in the years after her father's death: the boys would come up on Sunday mornings to play boisterous games with their small sisters in the nursery but otherwise there were few outlets, let alone opportunities for pleasure or amusement, in the grim atmosphere imposed by their mother's grief. 'It was an incredibly clouded household—incredibly overshadowed,' said Juliet Compton-Burnett. 'You ask about the days—they were *completely uneventful*. Nothing happened. Outwardly the same thing happened every day.' Inwardly there was intense mental activity. For most of the week Guy, Ivy and Noel, attending to their literary gifts in the study, had little to do with the younger ones, engrossed in elaborate games of make-believe behind closed doors ('It was very private') in the nursery. School barely touched this inner world, and secrecy was essential when so many people lived in close physical proximity, pursuing imaginary lives of utmost vividness side by side under the same roof. 'We had few toys and not many books,' said Vera Compton-Burnett. 'I remember often hearing the word retrenchment as a small girl.'

Retrenchment is a subject with which, as with the cold, draughts and generally arrant inconvenience of country houses, Ivy was intimately acquainted and in which she took a particular pleasure. The Calderons, inventing their own gods, their own penal code and their own board games from a makeshift assortment of cast-off pieces, are by no means the only children in her books left to amuse themselves from their own resources. Writing is one of very few activities which, though it has other drawbacks, escapes criticism at least on the score of expense:

'Less ambitious things need training,' said Sabine. 'We will leave her her own occupation, as it costs us nothing.'

'It does not save us anything either. But I am glad she has some occupation, and is not too sunk in black sulks to mention it. We will leave her to waste her time in her own way.'[6]

But children are as well aware as their elders that their entertainment ranks low on the list of problems they pose. The Lambs and Ponsonbys are publicly mortified by outgrown, outmoded or handed-down clothes; the Shelleys, Lovats, Grimstones, Challoners and Staces by the meagre appointments of their nurseries, generously renamed schoolroom and study as a means of acknowledging their advancing years at no extra cost; and nearly all are accustomed, like the Humes and the Middletons, to forestall the accusations of reckless expenditure constantly cast up against them by making their own shrewd calculations as to the price of food, clothes and lessons ('"The girls do not cost us much," said Sabine. "It would not be right that they should, but it is a fact that they don't."').[7] The university education required by boys is an especially sore point—'Grinning and chattering like apes and costing like dukes!' as Sir Jesse Sullivan says bitterly of his two grandsons in their last year at Cambridge:

'And where will they spend the next ones? Behind bars, I should think. I hope that will be less expensive.' . . .
'If we are fed by the public through a grating,' said Daniel, 'it will take our keep off Grandpa.'
'We should still carry our debt to the grave,' said his brother. 'Or to Grandpa's grave we should.'[8]

Dr Burnett had left the bulk of his considerable estate—£67,166—to his wife, in trust for her children after her death, on terms pretty well identical with the terms of Christian Stace's will: 'It was clear that Sophia would hold not only her former place, but her own and her husband's. Her children were little affected by the knowledge. They would hardly have been surprised if the whole had been their mother's. They knew how well their father knew, and did not know, Sophia; how equal and unequal Sophia was to her life.'[9] The joint income, from Dr Burnett's trust estate and from Mrs Burnett's own marriage portion, must have amounted to several thousand pounds a year but frugal practices unknown in their father's lifetime became a recognized feature of the children's lives in the next ten years. The family no longer kept manservants, and the four maids eventually dwindled to two under Minnie with a boy to clean the steps (though Mrs Compton Burnett permitted a telephone and a refrigerator, she set little store by newfangled gadgets and the idea of importing a vacuum cleaner filled her with such dismay—'taking all the goodness out of the carpet! She wouldn't have such a thing in the house'—that the matter was dropped). A great deal was done for show, as it was in so many respectable Edwardian households: 'My mother very rarely gave dinner parties, but when she did they were grand and formal with countless courses'. The children would watch over the bannisters as the guests went in and would be called down afterwards to entertain them, but these ceremonial occasions were in sharp contrast to everyday thrift. Normally their mother ate high tea with the family in the early evening, maintaining at the same time a strict pretence of dining nightly since owning up to high tea would have been unthinkable in fashionable Hove.

The result of this and similar economies, as of their mother's growing melancholia, was to drive the family in on itself. Mrs Compton Burnett returned formal calls but otherwise visitors were not encouraged, and the children had none of their own. 'We could never ask our school friends to the house—*I wouldn't have*—it was so strange and so peculiar. It took away the desire to mix with other people,' said Vera Compton-Burnett. Later, the four youngest girls began to attend children's parties at Christmas ('Going down to supper with little boys in Etons who would fetch you ice cream.' There were cards for partners, each with a little pink pencil, and a huge tea followed by conjurors or dancing before supper) and even gave their own in return, occasions as often as not of memorable embarrassment. The party rage had gripped Hove after Ivy left school, though one of her cousins remembered a party given by their step-grandmother for 'Ivy and Jimmy and Guy', and she had presumably noted in her sisters, if not from her own sad experience, something of Amy Grimstone's agonizing shame at the prospect of inviting schoolfriends to tea, or the marked lack of enthusiasm shown by the Lovats when asked what they know of other children:

'Well, we have been out to tea twice.'
'Both times I cried,' said Viola.
'Cried?' said Selina. 'Where they not kind to you?'
'Grown-up people have to be in a way. The children said we **were** different from them.'[1]

Much the same impression of strangeness and isolation was received by contemporaries of the younger Compton-Burnett girls at school. Their parties were considered 'very, very exclusive', and their mother uncomfortably strict. 'She never recognized you in the street or any-thing, and if they were with *her*, they'd hardly look at you,' said Marjorie Andrewes. 'I used to see the four little girls often, out walking with their nurse,' said Mrs Elliot who had been in the same form as Judy at school, and who remembered Minnie as 'a drab little figure—but I think they turned to her for everything.' One girl, who had gone to The Drive with a message, never forgot being shown into a room disused and covered with dustsheets, and being told to wait without moving or touching anything. Another, not even admitted to the hall, was kept waiting by the maid on the doorstep. At school the girls were reticent and given to stammering, with 'a terrible stutter' when called on to read or recite and a habit of giggling in class which their contemporaries attributed to nervousness. 'They were a funny family,' said Mrs Elliot. 'There was a sort of barrier up around them, you could feel it. They kept you off.'

It might be a description of the many families in the novels of I. Compton-Burnett who, like the Ponsonbys in *Daughters and Sons*, give rise to ceaseless speculation in their wondering visitors and a rather more sober reaction in the more experienced:

> 'Miss Hallam is seeing us as we are,' said Clare. 'Do families often stand revealed as soon as this?'
> 'Yes, fairly often,' said Edith. 'You would hardly believe about families. Or many people would not.'
> 'We have to belong to a family to believe it,' said France. 'But everybody does belong to one. It seems so odd, when you think of what is involved.'[11]

Muriel Ponsonby, a shy, plain eleven-year-old afflicted by dumbness which alternates with exasperating fits of the giggles ('"It is a nervous habit which we must hope she will leave behind." "It is hard to see how we can leave behind nervous habits," said Clare. "Probably most of our habits are of that nature"'), is the first of many whose inarticulate sufferings in childhood are as excruciating as anything endured by their elders. There can be small doubt that Oliver Shelley's attitude to children in *Two Worlds and Their Ways*—'They are always pitiful'—

was Ivy's own, though this was far from the impression left on her sisters. 'She had an incredible reserve,' said Vera Compton-Burnett. 'As a young girl she was never one with the family.' 'She put herself into the books, and she was a secret otherwise—known only to herself,' said her sister Juliet. Both remember Ivy in the years after their father's death as someone who took no part in their lives and who, as they grew older and were no longer confined to the nursery, became increasingly a repressive influence. The Compton-Burnetts learnt early, as members of large Victorian families had to do, to 'be alone in a room with other people' but Ivy, who had thankfully abandoned piano lessons herself, suffered much from the sound of her sisters' incessant practising and, as soon as she was in a position to do so, categorically forbade it. For years before that she would sit in the evenings between two candles at the schoolroom table, intent on her book, while one or other of her sisters 'thundered away at the piano'. Throughout their own wretched childhood, when the boys 'took great trouble to make us happy in what was not a very happy home', the younger girls had scant sympathy from Ivy. 'I can see her now standing at the window, twisting the blind cord and swinging it round—while we rampaged round the school-room,' said Juliet Compton-Burnett. It was a trick her sister later handed on to Isabel Sullivan in *Parents and Children*, another aloof adolescent absorbed by her own unhappiness in the midst of a family scene: 'Isabel went to a window and stood, throwing the blind cord over her finger, taking no notice when the tassel struck the pane.'[12]

Isabel, like other sensitive older children in the novels of I. Compton-Burnett, is by inclination a passive spectator, intervening only occasionally to protect her small brothers and sisters from their mother's depredations, accepting (as her elders cannot) the folly of interfering in and the impossibility of entering the children's world. Families in the books divide as the Compton-Burnetts did into groups sealed off from one another by age and occupation, and by 'that intense family shyness' which makes it so hard for Terence Calderon to establish relations with the schoolroom party ("We have no idea what impression this tragedy is making on them," said Terence. "We must wait for the time when they write their lives.").[13] If Ivy, unlike Guy, had no feeling to spare for her sisters, one cannot help suspecting that she watched them intently, storing things which she could not express, perhaps scarcely understood at the time. Beneath what seemed to them an impenetrable, sometimes positively hostile indifference lay an incomparably delicate understanding of the preoccupations and tensions of childhood. But it was something that remained dormant long after she had begun to explore other aspects of life before the first war. Children make only the most perfunctory appearances in her first six books and it was not until 1937, with Muriel Ponsonby in *Daughters and Sons*, that she turned her attention to the world of nursery and schoolroom: a world which to the end of her career as a novelist continued to cast strange shadows on the adults in the drawing-rooms below, and which must have been drawn in part from memories of her own early childhood, in part from what she had seen much later in these years of oppression at Hove.

'A figure in tragedy'

'I THINK THAT actual life supplies a writer with characters much less than is thought,' said Miss Compton-Burnett in 1944. 'Of course there must be a beginning to every conception, but so much change seems to take place in it at once, that almost anything comes to serve the purpose —a face of a stranger, a face in a portrait, almost a face in the fire. And people in life hardly seem to be definite enough to appear in print. They are not good or bad enough, or clever or stupid enough, or comic or pitiful enough.'¹⁴ Children gave satisfaction no more than their elders: 'When I meet them, they are open to the same objection, and fail to afford me assistance.'

By this time she had published ten of her twenty novels, and had long since set a sufficient distance between herself and the household at Hove which broke up in 1915 to look back on it with equanimity. All her books are sewn with retrospective allusions, but only the first three show a demonstrably closer connection with her early life. Traits belonging to several characters in *Dolores* (written in her mid-twenties and published in 1911) were borrowed, on Ivy's own admission, from various close relations, their setting from her family's Wesleyan background, and the novel's almost unbroken gloom evidently to some extent reflects her own when she wrote it. *Pastors and Masters*, published after a gap of fourteen years, belongs as much for its irresistible, ebullient gaiety, as for its urbane account of love and intrigue among dons in a university town strongly reminiscent of pre-first war Cambridge, to the world opened up by her brother at King's College in the first decade of the century. In 1929, with *Brothers and Sisters*, she turned back again to the family setting which afterwards remained the delight of her life, as it was of Jane Austen's. Children, dependants and servants, brothers and sisters in infancy, youth, middle and old age, power, love, death and the step-relationship provided abundant material. But the theme which, being the most violently dramatic, has most attracted attention is that of domestic tyranny; and—bearing Ivy's repeated disclaimers in mind, and though one must also sharply distinguish between the mature novelist who drew on the experience of her early years and the shy, secretive, immature girl who lived through them without apparent rebellion against the tenets of her class and age—it is interesting to see how far Ivy's mother may be said to stand behind the long line of her domestic tyrants; and what other models (supplemented later no doubt, since Ivy in her forties and fifties built up a small but choice collection of domineering, elderly women among her circle of friends) may have lain to hand in her childhood and adolescence.

Mrs Compton Burnett, who married late having been the youngest and one of the handsomest daughters of an uncommonly forceful father, seems to have possessed the kind of wayward, wilful, magnetic attraction, together with the emotional obduracy, often found in an only child. Her feelings, channelled exclusively towards her own family, were both demanding and fiercely possessive. She had once found Vera seated on her husband's knee and turned the child smartly off it saying, 'half in jest but half not' and with sufficient intention to wound, 'That's my place'. Her devotion to her husband in his lifetime was exceeded only by her cult of his memory afterwards. Her pride in her children was boundless, especially at the expense of their half-brothers and sisters or their 'rather more average' cousins; but it was a pride easily mortified, and often turned to exasperation ('Don't peer!' was her constant refrain to a short-sighted daughter, a phrase which Ivy also found useful as a critical elder sister). She had inherited from her father not only his excellent conceit of himself but also his histrionic gifts which, since they had no opportunity for public display, were freely developed in private. Her temper, never a strong point, grew reckless after her husband's death when 'she had nothing to hold her in': more than sixty years after her own death, her rages are still mentioned in awe-stricken undertones by the few outside her own immediate circle who witnessed them. 'She did get into terrible paddies,' said her daughter Vera. 'She made scenes over nothing at all, we never knew when she would have it. It was a pathological state.' The nervous uncertainty visited on her children grew steadily worse, exacerbated by Guy's sudden death, by their mother's increasing deafness, rheumatism and, in the final year of her life, by her painful last illness and a primitive and even more painful form of radium treatment.

All these quirks of a refractory personality devolved in turn on Sophia Stace: 'I sometimes find myself marvelling at the gulf between the average person and myself,'[15] says Sophia with the candour which is one of her more disarming traits. Another is the triumphant contrariness with which, having driven her children to their study, she interrupts them twice in a morning on grounds (that they are not working or, alternatively, moping over their work—work in any case so frivolous compared with her own that it barely merits the term) calculated to amount to a grievance of one sort or another. Attacks of the fidgets, common enough among Victorian ladies with no occupation beyond giving orders to a highly organized household, were a familiar complaint with Mrs Compton Burnett: 'She had *nothing* to do,' said her daughter Juliet. 'She had nothing to do with us—*she* bore no responsibility; if we were ill, *she* didn't do anything about it. She would look into the nursery or schoolroom in a kindly mood, or sometimes in the other. . . .' The daily routine was fixed, with times laid down for working, walking and meals. Permission was neither sought nor given to alter it, and it grew if anything stricter after their father's death. The three eldest children had possessed bicycles since Ivy was thirteen or so, a privilege later withdrawn by their mother: 'We weren't allowed bicycles in case we were run over, we weren't allowed to swim in case we were drowned, we weren't allowed to ride in case we had a fall.' Sophia, too, has vivid premonitions of death or disaster when her children leave the house, and vents this and other displeasures at the appalling meals which take place both before and after her widowhood:

'I don't think you all ought to sit, dreary and monosyllabic, and make no effort at intercourse, just because your mother is in great sadness and loneliness of heart, and never spare her an encouraging word. When my life is broken, I don't want less from people who are supposed to love me. I need more.'

'You exact too much from people in that position,' said Andrew. 'You have gone too far.'[16]

A similar constraint descended on the Compton Burnett household when, after Guy's death, Noel in his vacations from Cambridge was (like Robin Stace) often 'the only person at ease': 'At family meals Noel would talk to my mother about politics—I don't think anyone else ever said anything. I don't think any of the rest of the family would have spoken to my mother in a spontaneous manner, not Ivy even.'

Sophia is the first and closest but far from the only descendant of

Mrs Compton Burnett in her daughter's books. To the very end of her career Ivy generously distributed among her characters touches taken from her mother—her anxiety over her illness to the two masterful invalids, Matilda Seaton and Sukey Donne; her dangerous possessiveness to Josephine Napier; her ambitions for her children to Harriet Haslam, Eleanor Sullivan and Maria Shelley; her critical asperity to Sabine Ponsonby and others too many to mention. But the two who most nearly resemble the original pattern come quite close together near the end of their creator's life, Eliza Mowbray in *A Father and His Fate* (1957) and Eliza Heriot in *The Last and the First* (1970)—both described in almost the same terms as Sophia, whose looks had been borrowed in the first place from Mrs Compton Burnett. Eliza Mowbray 'cared little for looks in men . . . but demanded them in women and made much of her own. She was a short, fair, young-looking woman of fifty, with an almost beautiful, aquiline face, clear, grey, deep-set eyes, and lips and brows that were responsive to her emotions.' Eliza Heriot 'was a fair, almost handsome woman of fifty-five, with solid aquiline features and a short, upright frame, and active hands that seemed their natural complement. . . . Autocratic by nature, she had become impossibly so, and had come to find criticism a duty, and even an outlet for energy that had no other.'[17]

The two Elizas' likeness in character is as marked as in looks. Both are jealous, competitive women, both dramatically inclined ("'Mater sees and hears herself," said Hermia. "That ends my pity for her and transfers it to Father. He sees and hears her too'"),[*] both apt to congratulate themselves on the problem posed by an 'awkard temperament' ("'Oh, it is the highest type, you know," said Eliza. "But it is not so easy for the person who has it'").[†] Each wields absolute power in her family and each shares a humorous appreciation of the fact with her children who, slaves to their mother as the Staces had been to Sophia, find themselves almost daily constrained to admire their ruler's wanton, foolhardy, sometimes positively diabolical but always masterly sense of foul play. By no means can either be said to be a portrait of Mrs Compton Burnett, except in so far as each embodies an aspect— Eliza Mowbray is an inconsolable widow, Eliza Heriot a resentful

[*] *The Last and the First*, p.24; compare *Brothers and Sisters*: 'Sophia in her extreme moments, when she suffered more than most, never ceased to listen to herself.' (p.122.)
[†] *A Father and His Fate*, p.42; compare *Brothers and Sisters*: "'Oh, no one knows what people go through, when they have such a temperament as I have," said Sophia . . .' (p.189).

stepmother—in which Ivy's mother had once appeared. What seems to have happened is that Ivy used her early experience as other writers have used a body of myth, selecting from it images and archetypes which to the end of her life possessed her imagination and which, though they may retain certain essential and recognizable features, bear in the end no more resemblance to their starting point than to a face in the fire.

Vestiges of the original conception retained by Eliza Mowbray are easily identified. A widow with three sons, her considerable energies are equally divided between the past great romance of her marriage and the present great dudgeon aroused by her eldest son's desire for independence. Her brother-in-law, not a man easily daunted, is frankly frightened of Eliza, and says as much to her son:

'There is no one on this earth, whom I would not rather set myself against than your mother. I wondered how your father could undertake her. I put it in plain words. "My dear brother," I said, "you are a braver man than I am." But he heard no reason. And the marriage was a success. Believe it or not, it was.'

'I believe it,' said Malcolm. 'I was a witness of it. It lives in my memory. It casts its shadow over us. It was so great a success that nothing else can be so. No one can love her enough, admire her enough, give her enough. She can never be satisfied. And my brothers give a good deal.'[18]

The same dissatisfaction is evident in relations between Mrs Mowbray and her companion Miss Manders, known as Mandy, who serves at once as refuge and confidante to the young Mowbrays. Mandy has the 'long, thin face and large kind eyes'[19] bequeathed to Miss Patmore and others by the Compton Burnetts' Minnie, as well as the insatiable curiosity associated with this type (Miss Jennet, or Jenney, in *Elders and Betters*, Miss Griffon in *A Family and a Fortune* are obvious examples, besides a whole retinue of children's nurses); and her intimacy with the children provokes in Eliza a tirade of outraged betrayal preposterous in any but a person born, as one of her sons remarks, to be a figure in tragedy: 'I *am* a figure in tragedy, my dear. I was not born to be one. I was born for happiness and love and life. And they have been torn from me. You would think that people would extend to me a helping hand. But I am to have nothing; no kindness, no loyalty, no help in my hard place. I am a figure of tragedy indeed.'

Eliza Heriot, also a figure in tragedy and accustomed to trade on the fact, is interesting here chiefly in her capacity as disgruntled second wife. Her husband leaves the running of his home 'wholly in her hands', and has moreover bequeathed his property to her over the heads of his children in a will identical with Christian Stace's, or for that matter with Dr Burnett's. What is perhaps more curious is that in Ivy's last book (on which she worked intermittently for five or six years before her death) she returned to a situation which had loomed large in her first: Eliza Heriot's authority, in *The Last and the First*, is grimly challenged and ultimately routed by her eldest stepdaughter Hermia who leaves home just as, in *Dolores*, the eponymous heroine had done to escape the dominion of a coldly hostile stepmother. There is small point in setting the juvenile clumsiness of *Dolores* beside the breathtaking clarity and concision with which similarly gruelling battles are presented, at incomparably greater emotional pressure, in a book written almost sixty years later. But one may note in passing that the second Mrs Hutton in *Dolores* was in part at least a rough and superficial sketch of Mrs Compton Burnett ('let it not be thought that his wife was a virago or a termagant . . . Mrs Hutton was merely an irritable, jealous, sensitive woman'),[20] that her path is 'continually dogged by my stepchildren', and that she resents her husband's first marriage so acutely that he learns from 'dread of domestic friction' to suppress all trace of fondness for his eldest daughter. Hermia Heriot's father does the same; and both stepdaughters suffer not only from a loveless upbringing but also from the fact that any mention of their early childhood—Hermia was ten, Dolores nine years old when her own mother died—is forbidden on pain of their stepmothers' extreme displeasure.

Olive Compton-Burnett had been eight years old when her father brought home a second wife, and the first marriage was not thereafter a subject encouraged for conversation in her stepmother's household. Olive, like Hermia and Dolores, had once been especially dear to her father, and preserved the memory long after her privileged position had been undermined. But the gap in age and circumstances effectively prevented any great contact with the second family. She had been dispatched to boarding school when Ivy was two years old, returning for six or seven unhappy years before she left again for good ('A daughter leaving the family home to seek employment! It is not a thing she would be proud of,' says Eliza's son, discussing his mother in *The Last and the First* with a detachment matched in Hermia's sombre reply: 'There is no cause for pride. It has never been a home to me')[21] when Ivy was sixteen. Olive seems to have been the one who most actively smarted under the sense of inferiority fostered in all five step-children by their uncertain status at home, their separate education, their dullness when set beside the achievements of their half-brothers and sisters, their own mother's comparatively humble origins as the daughter of a provincial chemist, and the more or less complete break with her family. Always 'a difficult person', forceful and clever but not intellectual, Olive had never slackened the feud with her stepmother and 'vented it all round'. Inevitably one thinks of the submerged cruelties ("Of course stepmothers are cruel," said Hope, "but then so are stepchildren, though they don't have any of the discredit"')[22] inherent in this situation in the novels of I. Compton-Burnett. But one should remember that the two despotic second wives, Mrs Hutton and Lady Heriot, are easily outnumbered in the novels by stepmothers on excellent terms with their stepchildren—and that the kind of atmosphere which prevailed in the Compton Burnett household must have been widespread at a time when people had no alternative but to endure for years at close quarters what was perhaps no less a volume of suffering than the miseries of divorce, separation and broken homes which have since largely replaced it.

It was presumably a relief to both parties when Olive, after her father's death, severed close connections with her stepmother's family (though she retained to the end of her life a measure of financial dependence on her half-sisters). She earned a precarious living by journalism, mostly in London, always in straitened circumstances, and towards the end of the first war set up house with a friend called Emily Pope who remained her companion until she died at the age of eighty-seven in 1963. There are differing views of this ménage in which Olive, hardened no doubt by her early experience (to which she never afterwards referred), was the dominant partner, seeming something of a bully to outside observers who had small doubt that—at any rate when Olive was old and hearty, Miss Pope older and delicate—'there was tyranny there'.[23]

Iris and Daisy had spent more time at home though Iris, who helped with the housekeeping and maintained a mutual coldness with her stepmother, left home like her eldest sister at twenty-five to train at the Temperance Hospital in Hampstead (which she chose in preference to the Homoeopathic Hospital on the ground that she would not there be known as her celebrated father's daughter), where she eventually became a sister and remained—a faithful and respected nurse, a pillar of St Barnabas' Guild, the Bible Reading Fellowship and St John's Church, Ladbroke Grove—till shortly before her death in 1944. It is hardly surprising that Ivy had no special liking for any of her half-sisters. 'Though they lived cheek by jowl, and though there was certainly no enmity, I don't think there was any affinity,' said Vera Compton-Burnett. Ivy had cared perhaps least of all for Daisy, who was 'my mother's right hand. Daisy called her mother, which the others didn't, and I think she really felt herself to be her daughter. She was the daughter at home.' It was Daisy who paid calls with Mrs Compton Burnett, replaced on occasion unwillingly by Ivy who 'loathed calling. She didn't do it with a very good grace, and she hadn't a gift for it.' It was also Daisy who helped teach the small children, partly from inclination and partly because time spent in the nursery meant that so much less time need be spent in the company of Ivy and her brothers: 'She got out of the difficulty of relations with the older ones by being with the younger ones'. The chief difficulty seems to have been that Daisy, 'being so religious and Ivy so irreligious', provided an admirably accommodating butt for her younger sister's sharp tongue: while the pious and gentle Daisy sat staring dreamily into space 'Ivy would make remarks,' and turn poor Daisy's clumsy answers upside down. Part at least of Daisy's trouble was that she had too little to do. She would, according to her younger sisters, have made an excellent vicar's wife and, if one thinks of Ivy's attitude towards this calling as represented by the vicar's wife in Men and Wives—'I have had my fill of funerals, and mothers' meetings and parishioners' teas. The funerals are the best; they do get rid of somebody'24—one can very well see why the two had never got on. Guy sometimes held the peace between them ('And I should think he had his work cut out,' said Juliet Compton-Burnett), but 'Daisy was a target rather'.

Daisy's religious fervour first rose to a mania in the dark days after their father's death when Vera and Judy, coming home from school on weekday afternoons, would be captured and made to sing hymns at the piano by a sister who 'looked strange'. She was promptly sent away to visit her Thomas aunts in Cheshire, and came home restored again; but, round about her thirtieth birthday, after years of depression and strain brought on by the grinding monotony of life at Hove, her strangeness returned in a form which amounted to a serious breakdown. 'One Sunday afternoon, it was just after tea—we were so embarrassed we didn't ever speak about it—Daisy stopped at the door and said,

"There is something I wish you all to know. I have given myself to Jesus." We nearly fainted, I remember the awful tension,' said Vera Compton-Burnett. 'My mother said something like, "Well, I'm sure it's very nice that Daisy has done this." The rest of us were dumb with horror.'

Shortly afterwards Daisy departed of her own accord for a missionary training school, leaving a note explaining what she had done and saying goodbye to no one. She never returned to Hove and, having regained her health, volunteered in 1913 for service under the Church Missionary Society at Panyam in Northern Nigeria where she was held in considerable esteem, established a homoeopathic dispensary for the tribespeople, and was known as Mat-yen (woman of medicine). On her retirement some years later she became head of the school to which she had originally fled, the Carfax Missionary Home (later a refuge for retired missionaries) in Bristol. Here she was remembered in the 'thirties by her doctor[25] as a tall, imposing, self-possessed lady dressed in grey with an Edwardian coiffure: 'A *very* dignified lady, very austere, who had high standards of behaviour for herself and for everybody else. She could be very critical if you didn't live up to her standards.' She bore no resemblance to her father in looks, and in character she had become by then 'too controlled'. A clerical friend from Panyam, who had travelled out on the same boat in 1913 to Africa, recalled that 'she seldom spoke of any relative. We knew however that the members of her own family had little sympathy with her Christian principles and outlook.'[26] Her family for their part had not unnaturally lost touch with Daisy. Ivy herself in later life was frequently humorous at the expense of her missionary sister, though one may perhaps detect a hint of sympathy in her account of Rosamund Burtenshaw, the senior member of a trio of zealous and meddlesome spinsters distributing tracts in *A House and Its Head*: 'Miss Burtenshaw had retired from missionary work owing to the discomfort of the life, a reason which she did not disclose, though it was more than adequate; and was accustomed to say she found plenty of furrows to plough in the home field. . . .'[27]

Daisy's two brothers in their early twenties had made an equally dramatic break with the family. Both had already left Hove in their father's lifetime and neither seems to have made any great impression on their half-brothers and sisters before that. Charlie had had his first birthday ten days before his father remarried in 1883, Richard his fourth one month later; and Richard at any rate might have agreed with Fabian Clare in *The Present and the Past*, another melancholy small boy whose childhood had been overshadowed by his father's second marriage: 'My life was over when I was four. I wonder how many people can say that.'[28] Richard, who had come into a small income from property left him under his father's will, appears from the Law Lists to have practised as a solicitor in London between 1901 and 1903. Charlie never apparently qualified. He had been led astray by 'a set with money' and several times got into trouble, being finally discovered one night by the Salvation Army penniless on London Bridge with nowhere to go. Mrs Compton Burnett, who was promptly sent for from Hove, did her duty without hesitation on this occasion: 'My mother paid his debts and got him straight, and then he went abroad.' The rents from his share of his father's property—£28 10s. per quarter—had been paid to his stepmother until his twenty-first birthday, when he signed a formal discharge on 10 September 1903. Family legend later took a dim view of the doctor's two eldest sons: 'They were rotters and they ran through their money,' said a distant relative who remembered being taken up to London as a small child in the 'nineties to consult Dr Burnett for a sore throat.

Whatever the reason, the two brothers left the country some time in 1904, emigrating to America as their father in his youth had once half determined to do. Charlie, always a first-rate horseman, was last heard of by his half-sisters training cavalry in Canada during the first world war; he settled afterwards at Pasadena in California, was said to have become a fruit farmer, corresponded regularly with Olive, lived to a ripe old age and made a late marriage to 'an old friend' long after there was any prospect of children. Richard, who had set up as an attorney in Pasadena, was less fortunate: 'The financial slump in America in '29 ruined him and affected his health,' wrote Olive in 1949, 'and my brother Charles looked after him in his remaining years.'* He killed himself by jumping off a bridge in Los Angeles on 11 December 1935.

---

* Richard's death certificate says that he had been in the U.S. since 1900, Olive's letter (to her solicitor) that he emigrated 'just prior to 1905'. He died unmarried, childless and intestate, his sole possession consisting of a thirty-fifth share under the intestacy of his uncle, Alfred Henry Thomas, who had predeceased him in 1935; Richard's share, eventually made over by his brother Charles to Olive, came to £70.

'Always a little bit in awe of Ivy'

WHATEVER MAY HAVE happened after Dr Burnett's death, there is no reason to suppose that his two eldest sons had not got on well with their father in his lifetime, though one may perhaps detect a certain mistrust in his having in one sense passed over them both in his will. Dr Burnett left small parcels of property (mostly working men's cottages, together with two or three small farms, at Great Clacton and Walton-on-Naze) to his first five children, who would each have received an annual income from tenants of round about £150, and sometimes considerably less. Ivy and her two brothers had also come into similar but smaller bequests. The rest (apart from a conditional legacy of £200 to Minnie) was left in trust to his wife, to be divided after her death between her own children. The disparity between provisions for his first and second families in what was evidently a scrupulously fair will probably reflects the fact that his first wife had brought him little or nothing (as a 'struggling young doctor' in 1874, he himself had presumably only his prospects to live on),* and his second wife a fairly substantial dowry. But Katharine Compton Burnett became trustee and sole guardian of his infant children (who included Iris and Charlie at the time of his death), to be succeeded, if she should die, by Guy when he reached the age of twenty-one. Guy was also to assist his mother as joint trustee although Richard, who was entrusted with no responsibility, had been already twenty-one when the will was made, and even Charlie was three years older than Guy. Apparently the doctor, who had held strong, indeed reverent views on the supremacy of duty, trusted his wife to be fair to her stepchildren (and, when she was not, her daughters contributed annually after her

* No great capital outlay was required to set up in the late nineteenth century as a G.P.: Arthur Conan Doyle put up his plate at Southsea in 1882, in a villa rented at £40 p.a. and furnished for £3, having purchased '£12 worth of tinctures, infusions, pills, powders, ointments and bottles at a wholesale house', and prided himself on living expenses of sixpence a day (*Conan Doyle* by Hesketh Pearson, Methuen, 1943, p.66).

death to the comparatively meagre portions of their three half-sisters).

It is perhaps small wonder that Mrs Compton Burnett, left with nine children under twenty-one on her hands as well as two older, unmarried stepdaughters, should have been in the last years of her life so earnestly bent on retrenchment. She had moreover the additional strain of contributing to the expenses of her father's household. Rowland Rees died at Hove, sixteen months after his son-in-law, at the age of eighty-six on 22 July 1902, leaving a will which, though it makes ominous mention of his sons' debts, also includes elaborate directions for the getting in of all moneys and properties in a trust fund to provide for his wife, various grandchildren and all but three of his seven surviving children (excluding his eldest son Rowland, something of a black sheep in the family, as well as Allen and Charles who had all three received and squandered their inheritance). But the estate, when got in, amounted to £1,850 13s. 2d., barely sufficient to cover his few preliminary bequests—a discrepancy which, taken with the earlier move from his large house at Clacton to a small terrace villa in Hove, the fact that James Compton Burnett had for some years supported him, and that Katharine continued after his death to make an allowance to her stepmother, points to some kind of financial catastrophe.

Dr Burnett and his father-in-law had been fond of one another, and often played chess in the evenings. Katharine in later years would frequently take 'an evening prowl' to call on her stepmother ('I think I'll just go and see Mater tonight') and the second Mrs Rees returned her affection, though not without reservations ('She disapproved of Katie, you know, she thought the first family should've been treated better,' said one of Rowland Rees' granddaughters). Ivy's sisters had had little to do with the Reeses who did not care for small children, and who 'played no part in our lives at all'; but Ivy, eighteen when her grandfather died, had been old enough to take note of his character as of his dealings with a family which over three generations acknowledged him as its head. Records of his tempestuous career in Dover suggest a striking affinity with the many stiff-necked, contumacious fathers and grandfathers ruling their households by terror, and by an unshakeable conviction of their own divine right, in the novels of I. Compton-Burnett; and accounts of his years in retirement confirm that his temper had by no means worn thin in old age. 'A very peppery, aristocratic sort of a man, of an irritable disposition,' said his grand-daughter Vera; 'I should think his wife and family ran at his behest.' Vera never forgot her stepgrandmother, who was regularly snubbed at home, explaining that some indisposition was nothing worse than a cold, whereupon her grandfather growled: 'What would you have, woman—a plague?'

Rowland Rees shared with Sophia's father, the elder Andrew Stace in *Brothers and Sisters*, not only his early religious conversion and subsequent zeal but also his attitude to himself ('When he spoke of his Maker, he spoke simply of the being who had made him—and perhaps been pleased in this case to execute one of his outstanding pieces of work').[29] Indeed, when one considers Andrew Stace in his eighties— his gruff, disobliging manner with women, his likeness in temperament to his daughter and his preference for her husband's company, his habitual pose of self-pity, his genuine self-congratulation and his terrific fondness for self-dramatization—it is difficult to avoid the conclusion that the character must have been fairly closely modelled on Ivy's grandfather. Traces of his influence constantly recur in the novels, perhaps most forcibly in Miles Mowbray who (in *A Father and His Fate*) behaves abominably to his family and, when eventually thwarted, impudently turns his own public exposure into a scene of public self-applause: 'Everyone else has been able to be generous and heroic. And I have been ridiculous and pitiful and a sort of spectacle and butt. And doing more all the time than anyone else, and facing more into the bargain! Indeed no one else doing or facing anything! It has been a test on a large scale.'[30]

Alderman Rees had also frequently been, in the 'seventies and 'eighties, 'a sort of spectacle and butt' in Dover Town Hall, as in the local and national press. He had possessed, moreover, an ample share of that indomitable ebullience which enables Miles Mowbray, in common with many of Ivy's tyrants, not only to override other people with brutal indifference but, when his victims protest, to abuse them roundly for harbouring grudges. The Editor of the *Dover Chronicle*, writing evidently from personal experience, had hotly defended Councillor Rees in 1862 against this very charge: 'Mr Rees is the man to blurt out the fiery indignation of his Welsh ancestor, Ap Rice Ap Howell Ap Rowland Ap Rees; but when once the Welsh blood has effervesced in a genuine "tiff", he is the best-natured of good fellows.'[31] The celebrated vigour and obstinacy of the Mayor of Dover, his grief when his town clerk sought to 'insult and aggravate' him, his piteous remonstrances against 'dogmatic, impudent persons' who persistently gave him the lie, his blistering, virulent, but somehow absurdly fetching public tantrums, remind one again and again of Miles Mowbray whose particular talent lay, as Alderman Rees' had done, in carrying off impossible situations:

'I would rather be what I am, a weak, erring man, weaker than a woman I daresay, than a hard, hardly-judging person, who speaks with a second purpose all the time, and a malicious one at that. I bear no one ill-will, though something has been exposed, that I meant to be hidden, that had better have been hidden, as so many things in our lives had better be. Oh, I have not so much fault to find with myself.'

'But we hardly expected so much praise,' said Rudolf.[32]

A colleague and contemporary of Rowland Rees had been the chairman of the Gas Company, one W. R. Mowll, J.P., who, in company with the future Mayor, is several times reported in the local press as active in furthering the interests of the Young Men's Christian Association or relieving the poor in time of hard frost. William Rutley Mowll had several sons who entered the church or the law, and we have it on the authority of Arthur Waley (who presumably had it directly from Ivy herself)[33] that the figure whose shadow had lain over her childhood and who continued long afterwards to stand behind her tyrants was one of these sons—also in his day a prominent citizen of Dover, an evangelical churchman, staunch Tory, Town Councillor, East Kent's Receiver in Bankruptcy, Register of Dover Harbour and the Compton Burnetts' trusty family solicitor, Worsfold Mowll. Messrs. Mowll and Mowll of Dover had drawn up James Compton Burnett's marriage settlement in September 1883, and thereafter conducted his business transactions (including drawing up his will and his father-in-law's) to the end of his life. Worsfold Mowll had been named joint trustee with Mrs Compton Burnett during Guy's minority and much later, when Guy and Noel and Worsfold Mowll were all dead, his brother Martyn became joint guardian with Ivy to her four younger sisters. As a child, Ivy must often have seen Worsfold Mowll, who came with a clerk twice yearly to review the doctor's accounts and afterwards maintained the custom of lunching with his widow at Hove—solemn occasions which Ivy attended (and perhaps recalled, in a scene from *Men and Wives*, when another lawyer comes to condole with his client and review her finances: 'Dominic entered the house with a hushed tread, holding his bag as a secular object brought on a sacred occasion. He remained leaning over Harriet's hand in silence').[34] Worsfold Mowll, vastly tall, grave and portentous, ponderous in manner and person, made a memorable impression of omnipotence and omniscience on the small children who, though not present at lunch, would be dressed up and brought down for his inspection in the course of the afternoon. Vera Compton-Burnett, once reproved by her mother for stooping, remembered Mr Mowll launching at once into the cautionary tale of Little Johnny Head-in-Air: what infuriated the child was the injustice of being squashed simultaneously for looking down one moment and looking up the next. Later, she retaliated by putting a bulb under the plate of his brother Martyn—'rather less Worsfold than Worsfold'—and squeezing it so subtly that he could never be certain whether it jumped or not. But Worsfold himself had been more intimidating, a fearsome disciplinarian and not to be trifled with. 'He *was* a person . . .' said Vera Compton-Burnett; 'only second to God, I would think,' said her sister.

The Mowlls had long been a leading family in Dover. Worsfold, born in 1850, had founded the family firm in 1881 in partnership with his brother. His son Rutley (also in turn Ivy's solicitor) later won brief and no doubt disagreeable fame when, as Coroner for East Kent, he gave evidence at the Old Bailey on the inquest of Bessie Munday, one of Joseph Smith's Brides in the Bath murdered at Herne Bay in July 1912. Some forty years earlier, Worsfold's father had won an equally brief and perhaps even more disagreeable notoriety when, as President of the local Y.M.C.A., he had on moral and religious grounds successfully banned Shakespeare from the library and *Punch* from the reading room. The ensuing commotion afforded considerable amusement to the national and even international press from *Le Figaro* to the *Daily Telegraph*, and *Punch* printed a derisive riposte under the heading, DOLTS OF DOVER: 'Oh Mowll, Mowll. We cannot be serious with *you.* . . . But what of Dover? What of its Young Christians? What of people who can choose such rulers and submit to them? Well . . . we apprise Dover that its unhappy dulness shall be respected and tenderly cared for. Our pictures shall henceforth be explained (in foot-note or otherwise) for the instruction of Dover, and as the Essex Calf has been improved into average sense, Punch hopes that years of cultivation may elevate the Dover Dolt.'[35]

W. R. Mowll's two sons seem to have held the same stern belief in their own righteousness as their father who, undaunted by strenuous local opposition, had determined in 1871 to persevere in 'the cause of religion and morality, despite the ungodly press of England'. 'I have always gone on in the *old* groove,' was a saying of Martyn Mowll's when, as guardian to the motherless Compton-Burnett girls until they were twenty-four, he had earnestly attempted to curb their desire for independence. Ivy's sisters proposed to lead a musical life, chaperoned by Minnie and sharing a house with Myra Hess, a scheme which dismayed the heart of their guardian who envisaged prospects too frightful to contemplate if they were permitted any truck with however respected and respectable a pianist: 'Miss Vera, these *artist people* are very charming—very charming, Miss Vera—but unreliable. This friendship of yours may end in the law courts.'

Worsfold Mowll was also as godly, inflexible and assiduous as his father had been before him in prosecuting good works for local orphans, athletes and police constables who were regaled at an annual cricket match with the villagers and his family (he had eleven children as well as numerous nieces and nephews, one of them later at King's College with Noel Compton-Burnett) in the grounds of his house outside Dover. 'The police force will lose a friend,' wrote the *Dover Telegraph* when he died on 26 January 1906, lamented by the whole town with flags at half mast and the bells of St Mary's tolling on the day of his death, muffled peals at St James' and funeral sermons preached in almost every church the following Sunday. The Mayor and corporation followed him to his grave, together with over a thousand mourners and six carriages loaded with two hundred wreaths (among them one 'In loving memory' from Mrs Compton Burnett), in a funeral procession half a mile long. He is commemorated by a memorial window in Dover Town Hall and the *Dover Telegraph*, mourning his loss, suggests perhaps some of the reasons why he should also long afterwards have been commemorated in the novels of I. Compton-Burnett:

He was unlike other men. Worsfold Mowll was Worsfold Mowll. Without being pedantic, aesthetic or affected, he had a distinct individuality. . . . There was something great about Worsfold Mowll—one cannot bring oneself to prefix him with the ordinary Mr . . . a big man, truly, in every sense of the word—in stature, in the largeness of his heart, in his generosity and geniality. He had an overwhelming effect upon you—not the overbearing pettiness of the martinet, but a mannerism that enveloped you and drew you within its grasp with peculiar fascination. . . .[36]

Whatever the aspect uppermost in the minds of his townsmen in their hour of bereavement, there were undeniably traces of the pettiness of the martinet in Mr Mowll's relations with the Compton Burnetts. After their father's death, he had become their mother's chief guide and councillor and, though Mrs Compton Burnett may have found him congenial company, he seems to have appeared repressive and dictatorial to her children at a time when the three eldest were already beginning to assert their independence. One cannot help suspecting his influence on Dominic Spong, the Haslams' solicitor in *Men and Wives*, who exasperates the family by his interference in money matters (' "Oh, Spong is an old skinflint," said Godfrey rather uneasily. " . . . I don't know what we are coming to, if lawyers are to be father and mother and legal adviser all in one" '),[37] his laboured witticisms, his embarrassing habit of currying favour with their mother and his ill-concealed disapproval of the children's artistic and literary ambitions ('Dominic rose and took his leave, an extra heaviness in his breathing betraying his present unavoidable attitude to the house'). Both Arthur Waley and Jack Beresford, friends of Noel Compton-Burnett at King's, were familiar with Noel's imitations of Mr Mowll in a high, starched collar issuing oracular pronouncements from a great height, and both had the impression that he ruled the Compton-Burnett finances, as well as offering opinions on the children's education and upbringing, with an authority seldom gainsaid.[38] Ivy, too, made caustic comments on Mr Mowll; and it is perhaps worth noting that crushed and apprehensive children in the novels of I. Compton-Burnett often retaliate by aping the people who frighten them—Lesbia Firebrace, Duncan Edgeworth, Sabine Ponsonby and Jocasta Grimstone, four egregious tyrants, are all mimicked by their victims behind their backs.

Shapes and patterns which later sharply emerged in the novels must have surrounded Ivy in these years. Her mother, her grandfather and Worsfold Mowll all provided examples of the kind of moral turpitude which she afterwards accepted without rancour or indignation, and analysed with disturbing precision: ' . . . I think that life makes great demand on people's characters, and gives them, and especially used to give them, great opportunity to serve their own ends by the sacrifice of other people. Such ill-doing may meet with little retribution, may indeed be hardly recognized, and I cannot feel so surprised if people yield to it.'[39] But Ivy at seventeen was in no position to formulate her later philosophy, though she may well have lived according to its law of stoical acceptance. What little indication survives—descriptions of her attitude at college, letters and verses written in her early twenties,

the vicious doctrine of self-sacrifice embedded in her first novel—
suggests that she hardly recognized, any more than her mother, the
pattern underlying their mutual unhappiness.

Mrs Compton Burnett in the early part of her widowhood can have
had little enough to deter her from temperamental excesses, with
Olive and Charlie both treading roads to ruin in London, Daisy sunk in
religious melancholia at home, Ivy away at college, the four little girls
turning wholly to Minnie for affection and supervision. Guy and Noel
had been sent as day boys to Brighton College in the summer term of
1901, and both left again (whether on grounds of retrenchment, or
because they had as much difficulty as their sisters in adjusting to a
school where 'the day-boys were still pretty good mud, and the idea
of a Day-boy House still a little strange,'[40] or because the school itself
was at that time held in low repute and had even been up for sale the
year before) the following Easter. For a year they were taught by their
tutor at home until Guy, at nineteen, went up to King's to read classics
in 1904. No records remain of his two terms at Cambridge, though
his younger sisters were both convinced that 'he would have been quite
remarkable. Guy could have put the other two in his pocket.' Dr
Burnett had wanted Guy to take up medicine and they thought that,
if their father had lived, Guy would probably have acquiesced: when
pressed on the subject, he would reply that he meant to be a doctor of
divinity and headmaster of a school. But the plan to be a clergyman,
like Noel's to be a soldier, was no more than a childish ambition, and
both Ivy and her sisters maintained that Guy would have been a writer.
One should not perhaps attach much importance to a set of verses
composed on his father's death in April 1901, which, though they show
a certain 'fluency in words', reveal otherwise nothing beyond the
average capacities of a fifteen-year-old boy writing in the conventional
idiom of his period:

> There is a veiling curtain drawn before
> The eyes of men, concealing from their sight
> The hidden mysteries of the further shore,
> Till they were taught to bear the fuller light. . . .
>
> The curtain will be lifted, when 'tis time,
> The weary road will draw unto an end;
> They are the means to make the soul sublime
> To pass away, and meet each long-lost friend.

Noel, too, is said to have written a patriotic poem commemorating the deaths of his father and Queen Victoria, 'and God certainly came into it', so perhaps the earlier break with religion had not been as complete as it seemed to Ivy in retrospect. Her two younger sisters both agreed that (at any rate in the sense defined by France Ponsonby in *Daughters and Sons*) Guy had been truly religious. 'I think it was in a way his religious nature which supported us all,' said Juliet Compton-Burnett; and accounts of his forbearance towards their mother, his generosity to his sisters, suggest that he had reached in the last years of his life an extraordinary emotional maturity.

But the strain, coming so soon after his own dangerous illness on one whose health had always been delicate, must have taxed his strength beyond bearing. When the whole family caught influenza in the Easter holidays Guy, who had seemed to be getting well, suffered a sudden relapse and died within a few days of his apparent recovery on 29 May 1905. 'My mother put everything into Guy,' and she had received more in return up to the last few days of his illness when he would beg Minnie to prevent her coming into the sick-room: 'He hadn't the strength any more to stand it.' She never recovered from the two deaths. For months afterwards she would go for walks with Vera, urging her to talk about him, to dredge up memories of anything Guy had ever done or said, much as Sophia Stace in the early days of her widowhood 'begged with untiring eagerness for assurances of her virtues as a wife, that were given at first willingly, but by degrees with the last weariness'.[41] It was Noel, still young for his age at seventeen, who grew up to take the place of his father and Guy—'After Guy died, Noll changed almost overnight'—and Noel who became his mother's 'darling boy', though he could not respond to her as heroically as Guy had done: 'Noel had a lighter temperament than Guy, he didn't live in his nature so much.' Noel from this time became Ivy's inseparable companion. Both bore their own grief with resolute courage in silence; and both must have suffered from their mother's emotional collapse as the Stace children had done from 'the stress and pity of Sophia'.

But Ivy by this time was in her third year at Royal Holloway College and, having once escaped the confines of life at Hove, she never again submitted to complete subjugation. Guy's loss remained a source of almost unfaceable pain to the end of her life; and she was not able, as he had been, to offer their mother either consolation or intimacy. In later years the two would walk down to the sea together in the evenings, but it is unlikely that their conversation ever strayed beyond the bounds of Ivy's habitual reticence. 'Ivy very rarely put into words what was her real being,' said her sister; and Mrs Compton Burnett, though she was afterwards justly proud of her eldest daughter, was also, with reason, 'always a little bit in awe of Ivy'.

CHAPTER SIX

1902–1911

I

'Uplift was the keynote'

ROYAL HOLLOWAY COLLEGE, when Ivy arrived there chaperoned by Minnie on 2 October 1902, was a small, isolated and inward-looking community regarded with some suspicion by the outside world. It stood alone on the borders of Berkshire and Surrey, twenty miles from London, forty miles from Oxford, just outside the tiny country town of Egham, on a hillside overlooking Virginia Water and Windsor Great Park. Strange rumours about the doings of its staff and students circulated in the established universities, and stranger still among the wider public who considered education for women an unhealthy, even sinister attempt to undermine the nation's fabric. The college had been founded sixteen years before by the philanthropist Thomas Holloway, a baker's son who had built his vast fortune on a patent pill advertised in his lifetime as a cure for 'inflammations, abscesses and ulcerations . . . indigestion, biliousness, sick headache, nervousness, sleeplessness, loss of appetite' as well as 'skin diseases of the most revolting character'; but which proved, when analysed by the British Medical Association after his death, to contain aloes, powdered ginger and soap. The pill remained long afterwards a source of embarrassment and vexation to the grateful recipients of Mr Holloway's bounty. Queen Victoria had opened the college in 1886, and the following year twenty-eight students arrived to occupy an enormous French château, newly-built of local red brick and covering, according to a boastful prospectus, 'more ground than any other college in the world'. The Dean of Windsor, watching this strange, scarlet edifice rising in the neighbouring fields, had said: 'It is intended for the higher education of women; but the question I am asking is whether any women with facilities open to them at both Oxford and Cambridge are ever likely to go to Egham to be educated?'[1]

But education at Egham had several advantages over education elsewhere. Holloway College, for one thing, had an endowment of nearly a quarter of a million pounds which made it conspicuously richer than the foundations for women at Oxford and Cambridge. For another, its Founder's views had been in advance of his time and decidedly liberal: all students were to read for degrees (which was by no means the case for girls at the older universities), and their choice of subject was to be broader than the traditional curriculum based on Latin, Greek and mathematics—though these were still, in Ivy's day at Holloway, 'spoken of as genuine Schools and the others as soft options'.[2] Three years before she came up, the college, after long hesitation over the rival claims of Oxford, had finally been accepted as a part of London university: London, though new, inexperienced and widely despised at the time, was not only conveniently closer to Egham, but far bolder in its attitude to new schools and branches of learning, and far better disposed towards women than Oxford (where, some twenty years later, the Vice-Chancellor still prayed daily that women might not be admitted to the degree: 'Lord, if it must be, let it not be in my time').[3] Moreover the Founder, taking note no doubt of the sad fact that at Oxford girls were too often a downtrodden company compared with their brothers, had declared it his 'express and earnest desire . . . that the College shall neither be considered nor conducted as a mere training college for teachers and governesses'. He had been perhaps over-optimistic, since Ivy herself was one of comparatively few in her year not destined to become a schoolmistress. Most of the others seem to have approached the higher education in much the same spirit as the girl in *Dolores*, who bettered her mind 'simply because I must earn my bread, or go to the workhouse'.[4]

There were fifty girls in Ivy's year, 137 altogether, and the students continued to increase in number throughout the four years she spent there. They lived in a magnificent pile built round two quadrangles in the fancy French style—steep mansard roofs, round pointed turrets, pavilions at the four corners rising to a flamboyant skyline—which had been especially popular in the 'eighties and 'nineties among the nouveaux riches. So charmed was Mr Holloway by the châteaux of the Loire that he had sent his architect to spend a summer measuring the exact dimensions of Chambord, which he then reproduced for sound commercial reasons on his Surrey hillside in 'flaming red brick which fairly scorched the eye'. Even now, when the walls have mellowed to a rich poppy colour against green English lawns and a blue sky, one can well understand the visitor who said nervously in 1908: 'My dear, you really musn't show it broadside on!' A few years later this astonishing building, with its courtyards and broad walks, its terraced gardens threaded by drives, its greenhouses, summerhouses, ponds, streams, swimming pool and elaborate system of ornamental statuary, was chosen in a film called *Alf's Button* 'to represent the bathing establishment conjured up by the djinn, when Alf asked for a bath'. It had been designed to provide generous accommodation for some 250 to 300 students, a corresponding number of staff and the hundred or more servants required to attend on them. The girls' bedrooms opened on to corridors one-tenth of a mile long, so that it was impossible for people at one end to recognize anyone walking in the far distance at the other. Whole floors were still uninhabited in Ivy's day (it was rumoured that the unexplored range of closets and bedrooms above the attics had been intended by the Founder to house the girls' individual lady's maids); there were about eight hundred rooms, some of them so far flung that a contemporary of hers who stayed on as a lecturer had still, after a lifetime spent in the college, never even seen them.

Ivy used memories of Holloway twice in her novels, as the basis of the women's college in *Dolores* and for the girls' boarding school in *More Women Than Men*: people are apt to get lost in both these 'great, rambling, complicated place[s]', to be confused by unfamiliar faces and by the din of girls bustling 'in a chattering stream' along 'perplexing corridors' to unknown destinations. Girls at Holloway, coming straight from home with little experience of the outside world and no notion what to expect of life in an academic community, must often have suffered from the sense of bewilderment and lost identity which overcomes Dolores on her first day at college: 'As other days followed . . . she found herself with a place and purposes in a passionless, ardent little world—a world of women's friendships; where there lived in a strange harmony the spirits of the medieval convent and modern growth.'⁵ Other members of the college had also compared the enclosed atmosphere at Holloway—days spent moving between chapel and library, study and lecture room, according to a strict rule of decorum, silence and punctuality enforced by the ringing of bells—with the régime in a well endowed tenth- or eleventh-century convent where unmarried women pursued under close supervision a life devoted to religion, learning and the arts. Ivy's contemporaries prided themselves on their domestic appointments which were at once austere and comfortable, 'nicely feminine, yet learned'.

But the 'orderly, Christian household' enjoined in the Founder's trust deed was to be modelled on the standards of solid opulence brought to a high point in late Victorian country houses, vast establishments which sometimes housed as many as 150 people and maintained them by means of the latest technical devices: Holloway College had steam central heating installed from the first, and a tunnel built so that the sight of servants or their carts might not offend the resident ladies. The corridors were carpeted and the girls' studies—the 'narrow student chambers' of *Dolores*—each contained, besides the regulation set of severely plain dresser, two chairs and a table with brass fittings, a large looking glass (said to have been a stipulation of the Founder's will) and an open fire (rationed to one coal scuttle a day, which meant thrift and constant anxiety for those who, unlike Ivy, were not expert in the gentle art of lighting and tending coal fires). The college had been furnished throughout by Maples in massive mahogany, with carved oak, ornate plaster ceilings, oriental rugs and leather-backed chairs in the library. Maids swept and cleaned the rooms before breakfast. The Lady Housekeeper, a stern and fastidious martinet, was said to have been appointed by the Principal in 1891 on the strength of a sentence in her letter of application: 'I have been accustomed to keep a liberal table.'

Holloway, in sharp contrast to other impoverished and comfortless women's colleges of the day, was celebrated alike for its good living and excellent food. It had its own kitchen gardens, asparagus and strawberry beds, orchards and piggeries. Dinner in the great central dining hall was served by the butler and a line of starched maids off solid silver plate with specially woven monogrammed table linen. A procession in long dresses, often with trains on high nights, assembled every evening at seven o'clock and moved majestically in pairs from the drawing room through the library and museum under an avenue of candelabra along dangerously shining parquet floors (on which distinguished visitors slid and tripped, affording the students much simple pleasure) to the hall. The girls were expected to book their dinner partners beforehand, a precaution which Ivy generally neglected —several of her friends remembered her lurking with other latecomers at the back of the library, arriving sometimes so late that she was still doing up her buttons as she came, and a letter written in her third term to her cousin Katie perhaps explains why:

... The dramatic society are going to act a play.* The dress rehearsal is to be to-night, and to-night the first years are requested to attend. It is bad to be a first year; I am looking forward to next term, when I

* *The Rose and the Ring.*

shall be a second year, & have about fifty whole first years to sit upon. I trust that you will be able to interpret this scrawl, writing it is only by courtesy; I am in a hurry, writing in the quarter of an hour in which I should be dressing for dinner. I have been intending to write to you for the last 3 months, & I trust that you have also been intending to write to me, for intentions, when they are good are better than nothing, & I have certainly seen no sign of anything more substantial. . . . I must say goodbye now, & go & endeavour, in the short space of 6 minutes and ¾ to arrange my wig, an operation which Mother declares should occupy every lady at least half an hour. (1 May 1903.)

Dinner was the serious ritual of the day but private social life revolved (as Ivy's continued to do for much of her life) round substantial tea parties—'A good hearty time was had by all from 4–4.45 p.m.'—held out of doors in the summer, in every bay of the terrace overlooking shaven lawns and flower beds in a formally laid-out parterre. Picnics might be taken on the river, or beyond the double row of pines which ran along the west side of the college bordered by beds of white roses. Nightingales sang here in the evenings, pheasants and gold-crested wrens nested in the grounds, primroses and wild orchids grew along the broad grass path to the south-east where the girls picked punnets of wild strawberries and, on a fine day, the whole of the south tower was reflected in the waters of the lower pond. Ivy, always particularly fond of wild flowers, would go for walks alone or with a friend and bring back tiny posies, arranged so that each separate petal showed. Others gathered blackberries and made jam with sugar from the college pantries—stealing sugar and being late for chapel were the chief, apparently the only vices regularly practised in what seems to have been an idyllic, if severely restricted and in some ways rumbustiously juvenile community.

The girls were narrowly supervised, forbidden to speak at all at certain hours, to walk without permission outside the grounds, to invite male partners to their dances, male spectators to their plays or men of any description to tea without a staff chaperone. In the seclusion thus jealously guarded, they called each other by their surnames in imitation of their brothers, ran races in the corridors or tobogganned on college tea-trays in the gardens; and Ivy herself, though she joined in neither tennis nor hockey, cricket nor boating, did years afterwards recall with pleasure sliding on a tea-tray down the wide, carpeted staircases.[6] Enforced isolation (there were few trains to London and excursions, which were not in any case encouraged, could otherwise be undertaken only by horse-drawn cab, on foot or by bicycle) meant that energies left over from work were expended inside the college. There was intense religious and musical activity. The College Dramatic Society put on an annual play (including a performance of *Pride and Prejudice* in February 1904, which Ivy presumably saw and in which Lytton Strachey's sisters, Pernel and Marjorie, played respectively Mr Bennet—'exhibiting all the time a personification of slightly academic idleness'—and 'the oiliest possible Mr Collins').[7] Visiting celebrities* lectured regularly and there were at least a dozen clubs and debating societies which met in the evenings for literary, political, historical or scientific discussion. Ivy had certainly attended meetings of the Political Society, which was organized as a feminine replica of the House of Commons and hotly debated such issues as Mr Chamberlain's fiscal policy, alien immigration, the Licensing Act (on which the Conservative government inside the college was roundly defeated and fell in the Michaelmas Term of 1904) and women's suffrage (carried by a majority of 61). 'Everyone went to Political,' said Isabel Bremner, a friend and contemporary of Ivy (and often her partner at dinner). 'I know Miss Compton-Burnett did; when I made my maiden speech, they were very much amused.' Ivy, sitting among the back-benchers on this occasion, had called out, 'Let me have your notes,' which led to some ragging as 'we all thought she meant to put them in a book'. But when the Principal once warned her that she would never get used to speaking in public if she did not begin at college, Ivy had vehemently replied, 'Yes, I never shall, I never shall';[8] and, so far as I can make out from careful study of the minute books, Ivy took no active part in the transactions of any college society, spoke in no debates, acted in no plays, was neither elected nor volunteered to serve on any committee, and kept silence at both college and students' meetings—unless perhaps hers was the anonymous voice which asked (and received) permission to pick wild flowers at the students' meeting in May 1904.

Ivy in these years seems to have left two distinct impressions on her contemporaries, neither difficult to reconcile with what little is known from elsewhere. On the one hand, there are those who remember her

---

* Ones who may have interested Ivy were Professor Sidgwick on Addison and Professor A. C. ('Shakespeare') Bradley on Shakespeare's Theatre in her first year; A. E. Housman on Robert Burns in her second; and Henry Newbolt on *The Future of English Verse* in the summer of 1906.

spending most of her time in her room, ill-dressed, unpopular, reserved and shy: 'Compton-Burnett had her study a few doors down from me on E III when we were students at R.H.C. I used to meet her in the corridor and we just exchanged greetings. . . . She never mixed with the other students, and we never met at tea, coffee or cocoa parties. She always wore black.'9 Her friends, on the other hand, insist that she was neither diffident nor odd but 'pleasant and lively', excellent company— 'Oh, yes, she could make us laugh'—and a practised mimic:

> Miss Compton-Burnett's father was a doctor and she used to amuse us by telling us of the rapidly changing succession of page boys, thin boys, fat boys, tall boys, short boys—all had to wear the same uniform—the boy changed—the suit remained the same—with curious results [wrote Isabel Bremner]. Early in my stay at college, I had to ask permission to have a visit from a boy cousin. In fear and trembling, I knocked at the study door of the Vice-Principal (Miss Guinness). On entry I found Miss C-B. having a coaching. At dinner that night she described the interview, making the most of my faltering request—leading inevitably to refusal—followed by a demonstration of how I ought to have behaved to ensure success.

Miss Bremner's mother was the youngest of thirteen sisters, and the humorous doings of these aunts had greatly pleased Ivy: 'I remember her with a party of us—she wasn't shutting herself in her study *then*— when someone asked why we were laughing, she said: "All listening to stories about Miss Bremner's aunts."' Ivy's gaiety, and the malicious, quizzical wit recalled by her friends, are markedly absent from *Dolores* (in which a number of both staff and students at Holloway in her day are so faithfully drawn that the book was naturally read with attention inside the college, as well as by old Hollowegians). Miss Bremner herself, evidently expecting the kind of comical character sketches she remembered from Ivy's conversation, was disappointed and distinctly puzzled to find instead a moral tract concerned almost exclusively with the turbid emotional undercurrents of life in a women's college: 'I'm surprised it wasn't more humorous,' she said several times. 'I should've thought there would've been more fun in it.'

But Dolores' inner torments, which pervade that overwrought and joyless book, probably reflect a frame of mind that had little to do with Ivy's early experience at Holloway, where a measure of social and intellectual freedom provided a welcome respite from the oppressive atmosphere at Hove. By the time she came to write *Dolores*, her life at home must have seemed bleaker and her prospects more hopeless than anything she had known in her first three years at college. If she had then endured undue emotional strain, it would undoubtedly have been covered by her habitual reticence; but she had never made friends easily, and there is no reason to suppose that her apparent reserve with anyone outside her own particular circle amounted to anything more than the sense of dislocation she had felt at school in the first shock of separation from her brothers. All her contemporaries agreed that Ivy had only one close companion at college, a girl named Daisy Harvey, short, plumpish and rather pretty, whom she had known beforehand at Howard College in Bedford. Miss Harvey, who was nine months older than Ivy, arrived on the same day and remained, as Ivy did, for an extra year. She lived in Lewisham, read science at college and once went to stay with the Compton Burnetts at Hove where the family thought her decidedly dull. She seems to have become a schoolmistress and died unmarried in her seventies,[10] having long since lost touch with Ivy; and it is at least possible that she provided the model for Perdita Kingsford, the college friend whose frivolous charms give rise to so many of Dolores' afflictions: 'There was that in Dolores which yielded to womanhood's spells. She hardly judged of women as a woman amongst them; but as something sterner and stronger, that owed them gentleness in judgment. From the first hour to the last of their years of friendship, she read Perdita as an open page; and loved her with a love that grew, though its nurture was not in what she read.'[11] By all accounts Miss Harvey, who was neither as clever nor as entertaining as Ivy could be, shared something of Perdita's disingenuousness, her vanity, her intellectual shallowness and the unscrupulous ease with which she attempts to conceal it.* Perdita represents a type of pretty and predatory feminine wilfulness which reappears several times in the novels, and perhaps one to which Ivy had always felt especially drawn. Miss Bremner at any rate thought that, of all their contemporaries at Holloway, 'Miss Harvey was the nearest to Perdita'.

* Miss Bremner had read physics with Daisy Harvey, and remembered that she 'used to come to my room night after night with difficult questions'; Miss Harvey, who hated to acknowledge that she needed assistance, had a habit of sneaking across to other people's benches in the lab. for surreptitious advice and was once painfully confused at being caught out by their tutor—behaviour not unlike Perdita's when Dolores first meets her. (But the resemblance, if there was one, goes no further since Miss Harvey neither married nor died before the novel—in which Perdita does both almost straight from college—was published.)

It is perhaps worth noting that the two books which unmistakeably make use of Holloway College as their setting both deal, far more insistently than any of the other novels of I. Compton-Burnett, with strong currents of feeling between women. Miss Lemaître in *Dolores* (who was modelled on Marie Péchinet, the head of the French department at Holloway)[12] reappears in *More Women Than Men* as the teacher of modern languages, Maria Rosetti, and there are other points of resemblance between the staff common rooms of the two establishments. Feelings which, in *Dolores*, led to no more than a heady, platonic attachment take on, in *More Women Than Men*, physical expression described so plainly that, if the whole were not carried off with such studied lack of concern, one might well suspect the author of deliberately making a point. But the urbane homosexuality of the later novel, published in 1933 five years after the public furore which surrounded the prosecution of *The Well of Loneliness*, reflects the attitude of at least one section of Ivy's circle of friends in London when she wrote it; and her casual reminders of who sleeps where and with whom (matters invariably taken for granted elsewhere in her books) suggest a certain impatience with the mealy-mouthed euphemisms common at the time —as also perhaps a humorous contempt for the rabid denunciations in the popular press on the one hand and, on the other, for the absurdly high line taken in return by earnest propagandists on behalf of the Lesbian party. Whatever the explanation, *More Women Than Men* belongs far more to the comparatively sophisticated London society Ivy knew in the early 'thirties than to the 'passionless, ardent little world' of *Dolores*, which mirrors accurately enough the atmosphere of her girlhood before the first war.

Indeed, what seems to have happened at Holloway is that the more effusive aspects of communal life had led on Ivy's part to a guarded withdrawal. Hockey-playing stalwarts, strident feminists, impassioned high church ritualists or their stubborn low church opponents can have had little in common with Ivy though their exertions, and their disapproving, often indignant attitude to non-participants, may well have amused her. The domestic intimacy inevitable in so small a community, where first years were expected to know everyone by name within three weeks, was fostered by a system of 'College Families', groups of six or eight girls which 'coalesced under mutual attraction in a student's earliest days' and foregathered thereafter on every possible occasion, sitting together at breakfast and lunch, taking it in turns to hold tea parties in each other's rooms and meeting again for evening sessions

over coffee or cocoa. Ivy, who like Daisy Harvey and Miss Bremner
had refrained from joining a family, 'once wrote an article making fun
of R.H.C. cocoa parties. I believe she later on in her life was sorry to
have been so contemptuous.'[13] 'Slackers' were constantly reproved for
idleness, for lingering in one another's rooms at night, for staying up
after the last bell at 10.30 p.m. or for walking the corridors in dressing-
gowns with their hair down—all presumably attempts to discourage
the kind of over-familiarity which led to 'long and hot discussion' at
the democratic meetings held each term, when the students devoted
much time and energy to remonstrating with one another. Privacy, let
alone escape from the scrutiny of so many prying eyes at such close
quarters, must have been almost impossible, though sternly enforced by
the staff: '. . . bedrooms along one side of each of our main corridors
did indeed require decorum to be observed; it was an object lesson in
social behaviour to see Miss Block walking along the [ground floor
corridors] and closing her eyes as she shut doors carelessly left open.'
Ivy had closely observed Miss Block, had perhaps even attended her
'much-prized Sunday morning tea-parties' at which 'triviality or
gossip just didn't arise', and later reproduced her characteristically lofty
and repressive attitude in the person of Miss Cliff, who rules the staff
common room in *Dolores* as her original had been accustomed to
supervise the morals of both junior and senior personnel at Holloway.
    Moral fervour among the lower orders ran at times uncomfortably
high. 'When I entered the college, Uplift was the keynote,' wrote
Marion Pick who had arrived in 1903 and who, though far more
inclined to approve conventional observances than Ivy, nonetheless
found something distasteful 'to a sober judgment' in the sort of 'excitable, wayward emotionalism' which flourished among the college's
various religious factions. The Society of the Annunciation, the R.H.C.
Christian Union, the Bible and Foreign Missionary Circles ('a steady
stream of recruits was drawn to the Mission Field') met regularly; there
were daily Prayer Meetings, 'Lambeth teas', sewing bees, fund-raising
gatherings, a Waif and Stray Society (which adopted, clothed and
generally presided over a College Waif destined for domestic service)
and numerous other cells performing good works for orphans and
heathens at home and abroad. What Ivy made of these charitable
activities is not hard to guess. Her attitude to the mission field had
never been encouraging, and the various officious ladies who go about
doing good in her books exhibit at best a harmless complacency, at
worst a positively dangerous indifference to the feelings of the people

they patronize. At a tea-party held some fifty years later, Ivy described a fellow student who (like Hamilton Grimstone in *The Last and the First*) could never feel comfortable about skipping prayers till she had made up the omission next morning: 'You know, Mr Eliot says that if he misses tea he doesn't feel quite the same till tea the following day,' she said later on the same occasion, and much enjoyed the discomfiture of her staider visitors when a friend[14] remarked on the likeness between the poet and the girl at college.

But it is as well to remember that the nervous excesses and the 'ring of inner tensions' described by Miss Pick were an inevitable reaction to the combination of social sneers and material hardship endured by Dolores, as by many of the girls at Holloway, in the struggle for independence. Miss Pick (who, like Dolores, had escaped the drab lot of a country parson's daughter only by means of a scholarship) vividly conveys the solemn sense of daring incumbent on a pioneering generation whose mothers had anxiously followed the progress of Mr Holloway's experiment, whose own hearts had bled 'for poor Ethel May' in *The Daisy Chain*, and who had been brought up to understand 'only too well that there was a vast surplus of women over men, and that spinster aunts were a depressed race'. Miss Pick's own first inkling of academic delights had come from a serial in the *Boy's Own Paper* which gave her, at the age of eleven, sharp sensations of 'relief that I could be independent, and was absolutely free of the need to marry'. Ivy, too, describes in *Dolores* the burden borne by 'the earnest academic novice' in a community so vulnerable to the slur of impropriety, and so severely conscious of its own rectitude.

There were seventeen resident staff in her day and three men— Messrs Cassie, Donkin and Loney—who kept house at a discreet distance just beyond the college gates. Teaching was conducted by lectures, delivered to groups so small that they must have been more like classes, in 'lecture-rooms which, with their rows of desks, large blackboards, charts and pictures'[15] closely resembled school class rooms. Ivy was one of five in her year reading classics in a school which, under a classical Principal, enjoyed several special privileges: classical students had their own club, their own walk in the grounds called Peripatos where they planted out bulbs from their studies, their own lecture room decorated by their predecessors in grey-green, gold and white, and regular 'Classical treats' devised by the Principal. Miss Penrose (later Dame Emily), who became in turn Principal of Bedford College, Holloway and Somerville, came of a learned and illustrious family. She was descended from Archbishop Cranmer, a great-niece of Dr Arnold of Rugby, second cousin to Matthew Arnold and daughter of an architect who, having criticized the pitch of the pediment as 'steeper than I quite like', had himself personally measured the Parthenon: Miss Penrose's lecture illustrated with lantern slides on his findings was an annual treat for her pupils. 'She had statesmanlike vision, fairness of judgement, devotion to learning, and imperturbable faith in the ends for which she worked. . . . Deeply religious, reserved in all personal matters, scrupulously careful in expressing opinion, she was difficult to know, and formidable to those who did not know her. . . .'[16] wrote Helen Darbishire, who was briefly a lecturer at Holloway in Ivy's day. 'Miss Penrose . . . inhabited a region where no student trod, from which she came down when her Office required,' wrote Miss Pick, whose views Ivy in her first year also had reason to share:

> We have been having 'collections' at the beginning of the term. It is quite a new departure, and not altogether a pleasing one, for at the outset one's mind is painfully lacking in great ideas. After perusing my Roman History paper, which contained a map, shewing as I thought, considerable knowledge and artistic skill, the Principal impolitely informed me that it was evident that I had not much talent for drawing, would I do that map again please. I cannot say that she went up much in my estimation after that remark. To make matters worse, the only question she seemed to take satisfaction in, was one I had written in the exact words of the book. She praised my 'vivid description' & I discreetly refrained from telling her the sources of it. (1 May 1903)

Miss Penrose was not one of the six members of staff at Holloway whom Ivy later transferred to the senior common room of Dolores' college, and who are identified in a first edition at R.H.C. which contains at the back a pencilled key made by the distinguished mediaeval historian, Helen Cam (who came up in 1904, two years after Ivy). Neither was the Vice-Principal Miss Guinness, who had coached Ivy, nor the cheerful, absent-minded Professor Donkin who lived with his sister opposite the main gates, lectured on classics and occasionally entertained the college with dramatic burlesques written and performed by himself and his sister. But the head of the classics department, Margaret Taylor (known as Cato to her pupils because 'her standards were Roman') reappears in *Dolores* as 'the lecturer in classics, Miss

Butler . . . a small, straight woman . . . whose parted hair leaves the forehead fully shown, and whose hazel eyes have humour in their rapid glancing'.[17] Miss Butler resembles Miss Taylor not only in looks but also in the severity which frightens Dolores' more nervous companions, in her fastidious scholarship, her disapproval of all forms of slovenliness and her fierce championship of women's rights; it is an affectionate portrait and suggests that, as Dolores' appreciation of Miss Butler's exacting standards leads to the slow growth of mutual esteem, so Ivy had been on good terms with Miss Taylor.

The classical textbooks which Ivy had owned at Holloway, marked on the fly-leaf with her name and preserved to the end of her life, reveal little of her likes and dislikes, unless perhaps one may deduce from a note in Haigh's *The Tragic Drama of the Greeks* that she had imbibed something of Miss Taylor's feminism. Haigh sums up Euripides' 'conception of a model wife' as one who 'is careless of personal adornment when her husband is absent, and when he is present treats him with unreflecting reverence. . . . She humours his frailties, treats his mistresses with kindness, offers her own breast to his bastard children, and by such "virtuous conduct" wins and retains his affection.'[18] Ivy ended this passage with a small exclamation mark in pencil, and added her own laconic caption: 'An ancient Kipling'. But otherwise her markings are purely practical, consisting largely of underlinings, pencil strokes in the margin, useful sub-headings (as 'Soph. introduced third actor', 'Eurip. born 480 or 485', 'Aesch's disregard of probabilities') designed apparently to save herself the trouble of re-reading. Marks on the texts themselves are confined more or less to translations of hard words and phrases. Most of the *Iliad*, books I–V of Plato's *Republic* and the *Oedipus Tyrannus* in Jebb's seven volume edition of Sophocles are fairly copiously annotated. The rest of Jebb is almost untouched, the pages of *Electra* and *Trachinae* still uncut. *Antigone*— which was not one of Ivy's set books but which she must have seen, if not helped to stage, in an ambitious production by the classics department at Holloway on 5 May 1905*—has been read and lightly marked

---

* 'The stage was erected at one end of the College Picture Gallery and so admirably was it placed and arranged that even before a word had been spoken one seemed to breathe the very air of ancient Greece. . . . There was something in the quiet of this scene, with its comeliness of white stone and green boughs, which lent an added poignancy to the horror and pity that filled the mind when human anger and remorse had driven away peace. . . .' (R.H.C. *College Letter* 1905). Ivy was not in the cast but she must have found it hard to avoid helping in some capacity since the production,

throughout; a footnote on Eidothea, sister to Cadmus, a stepmother
who hated her husband's first wife and cruelly persecuted her two
stepsons, is heavily scored for no apparent reason save perhaps as an
indication of the direction in which Ivy's own interests already lay.
Some of the passages she has underlined in Haigh—on Aeschylus'
concern for the dangers of wealth, 'often leading men into insolence and
pride'; on Sophocles' use of conscious and unconscious irony; on the
conflicting motives discernible in Euripides' tyrants; on Aristotle's view
of crime ('the . . . most suitable for dramatic treatment are those committed against friends or relations'); and on the role of the chorus in
ancient and modern hands—make interesting reading in the light of her
own later development of all these themes. But careful study of her
annotations adds nothing to her own statement, made some forty years
later: 'The Greek dramatists I read as a girl, as I was classically educated,
and read them with the attention to each line necessitated by the state
of my scholarship; and it is difficult to say how much soaked in, but I
should think very likely something. I have not read them for many
years—another result of the state of my scholarship.'[19]

There were three seconds and two thirds in the London honours
school among the classical students in Ivy's year. Her family had confidently expected a first for Ivy but, by the time she took finals, Guy
had died and her sisters thought that afterwards she lost all interest in
examinations. His last illness began on Easter Sunday, 23 April 1905,
when he said to his mother that he 'wouldn't go to early service as he
wasn't feeling himself'. Ivy went back to Holloway the same week for
what was to have been her last term, leaving the whole family save her
mother and Noel in bed with influenza. Colds, chest complaints and
quinzies in one form or another were, as Ivy wrote later, 'a thing we
are all very prone to',[20] and there probably seemed nothing especially
alarming about the start of this particular epidemic. Minnie, who (with
Daisy as under nurse) had charge of the sick rooms, 'never took her
clothes off for weeks' and nursed Guy night and day: 'She was *incredibly*
tough and incredibly devoted. Above all to Guy.' Guy, too weak to do
more than lie still and listen, had asked for readings from the Bible.
'One tires of all other books but never of the Bible' was one of his last
reported sayings, and perhaps one of the reasons for Ivy's later bitterness

---

which was directed by Miss Taylor, had occupied the entire department for a whole
term and was generally held to mark the final triumph of Classics over all other
departments.

towards the religion which had comforted her brothers but which left
her without consolation. Variations on the same theme return throughout her books in conversation between brother and sister:

> 'We may die at any moment.'
> 'Not you and I. It is other people who may die young.'
> 'Why should we be exceptions?'
> 'I don't know. I wonder what the reasons are?'
> 'You don't think you and I will have an eternity together?'
> 'No, but we shall have until we are seventy. And there is no
> difference.'
> 'Can you bear not to have the real thing?'
> 'No,' said his sister.[21]

The four youngest Compton Burnetts had been put to bed together
in one room like a hospital ward and Topsy was feared to be dangerously ill, but it was Guy who developed double pneumonia, too swiftly
for Ivy to be recalled in time from college. Before she reached home, he
was dead. She spent the next four months at Hove, returned to Holloway that autumn, was awarded a Founder's scholarship[22] in April 1906,
and took a second in finals the following summer. 'Guy and Ivy were
everything to each other when they were young,' said their sister
Juliet; and Julian Mitchell's tentative comment perhaps goes as far as
anyone can on her life without him: 'Of the Latin poets, she liked
Catullus best: I wonder if this might be because of the celebrated line
"*Atque in perpetuum, frater, ave atque vale*".'[23]

'Wrestling along in the silent hours'

'PEOPLE WHO WERE born too late to experience in boyhood and adolescence the intellectual and moral pressure of Victorianism have no idea of the feeling of fog and fetters which weighed one down,' wrote Leonard Woolf,[24] who was born in 1880. 'It was not a question of unhappiness so much as of restriction and oppression—the subtle unperceived weight of the circumambient air,' wrote Lytton Strachey,[25] born in the same year. Neither had suffered an especially unhappy childhood, and both escaped earlier than most into the atmosphere of spiritual, sexual and religious freedom beginning to flourish at Trinity where, in the first few years of the century, both were regarded with horrified loathing by their more conservative contemporaries at Cambridge. No wonder if this sense of conscious revolt had not yet touched Holloway. Girls had been their brothers' inferiors for too long, and were too thankful to be educated at all, to care much for questioning the doctrines of patience, obedience and self-sacrifice which had traditionally governed their sex. The cheerful scepticism prevalent at Cambridge was something which does not seem to have reached Ivy till much later, perceived and percolated through Noel at King's.

In the summer of 1906, when Ivy arrived home from college to help teach the children and coach Noel for little-go, the feeling of fog and fetters must have seemed to close round her on all sides. Her mother, taking the practical view that talents so expensively polished should not go to waste, had removed the four younger girls from school and Ivy began without enthusiasm to supervise lessons in the schoolroom. Noel had been working alone since Guy's death under a new tutor, a Mr Bullick of whom neither his pupil nor Ivy thought highly. 'Noel always had a very strong imaginative life, he did have that, but in a family considered rather clever he was thought to be backward, or on the backward side,' said his sister, Vera. At eighteen, his chances of getting into King's were held to be touch-and-go: 'Well, candidly, Mrs Compton Burnett, he has very poor ability,' said the despondent tutor,

who was master at a prep school up the road and had been retained to
teach Noel history since a classical discipline evidently suited neither his
tastes nor his capacities. But, whether in response to his mother's urgent
emotional pressure or because Ivy had taken his education firmly in
hand (Noel's friends at King's always afterwards believed that she had
coached him, a rumour confirmed by her sisters), Noel did somehow
scrape through little-go, later taking a double first and the Gladstone
prize, whereupon his mother, charmed by her son's success—'it is of
course a very great pleasure to us all, and I am particularly glad for him,
it will encourage him so much, having lost his father and elder brother
he stands very much alone, and he has always been so brave,' she wrote
to Noel's Cambridge mentor, Oscar Browning—fondly recalled that
the disobliging Mr Bullick had himself taken a second at Dublin.

What seems to have happened is that Noel, who had been 'quite
satisfied until Guy died to be the inconspicuous one of the three', was a
slow mover whose gifts, like his father's, developed late but to spectacular effect. As a child he had been bored by lessons, scarcely read a
book, remained absorbed in his own private dream world, contentedly
overshadowed by his brilliant elder brother and sister. His arrival at
Cambridge coincided with a simultaneous emotional and intellectual
awakening, when he suddenly found himself with energies untapped
and whole new worlds unexplored. One of the reasons was no doubt
his brother's death. This was the explanation he gave later for abandoning all extraneous pursuits under pressure of work in the term before
his Tripos: 'I may perhaps say that it is not entirely for my own sake ...
I cannot forget the bitter disappointment caused to my mother by the
death of my elder brother. Any small worldly success which I might
gain would be to her perhaps the only recompense that would be still
possible.'[26] Another was the stimulus of intellectual pleasures hitherto
unknown, for which he had acquired already a voracious appetite in
the year before he went up to King's. At his entrance examination in
the autumn of 1906, he had met Oscar Browning, 'a man of bad
character and European fame' according to Rupert Brooke[27] who had
rooms that term (the same rooms as Noel two years later) on the landing
opposite O.B. O.B., who boasted with some reason that he had single-
handed reformed King's College itself not to mention the Cambridge
history school, was then a few years short of enforced retirement. Vastly
corpulent, prolix and obstinate, resembling in looks a degenerate
Roman emperor and in unbounded egotism his hero Napoleon,
accustomed to bathe naked in the Cam (he had once been bathed in his

own bathroom by the Prince of Wales in person), to hold *levées* in his rooms *en déshabille*, to sleep through tutorials under a red handkerchief and to teach by inspiration rather than by formal precept or instruction, O.B.'s vocation and delight was the guidance of young men: 'His information might be erroneous, his method of conveying it intolerable, but he did lead them to discover themselves and to bring to birth what would have lain in embryo,' wrote E. M. Forster.[28] 'He took these young men and made them into young Fellows,' said Raisley Moorsom, a friend of Noel's at King's, 'and Noel was the last one he made'.

Mr Browning had picked up this latest protégé at the entrance examination (as was his habit—another nervous scholarship candidate has described O.B. stumping through the examination hall and enquiring in a fiendishly unsettling whisper, 'How do you like the paper? I set it'),[29] and by the following March Noel was writing diffidently from Hove to take up his promise of advice: '. . . as I realize what a privilege it would be, and what an advantage to me in the future, I venture to ask if I may come next Tuesday' (22 March 1907). O.B., who spent his vacations at Bexhill a few miles along the coast from Hove, duly granted this request and laid down a stiff programme of reading, beginning with Maine's *Ancient Law* and moving on to Gibbon's *Decline and Fall* on which Noel submitted a weekly report that summer and, having finished all six volumes in almost as many weeks, promptly re-read the whole on O.B.'s instructions. In the next few years the friendship prospered not only at Cambridge but on regular visits, swimming expeditions (O.B. had a beach hut at Bexhill named Tilsit, 'so-called from the floating pavilion on the Memel in which Napoleon had signed his treaty with Alexander of Russia') and reading parties in the vacation. O.B. lunched several times and once spent the night with the Compton Burnetts at Hove, where the younger girls entertained him with Mozart sonatas and their mother placed his photograph (sent in characteristically regal acknowledgement of her hospitality the month before Noel went up to King's) in the drawing-room. Noel's letters in these years are interspersed with references to Topsy's prowess on the fiddle, and to O.B.'s kind enquiries as to Ivy's progress on her novel.

Impossible to say what Ivy thought in return of this witty, celebrated, half fraudulent, half genuinely inspired and wholly worldly mountebank, so far removed from the academic manner—'a something of greater than the common earnestness and ease'[30]—which she had known at Holloway, and later described with admiration in *Dolores*. Ivy at this time is remembered by her sisters as generally silent, but 'when she was in the mood she had such wit and sparkle. She could hit off anyone, hit the nail on the head—it wasn't always very kind.' She had been allotted her own study or wrote at the schoolroom table, working already on her novel though not even Noel was allowed to read it. It is tempting to see traces of Ivy's own experience in Dolores' sad return from college to a peevish and disgruntled stepmother demanding that she teach the smaller children, a morose father and a disconsolate younger brother all depressingly unchanged in the setting she herself had left 'four years earlier, on the threshold of her womanhood. Now that womanhood seemed old. Those four bright, troubled years, which had left this early world the same! As she spoke and moved beneath the pressure of her pain, she found herself simply dwelling through a dream on their difference. . . .'[31]

Certainly Ivy's own lot in these years must have seemed, like Dolores', a straitened one. Distractions at Hove were few and limited. In the first week of May 1907, she had travelled up to London accompanied by her mother and Noel to receive her degree, a triumph let fall with modest pride by her brother in a letter to O.B. The following autumn Noel left home for Cambridge, becoming in his first term an active member of O.B.'s Political Society, speaking regularly at the Union, joining the curious and exclusive King's society of poetical revolutionaries called the Carbonari, and rapidly making friends for the first time in his life. The new world which absorbed her brother must have made Ivy's future—immured in a dull provincial town without friends or diversions (unless, as Mrs Elliott believed, she attended Miss Laura's literature class for old girls at Addiscombe College)—seem even drabber by comparison. Noel's weekly letters to his mother were read aloud to the assembled family at Hove, and his friends from King's came to stay in the vacations before Mrs Compton Burnett became too ill, and the house too wretched, to receive them. Otherwise breaks in the routine at home were confined to occasional visits from relations and to the family's annual holidays, when they spent six or eight weeks each summer at a different country vicarage: at Brythdir near Dolgelly in 1907 ('We are in a very wild district here. Mountains are on every side. The Welsh language is prevalent,' wrote Noel to O.B. 'I think I heard you say you were acquainted with thirty languages; I suppose Welsh is not of the number'); at Dent near Sedbergh the next year (this was the family's first visit to Yorkshire, and perhaps a clue to the setting of Dolores in a Yorkshire vicarage, since Ivy must then have been still at work on the novel which was finished by the following summer); and at Sourton on Dartmoor in 1909.

Noel was meanwhile immersed in the literary and intellectual ferment brought about, among the more adventurous members of his own and Ivy's generation, by the books of Henry James, Hardy, Butler, Swinburne, Meredith and Bernard Shaw. His circle at King's was largely non-athletic, anti-philistine and hotly concerned with modern literature. He himself was writing poetry, as was his closest friend Jack Beresford (second cousin to the novelist J. D. Beresford, who became a few years later a considerable arbiter of contemporary taste, lectured on such subjects as 'Experiment in the Novel' and was the first person to encourage Dorothy Richardson in whom he saw an English heir to Proust). Arthur Waley, whose visits were remembered by Ivy's sisters with especial pleasure ('We always knew we should have a very gay time when he came down'), was later a distinguished poet, and Rupert Brooke, a friend of Noel's and one year ahead of him at King's, read aloud his early verses at meetings of the Carbonari. Much of this excitement rubbed off at home, where Noel shared it with his younger sisters. It was Noel who introduced them to Ibsen and Strindberg, Masefield, 'any number of books', paintings, plays and new ideas: 'It affected us to the bottom of our souls. In our family that kind of culture didn't exist inside the home. Noll arrived on the scene with a whole new world of literature.' But what came as an astonishment and delight to Vera and Juliet in early adolescence was apparently received with less enthusiasm by Ivy. Perhaps the revelation had arrived too late to stir her as it stirred the others. She had stoutly resisted when Noel urged her to write verse not prose and her own tastes, always more scholarly than his, seem to have settled somewhat earlier in a rather different direction.

She had been reading Plato's *Timaeus* the year after she left college (her parallel Greek and English text is signed 'I. Compton-Burnett June 1907' and the first part, judging by her pencil marks in the margin which stop abruptly half way through, has been read with close attention) but 'she had abandoned classics—that was a chapter she had closed', said her sister Vera. 'I don't remember her working, or reading even, she was always writing.' For years before that she had been accustomed, like her sisters, to read and re-read the classic nineteenth-century novels which were practically the only books they owned. When she left college her mother had given her £50 ('or anyhow a sum') with which to found a library, and she spent it on her own complete editions of Jane Austen and George Eliot. These two, with Thackeray and Hardy, Charlotte Brontë, Richardson and Mrs Gaskell, remained her staple favourites to the end of her life. She was reading *Vanity Fair* a week or so before she died,[32] and both her sisters remembered the tart flavour she had given Becky Sharp ('She liked that sort of bite') when she read the book aloud to them after Sunday supper in the schoolroom more than sixty years before. Trollope had her guarded approval ('Yes, he is good. He is so good one wonders why he isn't better'), Dickens is several times firmly shown off in her early books and so is Henry James ('I hate people whose golden bowls are broken'),[33] whose achievements she invariably deprecated and whose influence she repeatedly denied. Samuel Butler had clearly acted on her, together with the sceptical humour peculiar to the Cambridge mind and more particularly to Noel's friend and tutor Goldsworthy Lowes Dickinson, by the time she came to write her second novel in the early 'twenties. But Butler's influence had not apparently reached her—or, if it had, her imagination remained untouched—in the years between the autumn of 1906 and the summer of 1909 when she wrote *Dolores*.

The book is saturated in notions of self-abnegation—the temptations of the spirit and the flesh set against the austere claims of conscience—common among the heroines of at least a generation earlier. Dolores' struggles begin at nineteen when she leaves home for college and end at thirty-three when she looks back on a life of useless sacrifice in which she has successively crushed her own aspirations, her hopes of independence and, on five separate occasions, her chances of love and marriage for the sake of 'service to her kin': 'Dolores' survey of a crisis in her own experience was primitive and stern. For others might be honest doubt, and blameless wavering at a parting of the ways: for herself there was one road to be taken, and another to be left. On the one side lay effort for strangers . . . on the other the claims of kindred, of her father and her father's children.'[34]

The book's tone is repellantly extreme. Its moral doctrines are inhuman and its language the exalted terminology of religious passion and self-mortification: Dolores' voice is 'the voice of one taking a vow' and, although 'the sacrifice of her choice, lived day by day and silently, was hard to the brink of bending her will', she remains, regardless of the fact that 'her own experience was growing vexed to the utter clouding of her soul' as of the suffering she brings to others, 'faithful through all to her old religion of the duty she owed her kind'.

But Dolores' clenched hands, her trembling limbs, white lips, lined

brow and face prematurely aged in nights of sleepless torment are by
no means peculiar to herself. All these symptoms recur regularly in the
novels of both lesser and greater lady novelists over the previous half
century and more. Charlotte M. Yonge and Mrs Humphrey Ward, to
name but two, each of whom exerted immense influence in her day,
deal in precisely the kind of anguished conflict between home and
inclination, thankless spinsterhood and selfish freedom, which scourges
Dolores as 'she wrestled along in the silent hours . . . neither weeping
nor rising to pace the ground; but lying with dry eyes and worn face,
and hands clutching the coverings tensely.' Ethel May in *The Daisy
Chain* and its sequel (published in 1856 and 1864) and Catherine
Leyburn in *Robert Elsmere* (published in 1888) are both sadly prone to
nightly 'wrestles' ('But no wrestle had ever been as hard as this! And
with what fierce suddenness had it come upon her! . . . She laid her
head on her knees trembling').* Both shrink from the horrid tendency
to free thought bred among their male contemporaries 'at the University' and both, like Dolores, renounce the love of an Oxford man for
reasons which seem to the twentieth-century reader—above all to one
acquainted with the later work of I. Compton-Burnett—quite preposterously perverse.

But Ivy in her early twenties was still, at any rate in her literary output, almost wholly unoriginal. There is the same imitative facility in
the high solemnity of *Dolores* as in the set of album verses written 'To
Vera on her sixteenth birthday, 23 September 1907, from her sister Ivy':

> Sixteen summers passing swiftly,
> Borne on childhood's fleeting wing,
> Have they taught you truly, Vera,
> Lessons from the early Spring? . . .
>
> Will you pause today to ponder
> What the years to come will yield?
> Will your eyes with wistful wonder
> Turn to chapters unrevealed? . . .
>
> Well has childhood done its duty,
> Steadfast at your side has stood;

* *Robert Elsmere* by Mrs Humphrey Ward, p.100. A similar battle is fought over the
same ground to the same conclusion in *The Daisy Chain*, 'as Ethel tossed about listening to the perpetual striking of all the Oxford clocks, until daylight had begun to
shine in. . . .' (p.387)

Faithfully its care has kept you,
Clasped you closely while it could.
Never may it break the spell,
Never bid a last farewell,
Ever may its voices reach you,
Through your years of womanhood.

Among the 'lessons from the early Spring' which Ivy, as much as Vera, had learnt not to question was a stern sense, maintained to the end of her life, of her own and other people's obligation to their families. At Holloway she and Miss Harvey had remonstrated vainly with their friend Miss Bremner on what both saw as a clear dereliction of duty: 'They were of the opinion—they were very decided about it—that I oughtn't to have come to college. Because I was the eldest of the family and should have stayed at home.' Dolores' 'instinctive loyalty of service to that rigorous lofty thing, to which we give duty as a name' seems to have derived from Dr Burnett whose definition of 'Our Duty', laid down in a lecture to his medical students the year before Ivy was born, coincides (save only for his reference to 'our holy religion') exactly with his daughter's:

It is duty that places me here today; duty it is that brings many of you here also . . . there is a beauty in duty peculiarly its own—that moral beauty which makes one like to roam alone in the stilly eve or sit by oneself in the dark. When a man has done his duty purely and simply, he has a serene satisfaction not afforded by mere honour or public applause. Indeed, in this life, next to our holy religion, nothing will stand us in such good stead as a sweet consciousness of having done our duty.[35]

This view of the moral beauty and imperative nature of duty, especially when associated with roaming in the gloaming, was of course George Eliot's;* and, though this kind of relationship between master and

* See W. H. Myers' celebrated description of walking one evening in 1873 in the Fellows' Garden at Trinity, Cambridge, with George Eliot who, 'stirred somewhat beyond her wont, and taking as her text the three words which have been used so often as the inspiring trumpet-calls of men,—the words, God, Immortality, Duty,— pronounced, with terrible earnestness, how inconceivable was the *first*, how unbelievable the *second*, and yet how peremptory and absolute the *third*. Never, perhaps, have sterner accents affirmed the sovereignty of impersonal and unrecompensing Law. I

pupil is comparatively common among painters or composers, it is seldom that one finds one major author submerged so completely in the personality of another as I. Compton-Burnett, at the start of her career, in George Eliot.

It is not simply that the gaunt and angular Dolores possesses an uncomfortably large share of that 'strange impressiveness' with which George Eliot habitually endowed her outwardly plain ladies. Considering the number of more or less undistinguished copies strewn about the fiction of the period, there is nothing especially remarkable in a heroine who, plagued by a sense of duty keener and more casuistical even than Dorothea Casaubon's, set on a course of puritanical self-punishment yet more dour than Maggie Tulliver's, lacks the independent life of either. Further borrowings in *Dolores* may readily be multiplied: the luckless Perdita is marked down by her creator for the kind of doom which inevitably awaits George Eliot's pretty, flighty feather-brains like Hetty Sorrel or Rosamond Lydgate; Dolores' hero and beloved, Sigismund Claverhouse, embodies in one person the unaccountable attractions of neglect, deformity, advancing age, poverty and other social drawbacks associated, in *The Mill on the Floss*, *Daniel Deronda* and *Middlemarch*, with artistic or creative yearnings; acrimonious scenes between Dolores' stepmother and her middle-aged sister recall the covert warfare waged throughout Maggie's childhood among the equally uncharitable sisters Tulliver, Deane, Glegg and Pullet. The author of *Dolores* is evidently happier in the vein of comical exuberance opened for her by the last than at the rhetorical sublime, where she is altogether clumsier and more turgid than George Eliot ever was. But her debt is also more specific. Dolores' home in a country village owing something perhaps to the summer of 1908 spent by the Compton Burnetts at Dent in Yorkshire, and rather more to the topography of Great Clacton where Ivy as a child had visited her Blackie cousins, seems to have been taken in the first place directly from a literary source. Actual details of life in Dolores' Millfield (the combination of church, brand-new Wesleyan chapel and disused barn made over into 'a meeting place at general disposal for religious ends' and based presumably on the Coppins Hall barn used for Methodist gatherings at

---

listened and night fell; her grave, majestic countenance turned towards me like a sybil's in the gloom; it was as though she withdrew from my grasp, one by one, the two scrolls of promise, and left me the third scroll only, awful with inevitable fates.' (*George Eliot* by Gordon S. Haight, O.U.P. 1968, p.464)

Clacton before Dr Burnett gave the land to build a chapel; the social awkwardness arising from collisions between church and chapel factions; the feuds tirelessly prosecuted among rival local preachers) were unmistakeably supplied by the doings of Ivy's own evangelical relations. But it is surely not coincidence that the opening sentence of *Dolores*—'It is a daily thing: a silent, unvisited church-yard; bordering the garden of the parsonage; and holding a church whose age and interest spare our words . . . and at some moment of its lying in sight an open grave with its mourners'—brings to mind another funeral scene, identical in tone and treatment as in personnel.

This is the open grave, in a church-yard also bordering the vicarage, which comes at the end of 'The Sad Fortunes of the Rev. Amos Barton', the first story in George Eliot's first book, *Scenes of Clerical Life*. The chief mourner in each case is the parson of the parish, attended by a congregation whose former disaffection towards their pastor is momentarily subdued in pity for the loss of his wife. Both widowers stand with heaving breasts in grief further harrowed by remorse, and each receives a pale consolation from his eldest child—the Rev. Amos Barton from the nine-year-old Patty who closely resembles her dead mother, the Rev. Cleveland Hutton from 'the nine-year-old Dolores, with her mother's voice, and her mother's face, and her fitting part in her mother's name of sorrows!' Points in common between George Eliot's Mr Barton and I. Compton-Burnett's Mr Hutton seem too many to be accidental: both have been affectionate husbands and conscientious pastors to an ungrateful flock, both were educated at Cambridge, both wait vainly in their mid-thirties for preferment, driven meanwhile through penury to debt, and both are recommended to the reader's attention in similarly off-hand terms:

> The Rev. Amos Barton, whose sad fortunes I have undertaken to relate, was, you perceive, in no respect an ideal or exceptional character, and perhaps I am doing a bold thing to bespeak your sympathy on behalf of a man who was so very far from remarkable. . . . Yet these commonplace people—many of them—bear a conscience, and have felt the sublime prompting to do the painful right; they have their unspoken sorrows, and their sacred joys; their hearts have perhaps gone out towards their firstborn, and they have mourned over the irreclaimable dead. Nay, is there not a pathos in their very insignificance,—in our comparison of their dim and narrow existence with the glorious possibilities of that human nature which they share?[36]

No; there was nothing in the Rev. Cleveland Hutton to mark him a man apart. But it does not follow there was nothing about him to be written or read. Our deepest experience is not less deep, that it is common to our race. . . . There had been a strong, woman's heart to cleave to his own, through the struggles of the lingering unbeneficed time, the loss of his firstborn, and other things finding a place in his ordinary human lot. Standing by the open grave, dreading for the numbness of grief to pass, and leave him the facing of the future that was dark, he was as fitting a mark for compassion as if his name were to live.[37]

It is difficult to avoid the conclusion that Ivy intended a conscious tribute in choosing to take up the fortunes of her central character at precisely the point where George Eliot's concluding paragraph left off: 'Patty alone remains by her father's side, and makes the evening sunshine of his life.' This parting glimpse of Patty, prematurely lined at thirty and vowed like Dolores to spinsterhood for her parent's sake, is appended in the nature of a coda; just as the opening chapter of *Dolores* forms a pendant to the story proper which begins ten years later (with a second wife and stepchildren already installed at the parsonage by chapter two) and follows the process whereby Dolores' determination to make 'evening sunshine' is foiled at every turn. Both works are set back a quarter century or so from the time of writing—almost the only borrowing which (after a brief patch of indecision with *Pastors and Masters* and *Brothers and Sisters*) Ivy later kept, setting her novels to the end of her career in the same period as *Dolores*. Both writers start in the same slow focus ('If you had entered this straggling village at the time— somewhere in the latter half of the nineteenth century—when its parsonage was the home of the Reverend Cleveland Hutton. . . .'), assume the same stiffish intimacy with the reader, and alternate between lugubrious solemnity and a vivid, mocking, generally patronizing gaiety at the expense of the lower orders. I. Compton-Burnett's Millfield, with its teeming clerical life, stand-offish clergy and jealous evangelists vying for attention from argumentative and sharply critical parishioners, might be George Eliot's Shepperton thirty or forty years on. Dissent had been the principal thorn in the side of the established church at Shepperton ('that notable plan of introducing anti-dissenting books into his Lending Library did not in the least appear to have bruised the head of Dissent, though it had certainly made Dissent

strongly inclined to bite the Rev. Amos's heel');[38] drink and Roman
Catholicism ('You ask me . . . whether I consider—the spread of Roman
Catholicism—a *serious* thing. My answer is—that I consider it a *hopeless*
thing, a damnable thing, a thing that is sucking the very life-blood of
our religion') are held in equal loathing among the dissenting population of Millfield.

Prominence on Millfield platforms is anxiously disputed between the
two ardent amateur preachers, Dr Cassell and Herbert Blackwood
('the art of oratory had become Mr Blackwood's second nature—it had
been rather foreign to his first nature'), linked in an uneasy but indis-
soluble alliance by their identical views and the fondness of each for the
sound of his own voice, the natural resignation each feels at the sound
of the other's being tempered by their mutual reluctance to forego a
potentially sympathetic audience. The originals of both may be easily
identified among Ivy's own acquaintance. Just as George Eliot had
drawn the plots and characters of her early stories from her country
childhood, so Ivy's family background provided her with the more
engaging absurdities of nonconformist antics in *Dolores*, with the
complex series of intermarriages between Blackwoods and Huttons,*
and with an intimate knowledge of the step-relationship which bedevils
her heroine's home life. What she learnt from George Eliot† is the
combination of minute observation and humorous assurance which
informs all three stories in *Scenes of Clerical Life* as much as later scenes
from low life in *The Mill on the Floss* or *Middlemarch*. The resemblance
is at times uncannily close, so much so that the evening party given by
the Blackwoods to introduce the new Methodist minister ('a wholesome little man of forty with smooth, red cheeks and twinkling little
eyes, excellent both as a man and a Methodist, as his fathers had been
before him, but falling short of them in not being excellent as a grocer
as well') to the Huttons ('Mr Hutton shook hands with his host, gave a

---

* Herbert Blackwood in *Dolores* had married his fourth cousin whose sister Sophia
later became the second Mrs Hutton; Ivy's uncle Robert Blackie had married his
second cousin whose sister Katharine later became the second Mrs Compton Burnett.
In the course of the book the young Blackwoods, Elsa and Herbert, marry their first
cousins, Bertram and Evelyn Hutton—a connection suggested presumably by the dual
marriage in 1875 of Ivy's uncle and aunt, Elizabeth and Charles Rees, to their second
cousins, Robert and Esther Blackie (see family tree).

† Fifty years later Ivy told an interviewer that she had read a good deal of George
Eliot round about 1911, and less since: 'I like her books very much—the fresh and
lively part of them—not the instructive or moralising part. . . .' (*Review of Eng. Lit.*,
October 1962.)

covered glance at the Wesleyan minister, observed to Dr Cassell that the evening was dry, and fell into silence; feeling that the initiative due from an ordained Churchman in Dissenting company was at an end') presents the weird spectacle of I. Compton-Burnett in George Eliot's skin, and on the point of shedding it.

For it is in these comic interludes—barely more than a sideline in the book's serious business—that the immature author of *Dolores* comes closest to the urbanity of her later novels, and more particularly in recriminations between the second Mrs Hutton and her sister Mrs Blackwood: 'They were sisters in the fullest sense. . . . They were, in a word, in that stage of affinity where, with human creatures as with other complex things, contact is another word for clashing . . . the sisters' dialogue was charged with hidden currents. It became a series of thrusts with verbal weapons seemingly innocent, but carrying each its poisoned point.'[39] What is here laboriously described is precisely the kind of concealed collision which, when once she had learnt to catch and pin it in the act, provided the material of her mature and often terrifying triumphs. Tiffs between the sisters in *Dolores*, each bringing up her guns like generals who have spent a lifetime fighting over the same ground, remind one on occasion of Jane Austen as much as of George Eliot, and rather more of either than of I. Compton-Burnett's later manner—but already by fits and starts, in the malicious small talk tossed from hand to hand at the Blackwoods' party or in Mrs Hutton's peevish efforts at domestic friction, one may catch glimpses if not of her later passion, at any rate of her later coruscating wit.

The book contains several undeveloped instances of types later to be fully explored. Dolores' stepmother is an obvious example; Perdita, whose half-conscious falsity looks forward to the more sinister equivocations practised by a long line of unscrupulous flirts from Sybil Edgeworth in *A House and its Head* to Verena Gray in *A Father and His Fate*, is another; and Dolores' moody, deceitful, increasingly cynical brother Bertram provides a first faint sketch of other spiteful and dissatisfied younger brothers like Clement Gaveston in *A Family and a Fortune* or Esmond Donne in *Elders and Betters*. There are even occasional, faltering variations on favourite themes, such as the thorny question of food and shelter on which conversation is apt to run in later books: 'I have been so ashamed of being alive and well, and having to be housed and clothed and fed and provided for. It really is not reasonable . . . when people have to be provided for, death is the only thing.'[40] But the difference could hardly be more striking if one sets this kind of

casual irony, exchanged with an expertise born of long practice
between brother and sister in the later books, beside the awkwardness
caused in *Dolores* by Bertram's similar remark:

> 'Father takes credit to himself for having kept me sheltered and
> fed, while I should have starved or died of exposure, if he had not.'
> 'I suppose his income is really very much less,' said Dolores, in
> nervous uncertainty how to respond.[41]

Nervous uncertainty is marked on almost every page of a work
pieced together from a ragbag of styles, varying from epigrams as neat
as this one on Dr Cassell—'He had so long interpreted a conversation
as a didactic utterance by himself, that argument on equal terms struck
him as deliberate baiting'—to his startling descent into fruity Irish
anecdote ('"Talking of the drink in connection with Irishmen," said
Dr Cassell . . . "have you heard of the Irishman in the barn and his
bottle of whisky?"'). Phrases like 'this oft-lived heart-throb', 'a
generous dower of brunette comeliness' or 'the prime knit with a
nobler soul' suggest no more than a copious acquaintance with Victorian sentimental fiction, but elsewhere the author seems, like Samuel
Beckett's Mrs Rooney, to be struggling with a dead language. The
book reads at times as though she were alternately translating from the
Latin—'From toil for her bread, unfitted for her tenderness, he had
taken her to comfort unbought of weariness' (meaning that he had
married a girl obliged to earn her own living)—and coining her own
Homeric epithets, as 'smile-begetting naïveté', 'the outwardly genial,
bread-winning woman', 'no power of hiding that which was within
with lip-spoken words'.

This artificiality no doubt reflects Ivy's secluded background (her
brother Noel was noted for the same stilted turns of phrase, marked in
his case by a Gibbonian pomposity, when he first came up to King's)
and academic training. Slovenliness in speech, lax grammar and col-
loquial usage had been heavily frowned upon at Holloway, notably by
the Misses Taylor, Péchinet and Block (Miss Block had once reproved a
colleague for using the expression 'jolly well': 'You know perfectly
well, Miss X, there is nothing whatever jolly in your sentiments on this
matter'), all three of whom provided models for women dons at
Dolores' Oxford college. The atmosphere in this section of the book
reflects Holloway as closely as life in and around the Millfield parsonage
mirrors the world of Ivy's own relations at Hove and Clacton. One

would guess, from her habit of peopling the novel with minor characters drawn from life, that her college friend Miss Bremner (who had
'been told I am "in it"' by other Hollowegians who had read *Dolores*
and recognized the likeness) was the original for Dolores' astute and
witty companion, Felicia Murray; and that Ivy had liked Miss Cunningham and Miss Frost, two of the staff at Holloway who reappear in
Dolores as the amiable Miss Dorrington and the humorous Miss
Greenlow.

But, apart from the heroine herself who evidently in some sense
embodies her creator, the most intriguing of these portraits from a biographical point of view is the man who awakens Dolores' 'deeper
heart-throbs', Sigismund Claverhouse, 'the creature who filled her
heart and life, and on whom her lips were sealed.'[42] This is a hopeless,
though not ultimately an unrequited love. Claverhouse, long revered
from afar as a dramatist of genius, gives Dolores tutorials on the Greek
drama ('she stood, with limbs that trembled, at the door behind which
he awaited her alone') and later on his own plays, falls incongruously in
love with her friend Perdita and, when Perdita dies in childbirth after a
disastrous nine months' marriage, turns at last to Dolores who thrice
cruelly rejects him in the name of family duty. The depth and bitterness
of Dolores' protracted sufferings in this affair might suggest some underlying personal experience on her author's part but, of all the portraits in
the book, Claverhouse is the hardest to identify. Helen Cam's key names
him tentatively as: '? (looks only) T. Seccombe—visiting lecturer in
History 1905–'. Thomas Seccombe was appointed visiting lecturer at
Holloway in Ivy's last two years; he had been assistant editor to Leslie
Stephen in the 'nineties on the *Dictionary of National Biography*, becoming thereafter author, editor, critic and a regular contributor to the
Bookman—in short, a fairly typical Georgian man of letters whose
heart, like Claverhouse's, does not seem to have lain in an academic
career which culminated in his holding a chair of English literature first
at the Royal Military Academy, Sandhurst, and later at Kingston in
Canada. But Claverhouse, a taciturn and misanthropic recluse living
alone in penury with his aged mother, cannot have borne more than
the most superficial resemblance to Seccombe who was considerably
younger, a genial host and a familiar figure at London literary gatherings, cheerful, sociable, expansive and already happily married with
several children when he came to Holloway.*

* Seccombe (1866–1923) was, however, a generous talent-spotter among his youthful
friends who met brother men-of-letters at his house (and sometimes worked off their

Another possible model is Mr Salt, the tutor whom Ivy had shared with her brothers and who later coached her alone at Addiscombe College. Mr Salt, a cripple with 'an ethereal face, a look of great suffering and spirituality', seems to have had points in common with Claverhouse, whose 'aspect was grotesque at a glance; for his massive body and arms were at variance with stunted lower limbs, and his shoulders were twisted. His face was dark and rugged of feature; his eyes piercing, but unevenly set . . . his clothes and hair unkempt.'* Ivy's sisters both agreed that this description fitted Mr Salt, whom Ivy had evidently admired: 'He *was* rather untidy. He was very crippled, and twisted in the shoulders, and he had a suffering face.' Further details of Claverhouse's strange ménage and stranger marriage may possibly have been supplied by a legend, current at Holloway in Ivy's day, concerning the elderly lecturer in physics who lived with his mother outside the college gates, had once been engaged to a girl at the college, and whose life was said to have been blighted tragically for love when his marriage was broken off in dramatic circumstances on the wedding morning. It seems likely that Ivy incorporated in Claverhouse elements taken from all these, and perhaps from other sources—from Salt, her first introduction as a child to the heady pleasures of the mind and spirit, from Seccombe her first glimpse of a life lived outside domestic confines in the larger world of letters. But neither Mr Salt's private tuition nor Mr Seccombe's contacts with literary London, his seven hundred articles in the *D.N.B.* and his *'Bookman' History of English Literature* will provide a wholly satisfactory explanation of Dolores' attitude to 'the one, whom her young reverence had placed apart from the world, in the sphere which youth creates for those it sees as the world's great',[43] and whose lectures leave her pale, dazed and shaken with the effort to conceal 'tumult within her'. The most one can deduce is that Claverhouse's very existence points to a capacity in his creator at this stage in her career for ardent hero worship; and that, if Ivy had singled out at

* *Dolores*, p.111. Considering Claverhouse's evident staginess, one might well argue that he owes as much to Dorothea's lover, the elderly reclusive Mr Casaubon in *Middlemarch*—or for that matter to Maggie's, the crippled poet Phillip Wakem in *The Mill on the Floss*—as to either Salt or Seccombe.

own high spirits in boisterous games like 'Up Jenkins', see *The Early Life of Alec Waugh* by Himself, Cassell, 1962, p.90). It was he who introduced Frank Swinnerton to literary circles, and he who found a publisher for Alec Waugh's best-seller, *The Loom of Youth*, in 1917; and perhaps he encouraged Ivy, who was already known at college as one who meant to write.

Holloway or Hove a particular object for her affections, she would
scarcely have revealed it.

Probably in any case Claverhouse owed as much to her evidently
vague but awe-inspiring notions of the nobility of the artist as to any
factual model. His artistic genius provides, indeed, a curious comparison
with what she herself long afterwards called 'my sort of dramatic
novel, something between a novel and a play':[44] Claverhouse's plays
are 'obscure' and 'very profound. Read as they should be read, they
take one very deep.' They are not intended for the stage, ignored by all
save a handful of readers and declaimed aloud by their author in a voice
by turns swelling, trembling and tearful. They seem to be somewhat
macabre chamber tragedies of a kind not uncommon in late Victorian
literature, involving characters named Althea and Jannetta in sudden
death or madness. What is interesting is that (if one discounts the
romantic twitching fits which overtake the dramatist 'in the clutch of
the creative spirit') Ivy seems already to have had some inkling of her
own later working methods. Claverhouse draws his dramas from
recollections of past sorrow, a gift which leaves him during the upheaval
attendant on his marriage and returns only with the comparative
tranquillity in which he writes his final play: 'His own deepest experience, which had lain covered from sympathy's touch, was bared to the
probing of the world, which had shown itself unloving.'[45]

This seems a fairly accurate description of the frame of mind which
produced the mature novels of I. Compton-Burnett. Two of her
closest friends[46] in her last years recognized, when they came to read
Dolores, more of Ivy's private character—her intense shyness, her
shrinking from 'sympathy's touch', her tenderness and vulnerability
beneath the defences erected against a 'world, which had shown itself
unloving'—than in any of her other books. It is not that these traits are
absent from her later work, rather that what has there been absorbed
into the underlying emotional texture of the novels remains in *Dolores*
raw and unassimilated—and therefore however distressing from a
literary point of view, an open invitation to a more personal interpretation. One may see, for instance, something of Ivy's own habitual
discretion in Dolores' unremitting effort to preserve the 'unreal' or
'surface life' from the sufferings which drive her in secret to distraction:
'She was living in two worlds; darkly groping in the one for a spot of
solitude, that she might in the spirit live wholly in the other'.[47] Dolores'
two worlds—her clandestine passion for Claverhouse on the one hand,
the daily round of home or college on the other—may be said to

correspond roughly to the incomparably subtler cracks and fissures of the later novels in which a bland, smooth, elegantly artificial surface is threatened, on occasion dangerously ripped and torn, by pressure from below. The dichotomy was evidently already apparent to the author of *Dolores*, though she is unable to present it except by crude statement and assertion: 'She was saved from darkness only by the suffering need of living the surface life'; 'Calmness and conscious courage went; and a life opened whose every day was a struggle—a life to which she clung with the grasp whose slackening speaks destruction'.

But Dolores' surface life is put at risk not so much by any palpable forces of darkness or destruction as by their sheer absurdity. As Dolores repeatedly renounces her career, her independence, her college salary, her love for Claverhouse and his for her, all to less and less purpose for the sake of friends and relations who prove indifferent or downright ungrateful, she causes abject misery at first only to herself but eventually to others—so much so that her self-immolation comes increasingly to look like cruelty, and the objects of her sacrifice more and more like victims. One dies as a direct result, and another indirectly. It is Dolores who engineers the marriage of Claverhouse and Perdita (a marriage which makes both wretched, kills Perdita and leaves her husband prey to hideous remorse) at frightful cost to herself; and it is Dolores' triple desertion which finally brings the blind, helpless and despairing Claverhouse down to a lonely grave. She had left him for the third time, again at untold cost, to keep house for her father in his second widowhood: a sacrifice promptly and perhaps wisely repudiated by Mr Hutton who, seizing his chance while Dolores is briefly away at Claverhouse's funeral, selects in self-defence a third wife who makes it very plain that her stepdaughter's somewhat oppressive presence is no longer required at home.

But tribulations which may well seem laughable to the reader are bitter earnest to Dolores, and no less so to her creator. They are described in terms which, though evidently to some extent derived at second hand from literary models, nonetheless suggest a sufficient personal acquaintance with painful self-repression: 'It seemed to her ... that to suffer in secret daily, and lie in the night hours helpless under agony below the easiness of tears, was the lot that was natural for her.' This bleakness may, of course, reflect Ivy's own unhappiness from a suppressed and one-sided love affair; or simply the background of her life at Hove in the years after 1906 with a sick and fretful mother, irritating sisters, no prospect of escape from duty to her family, her

Ivy (*centre*) in her first term at Holloway with Daisy Harvey (seated on the balustrade) and Isabel Bremner (in white blouse, far right)

Mrs John Compton Burnett with her pupils at Howard College in the 1890s: Ivy's Aunt Sarah seated in the centre, Daisy and Iris Compton Burnett on her left hand

Members of staff at Holloway who supplied models for *Dolores. Middle row standing left to right:* Miss Pechinet (centre, in cap and gown), Miss Hayes-Robinson, Miss Taylor, Miss Block, Miss Cunningham. *Seated left to right:* Miss Frost, unidentified, Miss Guinness, the Principal (in centre)

Noel as a young Fellow, from a drawing by Kennard Bliss (King's 1911–13,
killed in action 1916) in the *Basileon*, June 1914

unassuaged grief for Guy and her loneliness in Noel's absence; or it may represent in part at least a kind of displaced emotion—the frustrations of struggling unsuccessfully with an intractable aesthetic form.

One may see much the same phenomenon in the painting of the period or a little earlier: in, for instance, the dark, heavy, sometimes even stiflingly Victorian interiors of Bonnard or Matisse which gave way, after a brief, imitative apprenticeship, to canvases suffused with light and colour. There is a similar sense of relief in turning from the morbid atmosphere of *Dolores* to the exquisitely frivolous lucidity of *Pastors and Masters*, published after a gap of fourteen years in 1925. The comparison is perhaps closer if one considers the spectacular transition from Mondrian's lowering, early landscapes, painted in the years when I. Compton-Burnett was writing *Dolores*, or the lurid purple tones and writhing forms of his paintings in 1910 and 1911, produced in what was evidently a frenzied wrestling with convention, to the clarity, simplicity and the delicate pale colours of his grid patterns which followed a few years later. It is easy to see traces of the same frantic, losing battle in I. Compton-Burnett's first novel: a battle which led from the turgid, overblown naturalistic style, carried to a logical if ludicrous extreme in *Dolores*, to the austerity and concision of her mature novels and which meant, for both novelist and painter, that the emotional charge released by each increased in direct proportion as the superficial convulsions of the early work receded before a surface of increasing formal severity.

Whatever the reason, the curious point about *Dolores* is not so much that it is a startlingly bad novel as its peculiar kind of badness. It was plainly written at a time when, as one of Mrs Ward's characters says of Robert Elsmere, its author was 'more struck by the difficulty of being morally strong than by the difficulty of being intellectually clear'.[48] Hence presumably the presence of a whole gallery of perfectly solid, peripheral characters—Dolores' father, stepmother, brother and close college friend—whose presence is essential only as instruments of torture for the heroine. Dolores herself is at best negatively convincing. Her character, whether one considers her saint-like heroism or its monstrous results, is unsatisfactory and her stony selflessness wrought to a pitch which is neither probable nor possible. She becomes interesting only in so far as one asks why any novelist should need to create a character whose sole purpose shall be to receive unending punishment at her own hands and at the hands of fate—punishments in themselves so pitiless, so constant and severe that (though the very act of suffering them makes Dolores necessarily implausible) they suggest nonetheless the presence of emotion frighteningly strong. Whether one prefers to approach the question from a biographical or a literary point of view— to see the answer in purely personal or aesthetic terms, or as a combination of the two—there can be small doubt that powerful emotion continued to run underground throughout the life and work of I. Compton-Burnett. Or, as someone says of feelings in a later novel, 'One is not without them, because they are one's own affair.'[49]

3

'Always secret and very dark'

In 1884, the year of her birth, Ivy's grandfather Rowland Rees had addressed some few pessimistic words to the youth of Dover on the perilous nature of novels: 'All books, he was sorry to say, were not healthy reading, and he would advise young men to beware of the mental poison, and to turn their attention to subjects which would afford real pleasure and improvement, such as history, geography, natural philosophy and the sciences. . . .' He went on to paint a grisly picture of any youth rash enough to discard the scriptures in favour of other forms of fiction: 'He could ruin his health and debase his intellect, he can deaden his conscience, fill his mind with debased ideas, and his mouth with impurity; he can break his father's heart and bring the blush of shame on the brows of his mother and sisters, and he can ruin his soul and bring it under the condemnation of God.'[50]

The Mayor of Dover's attitude was evidently not unlike Sabine Ponsonby's ominous reaction, on ferreting out the hidden manuscript of her granddaughter's first novel in *Daughters and Sons*: 'What is all this rubbish in your room, France?' Grandparents, in the work of I. Compton-Burnett, generally take a dubious view of literary activity: one thinks of Sir Michael Egerton ('It can't be so hard, or he could not write all those books. Long ones, too; I give him credit there') in *A God and His Gifts* or Jocasta Grimstone in *The Last and the First*. A curious, cancelled and unpublished incident in the draft of this last novel casts some light on what may perhaps have been Ivy's own experience as a child. The book itself, published posthumously in 1971, bears a sufficient likeness in point of plot and character to *Dolores* to suggest that Dame Ivy's thoughts, towards the end of her life, were running on things which had happened sixty or more years before, and the supposition is confirmed by this particular episode in which Jocasta forces her terrified granddaughter ('standing . . . so aloof that she might have been unconscious, indeed almost was') to disclose the text of a school essay.

Amy Grimstone's essay, like France Ponsonby's first novel or for that matter Dame Ivy's, concerns characters drawn from the author's own family circle. What is interesting is that the sentiments and stilted language of the essay* are unmistakeably a throwback to *Dolores*; and that Amy's feeling, as her grandmother reads her work aloud, is one of mortal trepidation:

> ... she suffered one of the extreme moments of her life. She sent up a prayer that it might pass, and a word of incredulous thanksgiving when it did. Jocasta let the paper fall from her hand ... and Amy was enabled to retrieve it and move away.
>
> She feared allusion to the matter, and lived in suspense for days; and the passing of the danger was a thing she could hardly believe, and was never to explain.

This atmosphere of secrecy and dread was well known to Ivy who, like France Ponsonby and practically all the budding authors in her books, refused to show her manuscript even to her brother. Years afterwards when she had long since disowned *Dolores*, consigning it presumably to the category of 'youthful agonies' ('I don't think anything in later life quite comes up to them, or makes one squirm as they did') so feelingly described by Miles Mowbray in *A Father and His Fate*, she even sought to shift the blame by claiming to several people that Noel had 'meddled in it': 'Yes, I did that piece of juvenilia, but my brother meddled with it, and I don't take any interest in it, because I can't remember how much I wrote and how much I didn't really. But people always *will* be prying into it, you know.'[51] Dame Ivy's memory must, as she suspected, have grown blurred with time since the inference that Noel collaborated on *Dolores* cannot have been strictly accurate. For one thing, his copy still survives inscribed on the fly-leaf in his sister's hand: 'Noël Compton-Burnett with the author's love'.[52] For

---

* The manuscript contains an extract from this essay, which begins by describing a tyrannical grandmother attended by her nervous grandchildren, and continues:

> A day of leisure is our theme. But through the leisured hour thoughts made their way, and almost deprived it of the name.
>
> For before the younger eyes the future lay, its promise already dim, and before the failing ones there moved the past, with its joys and sorrows, its suffering and sin —for we deal with an ordinary human life—its progress to the grave.

Compare the opening chapter of *Dolores*, quoted on p.169 (a much briefer version of the episode in *The Last and the First* comes in chapter three of the published text).

another, her younger sisters well remember the book being written throughout the years at Hove when the girls sat round the schoolroom table, supposedly taught by Ivy but actually drawing, painting, reading, 'browsing at what we liked', while Ivy slowly filled a series of exercise books in a small, cramped hand, crossing out and re-writing as was her habit for the rest of her life, 'digging a very sharp-pointed pencil—I can see her now—into the notebook. She went over and over them.' Both agreed that it was '*quite* false' that Noel had helped write *Dolores*. They had watched Ivy writing day after day when Noel was away at Cambridge and, even in the vacation, Juliet Compton-Burnett thought it improbable that the two did more than share a study: 'This would have been where they would have had their intimate talks about earnest things—*if* they ever had any. I think it quite likely that they just sat side by side and worked.' Lastly, there is Noel's own evidence in a letter to O.B., dated 1 August 1909, that he had not been permitted a sight of the manuscript until it was finished:

You were kind enough in your last letter to ask about my sister's novel. When finished she sent it to Blackwood as a venture. But alas! it was returned with the enclosed letter, which on the whole was not entirely discouraging. Since then I have read the book. I do not think I was influenced by fraternal prejudice, but I will stake all my pretensions to critical acumen, and vow that the book is filled with literary and dramatic excellencies. However 'Unhistoric Acts' (that is the book's baptismal dower) still is on my sister's hands. Before taking a further step I have been wondering whether I might remind you of your own very good natured suggestion to give her a letter of introduction to a publisher. We know that your influence would count for much, and I need not say that we shall appreciate its exertion. I may say that in my view the quality of the work is such, that you might possibly come to feel some pleasure in having helped to let it take its chance. In any case I am sure you will excuse this quite absurd imposition on your good nature.[53]

The mysterious *Unhistoric Acts* was almost certainly an early draft of *Dolores* under another name, since it is hardly likely that Ivy had time to write a whole new novel in the fifteen months between receiving her first manuscript back from Blackwood and submitting her second (which was conditionally accepted) in October 1910. What O.B. thought of the novel is unknown, though either his good nature or

Noel's shrewd appeal to his vanity as a patron prompted him to write to his own publisher John Lane, who apparently endorsed Blackwood's rejection. Neither publisher has preserved records of this correspondence which was conducted unbeknownst to Mrs Compton Burnett and her daughters so that Ivy's attempts to place her novel were kept, like France Ponsonby's, 'a dark secret' from her family and seem likely to remain one from posterity: 'People's first dealings with publishers are always secret and very dark. Especially when they come to nothing.'54

It seems probable that Ivy re-wrote the novel over the next year or so, perhaps with Noel's assistance, and perhaps incorporating advice contained in Blackwood's 'not entirely discouraging' letter (one cannot help speculating as to whether this might not have resembled the criticisms levelled against France's novel—that it was 'a string of beads' not welded into a whole, that it needed cutting, and that it was in parts so immature as to be unfit for publication). But these were also the months leading up to Mrs Compton Burnett's last illness, which fell heavily on both Noel and Ivy. Their mother had for years been afflicted by deafness which exacerbated her alarming nervous disposition and gave her terrible noises in the head. She was already gravely ill when, probably in the early summer of 1909, the family visited Clacton with the Blackies—and it was perhaps on this occasion that Robert Blackie, presumably not unaware of his eldest niece's dangerous tendency to fiction, prayed aloud before the two assembled families 'that his dear nieces might not be led into the sin of intellectual pride'. It was also this summer that Vera Compton-Burnett, at the age of seventeen, first realized the seriousness of their mother's condition. Ivy later accompanied her alone to Ryde in the Isle of Wight for a course of electrical treatment which lasted two weeks ('and they were hard weeks for Ivy'); Minnie nursed her, as she had nursed Guy, sitting up sometimes all night and running the household next day. Mrs Compton-Burnett would allow no one else near her for, like her eldest daughter, 'she had a horror of going to a hospital, a horror of going to a nurse'. Some time in the autumn of 1910 Dr Clarke, their father's friend to whom he had consigned his family before he died, took Noel aside and told him that she had cancer of the breast in an advanced and already fatal stage. Radium treatment was prescribed which produced fearful wounds and burns on the wrists; in July 1911, five months before her death, Noel accompanied his mother to London for a final radium cure.

In these last sombre years Noel's friends had long ceased to be invited to the house. Noel himself, who had spent industrious vacations 'reading six or so hours a day', taken a double first in 1910 and afterwards had 'little leisure owing to the very serious illness of my mother',[55] can have had no more time than Ivy for tinkering with her novel. By October 1910, the pair must have felt that time was running short if their mother were ever to see the book in print; and, after open family consultation since on this occasion money was involved, a new and more hopeful scheme was proposed to Blackwood, who replied to 'S. Compton-Burnett, Esq.' on 9 November:

Dear Sir,

We have now given our careful consideration to your MS. novel. We are willing to fall in with your wishes and to publish the story on the terms you suggest, viz:- at your own risk and expense. We would propose printing 1050 copies 6s fiction, allowing a sum of some £40 to be spent on advertising. The cost of production under these conditions would be approximately £150, and before putting the work in hand, we should like a payment to account of £75. . . .[56]

Jermyn Haslam in *Men and Wives* faced considerable domestic opprobrium when, having dismally failed to place his first slim volume of original verse, he was finally obliged to publish the book on payment by his father of a suitably large sum to Messrs. Halibut and Froude. Whether or not Ivy had had to contend with similar difficulties, *Dolores* was duly published on 20 February 1911, and, as Mr Blackwood (writing now to 'Miss I. Compton-Burnett') gracefully acknowledged, it sold immediately and well. 480 copies had gone by the end of the first month. The reviewers, conservative by nature then as now, were markedly more enthusiastic over the old-fashioned virtues of this eminently Victorian work than they were to be fourteen years later over the same author's first genuinely original novel; even Ivy found it barely necessary to conceal the pleasure with which she distributed among her friends copies of the *Daily Mail* and the *Times Literary Supplement* ('You must bear in mind for my benefit', she wrote modestly to Katie, 'that it is something to be noticed in the Times at all.'). The *Mail*, dismissing Ada Leverson's *The Limit* and Constance Smedley's *Mothers and Fathers* as second-rate efforts typical of lady writers, singled out the author of *Dolores* ('Who Ivy Compton-Burnett is, whether young or middle-aged, whether Mrs or Miss, I know not') as one who might yet vindicate her sex by rising to the dizzy heights scaled by Mr Wells, Mr Bennett, Mr Galsworthy and

Mr Robert Hichens: 'no one could call "The Limit" literature . . . But "Dolores" is literature; of that no competent critic can have any doubt'.[57]

The anonymous reviewer in the *T.L.S.* was Walter de la Mare who, noting that Claverhouse 'is somehow suggestive of Victor Hugo, whereas the rest of the characters have a just perceptible flavour of Jane Austen,' proved quite as generous as the *Mail* if rather less effusive: 'Miss Compton-Burnett has written with intense seriousness, her book lights up for the reader a serene and independent mind. . . .' Jane Austen, George Eliot and even Henry James were invoked gratifyingly often by, among others, Robert Ross (then 'rolling the Literary Log' in a gossipy column between sport and fashion notes at the back of the *Bystander*) who confidently predicted 'something really striking from the young author' in the future. Altogether the young author had every reason to feel satisfied with a début which seems to have left her with nothing but pleasant associations: Arnold Bennett's *The Card*, reviewed by de la Mare below *Dolores*, remained long afterwards a favourite with Ivy and, if she was struck by the possibilities of *Mothers and Fathers* as a title, she may also have noted and put by for future reference the name of another novel reviewed at the same time as her own: Mrs L. T. Meade's *Mother and Son*.

Ivy's mother was by this time too weak to resent, perhaps even to identify, the portrait of herself as Mrs Hutton. Whatever apprehensions Ivy may have entertained beforehand ended even more happily than Amy Grimstone's, for Mrs Compton Burnett was frankly jubilant at the book's reception. The staunchly Wesleyan Blackies were somewhat less so, and the Compton Burnetts' physician at Hove, a Dr Molson who recognized himself in Dr Cassell, was filled with such natural resentment that it became for some time a question as to whether he could bring himself to continue in attendance on the family. But, having once surmounted the dread of retribution at her mother's hands, Ivy treated querulous protests of this kind with characteristic insouciance. She freely admitted to her cousin Katie 'that I made use of your father and mother just to give a superficial touch to the personalities. That I intended no resemblance in character I should have thought was clear. Surely there is no real likeness? Jimmie and Grandma could not even see the surface suggestion. If people will insist that a cap fits, and further insist upon wearing it, it is not to be laid to my account.' (23 May 1911)

She took meanwhile considerable pains to sell 'my little book', explaining that she could on no account distribute copies 'as it is against my publisher's interest for me to do anything at all that checks the sale', and urging her relations to purchase instead the 'special edition for the Colonies, bound in paper, and costing only 1s' (this last was disingenuous, since they cost in fact 1s 6d or 2s). Miss Bremner received an even thriftier suggestion on a postcard which simply said in Ivy's sprawling hand: 'Ask at your local library for *Dolores*.' Of the 1050 copies printed, 850 at six shillings and 200 in cheap colonial editions, all but 146 had been sold by 31 December 1911, whereupon demand abruptly ceased. On twelve out of every thirteen copies sold, Ivy had received three shillings and seven pence per copy, less a publishing commission of fifteen per cent to Blackwood. By December 1920, three more copies had been sold. The remaining 143 were probably then wasted. Six years before, Blackwood's had proposed to clear their warehouse by selling off the stock on hand, offering Ivy as many copies as she liked at threepence or fourpence each. Olivia Manning said long afterwards that Ivy kept a cupboardful of remaindered copies of *Dolores*, which had been delivered to her in a truck. The whole affair puts one strangely in mind of Samuel Beckett's Krapp, meditating on his own laborious rise to fame: 'Seventeen copies sold, of which eleven at trade price to free circulating libraries beyond the seas. Getting known.'[58]

CHAPTER SEVEN

1911–1915

I

'Are we going to be broad and wicked?'

PHILIP NOEL-BAKER, then an undergraduate in his third year at King's, never forgot seeing Noel in May Week 1911, walking across the front court with a sister who 'knocked the college sideways'. This was Ivy, a few days after her twenty-seventh birthday, spending a week at Cambridge with her sister Judy to watch the races and perhaps to attend the King's Ball, which was held that year on Monday, 12 June.[1] Even allowing for the fact that women were rare at King's in those days (and, to say the least, not highly prized in what was still an almost exclusively celibate society), Ivy seems to have made a marked impression: 'She was stunning. Absolutely beautiful, and she had a wonderful figure.' Ivy had been justly proud of her figure ('a sort of well-covered slender', said her sister, 'and she dressed rather to show it'), as of her looks in general. 'I was a pretty piece, wasn't I?' she said long afterwards, of a studio portrait* taken probably round about this time. Mr Noel-Baker, watching appreciatively as she crossed the courtyard on her brother's arm and disappeared up the stair to his rooms, longed to meet her but never came near enough to manage an introduction.

Noel's rooms were in Wilkins Building, immediately to the left of the gateway as you enter the college, under the corner turret with what must be among the loveliest views even in Cambridge, looking directly across at the chapel from one window and down King's Parade from the other. O.B. lived until his retirement opposite on the same staircase, and seems generally to have selected a specially favoured undergraduate to occupy this particular set of rooms in which Noel had succeeded Rupert Brooke. Judy, who was then eighteen and 'only half finished', was properly impressed not only by the beauty of the buildings and gardens in early summer but by the grandeur of Noel's domestic appointments, his gyp, his amazingly talkative friends, the luncheon served in his rooms of roast duck and green peas and asparagus

* To Lady Ashton; the photograph is reproduced following page 240.

—so very different from her own home life at Hove—and by the general air of consequence accorded to her brother in what seemed, to a schoolgirl up from the country, positively palatial surroundings. 'Inside the college by 1911, Noel was regarded as one of the brilliant people,' said Philip Noel-Baker who had first got to know him well on Noel's return from four months spent learning German at Munich and Göttingen in the summer of 1910. 'I suppose one could say he was shy. He was very quiet and gentle: I don't believe he ever said anything disagreeable to anyone in the whole of his life. He was so clever and so well-read that I was shy of saying anything in front of him for fear it was wrong.'

Noel had by this time developed his own peculiar style of eccentricity, affecting a stiff wing collar and a mock-pompous style of delivery derived from his favourite author. 'Edward Gibbon, Esq.' is the pen-name assigned to 'Mr N. Compton-Bannerman, B.A.' in an 'Index of Standard Authors' supplied by the *Basileon* (the college magazine, which favoured a brand of anonymous, personal, often highly obscure under-graduate humour) for June 1911. 'He had this curious manner—sort of huffing and puffing, and at the same time making fun of himself,' said Raisley Moorsom who had come up to King's that year. 'My chief memory is of him standing with a walking stick in the court and pontificating—on nothing at all—in that Gibbonian manner,' said William Haslam, another historian and an exact contemporary of Noel at King's. The manner which intrigued his friends at Cambridge had first taken hold of Noel in the spring and summer of 1907, when he sat in the schoolrooom at Hove with Ivy and raced through the *Decline and Fall* twice over. The raw and enthusiastic schoolboy who began sending weekly bulletins to O.B. ('I should think that there could be nothing in History more marvellous than the Crusades') rapidly made way for the budding pedant who, barely three months after he had read his first page of Gibbon, wrote to congratulate his mentor on a whirl of end-of-term activity: 'The Pageant at Oxford seems from all accounts to have been an almost worthy celebration of the past it recalled; while a subsequent attendance at the King's garden-party must, I should think, have afforded a contrast not less striking than delightful.' (2 June 1907)

Similarly balanced and sonorous, though this time rather more polished periods form the opening paragraphs of his thesis dissertation written five years later in the summer of 1912. It was presumably the combination of extreme seclusion and a highly developed inner life, the effect of an upbringing that had acted as a forcing house to the emotions but left the intelligence untouched, which had made Noel as susceptible to Gibbon as Ivy had been to George Eliot, and which meant that, again like his sister, he had early felt the need to adopt some form of protective covering. Outside his own immediate circle at King's, he seemed a stiff, shy, unworldy oddity. 'He was quite unlike any undergraduate. He gave the impression that he hadn't been to a public school—he hadn't had the raw edges rubbed off him,' said Raisley Moorsom. As a young Fellow cast in O.B.'s mould Noel was known as 'the C.B.' to his humorous juniors, who once proposed as a promising subject for debate: 'C.B. is B.C.'. It took years to wear out this witticism: 'Thank God I've lived down C-B at last. I'm called at discretion Jim & Noel,' he wrote to his Cambridge friend Elliott Felkin in July 1914. Criticisms of his awkward delivery when he first took part in debates at the Union suggest that Noel had had initially to overcome a dislike of public speaking much like Ivy's own. But years at home which had driven her to a fine point of concealment and self-control had left Noel at once more exuberant and gentler than his sister, though with the same singular ability to detach himself at will from his immediate surroundings, informed by the same extraordinary sense of humour. 'His very distinct personality had never been blurred by school,' wrote the economist John Clapham, who had succeeded O.B. as History Tutor at the end of 1908. 'Partly, no doubt, because he was the only surviving son in a large family which had lost its father, he seemed curiously mature. He could be either in or outside his generation, as suited his mood. He belonged to the once notorious little society at King's, "the Carbonari", to which Rupert Brooke read some of his earlier poems; and, while still an undergraduate, he would tell you about it as a man of thirty tells of such things in retrospect.'[2]

Noel had in some ways an easier lot than his sisters, who had no option but to remain for another eight years at Hove: 'The cloud lifted for Noel a little earlier, King's was a magic world for him. He made friends easily, though he'd never had any at all before.' Chief of these was Jack Beresford, to whom King's had also come as 'an almost magical release' from the strain of an intense, self-contained and often melancholy family life in an isolated country rectory. Jack was a frequent visitor at Hove and the two families saw a good deal of each other when, after Mrs Compton Burnett's death, the Burnett and Beresford sisters exchanged visits on Noel's engagement to one of the three beautiful Miss Beresfords. Jack's gay and impetuous disposition is

nicely conveyed by, on the one hand, Noel's description of him to O.B.
—'He is in a state of lyric enthusiasm over the flowers of the field. He
is a charming fellow and the incarnation of the ingenuous; I like him
much' (1 August 1909)—and, on the other, a curt riposte sent from
Göttingen on 20 September 1910:

My dear Jack,
    I had your letter here, and more latterly your abusive postcard.
Many thanks for the former. As to the latter I must warn you that
should I receive any further missives from Wales breathing all the
fervour of the Celtic temperament I shall avail myself in my reply
of the German language and of German characters. I have not written
because I have not had anything particular to say. . . .

The two had been inseparable at King's from their first term, always
walking and talking together—'You remember our high Cambridge
talk, so up in the clouds and so insincere according to the way of youth,
and it's odd to consider how all of it is now brought to the rather sordid
touch of practice,' wrote Noel at the end of 1915 in one of his last letters
from the trenches.³ His wartime letters are shot through with references
to 'talk of literature and men' at Cambridge, Brighton and at O.T.C.
training camp together, to 'our headshaking mighty exchange of
argumentative broadsides' which had made Piccadilly reverberate on
Noel's leaves in London, and with his longing to see his friend again:
'Oh! my excellent Jacobus if you were here, what should not we two
veterans from the Cutlasses perform upon the Teuton. Alas! we are
scurvily separated—a perpetual irritation to us both.' (4 October 1915)
    Arthur Waley (then called by his family name of Schloss, later
changed to Waley in the war) also became a close friend in these years
and remained one of Ivy's circle to the end of his life. The Schlosses had
a country house in Sussex, not far from Hove, where Noel was often
invited to lunch (sometimes with Ivy, and once with his mother),
asking his friend back in return to spend weekends at Hove whence
they paid visits together to O.B. at Bexhill. 'Schloss . . . came over some
time back for the day,' wrote Noel in his first long vacation. 'He always
seems to me a very remarkable personality. He is unfamiliar, and
perhaps for that reason attracts one. I can never quite satisfy myself
whether he is cleverer than he seems, or seems cleverer than he is, but
of his cleverness I have no doubt.' (3 August 1908) Noel's friends in those
days were as beautiful as they were clever, judging at any rate by a

moving account of the King's college pageant performed on the banks
of the Cam in their second year:

> The Queen of the May (Mr Beresford) is in the act of crowning her
> pupils with nosegays of incarnadined tulips, when enter, R, the
> Christian slave-girl, Granta (Mr Schloss), fleeing in terror from a
> fresh punt-load of Jutes and Picts . . . who have surprised her washing
> her nightie on the bank. . . . Granta swoons and dies to Chopin's
> Funeral March (by request). . . . The whole of this tender yet stirring
> episode is the work of poor, dead, Robert Swithinbank, and copy-
> right by the Carbonari Society.[4]

The Carbonari, founded by Rupert Brooke and his Fabian friend
Hugh Dalton in their first term, was a fairly ferocious band of twelve
members who prided themselves on being intellectually superior to the
rest of the college, and who were regarded in return as an outrageously
odd lot. Brooke and Dalton, picking over the freshmen each year, had
singled out Noel for an invitation to join along with Arthur Schloss,
Philip Noel-Baker and Francis Birrell (first year in 1908, and remembered by Ivy's sisters as an occasional visitor at Hove). He read at least
two historical papers at the society's weekly meetings and certainly
attended the celebrated, ceremonial dinner held in Brooke's rooms on
5 February 1909, at which seven toasts were drunk including 'The
World, the Flesh and the Devil' and 'The King, God damn him'.
Unhappily Brooke's gyp, who had remained unobserved to witness
this incident, reported it next morning ('Well, they drank the King's
health, sir, but without much loyalty') whereupon, according to two
conflicting or perhaps complementary accounts, Dalton was debagged
and/or Frankie Birrell was chased round the courtyard by patriots who
wanted to duck him. The Carbonari were mostly Fabians, anti-
athletic, anti-philistine and ardently devoted to modern literature.
'There are only three good things in the world,' said Brooke according
to Dalton, 'one is to read poetry, another is to write poetry, and the
best of all is to live poetry!' A less exalted but perhaps rather more
accurate view of their proceedings is suggested by Arthur Schloss in a
programme note on promised delights at a Carbonari Ball: 'Finally,
Mr Rupert Brooke will perform a dream-dance on tip toe.'

Noel's life at Cambridge seems to have been bounded almost entirely
by college affairs: he had taken part in the second debate of his first
term at the Union, speaking thereafter almost every other week until

he was elected to the Committee in December 1908, and never spoke
again. He had been from his first term a regular attendant at the King's
Political Society which met in O.B's rooms, and became its secretary
in his third year (reading a paper on 'The Soul of Our Age' at the 490th
meeting and voting Aye, with Beresford, to the motion, 'Is there
one?'). His withdrawal from outside pursuits was no doubt partly
due to congenial company in King's, partly on account of his work
which prospered exceedingly. 'Everyone knew at once he was a certain
First,' said Leigh Farnell, another historian; and, on the constitutional
history paper in part one of the Tripos, Noel is said to have answered
only one question, writing fifteen pages on the hide, that most contro-
versial unit of land measurement in Anglo-Saxon England—so learned
and exhaustive was his treatment that he took a first by acclamation.
The Gladstone prize was awarded 'for the excellence of C.B.'s work on
the Special Period, Mediaeval History and Constitutional History,'
wrote Clapham to O.B. who, in retirement at Bexhill, had also received
a jubilant and characteristically consoling report from Noel: 'Out of
the second year History people, Toulmin, Beresford, Forbes-Adam
and myself are all scholars. That is pretty well for the last generation of
the disciples of O.B.' (1 August 1909)

   Geoffrey Toulmin, Jack Beresford and Eric Forbes-Adam all came
down from Cambridge to stay with the Compton Burnetts at Hove,
and were all well-known to Ivy. She herself paid visits to her brother
at King's and was presumably already unconsciously absorbing the
Cambridge attitudes which make her second novel so markedly
different from her first. Friends of Noel who met Ivy before the
first war remember her as giggly, cheerful, reserved in public but in
private no less witty than her brother. What had seemed to their
younger sister Judy a bewildering, bewitching glimpse of high life
must have been for Ivy, observing it with eyes not so easily dazzled,
quite as fascinating and almost as remote from anything she had
previously known at home or college. But her own direct contacts
with Cambridge, or with as much of it as was permitted to a woman,
were doubtless less revealing than the easy intimacy derived at second
hand from the gossip of her brother and his friends. These high-
spirited, intelligent young men who descended from time to time on
Hove, turning the house upside down for bouts of table-tapping,
dressing up and bathing parties, once even carrying off Ivy herself to
the continent, must have provided in these years almost her sole
window on the outside world. That she sat in it and watched with

unremitting attention is suggested by the reflection of what she saw in her next novel, if not by the procession of high-spirited, intelligent young men following one another across the pages of almost all her later work. Certainly Noel and his friends, or rather their dealings with their tutors, contributed largely to *Pastors and Masters*. Perhaps even the scandalous machinations surrounding O.B. in his last years at Cambridge—machinations whose intricacies must have been familiar to Ivy, since her brother was among O.B.'s most valiant supporters— have a bearing on the atmosphere of academic intrigue and narrowly averted scandal hanging over that novel.

It was O.B. who had first placed the King's history school on a level with classics and mathematics and made it the envy of the university. But by 1907 his work had long since been completed and he himself, superseded in his seventies by a younger generation of historians, was well on the way to becoming an indignant, irascible and mortified old man. 'As he grew older his off days increased,' wrote his biographer and, when Noel first knew him, his conceit had already grown more alarming than endearing—'his inner voice supported him for he too, like Socrates, possessed a singularly encouraging *daimon*, thanks to whom he knew that what he did was good'⁵—and his off days so frequent as to be almost insupportable. Twice disappointed in hopes (which he alone had entertained) of becoming first Regius Professor, then Provost of King's, he was finally obliged by what he regarded as a shocking manœuvre of his enemies to retire at the end of 1908 to Bexhill, where he morosely contemplated twin portraits in his dining room of Napoleon and himself. Noel, who became thereafter O.B.'s chief purveyor of college news, addressed himself in the next few years to the delicate business of condolence ('I think all those of my year have a right to feel sadly aggrieved' 3 August 1908), appreciation ('It was most good of you to let us come. Your talk I always look upon as an Educational advantage. Cambridge cannot be quite itself till you return to it' 5 October 1909) and reassurance ('I hope that Bexhill will not so win all your affection as to make your presence at King's too occasional. If we were to lose our chief celebrity the daughters of the Philistines at Trinity would rejoice past bearing. . . . I must plead guilty to a secret desire to see you the V.P.' 1 August 1909).

But, though Noel retained a vivid sense of gratitude to the end of his career at Cambridge, his early devotion to O.B. gave way to a growing respect and liking for John Clapham. Clapham's famous lectures on economic history (at which impassioned undergraduates stamped till the floor rang like a drum) had started the year after Noel came up to King's, just too late to fire him as they fired so many freshmen in the next twenty-five years and more. By the beginning of his second year, Noel was too firmly entrenched in O.B.'s camp—'I shall always think myself fortunate to have begun my study of history under you,' he wrote loyally in the long vacation. 'History studied as politics seems to me a vastly more important, not to say more attractive thing than history studied as economics or as anything else whatsoever' (3 August 1908)—to take readily to O.B.'s successor. It might have proved an awkward situation but any initial difficulties were resolved by tact on both sides. As President and Secretary of the Political Society at its five hundredth meeting in 1910, Clapham and Noel combined to organize the celebratory dinner which must have gone a fair way to mollify the society's founder, who was guest of honour. Clapham's own letters to O.B. suggest that he thought highly of Noel, and perhaps regretted losing him to a rival discipline ('You will be glad, I expect, to find him so well in the political tradition,' he wrote on 7 July 1911, of Noel's fellowship thesis, 'and not led astray by me into a study of the rural economy of the Godwin Sands as revealed in the Anglo-Saxon Chronicle or the origin of the two ways of dying wool'); and there can be small doubt that each thoroughly appreciated the other's combination of solidity with humour.

But stronger, or at any rate more lasting, than either of these relationships was Noel's affinity with Goldsworthy Lowes Dickinson, to whom he went for tutorials in his third year. 'Goldie admired Noel, and said he would have been a remarkable historian,' said Philip Noel-Baker; and it seems to have been from Dickinson that Noel absorbed not only the political and historical assumptions but also the underlying personal philosophy which, six years later in the trenches, were to sustain him in the bitterest months of his life. Not that there was anything especially remarkable about this friendship in its early stages, certainly nothing remotely comparable to Noel's dramatic schoolboy encounter with his first mentor. Dickinson was on every count the opposite of O.B.: modest, gentle, unassertive, shy to distraction and often ludicrously unworldly, he imbued his pupils with his own dry wit and unfailing tolerance. When he was awarded a travelling bursary in 1912 for the widening of Fellows' minds, Rupert Brooke said: 'If they widen Goldie's mind any more, it'll break'. He was not at first sight attractive —'Well, you know, he looked like the carpenter in *Alice in Wonderland*,' said a former pupil long afterwards. 'You know what I mean—

G

slightly seedy, badly dressed, dirty old grey flannel trousers, curious stoop and very curious walk with a long stride and threw his legs out in front of him; and he looked rather long-faced and gloomy, but I don't think one found him gloomy very long.'

'The hands were large,' wrote E. M. Forster, his pupil, friend and later his enthusiastic biographer. 'The clothes, except during his American visits, erred on the dowdy side—dark blue serge, shirts of indistinction, podgy ties. I dress like that myself, except for illogical flashinesses, and once when I invited him into one of these he replied that it is useless to dress well unless one's personal appearance corresponds.'[6] What charmed his pupils was his disinterestedness and diffidence, his lack of self-importance and his extraordinary power of clarifying muddled or irrational views. His preference in civilizations was for the Greeks ('I am one of the few people who have studied Plotinus from cover to cover,' he said in a rare moment of self-congratulation of his thesis dissertation on Plato and Plotinus) and the Chinese. His reputation rests not so much on his contribution to the League of Nations, still less on any particular distinction as an historian, rather on his vast and (considering the more or less dismal failure of his practical aspirations) disproportionate influence on generations of young men at Cambridge.

Dickinson represents very nearly to perfection both the virtues and the drawbacks of what he called 'the Cambridge mind so rare, so exasperating to so many people, and as I think so precious and so indispensable'. Its effect on Noel was pronounced, and perhaps even more on Ivy. Its cast was rational, enquiring, scrupulously truthful, as far removed from passion as from bigotry or bias, its characteristic tone sceptical and ironic. There have been more dazzling Cambridge minds—Bertrand Russell and Maynard Keynes are obvious examples—but none so representative as Dickinson, and few more persuasive. His failings were a mild but resolute melancholy in which he took such satisfaction that it amounted at times to weakness, a naïveté whether in practical or ideal matters carried sometimes to disturbing lengths, and a maddening tendency to reserve judgement. Hard experience in later years taught Ivy the dangers inherent in this kind of passivity, which recurs again and again in onlookers helplessly watching tyranny triumph from the sidelines of her books. But at the time when she was writing *Dolores* or just afterwards, the impact of one who, in Forster's words, 'came down, perhaps rather too heavily, on the side of limpidity and logic' must have struck Ivy with particular force. 'One may almost say of him that he held nineteenth-century opinions in a twentieth-century way. For him, as for the Victorians, life was a pilgrimage, not an adventure, but he journeyed without donning their palmer's weeds.'[7]

The author of *Dolores* had held nineteenth-century opinions in an almost exaggeratedly nineteenth-century way; and, if it is impossible to say exactly when she changed (though it is not hard to adduce reasons as to why and how), it is evident that by the time she came to write her second novel in the early 'twenties she had imbibed not only the general scepticism prevalent at King's but even the mannerisms of Cambridge conversation:

'I think I have found myself at last,' said Herrick. 'I think that, God willing, I shall have done my little bit for my generation, done what every man ought to do before he dies.'. . .

'Assuming God, you wouldn't do much if he wasn't willing,' said Masson.[8]

The plot of *Pastors and Masters*, in so far as it can be said to have one, concerns nefarious doings among dons at the college of which Nicholas Herrick, aged seventy, is a retired Fellow and his two friends, William Masson and Richard Bumpus, still active members. The setting is an 'old university town' (evidently Cambridge since the author makes it very plain that the only other claimant to the name is Oxford, which she did not know), and the book contains at least one portrait drawn from Noel's acquaintanceship at King's: 'William Masson was a tall, large man in late middle age, with loose limbs and loose clothes, and a weather-beaten, high-boned face. He seemed an example of all the uneasinesses combined into ease.'[9] Masson's looks (his character seems to have been pure invention on his author's part) were borrowed from the Dean of King's, W. H. Macaulay, who, like Masson, was a mathematician and a bachelor from birth with the same handsome, high-boned features tortured by a shyness so devastating that he seldom spoke. Noel, wishing to reassure his future brother-in-law in June 1915, wrote a week or so before his marriage: 'Don't think of me as likely to be an unsympathetic, impossible person in your family. I'm only the characteristic don (though disfigured in khaki) with the nervous Macaulayisms of that tribe.'

Macaulay kept a horse in the meadow behind King's and is said to have ridden with Noel, who had learnt to ride like Ivy in the summer of 1912. Dickinson, who liked horses but frequently fell off them, also rode with Noel in his last two years at Cambridge. Both habitually kept well clear of women but Ivy had presumably seen them both (Macaulay, whose rooms were directly below Noel's in Wilkins Building, could hardly have avoided being seen, however adroitly he may have dodged an introduction) on her visits to King's. Whether or not she ever actually met Dickinson with Noel, she must have heard a good deal about him and she certainly knew him later. Her sisters remembered her visiting him at his sisters' house in Kensington after the war, when the two had a number of London friends (Arthur Waley and Noel's two younger contemporaries, Raisley Moorsom and Elliott Felkin, as well as Arthur's and Elliott's widowed mothers) in common. Dickinson in those days read Ivy's books as they came out, and 'said they were very queer stuff'.[10]

Considering that his tastes remained on many fronts notably un-sophisticated, it is small wonder that Ivy's novels puzzled Dickinson, who had unwittingly contributed what was later to become a third strand—the type of detached and humorous observer who appears in almost every novel, perhaps most consummately as Mortimer Lamb in *Manservant and Maidservant*—quite as important as the theme of brother and sister or the archetypal tyrant to her books. This type is barely sketched in *Pastors and Masters* but already one may catch the character-istic tone. If one sets the book beside *Dolores*, the change in mood is very much that described by Forster in his comparison between Dickinson and Henry Sidgwick: 'Sidgwick wanted to believe in God and his inability to do so caused him a constant strain. Dickinson, equally conscientious, was somehow freer and less glum. It would never have occurred to him as it did to Sidgwick to compose his own funeral service. As soon as it came to the question of his own death, his own fate, he turned easy and modern, and one of the things which attracted the young to him was that he never gave them a sense of nursing a private destiny.'[11]

Ivy, too, had turned easy and modern by the early 'twenties ('"Are we going to be broad and wicked?" said Emily. "I like that, because I am not very educated, and so still young in my mind"'), and is plainly more at home in this atmosphere than she had been in the glum toils of *Dolores*. The difference is immediately apparent in a conversation—on God, and whether it is better to have Him or not—which pleasantly anticipates one of her favourite and most fruitful later themes:

'He always seems to me a pathetic figure, friendless and childless, and set up alone in a miserable way.'

'Yes, he has a touch of William in him,' said Emily. 'But you know he isn't childless. . . .'

'You can have him childless in these days,' said Bumpus. 'But if you have him, I like him really. I like him not childless, and grasping, and fond of praise. I like the human and family interest.'. . .

'And he had such a personality,' said Emily. 'Such a superior, vindictive and over-indulgent one. He is one of the best drawn characters in fiction.'[12]

Doubt and disbelief, which had led to desperate measures among an earlier generation of Cambridge dons, had become considerably less pressing by the turn of the century when O.B. kept a crucifix in his rooms 'to fwighten the agnoggers' and Dickinson was characteristically undecided. 'He hoped. He had no faith,' wrote Forster, and he had joined the Society for Psychical Research (which was known as the Ghost Club and met in O.B.'s rooms) just in case. At King's those who were not atheist or agnostic belonged to one of two parties. Floating voters were hotly contested between these parties, led on the one hand by the high church Father Waggett who lured likely undergraduates to his rooms with breakfast or luncheon invitations, and on the other by H. W. K. Mowll, a son of the Compton-Burnetts' family solicitor and leader of the low church party. Howard Mowll, a fervent evangelical supporter of CICCU who had drummed up converts for a series of revivalist meetings in Noel's day at Cambridge and ultimately became the Anglican Bishop in Western China with a seat at Szechuan, appears on the *Basileon's* index of standard authors for 1911 under the pen-name 'Aleister Crowley'. The general attitude seems to have been rather more relaxed than the 'ferocious agnosticism' practised a few years earlier up the road at Trinity ('"the College" is really enraged with us,' wrote Leonard Woolf to Lytton Strachey in 1903. 'They think you are a witch and given up to the most abandoned and horrible practices and are quite ready to burn us alive at the slightest provocation.')[13] But even Woolf and Strachey had been advocates of truth and beauty, pursued with clandestine earnestness in what was still, for all their lurid talk—'The whole place seemed to me more depressed and more sodomitical than usual,' wrote Strachey on a visit to Cambridge in 1906—an optimistic and largely innocent society. 'We found ourselves living in the springtime of a conscious revolt against the social, political, religious, moral, intellectual and artistic institutions, beliefs and standards of our fathers and grandfathers . . .', wrote Woolf: 'The battle, which was against what for short one may call Victorianism, had not yet been won, and what was so exciting was our feeling that we ourselves were part of the revolution. . . .'

Noel's generation at King's shared this effervescence, combined with an agreeable sense of moral and material well-being. 'We prided ourselves on being less sophisticated than Oxford,' said William Haslam. Whisky, rumoured to be widely drunk by undergraduates at Oxford, was replaced at Cambridge by tea taken with walnut cake or anchovies on toast in each other's rooms at night, or at the discussion societies where:

> The young men seek truth rather than victory, they are willing to abjure an opinion when it is proved untenable, they do not try to score off one another, they do not feel diffidence too high a price to pay for integrity; and according to some observers that is why Cambridge has played, comparatively speaking, so small a part in the control of world affairs. Certainly these societies represent the very antithesis of the rotarian spirit. No one who has once felt their power will ever become a good mixer or a yes-man. Their influence, when it goes wrong, leads to self-consciousness and superciliousness; when it goes right, the mind is sharpened, the judgement is strengthened, and the heart becomes less selfish.[14]

Forster's glowing account well illustrates both what Ivy took from Cambridge and—perhaps rather more important—what she discarded. One might say that in a sense she spent a lifetime assessing the price of diffidence in her books among self-conscious, supercilious young men, whose flippancy is a measure of their own impotence in novel after novel against the forces of tyranny and oppression. But Forster's characteristically banal conclusion, on the mind, the judgement and the heart, reflects a lofty vagueness which he shared with Dickinson and with the Bloomsbury group in London (of which Dickinson was an honorary and Forster a founder member). This kind of spurious comfort, leading either to complacency or to an equally spurious nostalgic disillusionment, is something wholly alien to the world of I. Compton-Burnett where self-consciousness is an essential armour and superciliousness conceals a grasp of realities bleaker and more brutal than anything dreamt of in Forster's philosophy.

But these have as yet no place in the light fantastic vein of *Pastors and Masters*. The book is pervaded, as King's had been when Ivy knew it, by an incipient homosexuality which, according to a contemporary of Noel's, 'gave that golden glow. The college was suffused with it.' In the meadows beside the Cam the undergraduates 'ran quite naked in crowds over the green grass',[15] pairs of dons like Masson and Bumpus in *Pastors and Masters*—who 'had meant romance for each other in youth'—were common, and marriage (though permitted since the 1880s, and even indulged in by some few hardy Fellows) was beyond the pale. Scant sympathy was reserved for married dons like the one who, complaining to O.B. of his wife's coldness, said he might as well be living with a deal board: '"Take care," [O.B. replied], "or you'll find that you'll soon be living with someone a deal bawdier."' The general view is nicely represented by another mot of O.B.'s when someone consulted him as to whether or not the Venus in Botticelli's painting was out of drawing: '"It's no good asking me, my dear fellow," he answered blandly. "I've never seen a naked woman."' Women at King's were not so much disliked as simply disregarded, an attitude by no means unfamiliar to Emily Herrick in *Pastors and Masters* who, when her brother suggests that married women should be seen and not heard, cordially proposes that single women be exposed at birth ('"How would it be known at birth which of us were going to be single?" asked Delia. "That is really clever of you," said Emily. "Though people exposed at birth would be single, wouldn't they?"').

One can't help supposing that, however little Dickinson may otherwise have made of the novels of I. Compton-Burnett, he must surely have approved an outlook in Emily which coincided so exactly with his own. 'What I do mind rather in his [Dickinson's] quite unconsciously donnish attitude to women,' wrote one who did not share the spirit of affectionate indulgence extended by Emily to her brother and his friends. 'He never forgets that one is a woman, a woman who will presently leave the room, and whose remarks in the meantime must be listened to with pleasure if amusing, with civility if they are not.'[16] It might be a description of Nicholas Herrick's behaviour to his sister, who treats him in return with a tolerance which perfectly appreciates the nervous depredations brought about, on a delicate masculine sensibility, by feminine penetration. Quite apart from its first tentative inklings of formal innovation, *Pastors and Masters* is already an assured and humorous compendium of attitudes which must have given Ivy much quiet pleasure in the years when, like Emily Herrick, she too had sat discreetly listening to the conversation of her brother and his friends. The dampening effects of marriage are explained by Emily to her friend Theresa, who had broached the possibility of a proposal from William Masson:

'But he wants to marry you, doesn't he?'
'As much as he can want to marry anyone. Anyone who is a woman. And that is not very much.'
'Oh dear! These dons and people!' said Theresa.[17]

Pastors and Masters is the only one of the novels of I. Compton-Burnett which takes place wholly within a contemporary setting. For all its echoes of pre-war Cambridge, it was written and set after the first war, and published when its author was forty (which perhaps explains why all its main characters are well advanced into middle or old age). It contains therefore no hint either of undergraduate immaturity or of the sober optimism which prevailed in the Cambridge history circles Noel had frequented. Both dons and pupils held an encouraging belief in history as an active, beneficial, educative and pacific force. When this creed was contradicted by the outbreak of war, the effect on Dickinson was one of mortal shock—'The shock broke something in him which was never mended, and when at the close of his life he again functioned he had evolved a new apparatus, not repaired the old'.[18] Ivy, who had sustained a greater emotional loss and was to confront its implications throughout her later work, had perforce to abandon the illusion, to which Dickinson still clung, that passion might be prevailed upon by reason, or that the lessons of history might one day be learnt.

The effect of relinquishing so comforting a faith cannot have been made easier by the fact that her brother had himself subscribed to it. 'Noel believed in history, as people did in those days,' said Philip Noel-Baker. He and Noel had both belonged to a group which shared what their friend and fellow historian, Charles Webster, described as a 'sense of social duty higher than that of any of its predecessors and a greater belief that remedies could be found for the evils of the time'.[19] It was this sense of social duty—as sharply defined to Noel as family obligations were to Ivy—which lay behind the Fabian programme of the Carbonari, Rupert Brooke's socialist enthusiasms and O.B.'s tireless efforts to educate and entertain the working classes. It produced among young men at King's the strong and satisfactory feeling voiced

by Nicholas Herrick, that each was required to do 'my little bit for my
generation'; and they knew that this bit might be accomplished as
much through the pursuit of history as through the holidays for
working-class boys arranged on the King's barge at Rye, or the literary
ambitions which preoccupied Brooke and appealed increasingly to
Noel.

Webster's own monumental work on Castlereagh and European
diplomacy had been undertaken at this time 'as a small contribution to
preserve the world's peace' (though, as he afterwards ruefully remarked,
'I had underrated both the pace at which history would be made and
the pace at which history could be written'). Webster, who had come
up as a scholar in 1904 and was elected a Fellow of King's in 1910, three
years before Noel, was one of the first among the coming young men
at Cambridge to realize, at a time of considerable excitement on all
historical fronts, that nineteenth-century foreign policy might be over-
hauled and virtually re-written in the light of close study of the records.
He himself set to work on Castlereagh at much the same time as his
friend, Harold Temperley, on Canning, and the two books, published
almost simultaneously some fifteen years later, subsequently became the
standard works on their respective subjects. Noel, who in the spring of
1911 had been 'vaguely on the look out for something to make a thesis
about' and applying to O.B. for suggestions as to 'something fairly
modern, and if possible with human interest', eventually picked
Palmerston, presumably in hopes of doing as much for him as his
colleagues at King's for Castlereagh and Canning.

Webster in the years immediately before the war systematically
combed the archives in London, Vienna, Paris, Berlin, Hanover,
Warsaw, Cracow and St Petersburg. Noel, working meanwhile at
Hove or on Foreign Office papers in London, corresponded regularly
with Webster, reporting progress, thanking him for 'various tips',
envying his trips abroad, noting that the Record Office and Chancery
Lane were 'now quite desolate' in Webster's absence, even picturing
him in verse—'In the city gay of Wien / There's a fellow to be seen /
Long grey coat and Guy Fawkes hat /You'd wonder what they're staring at'*—and proposing in March 1912 to join Webster in Paris where
he meant to examine the archives and learn French: 'thus shall enjoy at

* 21 January 1912. Professor Bindoff describes Webster's appearance nearly half a
century later: 'his disdain for clothes was ducal, and in the decrepitude of his black
hats he had no rival but Tawney'. ('Charles Kingsley Webster 1886–1961', PBA,
vol. XLVIII.)

one and the same time the nimble flippancy of the Gallic intellect and the wholesome race of your English wit'. (31 March 1912) But, though he had applied for permission from M. Poincaré to consult the *Archive Nationale*, the Paris trip never materialized and Noel, already 'pretty despondent about the chase', grew steadily more bored with routine work ('Anything to go down must be *documenté* to the marrow,' he had written disconsolately to O.B. in June 1911) and more displeased with Palmerston. 'I think of him meanly enough, and I am inclined to quarrel with my lot of having to hoe with such a fellow for a twelve month,' he complained early in 1912 to O.B. He was also somewhat apprehensive when the popular candidate, Rupert Brooke, was passed over that spring in the Fellowship elections, which meant that Noel himself would have to compete with Brooke the following year: 'Still everything is in the lap of the Gods; I fancy—to adapt Fielding's saying, that the intrigues of the fellowship electors would not disgrace the conclave of Cardinals.' (24 March 1912)

In the event he got his Fellowship, tying thirteen votes on 8 March 1913, with Brooke. But notwithstanding his exuberant relief, his telegram to Jack Beresford—'Rupert and I elected to fellowships. Jim'—and his grateful message to O.B. ('I must write to you at once because to you I owe everything I have had at Cambridge'), Noel seems to have regarded a return to King's with small enthusiasm. His thesis dissertation, on 'Palmerston and Europe 1847–1850',[20] remained unfinished and, in his own view at least, unsatisfactory. 'There was a most distinctive, broad, kind, penetrating humanity of judgement in the finished parts, I well remember, which was the ripening fruit of his earlier idiosyncrasy,' wrote Clapham in Noel's obituary. But the whole, though eminently worthy, remained a far from brilliant piece of work. Noel's aim, as he explained with justified and engaging modesty, had been to institute a strictly limited comparison between received accounts of his brief chosen period and the records preserved in Foreign Office papers: an undertaking which, if pursued on Webster's massive scale, would have carried its author to all the major capitals of Europe and been measured in decades. Noel had spent instead one year at the London Record Office, and emerged with a study which he hoped might 'at least be held to possess a certain negative value'. Its findings were unexciting, its style (save for the Gibbonian opening paragraphs) pedestrian, its bibliography slipshod and its final chapters incomplete or given up for want of time. It reflects in short his own dissatisfaction in a letter dated 26 June 1912, to O.B.: 'I am writing my thesis—the business though is a bad one in so far as I have made no *discoveries*. Everything is known already. I am not going to degrade myself into a retailer of new *and unimportant* details. I am ready to take an independent view of Palmerston but I can't do any more for him.'

The college made Noel steward in the summer of 1914 'in order if possible to secure him for Cambridge', but by this time the chances of his staying had grown slim. 'I have left scholarship for the PRESENT and am sowing—prodigal the spirit but arduous the labour—certain literary wild oats,' he had written the previous December.[21] Exactly a year later, when he had already joined the army and was waiting to be posted, he wrote from Aldershot to Webster: 'You know Macaulay is stewarding for me? Very much confidentially, I doubt if I shall ever go back to Cambridge. I think I shall turn wholly to literature; and not *quite* impossibly get married or go round the world. All this of course when I get my discharge.' Even as he wrote it, the thesis seems to have represented the same kind of false start for Noel as *Dolores* a few years earlier for Ivy. What he would have done eventually— whether he would have turned in the same direction as his sister—whether indeed, if he had lived, she would have developed as she did—are unanswerable questions. 'I long to do something at literature but it will be a life of real hardship,' he wrote to Jack Beresford in March 1915, during his last spring in England. What is certain is that both Noel and his sister had thankfully abandoned the roads along which both had toiled with such forced and uncongenial effort in the im- mediate past—a break which seems to have come to Ivy as decisively, and for much the same reasons, as a similiar realization to Emily Herrick in *Pastors and Masters*: 'So I know for certain that I could never marry William. For I find that I only like wickedness and penetration.'[22]

'Well, a house must have a head'

'I THINK IVY observed everything that happened in everybody's life and mind all the time she lived at Hove,' said her sister Juliet. The household at Hove broke up in the autumn of 1915; and it was not only Noel's friends, Arthur Waley and Elliott Felkin, who afterwards claimed that Ivy's family at home had sounded exactly like the people in her books. Harriet Cohen, at the start of her career as a pianist just after the first war, drew the same conclusion from talking to Ivy's younger sisters: 'Many were the tales they told of their extraordinary doctor father and the fantastic conversations that took place in that remarkable household. When I began reading Ivy Compton-Burnett's books, I felt I recognized if not the people, the conversations.'23

Mrs Compton Burnett died on 5 October 1911. The rule of seclusion imposed for years before that on her children ('We just had to live at home really, concealing the family tragedy') had bred a nervous resilience which must often have come close to exhaustion. She had been mortally ill for a year, tormented by deafness, by acute rheumatism and by sleepless nights which increased her weakness and pain. Only Minnie was permitted to dress the wounds left on her wrists by radium treatment, but there was little Minnie could do to lessen the strain of constant attendance on the two elder children, and on Ivy alone in Noel's terms at Cambridge. Even towards the end, when she had to be nursed night and day, their mother refused to take to her bed. In the last week of her life she would be carried downstairs in a chair to take the evening air on the porch. Approaching death had done nothing to slacken the force of a will bent, since her husband's death, on making time stand still. She had been proud of installing a telephone at The Drive but it was one of very few concessions made to the encroaching years after 1901. Her younger children could barely remember an existence not governed by a morbid emotional intensity at home and an almost complete withdrawal from life outside it. 'She was not progressive. She couldn't have got used to a changing world. I remember on the day she died Noel said: "Really we must regard it as a great mercy that she hasn't lived to be old. Because she never could have faced it." And she couldn't,' said Vera Compton-Burnett.

Their mother's death left the family listless, shocked and debilitated —'for the first year one was almost stunned'—much like the young Staces when Sophia died in *Brothers and Sisters*: 'The wave of emptiness and release that came over them, held them silent. It seemed that a weight had fallen, as a weight had lifted.'[24] The Compton-Burnetts had spent so long in confinement that it is scarcely surprising if it took another year for them to realize that the door was no longer locked, and three more before they too escaped, like the Staces, to London. The impulse, when it came, did not come from Ivy whose instincts seem to have lain, with Samuel Butler's, against 'change of any sort . . . as tending to unsettle men's minds'. She had discouraged all attempts to soften the harsh daily routine at Hove ('It went on of itself, through a kind of inertia,' said her sister Vera) and she resolutely opposed a concerted attempt to abolish it altogether. A few years later, when her tactics of resistance and delay had finally been worsted, she marked with a thick pencil line in the margin a characteristic note of Butler's against disrupting the established order ('. . . there is nothing so absolutely moral as stagnation') on grounds of strict moral economy: 'For there will be an element of habitual and legitimate custom even in the most unhabitual and detestable things that can be done at all.'[25]

The first few months of mourning were filled with family business, hampered by colds and lingering quinzies, and further complicated by the proofs of O.B.'s *General History of the World* which arrived from the printers thick and fast by nearly every post that winter. Noel had agreed to correct the proofs, issuing due warning ('I must tell you . . . that I am a bad speller, know little about punctuation, and nothing about names or facts' 11 July 1911) and, when neither his mother's death with the mass of work it entailed on top of his own researches nor his protracted influenza stemmed the flow, passing them to his younger sisters. By 30 December Ivy was writing politely but firmly to O.B. offering to return his proofs unread. Life at home meanwhile improved slowly and slightly. Permission was occasionally given to miss lunch, a thing unthinkable in their mother's lifetime, and friends could be invited to the house as they never had been before ('It wasn't much of a home to bring them to. It was so melancholy, and she was so nervous.'). The whole family began to swim for the first time in June

—'a somewhat refrigerating experience,' wrote Noel to O.B. 'My progress in the art is very slow. You, who like Charlemagne and other
historical personages, have always been a great waterman, would laugh
at my preposterous marine evolutions.' The younger girls had bicycles
and Ivy and Noel took to riding on hired horses over the downs behind
the town. Nearly half a century later, a friend happened to say that she,
too, had once ridden with her brother on the beach:

'Oh, the horses like that,' said Ivy.
'Even walking was lovely,' she said, with a sort of mild ecstasy.
'Oh yes, bliss,' I agreed. 'Ambling along on an old horse, hedge-
high. . . .'
For a few minutes we were away with our memories, with our
brothers, and our horses.[26]

But, though Noel spent much of that spring and summer at home, he
was also regularly away working at the Record Office in London and
it had never entered anybody's head that he should settle at Hove, any
more than it had as yet occurred to his sisters that they might settle
elsewhere. Vera, who was just twenty when her mother died, and Judy,
who was two years younger, had been for some time travelling up to
take music lessons at the Matthay school in London; Topsy and
Primrose, who were fifteen and twelve and who 'lived for each other'
like the two older pairs, studied under music teachers in Hove. The
gap in age and interest between these four and their eldest sister had
always been wide, and now became unbridgeable. 'Ivy had inherited
head of the household,' said her sister, 'and she was lost.'
'"Well, a house must have a head,"' says Miranda Hume in *Mother
and Son*, listening in silence to the reply when her twelve-year-old nephew
asks what it would be like without one: '"Someone would become
the head," said his sister. "It is a natural law."'[27] Under the terms of
their mother's will (a document which ignored the existence of her
stepchildren as its author had never wholly succeeded in doing while
she lived), Ivy and Noel became with Martyn Mowll trustees and
guardians to their four sisters. Ivy at twenty-seven had already come
into her money, Noel had a handsome allowance and would shortly
take his full share, the others would neither inherit their portions nor be
free of their guardians until they were twenty-four (which meant
another twelve years for the youngest). They were to remain with
Minnie as Lady Housekeeper in the house at Hove, where provision had

been made for their upkeep and maintenance under an unbroken
hierarchy—a point on which their mother, foreseeing perhaps a
possible source of contention, had left explicit instructions: 'and my
said daughter Ivy shall so long as she remains unmarried be entitled to
share the home . . . of my other children and take the head of it if she
so wishes.' Ivy saw the injunction as her plain duty, and promptly
set about eliciting from Mr Mowll the business secrets of a lifetime,
for her father's estate had been joined to her mother's in the trust fund
set up for their children and both largely consisted of property: farms,
villas, building plots, whole streets full of working men's houses, each
of which involved separate dealings with tenants. In September 1912,
Ivy as landlord granted permission to the tenant of 40 Sackville Gardens,
Hove, to attach a stop to her pier; a bulky envelope, dated April 1915,
is endorsed 'Argument with Post Office in respect of telegraph pole
and stay on land at Clacton'; and in the same year she paid the premium
on eighty-nine fire insurance policies. Noel, whose interest in adminis-
trative detail was at best perfunctory, must have been glad to resign as
much as he could to his sister. Another of her pencilled marks in the
margin of Butler's *Note-Books* suggests that, before 1911, monetary
transactions had been as darkly regarded among the Compton Burnetts
as they were in most Victorian households: 'Next to sexual matters
there are none upon which there is such complete reserve between
parent and child as on those connected with money. The father keeps
his affairs as closely as he can to himself and is most jealous of letting
his children into a knowledge of how he manages money. . . .'[28]

Managing money became henceforward one of Ivy's strong points,
and as head of the family she continued twice yearly to receive Martyn
Mowll or Worsfold's son Rutley (or, when Rutley Mowll died,
Worsfold's grandson) until the trust fund was wound up fifty years
later. She had also taken over the housekeeping—sorting linen, ordering
meals, engaging, supervising and dismissing maids—which remained
her province to the end of her life. The rest of the family found themselves set apart from their two elders, who had moved from one side
to the other of a traditional barrier which even Noel could not dismantle. The comical Gibbonian airs once assumed to conceal his
crippling sense of weakness at home and shyness abroad had taken on
an authority which, however much he might dislike it, was no longer
simply a matter of make-believe and self-mockery. He was caught as
much as Ivy in a system which proved stronger than either and
remained—in spite of occasional forays into the twentieth century

when friends from King's came visiting—frozen in all outward respects as it always had been since the year of Queen Victoria's death. To the schoolroom party it seemed as though nothing had changed, except that Ivy had stepped into their mother's place. From now on she kept their accounts, inspected their property, oversaw their investments, arranged their education, interviewed their teachers, dealt out their allowances and generally assumed power over her sisters. One thinks of France Ponsonby's forecast in *Daughters and Sons*, when her brother says that it would be good to have power: '"No, we should use it," said France. "No one can stand it. None of us could: think of the stock we come of."'[29]

The overcast atmosphere which had briefly lifted settled again on the house at Hove. Music had meant freedom since earliest childhood for Ivy's sisters, and their one means of escape from a 'dark and loveless home'. Vera, who studied under Tobias Matthay and later under his pupil Myra Hess, had passed her L.R.A.M. ('She is very young to have four letters to her name,' wrote Ivy to their cousin Katie, '. . . and we are quite proud of her') a few months before her mother died, and Juliet a year or so later. Topsy, the most gifted of the four and the most like her father, promised already to follow her elder sisters. All four were accustomed to retire to the nursery, now renamed the music room and furnished with Botticelli prints handed down from Noel at Cambridge, where they shared a private world as remote as possible from their background and upbringing. Their only close friends in Hove were the children of Topsy's Wagnerian violin master, Siegfried, Isolde, Ludwig and Elfrieda Menges (two of whom later became professional musicians), who with their parents made a string orchestra to which Vera and Juliet contributed piano parts. The Menges opened a window on all that was most frowned upon in smug, respectable, philistine Hove; and the young Compton-Burnetts, who in their mother's lifetime had been forbidden to invite the Menges to their parties, 'half lived' at their house after her death. In the last summers before the war Vera would also walk over the downs to meet Myra Hess, in lodgings at Rottingdean, for a bathe and a practice. Ivy, whose respect for outward convention equalled her mother's, viewed these proceedings with misgiving: 'You see, music to her was a pure debit,' said her sister Juliet. 'You'd have thought she'd allow it was a recognized art—but she wouldn't, and she plainly said so.'

The practising which had distressed her for years steadily increased in volume until Ivy could stand it no longer. Piano playing was

forbidden under her roof. The strings were still permitted to practise
upstairs but the Bechstein grand—a gift to Vera from her mother,
chosen by Mr Matthay when she passed her L.R.A.M.—was carried
out of the house and round the corner to a hired music room in Church
Road. Vera and Judy spent two hours there each morning, and were
perhaps glad of the daily respite from their sister: 'We didn't develop as
she would have chosen; she became very critical.' The three middle
girls were by this time past saving, but it must still have seemed possible
to retrieve the fourth from the hands of foreigners, artists, musicians,
all equally undesirable influences in Ivy's eyes. After a bitter battle
between Ivy and Topsy, which the elder and stronger inevitably won,
their youngest sister was dispatched against her will to Cheltenham
Ladies' College ('and it's *her* money that's being spent,' said Topsy
furiously). Primrose had been 'Topsy's child' and devoted follower
from birth, looking to her sister as Guy had once looked to Ivy for the
protection and intimacy which were not to be had elsewhere; their
mutual despair at parting led to a repetition of the miserable scenes
enacted fourteen years before, when their elders had also been parted
under duress. But Ivy remained as indifferent to tears and protests as
her mother had been before her. After two terms at Cheltenham, just
long enough for her to get over her first wretchedness and begin to
accept her new life, the child was brought back—again without reference
to her own wishes or Topsy's—and put to school at Addiscombe
College. The episode was typical of Ivy's arbitrary dealings: 'There
always *had* been a tyrant—she inherited the position, and she used it,'
said her sister Vera.

Ivy, unlike her mother, never made scenes and was rarely seen to be
angry. Her rule was quiet, orderly and cruel. Power seems to have
been to her less an emotional gratification than a tactical advantage
which she could no more help exploiting than her sisters could help but
concede. 'Those were years in which Ivy wasn't master of herself—
something was mastering her, and it wasn't the best part of her.' Her
discomfited sisters found themselves put down and kept under, their
proposals overruled and their attempts at retaliation hopelessly flattened
by Ivy's sharp tongue. Asperity remained her habit to the end of her
life, and so did a nerve-racking fondness for speaking aside, under her
breath, like the characters who 'barely utter' in her books. Several of
her friends in later life had much the same experience as Cicely Greig,
who recalled that 'Ivy once "barely uttered" at me'. The two were
sitting over dates and nuts at the end of lunch when Miss Greig, having

ignored a suggestion that she use her finger bowl, heard her hostess say 'Wake up!' 'This was "barely uttered", a sort of sighing whisper which I pretended not to hear. I had only delayed movement by about half-a-minute, but the half-minute had been too long for Ivy.'[30]

Ivy's sisters had learnt submission from years of worse treatment than this, which came at first as a relief from more open methods of oppression. Vera had been nine when her father died, Primrose too small to remember him: 'Ivy had had a hard life, but what had ours been? *She* was away all those years.' But Ivy's four years at Holloway had given her perhaps grounds for a sharper grudge than her sisters, who had after all never known any alternative to life at Hove. If they had learnt to accept constant rebuffs, she had learnt a stoicism which went too deep for her ever again to attempt anything other than passive acquiescence. Their mother's death had come too late for Ivy to be able, probably even to want, to alter the system under which she had suffered herself. When her sisters foregathered in the music room, she sat alone downstairs in her father's study. She disapproved of their friends, mistrusted their ambitions, seldom joined in their activities, often scarcely saw them except at meals for weeks on end. When the others went bathing and practised fancy strokes or dived off the pier, Ivy would swim out at a steady breast stroke so far that her family 'used to wonder sometimes if she would ever come back'. Her sisters thought that she resented, and would have liked to prevent, their enjoying opportunities she had never so much as contemplated for herself. 'She had had just about as miserable and dull an existence as any young woman ever had—a neurotic mother, we never knew from one minute to the next what was going to happen—Ivy had to endure that,' said her sister Vera. 'She was twenty-seven. The iron entered into her soul. Left at home with four sisters younger—much younger—than herself. Schoolgirls. Noel was her *only* hope.'

But, as the future closed round Ivy, it was opening on all sides for Noel. By the autumn of 1911, Jack Beresford, Arthur Waley, Geoffrey Toulmin, Eric Forbes-Adam, 'almost all my contemporaries', as Noel wrote enviously to O.B. from Cambridge, had already 'gone into the great world', whither he himself meant shortly to follow them. He retained his rooms at King's as a Fellow from the spring of 1913 but he seems to have spent much of that year and the following summer in London, sowing his 'literary wild oats', visiting Jack in digs at Kew or calling for him at his office in Whitehall—'Last night I went out to examine our wire,' Noel wrote from the trenches in France in August

1915, 'and lying in the open under the stars I thought of you and of our foolish talks in St James last year.' Jack, who afterwards published much pleasantly pastoral poetry besides his editions of Parson Wood-forde and others, was already preparing his first slim volume of verse,* and it seems likely that Noel was too. Both read, wrote and lived poetry as Rupert Brooke had advised. Jack's wife Janet, to whom he became engaged in 1914, was not a little disconcerted when her fiancé would have no truck with boxes of chocolates but gave her a volume of Wordsworth instead. Janet Beresford, later a close friend of Ivy's, well remembered going to literary parties to meet H. G. Wells where anyone as nicely brought up as she and Ivy had been was liable to end up in a corner talking to the governess. Jack's cousin, J. D. Beresford, was very much the coming man in these circles on the strength of his first novel, *Jacob Stahl*, a somewhat earnest but fearlessly frank account of its hero's social, sexual and sentimental education which rivalled Wells as essential reading for the younger generation before the first war. *Jacob Stahl* had been published in the same year as *Dolores*, and the success of the one was as marked as the oblivion which had by now overtaken the other.†

Not that Ivy in these years was by any means neglected. She and Noel had spent a holiday with Toulmin and his sister in Austria (where Ivy, greatly taken with the Tyrolean lakes, passed her evenings in the hotel while her brother hobnobbed with German students), and Noel was still much at home, frequently bringing one or other of his friends to regale his sisters with tales of the great world. But to the inmates of the unchanging household at Hove, Noel's accounts of amazing doings in London must have seemed as remote as the dens of vice and sinks of iniquity frequented by Robin Stace in *Brothers and Sisters*—dens and

---

* *Poems by Two Brothers* by Richard and John Beresford, Erskine Macdonald, 1915. Noel, who was already in France when the book came out, wrote to thank Jack for the poems: 'yours very familiar to me and bringing back very many walks and talks. I like them much and your brother's have a fresh beauty for me—these days they seem to cling about the cannon's mouth safe because so frail and light.' (18 October 1915.)

† 'Dear Madam, We beg to enclose herewith statement showing the position of your novel *Dolores* as at the end of 1913. There is, as you will see, no demand for the work, and as our warehouse space is of value we think we should try to dispose of the stock on hand as a remainder which would probably mean not more than 3d or 4d per copy bound. If you wish any copies we would let you have them.

We would be glad to have your instructions regarding the matter. We are, Yours faithfully. . . .' Letter from Blackwood, 26 March 1914.

sinks which prove such a disappointment to his family when they finally
decide to join him in town:

'We find that Robin's London life has nothing to conceal.'
'Oh, and I have envied it so,' said Julian. 'I have wondered how it
was I could do nothing with mine.'[31]

For years Jack and Noel (known as Jim to the Beresfords as he generally
was to his sisters) had exchanged visits and, when Jack still travelled
down from London almost every weekend to Easton Grey in Wiltshire
where his father was rector, Noel often went with him and sometimes
brought Ivy. 'I have not ever seen a brother and sister so devoted—so
essential—to each other,' said Jack's sister Dorothy. They seemed
uncomfortably solemn to the Beresfords' companion, Miss Fox, who
as housekeeper and general helpmeet spent a good deal of time at the
rectory and who found the Compton-Burnetts a difficult pair: 'I
thought they took life very seriously'.

Perhaps their diffidence stood out among the Beresfords who were
all voluble talkers, explosive, impetuous and erratic in temper, accustomed to fascinate by a desperate combination of the family magnetism
with the family's startling good looks. The three girls—Dorothy,
Tertia and Mary who were much of an age with Noel's sisters Ivy,
Vera and Primrose—were individually dazzling, and together they
must have seemed overpowering. It was always afterwards said that
Jack had found husbands for all his sisters, and Noel on their walks
early began to pair off with—was perhaps already writing poems to—
Tertia, though they were not officially engaged till the beginning of
1915. Tertia was the third of the Rev. John Jervis Beresford's four
daughters (one had died as a child) and the most retiring, with more
than her share of the strain of melancholy and pessimism which ran
through the whole family and a romantic disposition not belied by
her white skin, green eyes and blue-black, raven's hair. 'A very beautiful, rather sultry, George-Eliotish character,' said one of her nieces long
afterwards. Noel's sisters, who thought Tertia fey and none too bright,
allowed that she led an intense inner life nourished, like all the Beresfords', on a passion for poetry. A painting of her by Margot Asquith's
sister, Lucy Graham Smith, is so like the description of Ruth Giffard in
More Women Than Men—' "I have hardly had my own news yet,"
said her daughter, in her husky, languid tones, turning to her mother her
dark, unusual face, with its absent, indifferent eyes and curved and

protruding lips'[32]—that one can only suppose Tertia sat for both portraits.

Ivy, who later shared a flat with both Tertia and Dorothy in turn, seems to have borrowed traits freely from each for characters in her books; and indeed all the Beresfords may be said to have left their mark on her work. They were the first family she knew well who belonged to that narrow pocket of the upper middle classes—'large gloomy moderately rich families in largish, though not immense, houses in the country, going as a matter of course to Oxford or Cambridge, interested in acquiring property or money, yet lacking almost all contact with an outer world, living in a state of almost hysterically inward-looking intensity' in Anthony Powell's definition[33]—which has nowhere been more minutely explored than in her next nineteen novels. The Beresfords boasted a pedigree going back to the Conquest[34] and a seat bearing their name in the Staffordshire dales; their mother was a Margaret Hollinsed descended, according to family legend, from the chronicler who provided Shakespeare with plots; Beresford sons had been sent since the sixteenth century to Cambridge, and afterwards put to the church or the learned professions. The rector's children had inherited intact their paramount sense of the family's importance but (the Beresford fortunes having passed to a collateral branch in the seventeenth century) they lived on their father's diminutive stipend making ends meet, like so many of the less prosperous families in the novels of I. Compton-Burnett, at the brink of financial disaster. Jack had been sent for tuition to a neighbouring clergyman and his sisters 'crazily educated' by their father at home. Mr Beresford was blind, a bard and, even by Compton-Burnett standards, a creditable autocrat. His daughters, like Milton's, had for years been obliged to take turns at reading to him in languages ancient and modern ('In the scene of misery which this mode of intellectual labour sets before our eyes,' wrote Dr Johnson of Milton's domestic arrangements, 'it is hard to determine whether the daughters or the father are most to be lamented')*

* *Lives of the Poets*, World's Classics, O.U.P., 1952, vol. 1, p.102. Mr Beresford's daughters were more fortunate than Milton's in that they had been taught at least the rudiments of Greek, Latin, French, German and Italian, but less so in the poems which resulted when their father wove what he called the Woof of Song. One may serve as an example:

'The Coming Woman' 16.1.95.

Time hath been a girl was blushing,
Hesitating, shamefaced, shy,

or at writing down the poems he recited. His oratory seems to have been as fierce as his will. Asquith, whose wife's sister was married to the squire of Easton Grey and who seldom gave his undivided attention to sermons, once confessed to Dorothy Beresford: 'I never read the collects when your father is preaching'.

Tart tongues and short tempers bred a high standard of wit at the rectory. The Beresfords lived in very nearly complete isolation, seeing no one save the few families in country houses round about, natural overlords in the village, revolving round an elderly tyrant at home— 'an ancient Roman, man most excellent,' wrote Noel of Jack's father, 'though poles apart from me as such a man must be'—and preserving a fair crop of dark secrets in their past. Mr Beresford had been blinded in infancy by a twin brother who poked out his eye with a pair of scissors; the brother, dying young, was afterwards expunged from the family tree. Mrs Beresford—'a racehorse put to do carthorse work' according to her daughter Dorothy—had found family life too much for her and retired for good to a nursing home in Somerset soon after Mary was born; though she lived for another fifteen years, her daughters never saw her again, her name was not mentioned and there was no picture of her in the rectory. Jack's elder brother Dick, a King's choir scholar and a captivating child who had failed to live up to his promise, was finally dispatched round about this time to South Africa (as secretary to Lord Gladstone through the Asquiths' kind offices) and never came back. The whole family was given to freaks of temperament pricked on by an imagination which furiously coloured even their most humdrum transactions. 'They were a potent family to marry into,' said Jack's wife Janet, whose sisters-in-law must have proved on occasion a trial and who, though not often daunted, stood in considerable awe of old Mr Beresford.

It is not hard to see why the family made a lasting impression on both Noel and his sister: 'It was all observation with her,' said Juliet Compton-Burnett, who thought Ivy in these years spent her time watching and noting. 'If you came into a room, she would look you up and down in an instant, from head to foot.' Noel, less aloof than his sister and far

---

Time hath been: now she is crushing,
Or she will be by and by.
For she learns to play at Hockey
And at Hare and Hounds and Fives
Till, with hands and heart right rocky,
She will make the worst of wives.

more at home with the Beresfords, seems to have found in their company something of his father's boisterous spirits: Dorothy remembered him rising up with cries of 'My turn!' at one of Mrs Graham Smith's dinner parties, flagging his napkin in an attempt to shout down the assembled Tennants, Asquiths and Beresfords. It was not only their forcefulness which had impressed Noel since his first meeting with Jack at King's ('having my first friendly talk at Cambridge, and infinitely admiring your mastery of a very formidable landlady'). He liked also their extravagant vagueness, their indifference to shabby clothes and short commons, their habit of declaiming Matthew Arnold aloud at the hills or enthusing over 'the flowers of the field' with a fine rhapsodical buoyancy which matched his own. Ivy, though resilient enough if need be, took a firm line with people or facts she deplored: 'I daresay you are depressed. We most of us are that,' she wrote to her cousin Katie on 22 September 1914. 'Indeed, if long faces were of any help to anyone, it would be refreshing to reflect how much good we should some of us be doing. However, efforts in that line being no good, the other is the one to be taken. I suppose though economizing, & subscribing, & meeting folks with folks at the war, are things not to be welcomed by the most stoic.' Noel was as crisp as his sister but better disposed towards circumstances which might well have depressed him. 'There is a strong and very unexpected beauty about a camp,' he wrote in the spring of 1915, waiting for his posting to France under canvas in pouring rain on Salisbury Plain. 'There's a freedom about this swaying windy wet dwelling that more than makes up for not feeling comfortable . . . I would rather live in a tent than in a house for ever. But to that Tertia though she agrees to much, certainly will not agree so dont be alarmed. Its rather cold though. . . .'

'No suitable material to work on'

ON THE OUTBREAK of war the Compton-Burnetts, who had finally decided to move as a family to London, had just taken a house in South Kensington. Noel had fixed on the first weekend in August to go down from Cambridge 'to pay a few visits, and then home' where his sisters were already preparing to shake the dust of No. 20 The Drive from their feet for good. Cambridge was no less surprised by the war than Hove, or for that matter the British Cabinet, which had spent the better part of July urgently discussing the Irish question. On 28 July, exactly a week before war was declared, Noel wrote to Elliott Felkin from King's complaining how bored he was by 'dull dull English academicians' and proposing to spend the summer abroad. In the event, he spent the summer at an army training camp in Cambridge with Jack Beresford. Like most of his friends, Noel supported the anti-war movement hastily mounted by Dickinson and others, but by the end of August Cambridge had succumbed with the rest of the country to a violent fever of jingoism. Military hospitals were set up in college buildings, the O.T.C. installed at Pembroke and Corpus, boy scouts bearing messages buzzed about all over the town, railway bridges were guarded, telephone lines patrolled and troops so thickly billeted that, according to the *Cambridge Review*, 'you could hardly step in the streets without bumping into khaki'. Of the Fellows of King's, Maynard Keynes had been summoned posthaste by the Treasury to London, Rupert Brooke was negotiating with Churchill for a commission and Noel had been told by the local commanding officer 'that he thought I had very little chance of a commission. There are 50 very likely people in King's, all of whom have been refused. The doctor reported me as fit ... but my chest measurement is absurdly small—not good enough for a private. Meanwhile I shall join the O.T.C. There is to be 3 hours drill daily.' (8 October 1914)

Noel, always pacific, was also like his sister a realist. He had voted

No to the motion, 'Is war preventable?', at his first meeting of the
Political Society in 1907 and, in a debate on conscription at the Union
the following spring, 'Mr Compton-Burnett rose with loosened joints.
If he had to serve in the army, he would be a demoralizing influence
since he would be the last to advance and the first to retire. It was
useless to force those to fight whose natures were against fighting.
Mr Compton-Burnett has a neat, gentle way of putting things.'[35]
Two years later Noel was describing local German manœuvres ('All
looked very efficient and, to English eyes, regrettably formidable') to
Jack from Göttingen. 'Personally I believe the war will be over in less
than a year,' he wrote in October 1914; and in November he read a
paper for the last time to the Political Society on 'Peace'. 'It was, as I
remember it, a moving defence of the love of peace, because peace is
life,' wrote John Clapham after Noel's death. 'He had already decided
to take his risks in war.' The reasons underlying this decision are
sufficiently clear in a letter written that autumn from King's:

Dear Charles Webster,
    Your dissertation on college wine politics showed the grasp of
the master. Many thanks. I won't trouble to get the Wine Committee
to meet this term.
    You are occupied indeed, and that is to the good if it prevents
thought. Nothing comes of thinking of the good friends who have
dropped out of our lives, whose death has done so little for the world
they would have served so valuably with their lives. Nothing comes
of thinking of it but one must think.
    You want college news. Well of course there isn't any. We have
no history but all the same we aren't happy. Various young men
come up for a few days liberated from the front or from training
camps. Stackard was in Hall tonight. How horrible *him* to be
mentioned in dispatches and poor Freddie to be dead and done for,
how horribly ironical and typical of war! . . .
    I get more and more anti-war. I realise more completely how
impossible it is to reconcile the intellectual attitude to the war with
the popular politician's attitude. Ramsay Macdonald and the I.L.P.
are my only hope in the home situation. The situation at the front
seems uncertain enough.
                                            N. C-B.*

* Freddie was F. M. Hardman who had come up to King's in 1909 and was killed in
action on 27 October 1914; Dickinson shared Noel's contempt for all politicians 'with
the exception of the I.L.P.' (*Goldsworthy Lowes Dickinson* by E. M. Forster, p.165).

Noel's attitude to the prevention of thought, and even his turns of phrase, bear an almost uncanny family likeness to the terse stoicism with which his sister in later years marked and mourned the loss of friends. He seems to have arrived early at that mood of uneasy resignation described by Robert Graves and others who, with few illusions as to their own heroism or the conduct and aims of the war, were driven to return again and again to the front by a sense of personal loyalty to their friends and their men which came to seem infinitely more real than the cloud of fraudulent emotion and dishonest propaganda covering political and military incompetence at home.

It was considered monstrous by his friends at Cambridge that Noel of all people, so dreamy, impractical and sweet-tempered, partly disabled since childhood and still in indifferent health, should be swept up and tossed away as a second lieutenant in the trenches. 'We thought it an outrage,' said Philip Noel-Baker. Elliott Felkin, who had written bluntly to ask why anyone should of his own accord abandon civilian life, received an answer which makes it clear that Noel stuck as firmly as his sister to their father's view of duty: 'The explanation of my soldiering is simple enough. Having searched my conscience very severely I decided that my main reason in not "rolling up" was personal aversion to doing so. That point having been reached for a man of my character my dear Sir the resulting action necessarily followed. Don't think tho' I'm a jingo. My view of the war remains. *Only* desiring as I do the defeat of Germany, or at least desiring Germany not to win, I couldn't stand out.'

This letter was one of the very few mementoes of her brother which Ivy afterwards kept to the end of her life. The two surviving letters from him to her, both written just before the battle of the Somme, suggest that the pair were so close, and so wholly at one in their view of the war, that they probably felt little need to discuss it. Noel's reasoning must have seemed self-evident to Ivy, whose whole adult existence had been a matter of submitting personal inclination to the severest search of conscience. It seems likely that she accepted from the start her brother's attitude to the wastefulness and futility of what seemed to so many of their contemporaries 'a war of defence and liberation'. It is almost impossible to over-estimate now the patriotic exaltation which then swept the country, a communal hysteria so powerful that, as casualties mounted to a point which still beggars belief, families at home took to placing cards in their windows proudly detailing their losses at the front. White feathers were distributed, and dachshunds stoned in the streets for German dogs. In October the Schlosses changed their name to Waley because, as Arthur told Raisley Moorsom, he was tired of being arrested six times in one month as an enemy spy. 'Thus do the mob and the idols of the market place reign in triumph,' wrote Noel to Elliott when he heard the news, 'all aesthetes and men of independent intellect palpably most prone before them.' (15 October 1914)

Noel embarked on a military career without rancour and without repining, though with a passionate sense of all he had already lost that autumn and of all that he still stood to lose. His sober estimate of the situation meant that he faced sooner than many of his more idealistic contemporaries the need to reconcile himself to his own extinction in a cause for which he felt no enthusiasm—' "for neither in law nor war is it right for any man to take every means of escaping death". Thus Socrates and also one's own inner mind,' he wrote to Jack the night before a raid which he did not expect to survive in October 1915. Two months in the front line had taught him to confront death with an equanimity which, though more solidly based, was not essentially different from the feeling with which he had first joined the army almost exactly a year before. People who entered the war without illusions in 1914 were at least protected from the bewildered disillusionment of those in whom an unsuspecting patriotism only gradually gave way to a proportionately bitter sense of betrayal till, as the war dragged on, 'its continuance seemed merely a sacrifice of the idealistic younger generation to the stupidity and self-protective alarm of the elder'.[36]

The practical uselessness of this kind of theoretic knowledge, and the impotence of a younger generation ruthlessly suppressed by its egotistical elders, are constant themes in the later novels of I. Compton-Burnett; and so is the vanity of struggling to achieve the independence which had eluded both her brother and herself. Otherwise there is little direct evidence, beyond one brisk, reproving letter to her cousin, as to how Ivy felt that autumn. The few people who discussed the '14-'18 war with her long afterwards were all considerably younger, and all agreed that it was a subject she still found almost intolerably painful. Nearly thirty years later, casual visitors in the second war were warned by her closest friend that the fighting must not be mentioned in Ivy's presence. The people who knew her well enough to talk about the first war at the time are nearly all dead now. Perhaps one of them was Lowes Dickinson, who certainly had Noel in mind after the war when Ivy knew him, though it is quite probable that neither overcame their mutual shyness sufficiently to say much about her brother. Dickinson had been appalled by a catastrophe which destroyed his whole basis for living: 'The outbreak of the Great War was an almost paralysing shock to Dickinson,' wrote Roger Fry. 'He had as it were staked everything on his belief that human beings were fundamentally reasonable, that the appeal to reason must find a response. . . .'[37] He had discussed matters with Noel at King's in the autumn of 1914; and, though Dickinson shrank all his life from giving advice, he did at least confirm Noel's feeling that there was nothing to be done but fight.* Afterwards he seems to have felt Noel's death as an extra burden added to his general crushing discouragement: 'Goldie felt a mild sense of— not exactly remorse—a mild sense that perhaps he should have told him something different,' said Raisley Moorsom who knew Dickinson well between the wars. 'I remember so often his saying that, more than once to me, how he felt that about Noel and how sad he was.'

Whatever Noel's private struggle may have cost him, there is small trace of it in his wartime letters which suggest rather a cheerful confidence in his own adaptability. In spite of the forebodings of his friends he inclined to like the army, living 'in very passable comfort . . . at the nation's expense', growing 'more stupid and lazy with every day that passes' and agreeably impressed by the unfamiliar charms of white tents against the sky or, later, by 'old gold dawns' in the trenches. Ivy, as philosophical as her brother, watched his pleasure with indulgence and amusement: 'Jimmie was here with Jack Beresford for some days last week,' she wrote to Katie from Hove, where the pair had spent their leave from the Cambridge training camp on Royston Heath. 'He has so enjoyed his taste of soldiering, & looks so strong and well—with a *cropped* head, quite in military style!! Can you think of him?' By the late autumn the Compton-Burnetts had abandoned their move to London, Jack had returned reluctantly to his office at the Board of Education in Whitehall and Noel had become a member of Kitchener's vast new civilian army, receiving his commission on 23 November from the Leicestershire Regiment and his training at barracks in Aldershot, where he found little to console him among his brother officers: 'pleasant fellows enough—for them life and art being the

---

* Information from Raisley Moorsom; Dickinson was fifty-two when war broke out: 'there was for me no question of enlisting though I think I should have enlisted if I had been younger, for I was not "a conscientious objector", though I had no illusion about the war nor anything but despair in my heart.' (*Goldsworthy Lowes Dickinson* by E. M. Forster, p.156.)

latest musical comedy. I like and feel for the privates: they are just humanity, suffering and patient. I've just been inspecting their feet, 600 of the dirtiest, poor tortured feet you can think of. I felt my sympathy for them almost too much. It's this damned sentimentality that plays the dickens with a man's constitution.'

Jack and Janet Beresford were married on 11 February 1915, and settled in a flat on Queen's Road, Bayswater. Noel's letters at this time to Jack (who, with a new wife besides three sisters to support and an ailing, elderly father, had for the moment no choice but to remain at home) are unfailingly generous, showing no sign of envy or even despondency, only a persistent desire to reassure his friend which underlies any number of blithe and ingenious attempts to divert him. But Noel, marooned at Aldershot and later in billets at Andover, was increasingly caught up that spring in his feelings for Tertia, to whom he became engaged round about the time of Jack's wedding. 'I dread going back to Andover leaving behind all that I value. I wish I was settled with Tertia and that you and Janet were coming to stay with us. I feel a pleasant certainty that things—even small delightful things like that—are predestined,' he wrote at Easter, after a brief leave spent visiting the Rodin exhibition with Tertia from Jack's flat in Queen's Road. His letters turn constantly on their hurried, unsatisfactory meetings ('Tertia and I are getting one of our snatches next weekend ...'), on their plans for the future ('Tertia and I will be lamentably poor ... Still ... my friends will stick to me and hers to her, both of them to us, so what does in the name of friendship money matter in any degree?') and on arrangements for procuring a ring from Liberty's ('a diamond to be set in silver . . . engraved inside "as rivers in the south" . . . this must be *slender*; very light and slight: see to that'). By the beginning of April he had made a will and moved to the transit camp at Perham Down, quoting nonchalantly from the Bible: 'The people complained in their tents'. From now on his letters become steadily more clouded by dread of the future, by news of Rupert Brooke's death at Gallipoli, by his anxiety for Tertia, the misgivings of her family, and ominous signs of his own impending departure: 'The report this morning is that we're going to Turkey in 6 weeks but I don't believe it . . . I trust and pray we don't go for poor Tertia. Oh Jack how terrible! I lie awake often and think of that till I'm as cold inside as out.' (11 April 1915)

Noel's preoccupation with Tertia can have left little time for his sisters, whose troubles meanwhile had multiplied. Their delight at the prospect of escaping from Hove had turned to desperate dismay when the war put a stop to their plans. 'For my part, I am quite dreading to see Mowll next week, & hear what effects the war may have on us,' wrote Ivy to her cousin in September. 'I have cut down the girls' musical expenses as far as I can, without really interfering with their progress. And they are all very good and sensible about it.' But Ivy's categorical directions were by this time more than her sisters could stand; and they were convinced that the household would have continued unchanged, with Ivy installed at its head in perpetuity, if she had not been faced with open revolt. She had written nothing since their mother's death, concentrating instead on home affairs and putting her manuscript, if she had one, in a drawer like the two novelists in *Mother and Son* whose youthful ambitions had likewise come to nothing ('"I wonder there is any drawer space left," said Miss Burke').[38] Domestic supremacy, combined perhaps with the stationary sales of *Dolores*, had for the moment suspended her determination to write. But Ivy at thirty must still have aspired, like the authors in *Mother and Son*, to higher things—even apparently contemplating their pursuit at a fashionable establishment for young ladies in Kensington, which was another scheme scotched by the war. 'I don't think I must think of Amica's college while we are living in Brighton, though in some ways I should like very much to join the essay class. I daresay I shall, some time. . . . Both my nice maids leave this Saturday, and two more come,' wrote Ivy who, though she pinned no hopes on the efficacy of prayer herself, was not above asking her cousin to arrange 'public intercession at the after-breakfast ceremony, on my behalf, at this crisis'. The letter bears out her sisters' view, that Ivy at this time did indeed behave as though she were the only person on the premises: 'It was *my* servants, *my* house and not ever ours. . . . She was desperately holding on to my mother's place. She had no conceivable notion of equality between sisters.'

Myra Hess, who as the friend and teacher of Vera and Judy had been invited to stay at Hove, seems to have reacted with much the same startled incredulity as the Ponsonbys' visitors in *Daughters and Sons* ('"I rather wonder that your grandmother welcomes strangers in the house." "I can't think how she dares to," said Victor. "It is sheer impudence and dare-devilry. It comes of a lifetime of having her own way."'). Myra had pronounced that things could not go on. 'She couldn't believe the household she'd come into. She said, "You're all in fetters. You must get away."' The astonishment was mutual. 'When we saw other people who hadn't been brought up in that way,' said Vera Compton-Burnett, 'we perceived for the first time what an astonishing situation ours was.' Details of the struggle that followed—a struggle in which Ivy herself, unlike most of her tyrants, ultimately sustained defeat—are paralleled again and again in the state of simmering mutiny which pervades so many of the novels of I. Compton-Burnett. The Sullivans, discussing their governess in *Parents and Children*, give perhaps a sympathetic hint of the difficulties with which Ivy must have had to contend in these months at Hove:

> 'She still seems to me in her own way a person born to command,' said Luce. . . .
> 'I wonder if anyone is born to obey,' said Isabel. 'That may be why people command rather badly, that they have no suitable material to work on.'[39]

The Mowbrays speculate on similar lines about their father; and the Ponsonbys, Haslams and Edgeworths react to a brief respite from oppression with a mixture of uneasiness and relief not unlike the feelings of Ivy's sisters when, in the spring of 1915, she fell ill and was laid up for some weeks with bronchitis: 'Of course we went up to see her, there was no open breach at that time. But we felt so free—of her. There was no constraint at meals.'

The break was decisive. Ivy's sisters had been much moved by reading Emerson, and by a general stirring against the old order in the world at large which confirmed their own restiveness. Being still powerless to loosen Ivy's grip on the household, they determined to leave it. Minnie was consulted and took, as her descendants generally do in the novels, a pessimistic view: 'Minnie said, "You'll never manage it. We shall be here always, we can never change it."' But all four were now irretrievably bent on escape, led by Vera ('It became unendurable. One was twenty-three and one had had no life of any kind') who wrote to Noel at Perham Down saying she had urgent secret business to discuss. When Noel, suspecting a love affair, replied that this was neither the time nor the place for a visit, Vera delivered her ultimatum by post.

Noel's state of mind was by this time nearly desperate. 'Tertia and I have long had a plan which I think we will stick to,' he had written at the beginning of April to Jack: 'If all goes well and I am not sent to the wars we will wait for peace to be married, as in such things turmoil and haste, and waiting upon trains when one should wait only on the sun and moon, are all discords and hard to reconcile oneself to. If on the other hand the summons seems likely we will marry out of hand and get what comfort we can.'

In the meantime they had to make do with meeting uncomfortably at other people's houses in London for odd weekends before he returned to Perham Down and she to Easton Grey where old Mr Beresford, not best pleased by Jack's marriage, looked with open disfavour on Tertia's. Even Jack had his doubts about a match between two such highly excitable people. Tertia was by nature unstable, being prone like her mother to nervous trouble, and Noel himself, though calm enough to the outward eye, seemed to his friends to possess neither the robust temperament nor the physical stamina required to sustain prolonged emotional strain. Jack's mistrust must have been especially bitter to Noel. 'If I marry Tertia *now* it can only be a nominal marriage,' he wrote on 13 May in a letter which, though he felt it 'impossible [Jack] should understand', makes a last, sad attempt to dispel his friend's forebodings: 'I won't run the risk of anything else; and not being able to live together, if we marry before I go it *must* be at the last minute. . . .' Neither family can have been much reassured but no one could long withstand Noel's urgency or, as rumours multiplied and it became clear that his posting could not be much further delayed, his sound reasons for snatching at happiness. By the end of May he was arranging details with Jack:

How speedy can the thing be done. I can only get four days so time is precious—the glass runs out sands of gold. Will you find out. I am so far from things here. Can one just go to a church and be married. . . . If ecclesiastical marriage is difficult, we will content ourselves (very willingly, and perhaps preferably) with the civil. You wouldn't mind would you. If you would that settles it for Tertia and me. We always call Janet and you our only friends—and neither of you can know the gratitude we have in our hearts. Write at once. I rather think I could get next Friday week—till Monday but I'm not sure. I've been practising with a pistol (leaving nothing to chance) Jim.

In the event, after some tactful negotiations on Jack's part, they were married on 12 June by Tertia's father in the church at Easton Grey. Jack was there but Ivy was not. On 16 June, after four days' privacy and peace at a farmhouse in Wiltshire, her brother was back at Perham

Down still without knowing the date of his departure for France (which came at short notice six weeks later). From Noel's point of view his family could hardly have chosen a more wretched moment to quarrel. Distracted by preparations for the front, by fears for Tertia, by haste and uncertainty and the difficulty of conducting affairs through the post at long distance, he had replied to Vera, defending Ivy and upbraiding his younger sisters for what must have seemed an ill-judged and mischievous squabble, erupting at the worst possible time. 'But for us it was the *last second*. Flesh and blood couldn't stand it any longer. So in a way there was a rift with Noel too,' said Vera Compton-Burnett. 'He took it very hard.'

What Ivy's reactions were at this point—what part Noel's marriage or his dangerous future played in her feelings—one can only surmise. It was years since the two had held all things in common but, though his defection had been both gentle and gradual, one may perhaps suspect that Ivy suffered as keenly as Noel from the isolation described in his sombre letter of 13 May to Jack: 'I feel the profound loneliness of life, deepened and darkened, as I realise that only the heart knows its own weakness and bitterness.'* If Noel's engagement had come as a shock, perhaps a violent one, Ivy bore it in silence as she bore the prospect of his imminent departure, and the last phase of the long drawn struggle at Hove. 'It was a time of pain and difficulty, as it must be, like an abscess before it breaks,' said Vera Compton-Burnett. The four girls had agreed that, in spite of Noel's disapproval and no matter what Ivy might do, they would take their own house in London and share it with Myra Hess. They had calculated that they might 'live and pay for music lessons and get on quite well' on their combined allowances, eked out by the sale of their mother's jewellery ('She was very fond of diamonds. I remember I had a diamond pansy which I lived on for quite a while') which had been equally divided between her five daughters. They drew lots to decide who should break the news to Ivy.

'I never shall forget the day it had to be done. Or the meal at which I did it,' said Vera, who had drawn the shortest. 'I remember my voice dying away. And having to take a new breath to continue. And being kicked by one of the others under the table.' This was at an evening meal towards the middle of the summer. Ivy's only reply was to point

---

* 'The heart knoweth his own bitterness; and a stranger doth not intermeddle with his joy' (Proverbs 14: 10). Violet Powell (*A Compton-Burnett Compendium*, Heinemann, 1973, p.85) points out that 'the heart knoweth' is a phrase Ivy later used twice, in much the same context as Noel, in her novels.

H

out that both parties might conveniently live without meeting in a house with two staircases: 'One would be the servants', and the other would be hers—that was the way her mind worked.' For the next few weeks the matter was not mentioned again. Silence became Ivy's weapon. She might accept their decision but she would do nothing to implement it—'She would take no part. She took no steps'—though she did summon the family solicitor from Dover. 'He came to prevent it. A Victorian if ever there was one,' said Vera Compton-Burnett. But the girls' determination defeated even Martyn Mowll who said heavily, as he rose to go: 'Miss Vera, you have made your bed. And you must lie upon it.'

By the first week in August, Noel was reporting distant gunfire as he marched towards the western front. By the beginning of September, his younger sisters had signed the lease of the house in St John's Wood where for the next twenty years they lived with Myra Hess. By October they had left No. 20 The Drive, chosen what little of its contents they wished to retain, and organized a sale of the rest which took place on the twelfth, thirteenth and fourteenth of that month. They spent the week of the sale at a boarding house in Holland Road and immediately afterwards followed their furniture to London, chaperoned by Minnie whose feelings—after thirty-three years spent serving the family with a devotion which had survived their father's death, Guy's, their mother's alteration in character and what seemed a similar change in Ivy's—may well have resembled Miss Patmore's at the end of *Brothers and Sisters*: '"Oh, well, things are over now," said Patty. "We shall be off to London, to start afresh. Well, anyhow, it will be a change." Her voice betrayed the craving of years, and the young faces fell and brightened at the thought of it, and its being satisfied.'[40]

Ivy, having accompanied her sisters to the boarding house and put her own furniture in store, had nothing to do and nowhere to go. Again, there is no clue to her feelings save that, after the publication of *Brothers and Sisters* in 1929, she continued to the end of her life to return to the situation in which she had first been oppressed and later become the oppressor herself. She had set her face resolutely against her sisters' departure but there is some evidence, in the copy of Butler's *Note-Books* which came into her hands at the end of the war, that her mind still dwelt on the dissolution of the household at Hove; and that, whatever her views at the time, she had moved in the interval very much closer to the attitude which afterwards prevailed in her books. A dozen of Butler's notes are variously underlined, annotated in Ivy's hand, marked with an ampersand or a pencil stroke at the side, but of these a single passage stands out, being scored with not one but six thick, heavy lines in the margin:

The Family

I believe that more unhappiness comes from this source than from any other—I mean from the attempt to prolong family connection unduly and to make people hang together artificially who would never naturally do so. The mischief among the lower classes is not so great, but among the middle and upper classes it is killing a large number daily. And the old people do not really like it much better than the young.[41]

CHAPTER EIGHT

1915–1919

I

'My mind baulks at it'

'WE LEARN STRANGELY how to endure,' wrote Noel whose letters
from the front quickly settled into that subdued and reticent tone
which must have been familiar to anyone with a friend or brother in
France. In the autumn of 1915, it was becoming increasingly clear that
the war which was to have ended the Christmas before would not even
be over by next Christmas. No hint of disaster reached the press but
shrewder and more apprehensive readers were by this time schooled
in a dreadful expertise to note the apologies and qualifications which
monotonously followed each 'great victory' and each 'staggering blow',
with nothing to show save a fresh row of deaths in a lunatic sum
already beginning to be reckoned in millions. Conditions in the trenches
could barely be guessed at between the lines of inadequate newspaper
reports. Ivy seldom afterwards spoke of these months when, for
people at home with nothing to do but watch the papers and wait for
letters, the worst fate of all was to be cursed with an active imagination:

'We may as well imagine the scene.'
'No, my mind baulks at it.'
'Mine does worse. It constructs it.'[1]

Others have described how, after each new offensive, 'the awful
sluggishness of the hours seemed a specially devised torture of hell',[2]
how every knock at the door suggested a telegram, every telephone
call might mean bad news, even the striking of a clock fell with
shattering force on nerves strung up for days and weeks on end. There
was small reassurance to be had from letters when the post took as much
as four days to reach England from France, and the writer had time to
be killed over and over again in the interval. 'I'm in for some danger in
the next few days, but if by the time you have this you hear nothing
all will be well,' wrote Noel, whose letters must often have been read

with a lurch of sickening apprehension. But even to Jack he never mentioned a risk until it was over, and seldom referred to his own safety at all. The curious detachment which he shared with his father and Ivy was if anything sharpened by his first sight of the trenches —'rather like a manufacturing district, only the smoke is white not black'—or his first excursion by night into No Man's Land: 'As the rockets went up from either trench I saw the cornflowers thick and tall round me, covering with burial flowers so blue and hopeful the poor crumpled form of some enemy, who had been there long dead, for whom Ezekiel wrote an epitaph in the days past "Son of man, can these bones live?".' (16 August 1915)

After a brief spell at the front in early August, he was sent back for a course of instruction to Etaples where the archaic training in obsolete open warfare manœuvres, and the homicidal ferocity of the bayonet instructors, must have seemed as weirdly inappropriate to Noel as they did to other incredulous young subalterns fresh from England. By the beginning of September he was billeted just behind the line, engaged on last-minute preparations for the forthcoming offensive at Loos, and more amused than otherwise at the prospect of imminent death: '. . . we have been told by the general in a most dramatic Boys' Own Paper way, that the village is to be held at any cost. I wonder if you picture how peaceful life is here with the Germans not a mile away. I am writing at my table with roses and hollyhocks outside the window, and with the church bells sounding as peacefully from the ruined tower as at Easton Grey.' The incongruity of roses and hollyhocks, apple orchards and lanes full of elderberries, of listening by night to an enemy in the opposite trench whose 'guttural Bavarian talk' he had last heard as a student in Munich, appealed strongly to Noel. In the last few days before the battle, he still described a bombardment to Jack as sceptically as he had once discussed the antics of the Carbonari with his tutor at Cambridge:

For one minute, lying alone together and close we seemed in the midst of a flaming fiery furnace, or like one of those immaculate heroes who stand in a perfect hail of missiles to advertise Dri-ped shoes or some military tailor. But really no shell came within 30 yds and soon they got more distant. I feel something of the fascination of modern war—this strife of midgets who hurl the thunderbolt.

The noise is rather a bore. Will you get me the Mallock Armstrong Ear-Defender 4s. . . .'

This letter is postmarked Thursday, 23 September. On Friday Noel moved back to the front line and sent Jack a sealed letter 'for Tertia in case I am killed', on Saturday the first offensive began and on Monday the London papers carried news of a 'splendid victory' at Loos. Noel survived that battle but, for his family and friends searching the terrifying casualty lists which followed, piecing together what had happened from laconic references in letters like this one, from sketchy accounts in the papers and from the wild rumours accompanying the wounded troops who filled the platforms at Victoria and Paddington for weeks afterwards, this must have been a war of attrition at home as it was on the western front. Nearly twenty years later Vera Brittain, whose brother and lover had both been killed in the war, wrote that she could still not work comfortably in a room from which it was possible to hear the front door bell. Ivy herself wrote in 1948 to Robert Liddell: 'I find I cannot read the news and do not do so. After living in mature awareness through two wars, that side of me is worn out and can do no more.'

In the autumn of 1915, Ivy was homeless. She had accepted her fall from power as dispassionately as she had earlier undertaken to wield it, and she wrote at the end of October proposing to stay at 8 Carlton Hill with her sisters, who flatly refused. They made no objection to her coming to tea, but any attempt to contain in one household two such formidable characters as Ivy and Myra Hess must have seemed tantamount to inviting disaster. There was one small spare room, known as the Developer because Ivy on a tour of inspection had said that in such a small house with no space to turn round her sisters would find no room to develop: it was at any rate abundantly clear that they could not hope to remain independent for long, once Ivy had taken up residence in the Developer. For the first time in her life she was free, through no choice of her own, from the family claims which had governed all her adult existence. One may perhaps suspect 'tumult within her' from the way in which her attitude to duty—'that rigorous lofty thing' which had meant mortal misery for Dolores—capsized between her first and second novels: '"The sight of duty does make one shiver," said Miss Herrick. "The actual doing of it would kill one, I think."'[3]

Probably the only person who could have appreciated Ivy's feelings at this time was Noel, whose departure had already snapped her last link with the past and whose future it was not safe to contemplate. That he perfectly understood her frame of mind is clear from one of the letters she afterwards kept. On 17 May 1915, when he believed that he had only three weeks left in England and was engaged in frantic preparations for his marriage, Noel still found time to write from Perham Down to Elliott Felkin:

> I wonder if you would ask your sister . . . whether she would put my sister Ivy up for her club. I should like my sister to know yours as I think they are rather kindred—at one in their contempt of the human race (tho' perhaps not quite primitive Christians for all that!) Ivy is often wandering about in town; the foxes have holes, the birds have nests, cabmen repose inside their hackneys, but my sister has not etc.
>
> I wonder if yr sister wd write to Ivy 'if willin'.*

Elliott's sister Winifred had probably joined a club for the sake of some respite from a masterful, widowed mother (at whose house Ivy became a regular visitor after the war), and because it was by no means easy in those days for single women living at home to meet congenial company. Four years older than Elliott, without either his considerable charm or his Cambridge education, Winifred appeared to his young friends from King's a somewhat condescending blue-stocking in pince-nez with a habit of intellectual name-dropping. But it is small wonder if she found her spirits severely dampened in their presence. Her mother had been Henry Felkin's second wife and, as her stepbrothers and Elliott each in turn became independent and went, leaving Winifred alone at close quarters with their formidable parent, her nerve seems to have failed at the prospect (later it broke altogether when, after a miserable accident which cost her the sight of one eye, she could no longer support life at home). Ivy's sisters remembered Winifred being brought by her brother to spend a weekend at Hove, where she was no doubt drawn to her hostess by the sense of a blighted youth which had given both their sardonic attitude to the race at large (and perhaps to the younger members of the party in particular). Moreover Winifred's mother was descended, like Ivy's, from an old farming family at Clacton and had inherited in 1907 Lilly Farm,[4] which stands between the Compton-Burnetts' Valley Farm and the sea. Both families spent

* 'The foxes have holes, and the birds of the air have nests; but the Son of Man hath not where to lay his head.' (Matthew 8:20) '"When a man says he's willin'," said Mr Barkis . . . "It's as much as to say, that man's a-waitin' for a answer."' (David Copperfield, chap. 8.)

occasional holidays at Clacton and, if the link perhaps explains Noel's interest when Elliott first came up to King's in 1911, it was certainly the kind of thing calculated to appeal to Ivy, who had for years been supervising her own family's property all round the Felkins' at Clacton.

Whatever the reason, the two took to each other as Noel had predicted, and Ivy may well have stayed with the Felkins when, some time in November or December, she finally left Hove for London. Here, in spite of all her precautions, in spite of the policy of passive resistance which she had pursued for so long and probably proposed to pursue for the rest of her life, she was once again obliged to construct a life of her own among strangers in that state of anonymous flux which had so alarmed her at school and college; only this time the world to which she had previously retreated was itself disintegrating under her feet. People from all over England were 'running away', like the Staces in *Brothers and Sisters*, 'and seeking cover in London, where it is easiest to keep it'.[5] Single women who, even a year earlier, would have thought it imprudent to travel unchaperoned were already beginning to elude established controls, living alone, mixing without reference to their parents or families, moving almost as freely as men, expending energies, which for years had been permitted no outlet, on war work of one kind or another. In the circles to which Winifred introduced Ivy, even the need to earn a living seemed less disreputable in the light of what was happening to their male contemporaries at the front.

There were few of Noel's friends left in London, and those few either, like Arthur Waley, immersed in the agonizing dilemma which confronted men who could not join the army in wartime or, like Jack Beresford, preparing that winter to join it. Ivy's relations with the Beresfords were comparatively formal at this stage in the war: she scarcely knew Jack's wife Janet as yet and Tertia, who was still living at Easton Grey, was not on close terms with her sister-in-law. Tertia was six years younger than Ivy and her opposite in almost everything: graceful, dreamy, highly strung and easily upset, with a strong taste for poetry but no intellectual leanings whatever and none of Ivy's scorn for cultivating traditionally winning womanly ways. She had spent the first months of her marriage furnishing a cottage for herself in the village, 'she having much the home instinct,' as Noel wrote admiringly to Jack. Apart from wide reading in the standard poets, Tertia's education had consisted solely of a short course at a domestic science college. The only things which linked the two—their deep mutual reserve, and the fact that Noel mattered more to both than anyone else in the world—were perhaps as likely to drive them apart as to draw them together. It cannot have been easy for Ivy to approach the girl for whom her brother waited 'only on the sun and moon' and with whom he felt himself 'almost mystically one'. Tertia for her part may well have found her first encounters with Noel's elder sister, who must have seemed in some ways to belong more to her parents' generation than her own, a fairly frightening experience.

In a motherless household, Tertia had grown up under the stern eye and firm thumb of her elder sister Dorothy, whose stormy temperament and scathing tongue were rather more to Ivy's taste. A lively dissatisfaction with their own affairs brought these two together at a time when they must have been pretty evenly matched, whether in point of sarcastic humour, strength of will or their wholesale 'contempt for the human race'. Perhaps, too, Dorothy's social success appealed to Ivy who, though she never shone in company herself, became in her middle years increasingly appreciative of the glittering as well as the seamier sides of London society. As a small girl Dorothy at the rectory in Easton Grey had been bosom friends with Violet Asquith at the manor* and afterwards became, as did several of his daughter's friends, one of the young ladies whom Mr Asquith enjoyed escorting and with whom he conducted a leisurely correspondence from 10 Downing Street. People who knew both the elder Miss Beresfords in those days found it hard to decide which was the lovelier but Tertia, persuaded of her own inferiority since childhood, believed that Dorothy was; and Dorothy possessed in any case a *savoir faire* far beyond her retiring younger sister. Tertia's marriage had not pleased Dorothy any more than it probably pleased Ivy: in the summer of 1915, Dorothy had gone so far as to become engaged herself from pique to a passing curate (she had done the same when Jack married, and the arrangement proved in each case a purely temporary expedient).

Tertia, always inclined to feel herself misunderstood at home, had meanwhile left the rectory for the cottage which she shared with a friend from college whose husband was also away at the front (this was the Mrs Hilda Harrisson who, to Tertia's annoyance, followed Dorothy as one of the Prime Minister's young ladies, and subsequently published

* After his marriage to Margot Tennant in 1894 Asquith and his family often stayed at Easton Grey with her sister, Lucy Graham Smith, who was 'a kind of fairy godmother' to the young Beresfords. When one was thirteen and the other fourteen, Violet Asquith and Dorothy Beresford held a joint Sunday school class in the village, shared Christmas parties, tobogganned, wrote poems, went for long walks together and corresponded regularly when apart.

her correspondence with him in two stout volumes). But letters from France took even longer to reach Wiltshire than London, and an arrangement which had never been satisfactory must have seemed even less so as Noel's first leave approached. By the beginning of December, he had spent just over three months in the trenches and was nearing the point when, according to Robert Graves, an officer began 'gradually to decline in usefulness as neurasthenia developed in him'. Noel's part of the line had been out of the action that autumn but he several times described 'mighty narrow shaves' in his letters to Jack, and had already received a green card (three of which were believed by the troops to mean a decoration for gallantry) congratulating him on distinguished conduct in the field. On 3 December he wrote that he hoped to be in London on the seventeenth of that month: 'I shall be glad to get away because my nerves are getting a little shaky—nothing at all to speak of— but it's odd how tiring a hazardous life gets after a few months. You know the tag? "Skin for skin, yea all that a man has will he give for his life" and I've felt that rather too much in my bones lately.'

Tertia, who had taken a suite at the Savoy to celebrate the first time she had spent more than four days alone with her husband in six months of marriage, travelled up to London only to find that Noel's leave had been postponed for a week. Disaster was narrowly averted by Jack and Janet, who lent their Bayswater flat, spending Christmas night themselves at the Paddington Hotel and Boxing Day in their own spare room. After so long apart, this bare week together can scarcely have left Noel much time for seeing other friends, or even his sisters. On 31 December he left England again, with thoughts of a kind which were to preoccupy him increasingly in the next few months:

I saw the New Year in from the ship's deck. . . . Thank you dear Jack for the home you gave Tertia and me. We were happy, and wise enough to live for the day and the hour, and now we have what we had. We must be content. This you remember I expect from the Apology and school-days 'For so it is O Athenians in truth whatever is each man's post, chosen by himself as the better part, or appointed by his leader, there as I think he must stay in spite of danger, reckoning not of death, nor of anything except of disgrace and of honour. . . . For to fear death, O men of Athens, is to think oneself wise when one is not so.' One remembers this too from earlier days and from a profounder book 'And yet I am not alone because the Father is with me.'

In years to come we shall perhaps look back not with horror to this year when these thoughts are the most natural. . . .' (3 January 1916)

The prospect of returning alone to her cottage was too much for Tertia. She found instead a flat in Queen's Road next door to her brother (who had himself newly joined the Army Service Corps, and by January was already in barracks at Aldershot) where Ivy joined her. Ivy, seldom at ease under any roof but her own, seems to have accepted this arrangement without any special enthusiasm as a means of combining practical advantage with family duty for the sake of her brother, who certainly thought his wife too tender a plant to be left to struggle untended. His letters to Jack are filled with solicitude for Tertia, requests to cheer and console her, enquiries as to her health, her safety, her nerves which bothered him far more than his own. Up to this time he had carefully concealed from her any hint of his four months in the trenches: 'In my letters to her I say nothing of the war. I daren't. I beg you also not to. . . .' What is striking, amid such constant concern for preserving Tertia's peace of mind, is the absence of so much as a mention of Ivy's. No doubt he rightly judged her to be self-sufficient, which Tertia palpably was not; and perhaps he even counted on his sister's presence to weather the shock when in February 1916, the month of Verdun, he at last broke the truth to Tertia: 'I had to tell Tertia that I was actually at the front, driven to this partly by a lonely feeling of my own, partly by an idea that she would *wish* to know, and also by fear that she should notice my battalion in the casualty lists; and that the cat suddenly jumping out of the bag might terrify. She has been very brave about it, and I hope will bear up, though its hard for her and I can't but feel anxieties.' (14 February 1916)

It is a moot point whether, in these months when he wrote nearly every week, sometimes oftener, to Jack and probably almost daily to Tertia, Noel found time to keep up a third regular correspondence with Ivy. Their sister Vera, who had seen some of Noel's letters and poems to Tertia on a visit to Easton Grey in the summer of 1915, said she would not have been surprised to learn that Ivy had few. Janet Beresford had a similar impression: 'I somehow do not think Jim wrote regularly to Ivy though I do not really know—I think probably he meant much more to her than she to him though he definitely felt a responsibility for her. She was not a quick sensitive person anyhow on the surface as he was.' Ivy of course spoke of her own anxiety to no one.

Once Noel was gone, she had indeed no one to whom she could speak freely. At a time when people dreaded the post as much as they longed for it, she must often have found it a trial to watch his letters coming for Tertia; and perhaps she felt that in sharing a flat she had shared enough with the person who meant life itself to her brother: 'having as I do' (he wrote to Jack) 'an assurance—so deep and faithful—that I shall come back to Tertia, for this is how it now solely seems—with no hair of my head harmed'. If this was how it solely seemed to Noel, then simple wisdom as well as the habit of years must have confirmed Ivy's inclination to keep her own counsel.

The two letters from Noel which Ivy afterwards kept suggest that brother and sister had preserved from infancy a tacit understanding free from the agitation of his feelings for Tertia, and probably almost as remote from the abstract speculations which became increasingly urgent in his letters to Jack. In practical matters he relied on his friend, sending a steady stream of requests for the various necessities of life at the front: a cholera belt and a canvas bucket, cigarettes, chocolate and copies of the *T.L.S.*, ear-plugs, 'wound stuff' and trench boots. These last arrived by return and proved, as heavy rain filled the trenches with liquid mud: 'a mighty comfort . . . and a symbol also of civilisation and artificiality, things it is good for one's nerves still to believe in. Do you know it's odd what courage is induced in the timid heart by respectable clothes. I'm sure anybody would face bullets with greater equanimity after putting on a new coat, than after reading the New Testament and Plato rolled into one.' (10 October 1915) Noel's respect for his boots goes some way towards explaining a similar outlook in Ivy who had set such store by preserving conventional appearances at Hove, and who later became a lifelong exponent of civilization and artificiality—things which provide a frail enough protection for the timid heart against the bullets ricocheting between the lines of her books.

But in the autumn of 1915 and the following spring Noel was evolving for himself a philosophy drawn directly from the *New Testament* and Plato; and it seems likely that he knew Ivy's views on the former too well to quote without scepticism from the Bible to her. Indeed, at the beginning of the war he could hardly have done so to Jack. 'Like you I pray now, and I pray for you,' he had written from Aldershot the week before Jack's marriage. But up to the time he left England his letters still mostly make fun of the future, and glance if at all only shyly at death: 'Tertia will be a weight on my heart when I go, if ever I do, but I fancy I shan't fear for myself, death being easily recognizable as the beautiful liberator. The sentimental subaltern thus writes to his friend. The brigade is indulging in a garden party this afternoon which accounts for this portentous gloom. How hateful such things are!' (13 July 1915)

Over the next few months Noel's style changed under the pressures which brought so many of his generation to a sudden maturity in the trenches until by December, when Jack proposed joining the army, it had shed all trace of self-mockery:

Dear Jack,

I was glad to have your letter and to know that you aren't doing anything militarily desperate. I think you intend what's right, and in this matter are choosing the better way. Life gets so obscure in its ends and means, and the common life of the world so heart-breakingly suicidal, that one thinks the best is to hold to what is nearest, the domestic responsibilities and affections. I feel these days that the only hope is the law of Christ, 'But I say unto you that ye resist not evil'. No doubt the world must go its way, and this is too hard a saying to be received—too spiritual and too intellectual. And again 'Blessed are the meek for they shall inherit the earth'. Personally I find this attitude the only satisfactory one so far as it touches the world, and for one's inner life its even more so. Religion, which is life, reaches its highest here 'Ye shall indeed drink of my cup, and be baptised with the baptism that I am baptised with, but to sit on my right hand and on my left is not mine to give but it shall be given to them for whom it is prepared of my father'. That's 'high as we shall go' with a vengeance, that promise of the suffering but not the reward. Quite a sabbath address. Goodbye. I shall turn up in London I think about a week today but dates aren't fixed. Yrs affectionately Jim.*

Perhaps Noel was prevented from writing as freely to his sister for fear of her disapproval; more likely, he had fallen with Jack into a habit of abstract discussion which, beginning with life and art in their earliest days at King's, moved on as their friendship deepened to the pressing question of death. It is in any case impossible to say how far Ivy's unforgiving attitude to religion had already hardened, and how

---

* Dickinson, still a follower of Socrates, was also beginning round about this time to turn to Christ, whose essential teaching came to seem to him 'sheer common sense and sanity, and not the paradox I used to think it'. (*Goldsworthy Lowes Dickinson* by E. M. Forster, p.160.)

far it was shaped afterwards when she had to reconcile the knowledge that her brother had chosen the suffering with the certainty that there was no reward.

Noel's letters to Jack keep the nice balance between gaiety and gravity which both had practised at Cambridge. But a correspondence which, though it often mentions the tedium of the war, never refers to other more sordid, ugly or pitiful aspects probably gives a lopsided view of Noel's activities. It seems to have served as a safety valve, a means of discussing matters unmentionable in the trenches where cold, mud, exhaustion, misery, the constant spectacle of comrades mutilated or dying, the company of live rats and rotting corpses, the alternation of boredom with terror had bred a profound, quiet, deflationary cynicism. It must have been a considerable relief to Noel to be able to write in private to Jack of sensations better not broached in public:

> I've just come back to my dug-out, and have lit a candle to write to you. The first snow of the year is falling, and one's heart is quite heavy with its marvellous beauty. Our trenches and the Germans', the earth cast up irregularly and now white in the dawn, seem like a tempestuous sea of crumpled and curling waves; one waits for the crash as they break, and even when one has destroyed the illusion it recreates itself, and one wonders at the skeleton trees, marking the German positions and rooted as it seems in the surf. (Autumn 1915)

Poets were heartily despised at the front, along with staff and field officers, home service units and conscientious objectors in a carefully graded system of contempt which embraced all military and civilian forms of life from generals down to the detested ranks of journalist and politician. That Noel shared the general view is evident from an uncharacteristic tartness underlying his humorous reproaches when Jack joined the Army Service Corps, a race of notorious shirkers accustomed to feast on food meant for the troops who were 'scattered . . . to the right and left' by 'luxurious overpaid A.S.C. gentlemen' cruising about in large cars. Senior officers, whose contact with direct action at the front was largely confined to issuing unrealistic orders beforehand and compiling equally unrealistic reports afterwards, were especially loathed. 'In the army you *must* push yourself or you get nothing,' wrote Noel in another uncharacteristic spurt of resentment. 'Consider me, still a 2nd lieutenant though (as I say it who oughtn't) more militarily competent than the average field or staff officer.'

He seems to have felt the same disgust as other supposedly incompetent poets who found themselves driven, through a combination of self-mistrust, despair of their superiors and sympathy with their men, to acts of conspicuous courage. Noel's fear was the common one, described by both Graves and Siegfried Sassoon, of cowardice when put to the test: 'This particular fear (certainly not the fear of death or wounds) is the burden of active service'. He sent Jack only one detailed description of a raid, set down next morning in the rush of relief at having lived to report on a mission from which there had been no survivors two nights before:

At 1 a.m. myself and a fellow subaltern from Trinity, with pistols, two desperate non-coms with bombs and bludgeons, all with faces blacked and wearing cap-comforters, got out of one of our listening posts and started on our voyage. . . . We went in pairs, the two timid officers in front, the two desperate sergeants five yards behind. We chose the clearest night we could—it was possible to read in the moonlight—so as to outwit the Boche who would surely think none likely to approach under such conditions. . . .

The result of this cheerful adventure was the capture of a flag marked 'Gott strafe England' from the German trenches ('The men want to keep the flag or else I would send it to you as a curiosity'); the general atmosphere of skulduggery confirms the remark of a fellow officer from Cambridge, reported by Professor Clapham, 'that it was hard to keep from laughing when on patrol with Burnett because of his whimsical comments'.

People who lived through the first war have described often enough the glazed eyes, lined faces and blank looks of troops returning from sights and sounds too raw and recent to be put into words. Noel himself had suspected this wall of incomprehension in the months when he waited at Perham Down for his own initiation in the trenches: 'It's odd how anxious we of Kitchener's army are to hear from those there, as if by much reading and hearsay we could guess at it', he wrote to Elliott on 8 May 1915. Soldiers on leave were so bewildered by the spectacle of patriotic hysteria feeding on public gullibility that it was often a relief to get back to open madness at the front from what seemed a more shameful madness at home. Robert Graves found it 'all but impossible' to attempt anything but the most desultory small talk with his family and friends. Siegfried Sassoon had nothing to say to his.

Vera Brittain, one of the few who described the shock of meeting this
numbness from the other side, waited miserably for the war to divide
her from her lover and brother, 'putting a barrier of indescribable
experience between men and the women whom they loved, thrusting
horror deeper and deeper inwards, linking the dread of spiritual death
to the apprehension of physical disaster'.[6] Whether or not the barrier
operated between Noel and Ivy, it was by his own choice impassable
with Tertia; and it fell across much that he could not write about even
to Jack, whose patient encouragement meant a brief, necessary oblivion
from 'it'. 'It will be good and refreshing to see you, my Johannes,'
wrote Noel just before his first leave, 'for these days sometimes I feel
almost dotty, surely very pardonable to anyone living in this lunatic
world.'

In a lunatic world the Beresfords stood for sanity, affection, con-
tinuity, all things which Noel knew well enough that he must almost
certainly and probably very soon relinquish. His love for Tertia
cemented his friendship with Jack and both drew him into a family
circle which inevitably excluded Ivy. It was not that anyone meant to be
unkind (though there must have been some constraint, if not a coldness
between brother and sister over Tertia), only that the young Burnetts
and the young Beresfords shared a whole new set of domestic pleasures
which seemed especially precious in wartime, and in which Ivy played
at best a peripheral part. 'Small delightful things', like the prospect of
exchanging family visits, of owning a home of his own or the birth of
his niece Rosemary Beresford in the spring of 1916, held a tantalizing
charm for Noel, who had long since laid his plans for entertaining
Jack's children 'with Othello-like stories of peril in the deadly breach,
they being seated on the avuncular knee'. As it turned out one of them
was dandled on Noel's knee, for the authorities were generous with
leave in the months leading up to the battle of the Somme and, by the
end of April, he was once again in London where Rosemary's mother
remembered him 'looking very quizzically' and with unusual emotion
at 'Jack's child'. Noel, unlike his sister, had always been fond of small
children and this one must have seemed to give a kind of vicarious
substance to his own hopes of a happiness he dared not yet contemplate
with Tertia. He had already a ring, given him by Jack the summer
before, which was destined for Rosemary: 'In the good future when I
am godfather to a girl of yours and Janets, when she is ten years old, I
shall produce it from the treasury of the past.'

There was a fastidious sharpness in Ivy that would have made it

The Compton-Burnett family with cousins in the summer of 1912. Ivy in
the centre with Topsy beside her on the left, Stephanie (Baby) standing
behind on the right, and Noel on the right in front

The Family

i

I believe that more unhappiness comes from this source
than from any other—I mean from the attempt to prolong
family connection unduly and to make people hang together
artificially who would never naturally do so. The mischief
among the lower classes is not so great, but among the middle
and upper classes it is killing a large number daily. And the
old people do not really like it much better than the young.

'The Family' from Ivy's copy of *The Note-Books of Samuel Butler*, p.31

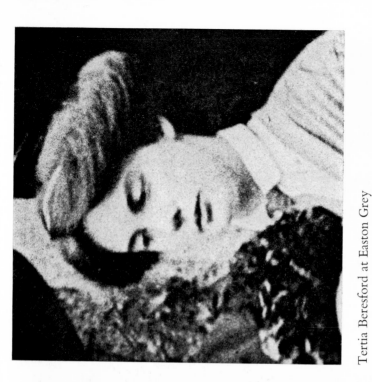

Tertia Beresford at Easton Grey

Jack Beresford, from a painting
by Lucy Graham Smith 1913

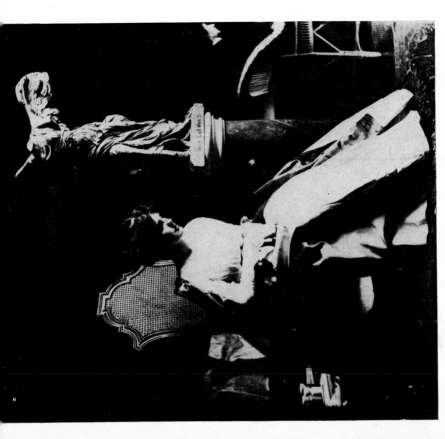

Ivy (*left*) and Dorothy Beresford (*above*) round about the time of the first war

The whole life of some people is a kind of partial death—a long, lingering death-bed, so to speak, of stagnation and nonentity on which death is but the seal, or solemn signing, as the abnegation of all further act and deed on the part

I am a living witness of this continuing life-in-stagnation of the ?

Note in Ivy's handwriting after Noel's death, from her copy of *The Note-Books of Samuel Butler*, p.22

7TH BN
THE LEICESTERSHIRE REGT,
B.E.F.

First page of Noel's last letter to Ivy, written from the Somme on Saturday, 1 July 1916 impossible for Noel to write unselfconsciously and optimistically to her, as he did to Jack, about the good future or the treasury of the past. He looked upon Jack as a brother to whom he confided raptures— 'Why, Tertia and I know each other to the end of things; probably as unreservedly as any two souls ever have'—which his sister could hardly have welcomed. But neither Jack nor Tertia had known him in more distant, comfortless times; and one cannot help wondering how much, in these desperate months, he turned to the permanent, perhaps almost silent consolation of an older intimacy with Ivy. The strains which drove him 'sometimes . . . almost dotty' were well known to his sister. These two after all had looked to each other before in fear and uncertainty, in grief for their father, in their desolation after Guy's death, as well as in years of dull daily endurance at Hove from which both derived a fund of stoicism drawn on still more deeply by the war. Ivy possessed little of Noel's spontaneity and none of his ability to keep open heart for his friends. Noel, in so far as one may judge from his letters and from his sister's borrowings from him for Robin Stace in *Brothers and Sisters*, had a smoother temperament than hers, sunnier, more direct, certainly more sociable, and one on which profound emotion left a shallower imprint. But if his straightforwardness made him more tender, it also made him if anything more vulnerable and apt in a crisis to depend on his sister's reserves of strength. However much his marriage had separated the two, one may suspect that it had not at bottom damaged a relationship based on unconditional sympathy and trust.

Much went without saying between Noel and Ivy, as it does between brother and sister in her books. This far at least one may go on the evidence of an unemotional letter, largely concerned with family business and written from behind the lines on Saturday, 24 June, the day on which the British artillery began its preliminary, supposedly lethal bombardment on the Somme. Bets had been laid on the date in the trenches for weeks beforehand, and the forthcoming 'Big Push' had been common knowledge all over England since the middle of June. The final seven days' bombardment could be heard from Kent and from the southern suburbs of London. But Ivy, who seems to have been unwell, had fled London (as, twenty-five years later, she frankly declared she had fled the bombs in the second war) with Dorothy for Wales. This letter was forwarded from Bayswater to Easton Grey, and on to a boarding house on the Mumbles near Swansea where it must have reached her the following Saturday, which was the first day of the battle of the Somme:

Saturday.

This letter will find you somewhere in the wild, and not too much bored I hope with life. You must have had an ill time,—yet we survive, such is the mercy(?) of Providence. These days that the locust devours, and an unappetising dish must he find them, shall according to the scriptures be returned to us again. I suppose the scriptures will be fulfilled when peace comes, which I truly think *will* be this year. The day and hour knoweth no man. I leave my school in a few days, so write to my old address. If you are with Dorothy, dont let her nerves get on your nerves.

I had the documents for the letting of No 20 and a Sackville mansion yesterday & have sent them back to Rutley. I think on the whole you do well, that is to say you couldn't do better, than accept the £150 for No 20, though it is enough to make our parents curse God to his face. 'Tis of a badness. I'm quite well and shall remain so, unless the Kaiser succeeds in his attempts upon me.

What are your permanent plans. I take it you return to your apartment in Queens Rd? I have nothing to say. I am your servant

N

This is the tone of voice of someone with no front to keep up, almost as though Noel were talking to himself or writing in a diary. The contrast is marked if one sets this letter beside a characteristic passage to Jack, in which he imagines being rudely wakened by a bullet to find himself a star. 'Do you know these endless days in the open, and even more these nights, looking at Jupiter flaming like a torch and the Pleiades like distant tiny candle points, fill me to bursting with the love of life and the desire for it? The thought that the lights would still shine for other eyes, if one slept, in some moods only chills. . . .' This was as far towards pessimism as he permitted himself to go in writing to Jack. Admittedly, Noel was perhaps not yet so deeply inured to horror in the months before Jack also left England for the front, but there is a resignation bleaker than anything he shared with his friend in his last, terse, flat letter to Ivy.

This was written on Saturday, 1 July, a day of blazing sunshine on which the British army suffered more casualties than on any other single day in its history. Noel's battalion was part of the 37th Division in the VII Corps detailed for a purely diversionary attack on the Gomme-court Salient at the northern tip of the line, probably the strongest point of a German system which, according to Winston Churchill, 'was undoubtedly the strongest and most perfectly defended position in the world'. The task of the VII Corps was peculiarly wretched: to attack without taking and with desperately inadequate resources an impregnable fortress under a German barrage which was fiercer on the first day of the battle than in any other sector of the Somme. Officers, batmen, even grooms in Noel's division had dug day and night for a week. The first line went over the top at 7.30 a.m. and by nightfall the VII Corps 'had lost 7000 men for no reason whatever'.[7] Observers like Noel, whose division was ordered simply to hold the line, watched wave upon wave of men mown down as they advanced shoulder to shoulder over the ranks of their dead and dying predecessors. By Saturday evening it was clear to the survivors, back where they had started from in their own trenches, that the battle was lost, though no thought of failure had reached Haig and his generals who, far from calling off the whole catastrophic attack, ordered a renewed offensive to begin at once. Noel's letter, which has neither superscription nor signature, was written in two parts and posted on Sunday. By 6 or 7 July, when it reached Ivy in Wales, the English papers were ecstatically celebrating a wholly illusory triumph:

Saturday.
This is a short letter written just on the fringe of the battle. So far as I know I shan't be in it; but in any case the ordeal can't last long. It must be 'too hot to last'. I wish I could finish the remark but the truth is I would give a thousand pounds *to* miss it. In any case its foolish to reckon up the gain and loss of Death. The comfort is that Death puts all one's arguments out of court. Its a hot day, and one pities the wounded jolting by in waggons. Lucky fellows really! I'm *not* depressed, only I defy anyone not to get a headache from the guns. The posts are likely to be irregular for the next few days but I'll write again as soon as I can.
II/Should I by any chance get 'done in', I should like you to take any books of mine you like, & especially my Gladstone Prize[8] in pious memory of our Greekish youth. Oh! we *were* clever. I hasten to add I intend to attain a grand old age.

What Ivy did next is uncertain. Noel's battalion was shortly moved down from Gommecourt to Mametz Wood near the point where, as depressing reports gradually filtered back to the general staff, Haig planned his second major assault to take place on 14 July. This was the day on which, for the first and last time in the war, the cavalry, who had waited in vain for the gap through which they were to gallop against machine guns to victory, charged with lance and sabre across a cornfield just beyond the two Bazentin villages which had been taken with comparatively little fighting in the first surprise attack of the morning. Noel was killed that day at Bazentin-le-Petit.*

* Noel's battalion was the 7th Leicestershire in the 110th Brigade, deployed before dawn just outside Mametz Wood: 'In the front line were to be the 6th and 7th Leicestershires, each with a Stokes mortar attached. . . . The 6/Leicestershire moved up via the eastern edge of Mametz Wood and the 7th and 8th by the light railway where Lt.-Col. W. Drysdale of the 7th was wounded. By 2.35 a.m. in spite of shell-fire . . . the battalions were formed in four lines on the tapes. . . . When the barrage lifted at 3.25 a.m. the leading companies [of among others the 7/Leicestershire] rose and advanced through the ground mist at a steady pace . . . the enemy made but a feeble and spasmodic resistance to the first onslaught. The leading British wave reached the German line before a shot was fired. . . . The second line was taken without much resistance, by 4 a.m. . . . and the Leicestershire battalions passed on to occupy Bazentin-le-Petit Wood. The wood was taken with little fighting, except at the north-western corner, where the Germans held out all day. . . .' (*Official History of the War. France and Belgium 1916*, Macmillan, 1932, vol. 2, pp.75–81.)

Noel was killed in the initial attack on the wood (this was to have been part of a larger combined offensive which was first postponed and then abandoned in the course of the afternoon because of heavy losses and a determined German counter attack; some six hundred yards of ground were gained on 14 July at the cost of nine thousand British casualties—'as brilliant a success as British arms have ever gained,' according to that day's dispatch in *The Times*).

2

'It quite smashed my life up'

TERTIA WAS THE first to hear of his death in a letter from his commanding officer commiserating with her on her loss. She ran out on the street in her dressing-gown, beat on the next front door and implored Janet to go at once for news to the Asquiths. Janet set out for 10 Downing Street and was shown upstairs where Margot Asquith, in bed with a breakfast tray, was kind but not reassuring. She well understood what Janet must have feared, that Tertia was 'more sensitive than Dorothy' and might prove in despair the wilder of the two. But nothing could be done or found out. Janet returned by way of Paddington to meet an old family friend who had been summoned first thing from the country. By the time they got back to Queen's Road, Tertia had swallowed what she hoped was a fatal dose of sleeping tablets.

Her suicide was impulsive and unsuccessful. The doctor who brought her round advised her to wait another three or four years when she would know her own mind better. Or, as someone says in *More Women Than Men*, people do not so easily let go of life: 'What kills them is their own death, and not the loss of anyone else at all.'[9] It is a hard saying and a characteristic one. Ivy, in the days of Tertia's initial collapse, presented a granite front which supported her sister-in-law 'like a great rock'. The story that, on the day she heard of her brother's death, Ivy calmly discharged her duties as a V.A.D. nurse contains, like many of the legends which later sprang up around her, a basis of truth: its mistake lay not in assuming Ivy capable of carrying on business as usual but in the fundamentally misguided belief that it could ever have occurred to her to undertake war-work. She held the war, its works and the human race in contempt; and (even if her own early life had not given her a horror of nursing) she had endured too much at their hands to do anything but abhor public spirit.

Tertia in any case required attention. 'It is too sad to think that T's husband is killed,' wrote the Prime Minister on 25 July to Hilda

Harrisson, 'but I am afraid it is so. I tremble to think what will happen to her. And his loss is a terrible waste. He was not chair à canon.'[10] If Mr Asquith trembled for Tertia, so did her family who had to witness her first pitiful paroxysms of grief. Rumour got about that she was pregnant. Distracted and inconsolable, she could not endure the company of her family or friends or anyone save her father's faithful attendant, Eva Fox, who over the next eighteen months nursed her slowly towards recovery. 'Walking and talking and being with nature,' said Miss Fox, 'that seemed to bring her back more than anything.' It was Ivy who found the nursing home at Bexhill to which Tertia was dispatched with Miss Fox; Ivy who attended to winding up affairs in Queen's Road and at Easton Grey; Ivy who, as joint executor with Tertia, applied for probate of her brother's will;* and Ivy who paid regular visits to his widow in Bexhill, and a year or so later, at the cottage in Essex where Tertia was sufficiently restored to receive the attentions of another admirer. At the end of 1919, Ivy told her cousin that she still saw Tertia 'nearly every day'. Her attitude perhaps reflects the sympathy not untinged with distaste extended in her books to lovely, irresponsible egotists like Perdita Kingsford or Verena Gray who, helpless prey to their own emotions and perfectly impervious to other people's, are called to account less severely than their more stoical sisters for the consequences, always disastrous, of their own actions. Ivy's feeling for Tertia became, according to Vera Compton-Burnett, 'motherly almost'—a protective surveillance to which Tertia not unnaturally failed to respond. 'Tertia *didn't like* Ivy. She was not grateful to her at all.'

Nobody in the aftermath of Noel's death could do more than guess at his sister's grief: the more Tertia suffered, the less Ivy showed. Tertia's father had died a month before Noel on 11 June 1916, and it was again Ivy who went down with Dorothy to sort out and clear up at the rectory where, on 5 August, she too received a letter from one of Noel's fellow officers:

* The fact that probate was granted to Ivy alone means either that Tertia resigned as executor, or that she was declared unfit and incapable; Noel left her his personal belongings, the property inherited from his father, and the £200 a year provided for his widow under the terms of his mother's will (which meant virtually everything, since his estate came to £2,751), and the rest to Ivy.

> 7th Bn Leicestershire Regt.,
> B.E.F.
> 30 July 1916

Dear Miss Burnett,

How terrible it must be for you all at home. I'm sure we fellows in the midst of it all can't half realise what these losses mean to the people at home. From all the news I can gather Bumby fell in the greatest excitement of the attack, just as he and his wonderful platoon reached the German 1st line. He was hit in the head by a revolver bullet and passed away instantaneously, suffering no pain but falling like the wonderful hero he was. This was all just near the south edge of Bazentin-le-Petit wood and he would be buried on the battlefield by the chaplain and R.A.M.C. Do please write if I can do any little thing for you. . . . This is such a sad letter but please accept my deepest sympathy on your great terrible loss.

> Yours very sincerely,
> T. Cecil Howitt.[11]

A few days later Ivy wrote to her cousin Katie, on the black-edged mourning paper which had served for so many of her letters and Noel's in the fifteen years since their father's death:

Just a word to say that I *am* feeling braver, and that your letter *has* helped me to feel so.

It is a sorrow with a great pride in it—a terrible bitterness too, and a disappointment one cannot face as yet—but a great pride for—as the Provost of King's writes to me—the most complete and fullest sacrifice that any man has made.

Exact news has come to us too, and that is comforting. He was killed instantaneously, hit on the head by a revolver bullet, and had no pain. He had led his men right up to the German line, and secured it, and fell in the greatest excitement of the battle, and is buried on the battlefield. Well, one thinks how, as a little boy, he always said he would be a soldier.

It had haunted me to think that perhaps he had suffered, and longed for people who loved him, and now I am happier. Tertia is well again, but often very low spirited. What can one expect? No, there is no prospect of a child, dearest, I did not mean to give you that idea. There is no ordinary comfort, you see.

It will not do to build much on a letter written when Ivy was probably so stunned that she could barely apprehend the fact of her brother's
death, far less deal rationally with it. But, even allowing for the conventional formulae of grief, her letter does suggest how far she still had
to go before she reached the philosophy worked out in her books
(where self-sacrifice is invariably, often criminally unwise, and its
recipients neither proud nor grateful), and how difficult the journey
must have been. Vera Brittain has described the mental inertia of people
bereaved by the war who dared not look beyond the platitudes which
stood between themselves and madness: 'My only hope now was to
become the complete automaton. . . . Thought was too dangerous; if
once I began to think out exactly why my friends had died . . . quite
dreadful things might suddenly happen.'[12] More than a quarter of a
million British soldiers were killed or maimed for a territorial gain of
at most eight miles in the Battle of the Somme. Out of 12,500 Cambridge men who like Noel had joined the army, nearly a quarter were
reported dead or wounded by October 1916. 'It was a terrible war,'
said Ivy, 'it got into every life, it got into every home.' Private despair
was multiplied on an inconceivable scale, and reflected in the public
confusion which tried frantically to make sense in terms of sacrifice out
of the loss of almost a whole generation. Long after the war people still
clung to the 'perfect patriotism' of books like *Tell England* in which
the country's population is likened to a Holy Family 'composed of
fathers who so loved the world that they gave their sons', mothers
similarly inclined and sons so ennobled by this parental generosity that
they gladly died: 'To be eighteen in 1914 is to be the best thing in
England. England's wealth used to be counted in other things. Nowa-
days . . . boys are the richest things she's got.'[13] It was not for another
ten years and more that books like Robert Graves' began to put the case
that England's boys had been squandered to no end save to pay for the
complacent, callous stupidity of their elders.

'In these days we do not look forward,' wrote Ivy at Christmas 1916
to Katie. 'The hour is enough.' Since Noel's death she had lived with
Dorothy who, though hardly a consoling companion, must have
been a distracting and often a provoking one. People ignored Dorothy
at their peril. Life at Easton Grey had cramped but not curbed her
instinct for operating on the grand scale: 'Poor as church mice we may
be,' said Dorothy, 'but proud as Lucifer'. Years later she compiled a list
of the austere joys of her youth: almond blossom, bluebells, fine china,

'intense literature', days 'filled with plain living and high thinking'. 'Living vividly' was an article of faith with Dorothy who, as she said, had all her life 'a dread almost amounting to obsession of doing anything unless the Spirit moved'. It moved a great deal, always vehemently, and not always as harmlessly as the programme outlined above might suggest. But Dorothy's malevolence, brought on when the disobliging facts of plain living impinged too sharply on the raptures induced by high thinking, no doubt suited Ivy whose bitterness was not the less terrible for being shared. 'We were both witty women,' said Dorothy. 'I should think very few women have meant as much to each other as Ivy and me.' More than fifty years later Dorothy still had the exquisite carriage and the graceful, incisive gestures of a legendary Edwardian beauty; the classical perfection of her features, and the shyness carried off with such a high hand that few of her admirers can have had the nerve to suspect it, are nicely illustrated by her story of 'one of the greatest compliments I have ever received from a half-Russian dress maker who I had urged not to let me be too dowdy— "How can Madame ever hope to be fashionable with a face like that?"'

It was the combination of devastating looks with an equally devastating malice which appealed to Asquith (known as 'the Oracle' to Dorothy, who habitually annoyed her family and friends with often rather more opprobrious nicknames), and probably also to Ivy, who seems to have enjoyed the company of pretty women in something very like the Prime Minister's spirit of more or less platonic appreciation. One of the things which had irritated visitors to Easton Grey in the days when Dorothy was 'Queen of the rectory' was her ostentatious devotion to her father: 'Tertia did the housekeeping and Dorothy did her father's business,' said Miss Fox (who had herself copied out the whole of *Ecclesiastes* in braille on the rector's instructions). Dorothy had never forgiven her mother for, as she said, 'taking the easy way out of life at Easton Grey'. This was a kind of truculence which Ivy well understood and perhaps passed on to Tullia Calderon who, in *Elders and Betters*, retaliates against the defection of one parent by dedicating herself to the other: 'Father may spring a demand on me at any moment. I must turn a blind eye to general claims . . . my time, as you know, involves Father's . . . I can hardly leave my father for an hour, and must just submit to fate.'[14] One cannot help suspecting in Tullia's boastfulness echoes of much that must have amused her creator in Dorothy, who could on occasion show the same baleful candour as Tullia and who plumed herself on the same lofty indifference to practical affairs:

'She held it beneath her to talk or think of money, and assumed it was always there, which would indeed have disposed of its problems.'

Ivy's dryness was more than equal to Dorothy's condescension, and the two got along sufficiently well to contemplate setting up house together on Ivy's means. By December 1916, they were living temporarily at 30 Westbourne Terrace: 'The Christmas institution is truly a trial, and I have been in low spirits, I confess,' wrote Ivy. 'Dorothy too has been depressed—the many troubles of the year being enough to make her so—and the Asquith disturbance* has done what it could to worry people intimate with them . . . to be just and cheerier, a growing circle of congenial friends is doing a great deal for me.' One of these was Winifred Felkin and very likely another was Margaret Jourdain, whom Ivy met through Winifred or Elliott round about this time. A third was Alan Kidd whom she had encountered with Eric Forbes-Adam at a dinner party given that autumn by Janet for Ivy and Dorothy. Alan Kidd, a charming and eligible bachelor, comfortably off and strikingly handsome after the romantic Sherlock Holmes school of looks, was a friend of Jack's from Whitehall and promptly became a regular caller on Ivy and Dorothy, presenting each with identical bound volumes for Christmas. It was at first far from clear which of the two he was courting and Janet, well placed to observe the affair from the start, believed that Ivy would have been by no means displeased if his choice had lighted on her. But, as an unmistakable preference for Dorothy emerged, Ivy tactfully took to spending her evenings that winter in Queen's Road with Janet. Gallantry alone, according to Dorothy, prevented Alan from proposing until she and Ivy were settled in their new home. He had not wished her decision to be taken in haste or spoilt afterwards by hankerings for what Dorothy called 'the perfect rooftree', which was a flat at 59 Leinster Square taken by Ivy in the summer of 1917. Here the two entertained among others O.B. (on a visit from Rome where he had retired to an apartment largely furnished with revolving busts of himself) who, in spite of his vast bulk, insisted on being hoisted up to the roof to admire the Bayswater view laid out at his feet. Dorothy had confessed her engagement in some trepidation to Ivy—'I thought she'd think it weakminded of me'—but Ivy accepted the news as blandly as if she had planned it herself: 'That was her attitude to life, that what she chose went, so to speak. What it came to was it would keep me quiet and calm while she had more time for her writing, and she still had me there to say any wild thing that

* Asquith resigned as Prime Minister on 5 December 1916.

came into her head.' Dorothy was married from Ivy's flat on 31 August 1917; Asquith was witness to the wedding and Ivy dressed the bride who 'looked lovely', as Ivy complacently said.

It is of course possible that Ivy was writing again by this time but perhaps more likely that Dorothy, whose memory was not strong on facts, had confused this with a later period in her mind. 'One was a good deal cut up by the war; one's brother was killed, and one had family troubles' was Ivy's own 'masterly understatement'[15] when asked, as she often was afterwards, what had happened in the fourteen years between her first and second novels. By the summer of 1917 Tertia seemed well on the way to recovery, Ivy's sisters had apparently dropped out of her life and she herself presented a resolutely cheerful face to her friends. 'She was a creature of tremendous tenacity of feeling,' said Dorothy. But even Janet, who spent nearly every evening with Ivy when Jack was away for months on end at the front, was permitted scarcely a glimpse of anything below the surface of Ivy's inscrutable small talk. In the middle of July Janet returned for the birth of her second child to her parents' house in Lancaster Gate, where Ivy paid her a visit and kept the conversation as always to scraps of gossip and news: 'I remember thinking then that she was completely overcome,' said Janet. 'Jim meant the beginning and end of life to her.' A full year had passed since his death. One thinks of the bleak rejoinder in *Darkness and Day*, when someone says that time must help people get used to if not get over a loss:

'Time has too much credit,' said Bridget. 'I never agree with the compliments paid to it. It is not a great healer. It is an indifferent and perfunctory one. Sometimes it does not heal at all. And sometimes when it seems to, no healing has been necessary.'[16]

Janet had learnt a good deal that winter about the Compton-Burnetts in conversations from which she chiefly remembered how much Ivy had loved her father and how little her mother, to whom she had nonetheless remained 'a dutiful daughter' at Hove. Her sisters were by this time a lost cause so far as Ivy was concerned: though she still stood guardian and punctually discharged their business affairs, they had forfeited all further claim on her sympathy. They can hardly have missed it, being by this time so taken up with hard work and friends of their own that it seemed small hardship to be 'kept rather tight' by their guardians. Freedom and the Bohemian life went far towards compensating

for the rigid restraints of their childhood (though they were not yet
sufficiently emancipated to realize that they might dispense with a
boy for cleaning the knives, or manage without a maid who wore pink
or blue print in the morning and white in the afternoon, and whose
laundry placed a considerable strain on their slender finances). Otherwise their circle consisted largely of musicians and mystics, two callings
which Ivy could never abide. She and her brothers had early abandoned
religion on aesthetic and practical grounds; her sisters inclined rather to
the spirit world, taking comfort in the life force, reincarnation, the
mastery of mind over matter, the teachings of Mrs Besant and Emerson's American disciples which, like a good many other quasi-religious,
quasi-philosophical faiths, were much in vogue both before and after
the war. Vera and Juliet later became lifelong followers of Rudolph
Steiner and Anthroposophy. Topsy and Primrose were especially
attracted by what was then called New Thought. Their music master
had introduced them to *In Tune With The Infinite* by Ralph Waldo
Trine, who writes with a fervent, higgledy-piggledy effusiveness not
unlike Dr Compton Burnett's style of chat. It was perhaps Trine's
rousing optimism, expressed with more vigour than clarity, which
appealed to a similar strain in Dr Burnett's daughters; but it is hard to
believe that the doctor would not have made short work of Trine's
views on bodily health, or that he would have entertained Trine's
general conclusions—on 'God-thoughts' inducing 'God-power' and
eventually turning 'God-thinkers' into 'God-men'—with any more
patience than Ivy. 'Mystical means muddle-headed'[17] was one of her
sayings and her father, equally firm, had disposed of faith-healing as
'to my mind, rank nonsense'.

   The gap in age and status had precluded much feeling between Ivy
and her two youngest sisters, whose tiresomeness must have seemed
not the least of her problems at Hove. From their point of view, Ivy
meant trouble: 'Being held in the way they were, and being spoken to
in the way that they were . . . that was unpalatable to them.' Primrose,
who had been presented at birth to the infant Topsy as 'your baby', had
scarcely had cause to feel herself much wanted afterwards by anyone
else. She had been nearly two when their father died, Topsy five years
old and so like him that he called her 'wee Daddy'. Their lives had been
almost from the start so abnormal that the exchange of one tyrant for
another on their mother's death had probably made little difference,
though perhaps it increased their sense of their own helplessness. They
turned to each other with an absorption which increased as they grew

older to a point at which it involved a practically complete rejection of the outside world. By the summer of 1917 they had withdrawn into a dreamy, lethargic, secretive indifference which desperately worried their sisters. Veronal had been prescribed for Topsy's toothache before the family left Hove and, long before anyone suspected the reason, the drug which had provided at first a temporary oblivion, more soothing even than music, had become a permanent refuge. Topsy, once a passionate reader of Shakespeare, had not opened a book for months. Primrose had been an especially lively child, Topsy by common consent the brightest of the four and the one who was to have made a career as a concert violinist: she had played for O.B. at the age of eleven and given a public recital with Vera at Hove, but in London the two youngest sisters both gradually gave up practising.

The common front against interference which had been necessary in childhood had given all four girls a regard for privacy and a dread of intruding on one another which perhaps partly explains what happened next. Topsy and Primrose shared a bedroom and habitually kept the door locked. On 10 December 1917, they proposed spending a few day at a farm in West Wickham where they had gone for holidays before. Minnie, who left out a tray that night in the dining room, found the food eaten next day and the girls apparently gone. When, several days after they should have returned, she became sufficiently alarmed to make the journey to Wickham, the girls had not been seen at the farm. Their bedroom door remained locked. Iris, who had remained on friendly terms with her half-sisters, arrived from the Temperance Hospital and advised breaking down the door. On 27 December the lock was forced and the girls were found dead in bed, with five bottles of veronal, a water jug and a tumbler standing empty on the chest-of-drawers.

They were wearing dressing-gowns over their nightdresses, both lying on their right sides, Primrose's left hand clasping the dressing-gown of her sister. She had died first, twelve hours before Topsy, and both had been dead for at least two days. The two doctors who examined the bodies found it impossible to say whether the sisters had swallowed a lethal dose simultaneously, but they agreed that in spite of the cold it was almost inconceivable that either had been dead more than four days.* They were last seen alive on 10 December. What had

* It was at first assumed by the family (and by the local doctor) that the sisters had lain dead in bed for two and a half weeks before their bodies were found, but Dr (later Sir)

happened in the interval behind their locked door never emerged. A copy of Trine's *In Tune with the Infinite* was found in the room, and adduced at the inquest by Rutley Mowll as evidence that the girls had not deliberately killed themselves. Certainly the book unequivocally discourages suicide which, since the spirit body coexists with and outlasts the physical, seemed to Trine not so much criminal as pointless. Evidence at the inquest showed that Primrose had bought the bottles of veronal one at a time from the same chemist over the past six months (and had said, in reply to his warnings, that she used it 'entirely to obtain sleep'). But the motives behind what *The Times* reported as 'Mystery in St John's Wood' remained uninvestigated, and the coroner recorded a verdict of death from an overdose of veronal with a rider for which the family was thankful: 'Under what circumstances such overdose was taken there is not sufficient evidence to show.'[18]

Ivy attended the inquest but was not called to give evidence. Having lost her father and both her brothers, settled her account with her mother and disowned her sisters, she seemed already so thoroughly detached from the past that Janet at least had supposed 'family troubles' could never hurt her again. But even Ivy's reserve could not wholly conceal the effect of a tragedy for which no one had been prepared. She could not sleep afterwards and lay awake coughing night after night; insomnia was always an affliction with which she sympathized in her friends, and from which she suffered for the rest of her life. Pity for her sisters was perhaps compounded with pity for herself—one's own grounds for self-pity being, as Oliver Shelley says in *Two Worlds and Their Ways*, generally too deep for words: 'Mine are the knotted and tangled kind, that lie fallow in the day and rise up to torment people at night'.[19] The double death was too drastic, and its implications too grievous, to be explored much at the time. Drug addiction was not in any case a subject which could be readily discussed in 1918. Dorothy had her own highly characteristic explanation: 'They were bored with life—they lived vividly even at that age. They were very highly tuned, and they could bear it no longer.' Ivy at the very end of her life advanced another theory to Vera: 'You know, I think Topsy and Baby had too much music in their lives. I think it was all that music. John

---

Bernard Spilsbury, who carried out the post-mortems as Home Office pathologist, maintained that this was virtually impossible, and that they had almost certainly died on Christmas Day.

always thought so, I know.' (John had been Ivy's name for Noel, not used by the rest of the family.)

In later years, when wild rumours which she did not entirely discourage tended to circulate about I. Compton-Burnett, it was inevitably suggested that her sisters had killed themselves in despair at being detected in an illicit affair with one another. But the notion of Lesbianism, with or without incestuous connections, involves a misconception about what was and what was not accepted as normal behaviour in Victorian families, whose permissiveness in some directions seems often as startling as their prudishness in others. Caresses between girls, between men, between brother and sister were freely indulged as signs of a tenderness which might well now bear a more prurient interpretation. In Ivy's childhood it would have been considered incomparably more shocking that a respectable married woman should openly refer (as Ivy's mother apparently did) to sitting on her husband's knee than that two sisters should sleep together. Girls commonly shared a bedroom and often a bed. If Freud opened the door on much that was murky in family relations, he also put a stop to much that went on in perfect ignorance and innocence. People who grew up before the first war say that it is impossible today to conceive of the barbaric sexual darkness in which children of both sexes were brought up and expected to remain till they married. Ivy herself must have resented this suppression acutely, or so at least one would suppose from a note of Butler's in which he proposes that the facts of sex be fully and frankly explained to adolescents: 'There should be no mystery or reserve. None but the corrupt will wish to corrupt facts. . . .'[20] This was, even in 1918, a preposterously provocative suggestion, and meant to be so. Ivy marked the whole passage in her copy of the *Note-Books* with a stroke at the side, underlined the last sentence and added a pencilled note in the margin: 'Then what a mass of corruption is the average person!'

In this kind of atmosphere passionate attachments flourished as a matter of course. Novelettes of the period regularly contain brothers whose behaviour to their sisters is unashamedly 'lover-like'.* Such

---

* e.g. the intense relationship between the chaste heroine of Maud Diver's *Captain Desmond, V.C.* (Blackwood, Popular Edition, 1925) and her favourite bachelor brother: 'He led her into the dining-room with more of lover-like than brother-like tenderness; for despite his forty years no woman had yet dethroned this beautiful sister of his from the foremost place in his heart.' (p.10) There is an excellent account of the physical relations considered perfectly proper between Victorian women to whom Lesbianism was unknown, whether in theory or practice, in John Fowles' *The French Lieutenant's Woman* (Cape, 1969, pp.154–6).

things could hardly have been encouraged in a society which less ruthlessly inhibited the discussion, let alone the practice, of sex or anything
remotely connected with it; and, though it is tempting, it would be
unwise to interpret Ivy's early life in the light of the relish with which
she afterwards confronted all shades of homosexuality in fact and
fiction. Habitual discretion among the Compton-Burnett children,
reinforced perhaps by the havoc they had seen spread from their
mother's love for their father, had bred if anything a more than usual
delicacy in sexual matters. It was generally believed by their closest
friends that Noel had never consummated his marriage to Tertia, and
indeed he himself said as much in one of his letters to Jack; but, though
one might ascribe this abstention to a vestige of what Noel called 'my
old morbidities', it was more likely due to a characteristically generous
resolve that, if he must leave a widow, he would at least avoid the
additional suffering that his death would have brought to a fatherless
child. The fact that neither Ivy nor any of her five surviving sisters and
half-sisters married was the rule rather than the exception among their
contemporaries. The slaughter of men of their own age was one of the
privations Ivy's generation had had to endure, and she accepted it
philosophically as part of the illimitable damage done by the war. She
herself had for years relied for amusement at Hove on the company of
Noel's friends from Cambridge; and Janet Beresford was positive that,
in spite of her shyness, 'Ivy wouldn't have minded at all' if Alan Kidd
had asked her to marry him in 1917. Fifty years later there was even a
hint that Ivy had been fond of, perhaps in love with, someone else who
was killed in the war[21] which is possible though deeply improbable in
the light of her character and circumstances. Both her sisters and Janet
are certain that there was no truth in this rumour. If Ivy had suffered a
further loss, it was in any case negligible compared to the pain of
Noel's death which reinforced and brought back Guy's: '"Them both
dying like that," she said many times, "quite smashed my life up, it
quite smashed my life up." The violence of the phrase was most uncharacteristic, but she never varied it.'[22]

Her efforts to subdue and contain the long series of shocks culminat-
ing in the suicide of her sisters must have lowered Ivy's resistance for
she was desperately ill in the influenza epidemic which ran through
London like the plague in the late summer of 1918, raging with such
virulence that by October the casualty lists from the front were matched
by columns almost as long in the papers of people who had died from
'flu at home. Shortage of food, light, heat and domestic help, rising

costs, frequent air raids and perpetual anxiety in the past four years had weakened the civilian population. The sickness struck mostly at young people and developed so swiftly into acute pneumonia that death followed often in a matter of days, sometimes hours. Ivy, who had remained alone in her flat at Leinster Square with a daily woman to clean it, declined to summon help or take to her bed and was found by chance almost unconscious in the empty flat. Nurses were not to be had for any money so for the next few weeks Minnie came over each day from St John's Wood and was replaced by Vera at night. 'We didn't have the antibiotics then,' said Ivy. 'One just fought for breath for about a month.'²³ She was often delirious and would struggle to climb out of bed.

Personal acquaintance no doubt accounts for the particular excellence of sickbeds and deathbeds in her books, and for her intimate knowledge of the pneumonia which draws Ruth Giffard 'down into depths of fear and suffering' and very nearly kills Dudley Gaveston. Dudley's illness, in *A Family and a Fortune*, closely follows the course of Ivy's own. His strength, like hers, had been undermined by what his family call 'the troubles', he too had gone away by himself and been discovered alone, barely conscious, close to delirium and fighting for breath: 'The crisis came, and Dudley sank to the point of death and just did not pass it. Then as he lived through the endless days, each one doubled by the night, he seemed to return to this first stage, and this time drained and shattered by the contest waged within him.'²⁴

Ivy lay for several months in this state of extreme debility, unable to read or write though she liked to be read to and gave specific instructions to Vera: 'Read, but don't put any expression into it. Read in a dull, monotonous voice.' Dudley Gaveston had made the same proviso, which is several times invoked in the novels among those who dread the excessive feeling and 'the beautiful self-conscious voice' displayed in reading aloud by Sophia Stace and other descendants of Ivy's mother.

As her strength slowly returned, Ivy began to see people again and to take more interest in books, though she herself said she could stand nothing stronger than Wilkie Collins. Margot Asquith came to visit her, and so did Arthur Waley who later maintained that for years after Noel's death Ivy refused to do anything but lie on a sofa all day eating chocolates: 'We all used to urge her to stop reading library books and write some of her own.'²⁵ He attributed the elaborate and, for a twentieth-century novelist, highly idiosyncratic machinery from which

I

she eventually evolved her plots to her weakness for melodramas constructed around secret passion and sensational revelation, mistaken
identity, misappropriated funds, missing wills, lost, stolen and always
fatally compromising letters. 'That', according to Arthur, 'was Ivy's
idea of a novel.' To help pass the time she had also taken to needlework,
and covered the seats of her chairs: 'I couldn't do brainwork, you see,'
said Ivy, 'but then my brain came back.'

3

'And then she went into a retrospect'

THE TAPESTRY PATTERNS for Ivy's chairs were said to have been chosen for her by Winifred's friend, Margaret Jourdain, whose *History of English Secular Embroidery* had been published in 1910. Margaret was the youngest but two of the nine clever children* of the Rev. Francis Jourdain, who had been vicar of Ashbourne in Derbyshire and whose family was in its own way as remarkable, almost as indigent and quite as old as the Beresfords. The Jourdains descended from French Huguenots (Raymond, Guillaume and Alphonse Jourdain had given distinguished service in the First and Third Crusades)²⁶ who crossed the channel in two waves at the beginning of the sixteenth and end of the seventeenth centuries. A John Jourdain was Mayor of Lyme Regis in 1584, his son a founder of the East India Company and his cousin Sylvester was shipwrecked with Somers and Gates and one of Lytton Strachey's forebears off the Bermudas in 1609 (accounts of this voyage by Sylvester Jourdain and William Strachey are thought to have given Shakespeare ideas for *The Tempest*). Another ancestor, Renatus Jourdain, was drowned off the Scillies with Sir Cloudesley Shovell in 1707, several more rose to high command in the British army and the extraordinarily varied achievements of the inmates of Ashbourne vicarage suggest that by the late nineteenth century the family had by no means lost its taste for adventure.

Two of the Rev. Jourdain's five sons travelled widely in Africa and the arctic, three of his daughters were among the first women at Oxford and, though he himself seems to have published nothing more ambitious than a guide to his parish church, seven of his children wrote books as easily and often as most people write letters. Margaret's eldest

---

* Mrs Jourdain, on being told by a parishioner that a bus route had been opened between Jerusalem and Jericho, is said to have answered tartly: 'How I should like to fill it with all his clever children!' (*The Ghosts of Versailles* by Lucille Iremonger, Faber, 1957, p.65.)

brother was a pioneer and scholar as distinguished in ornithological circles as she herself was to become on furniture and the decorative arts. Her eldest sister was Principal of St Hugh's in Oxford, and something of a celebrity outside it on account of having seen the ghost of Marie Antoinette at Versailles; another sister, Charlotte, had been governess to the Asquiths before joining the community of the Sisters of Mercy at Truro (a sisterhood which, some dozen years earlier, had been suspected of having designs on Lady Ottoline Morrell)[27]. Her brothers Charles, Henry and Raymond had all fought in the war, the first two commanding battalions: Raymond was wounded, Henry was the only officer in his regiment to survive Gallipoli, and Charles was killed in France three months before the armistice. There is nothing to suggest that Margaret had been especially attached to Charles (who was considerably older, married, and had in any case spent the better part of the past thirty years defending the empire in India, Ceylon and South Africa), but the loss of a brother in the war must have deepened a friendship already beginning to prosper with Ivy.

Stories about Margaret from childhood onwards suggest a shrewd, self-reliant and singularly unorthodox character. Charlotte Jourdain's decision to take the veil can hardly have met with any great sympathy from a younger sister who, almost before she was out of the nursery, had understood and rejected her elders' exploitation of Christianity: 'Margaret saw that when she was a little girl,' said Ivy long afterwards to Elizabeth Taylor. 'She said to her governess, "I don't want to hear any more about that poor man," and walked out of the room.' Margaret in middle age, when Ivy first met her, seems to have had points in common with Emily Herrick in *Pastors and Masters*, including an attitude to religion which held that things might have gone better if the mediaeval church had kept the Bible chained up. She had freely declared herself an atheist for years before that (though she still sat on Sundays in the family pew, for much the same reasons as the civilized, tolerant atheists in Ivy's books). She had taken a third in classical Mods at Lady Margaret Hall in 1897, returning home afterwards to live with her widowed mother at Broadwindsor in Dorset and to found, with her younger brother and sister, what became almost a family industry.

Philip and Melicent Jourdain had been crippled from birth by an hereditary paralysis (Philip so severely that he could not hold a pen), but both contributed over the next decade and more to the steady stream of publications issuing from Broadwindsor Manor. Margaret and Melicent wrote poems; Philip, a Cambridge mathematician specializing in transfinite numbers, edited a couple of scientific and ethical journals; Melicent published an autobiography; Margaret and Philip produced between them fifteen books in the first sixteen years of the century (these included an English edition of Horace's *Odes*[28] in which Margaret, still in her twenties, placed her own translations side by side with renderings of the same lines from better known hands such as Milton, Ben Jonson and W. E. Gladstone). Margaret's output meanwhile had risen from three published articles in 1903 to nearly sixty in 1910, on anything from chintzes to Chinese wallpapers, stump work to samplers, card tables, knife cases, old grates and trunks, cradles, tea pots and royal gloves. These provided, if not an adequate income, at least a foothold in London and, by the beginning of the war, Margaret had taken rooms with a college friend engaged on relief work (which no doubt meant for them, as it did for so many women at the time, relief in more senses than one) in Trafalgar Square, Chelsea, where her scope widened to cover patriotic pieces on the Germans, on soldiers' letters from the front, on air raids for Philip's *International Journal of Ethics*, and a war-work series for *Country Life*.

Margaret belonged to the genre of New Woman which had once dismayed Dr Burnett, a small but growing band of unattached, self-assured, purposeful spinsters accustomed to make their own way in the world. By the end of 1918, she meant to make hers as a freelance from journalism, catalogues, handbooks and articles on the great country houses which she, being better connected and far more determined than many of her colleagues, was often the first professional to penetrate. Her tastes were rather more worldly than Ivy's on both social and literary fronts. She knew many of the writers and journalists who had revolved round literary hostesses like Violet Hunt before the war, and she had been a protégée of Lord Alfred Douglas during his short and stormy editorship of the *Academy*, when he took her about, lunched with her at the Café Royal, published her poems, encouraged her to write about nature or the French symbolist poets, sent her a weekly parcel of books to review and generally succeeded for almost two years in diverting her attention away from the decorative arts. Lord Alfred, cramped but not crestfallen after the Wilde trial, had prided himself on an eye for spotting young poets, publishing Rupert Brooke and Siegfried Sassoon as well as 'M. Jourdain' in the intervals between steering his paper on a fairly disastrous course of litigation. The *Academy* folded in 1910, but not before its editor had brought out Margaret's *Outdoor Breviary* (a set of pastoral prose pieces which appeared in the *Academy* throughout 1909) in the same format as his own *Sonnets*: Margaret had a copy of these inscribed 'To Miss Jourdain (author of so many good sonnets)—Alfred Douglas. 1909.' Her own *Poems*, published in the same year as *Dolores*, were dedicated 'To Janette'.

Margaret had shared rooms when she first came to London with Janette Ranken who, having gone down from Oxford after two years and pursued a brief career on the stage, left her companion in 1917 to marry the actor Ernest Thesiger—a marriage which astonished their friends, since neither bride nor groom had previously taken any great interest in the opposite sex. Ernest Thesiger became for Janette's sake a friend of Margaret and, for his own, a lifelong friend of Ivy. He was not only irresistibly fetching himself, but typical of much in Margaret's circle that greatly appealed to Ivy: a renegade from an impeccable family (his grandfather had been the first Lord Chelmsford and his father, as Ernest recorded with pleasure, 'knew nearly all the Peers of the Realm')[29] and an eccentric of the first water, a man who wore pearls next the skin and had told Réjane that her nose was even more ugly than his. His looks were extraordinary: he had been drawn by Sargent, caricatured by Max Beerbohm and painted on fans by Charles Condor ('as Death, in black draperies, with a skull-mask wreathed in scarlet poppies'). He had enlisted as a private in 1915 and baffled his commanding officer by taking his needlework with him. Ernest Thesiger was the man who said, or is supposed to have said, when asked for a first-hand impression of Ypres, 'My dear, *the noise*!! and *the people*!!!'

All this must have come as a pleasant shock to Ivy, though it can scarcely have come all at once. Winifred had introduced her to Margaret before or just after Dorothy's marriage and for a time they formed a congenial trio, so much so that when Ivy and Margaret showed signs of becoming a pair Winifred was hard put to conceal her resentment at being left out. Ivy had probably proposed sharing her flat (though neither party can as yet have envisaged that the arrangement would work on a permanent basis) round about the end of 1918 when Margaret moved out of her old rooms in Trafalgar Square; an entry in Margaret's diary suggests that she was already staying at 59 Leinster Square by the following May. She was away for most of the summer, and on 1 October her brother Philip died. Of all her brothers Philip had always been closest to Margaret in interests as well as in age: the two had lived and worked together for years and, long after Margaret's departure and Philip's marriage in 1915, each had continued to put work in the way of the other—Margaret acting as Philip's editorial assistant, Philip putting forward her name for articles on anything from 'The Victorian Spirit' to 'What Bolshevism Is' for the *Daily Mail*. His death, fourteen months after Charles', must have been hard on his sister, and perhaps it provided a more intimate bond than anything else could have done when Margaret finally moved into Ivy's flat on 6 October 1919.

Margaret was forty-three that autumn, Ivy was thirty-five. Each had been at a loose end and each no doubt found in the other a convenient solution to their respective problems of where and with whom to live. Part of Margaret's attraction for Ivy lay perhaps in the fact that she had no connection whatever with the miseries and mistakes of the past; part also in her vitality, her formidable organizing powers, her decided opinions, multifarious interests and countless friends. But Ivy at this time was still 'drained and shattered' and in no state to cope with anything save a prolonged convalescence, which probably explains why Margaret fell into the habit of pampering her, fetching her book or her bag and saying indulgently, when Dorothy suggested that Ivy might fetch things herself, 'You see, she's like a child.' It was years since Ivy had mattered in this way to anyone, far less been able to depend on anyone as she had once done on her brothers; and it must have been under the reviving influence of Margaret's courage and humour and affection that Ivy's 'brain came back'.

One may also date from much the same time what seems to have been a crucial encounter with Samuel Butler. His *Note-Books* had been published posthumously in 1912 but Ivy's copy is a fourth impression of the second edition published in 1918. The first, and perhaps the most startling, of all her marks in the book was prompted by a passage on the life after death of great artists—on whom 'death confers a more living kind of life than they can ever possibly have enjoyed while to those about them they seemed to be alive'—in contrast to the death-in-life endured by their less ambitious contemporaries: 'The whole life of some people is a kind of partial death—a long, lingering death-bed, so to speak, of stagnation and nonentity on which death is but the seal, or solemn signing, as the abnegation of all further act and deed on the part of the signer. Death robs these people of even that little strength which they appeared to have and gives them nothing but repose.'[30] There is a note at the foot of the page in Ivy's hand, wild and sprawling and ill-spelt, as though forced from her at some moment when even she could no longer keep up her calm front of civilization and artificiality: 'I am a living witniss of this crushing lifless stagnation of the spirit.'

Ivy's was scarcely an excessive or even an uncommon reaction to a cataclysm which had taken all that she valued, smashed her private life and smashed with it the social and moral foundations on which the world had seemed so solidly built. People who emerged from the first war sore, angry, depleted and desperately in need of consolation suffered often enough from what Dr Compton Burnett called 'a kind of dead-all-over feeling' which simply increased the pain when their rational faculties returned. Many succumbed altogether to a mental and emotional numbness from which others only slowly or partly recovered. One of the hardest things for the survivors to bear, apart from their own personal losses, was the irretrievable collapse of standards and assumptions for which it seemed that their contemporaries had died in millions: '. . . my mind groped in a dark, foggy confusion, uncertain of what had happened to it or what was going to happen,' wrote Vera Brittain, whose experience is paralleled in a good many autobiographies of the period. 'Still partly dominated by old ideals, time-worn respectabilities and spasms of rebellious bitterness, it sometimes seized fleetingly the tail of an idea upon whose wings it was later to ascend into a clearer heaven of new convictions.'[31] For Miss Brittain, as for many others, wings were provided by the study of history and the new heaven meant campaigning for internationalism, the League of Nations and women's rights. For Ivy the quickening impulse apparently came from Butler, who provided her when she needed them with texts from which she was to work for the rest of her life. It was presumably at some time in the years when she lay on a sofa, tended by Margaret and teased by her friends, that she marked (with a recklessness quite unlike her usual caution) his passages on 'The Family'; on 'Religion'; on 'Change and Immorality'; on sex, money and the dangers of keeping young people from knowledge of either.

Butler had died in 1901, when he was known if at all as the eccentric author of *Erewhon* and various other more or less obscure and peculiar works, including one devoted to proving that a woman wrote the *Odyssey*. His vogue, which reached its height in the 'twenties, had been gathering strength since the publication of *The Way of All Flesh* in 1903. If Ivy had read Butler's novel before the war, it had made no impression or none that affected *Dolores*. The *Note-Books* contain a selection from the common-place books in which it was Butler's custom to pare down and polish reflections which, when they came out, were considered according to which way you looked at them either delightfully or dreadfully bold. The scored and pencilled pages of Ivy's copy suggest that she responded as readily as she had once submerged herself in George Eliot to a set of proposals for radical subversion laid down with Butler's most disarming and deceptive mildness. Both the subversive content and the sweetly reasonable manner are reflected in *Pastors and Masters*, and throughout Ivy's subsequent novels in which— though she retained her preoccupation with duty, self-sacrifice, power and its crippling effects on both those who wield and those who submit to it—she nonchalantly reversed the conclusions drawn in *Dolores*.

Up to 1911, and probably much later, Ivy had shown small sign of deviating from the conventional outlook of her class and age. Though she objected to society's blatant use of religion for highly dubious ends, she was not apparently inclined to cavil at its moral underpinning. One may at least suspect as much from a letter to Katie, dated 24 March 1913, expounding the improving power of sorrow—a theory Ivy afterwards had cause to revise, if not disown:

> If you do not let it embitter you, as you are less inclined to do than I, and even if you cannot help its embittering you a little, it will make you larger in the long run. And as you grow larger, you grow more useful, to others anyhow, and in a way to yourself. No experience is ever wasted; and an experience like this will come to seem to you in years to come, to be the cause of the best of what you are—and will no doubt be the cause of much you would never have been without it. Real charity and a real ability never to condemn—the one real virtue—is so often the result of a waking experience that gives a glimpse of what lies beneath things.

The lesson Butler taught is easily seen if one compares this letter with Ivy's later views on real quality. It is not simply that the advantage in her novels seldom lies with people who aim at true success ("'The other kind of success is better,' said France. 'True success seems to be effort and achievement without any reward. It is as bad as true kindness or honest advice or anything else of that kind'")[32] or show true dignity ("'I always wonder if the true kinds of dignity, the dignity of toil and simplicity and frugal independence, are as good as the other kinds'"). This sort of thing might be dismissed, and indeed often has been, as a superficial playing on words, though one might as easily argue that a more fastidious use of words reflects a greater delicacy of feeling on Ivy's part than the conventional comfort handed out to her cousin in 1913. The unselfish conduct outlined in her letter had not proved a practical programme for Ivy in the years when she ruled her sisters at Hove. It is a short step, though a hard one, from tacitly condoning this gap between practice and precept to recognizing that the gap favours the powerful at the expense of the weak; that it promotes the worst excesses of hypocrisy and callousness; that it bedevils people's dealings with one another at all levels from international politics to the most humdrum transactions inside a family; and that it is not to be closed. What passes for cynicism in the novels of I. Compton-Burnett is more often than not a casual acceptance of these harsh facts, the last being generally the one people find hardest to stomach. Their justification is given in an unusually explicit discussion, from *Elders and Betters*, on unselfishness:

'Most things that are good, or called good, are founded on that,' said Thomas.
'And those things are very good indeed, too good to be possible. It comes of a foundation that must break down. Most people have tried to build on it. And they remember it, and respect themselves, and are exacting with other people; and I think they are justified. A person who can really be called an unselfish person, has no place in life.'[33]

This is the philosophy implicit in all but the first of the novels of I. Compton-Burnett. It underlies her singularly persuasive portrayals of virtue as well as her sympathy with vice. And, though her readers must often have felt that it sprang fully armed from her head on to the pages of *Pastors and Masters*, its first inklings seem to have reached her from the following passages marked with her pencil in Butler's section on 'Elementary Morality'—passages which suggest that not the least of the things that pleased her about Butler was his fondness for speaking the truth with a thoroughly disingenuous air:

Vice and Virtue

i

Virtue is something which it would be impossible to over-rate if it had not been over-rated. The world can ill spare any vice which has obtained long and largely among civilized people. . . .

As a matter of private policy I doubt whether the moderately vicious are more unhappy than the moderately virtuous; 'Very vicious' is certainly less happy than 'Tolerably virtuous', but this is about all. *What pass muster as the extremes of virtue probably make people quite as unhappy as extremes of vice do.*

The truest virtue has ever inclined toward excess rather than asceticism; that she should do this is reasonable as well as observable, for virtue should be as nice a calculator of chances as other people and will make due allowance for the chance of not being found out. Virtue knows that it is impossible to get on without compromise, and tunes herself, as it were, a trifle sharp to allow for an inevitable fall in playing. So the Psalmist says, '*If thou, Lord, wilt be extreme to mark what is done amiss: O Lord who may abide it?*' and by this he admits that the highest conceivable form of virtue still leaves room for some compromise with vice. . . .

ii

The extremes of vice and virtue are alike detestable; absolute virtue is as sure to kill a man as absolute vice is, let alone the dullnesses of it and the pomposities of it.

vi

*Virtue has never yet been adequately represented by any who have had any claim to be considered virtuous. It is the sub-vicious who best understand virtue. Let the virtuous people stick to describing vice—which they can do well enough.**

It would be easy to find parallels for any or all of these passages in Ivy's books. Butler pointed her in a direction from which she never turned back, just as George Eliot had once misled her down tortuous paths to a dead end. What George Eliot blocked up, Butler unblocked, and there is evidence that Ivy retained her respect and affection for him long after she had discarded him as a pointer. Her fifth novel contains what I take to be a portrait of Butler himself, modelled so closely on material taken from Festing Jones' *Samuel Butler: A Memoir* that it is hard to believe it was not meant as a discreet but deliberate tribute. The

* *The Note-Books of Samuel Butler*, pp.27–8; the italics are mine throughout, and I have used them to mark the sentences singled out by Ivy's pencilled scorings in the margin of her copy.

Memoir came out in 1919, and was one of the library books that Ivy persisted in reading despite all Arthur Waley could say ('Have you seen the new life of Samuel Butler—by H. F. Jones?' she wrote to Katie in November 1919. 'Pleasant to get from the library—too dear to buy.'). From it she must have borrowed much that reappears, more or less thinly disguised and sometimes almost word for word, fourteen years later in *More Women Than Men*. Jones' book is immensely long, detailed and, as Asquith said, skipworthy; interesting at that time chiefly because it confirmed what a good many readers must have suspected, that *The Way of All Flesh* faithfully describes its author's own appalling childhood; and perhaps also, from Ivy's point of view, for a number of curious facts such as that Butler was a lifelong homoeopath and had once proposed becoming, if only to annoy his father, a homoeopathic physician himself. What he liked about homoeopathy, indeed what he liked about most things that appealed to him, was that 'It can't do you any harm'.[34]

The harm people do one another was an abiding horror to Butler. His own suffering at his father's hands had given him a driving sense of pain and punishment matched by the stoical conviction that, since people will inevitably inflict the one and suffer the other, the most one can do is limit one's power to hurt and to be hurt. He had escaped from his father at immense cost to his own emotional life. But the escape left him free to pursue, with unimpaired energy and greatly increased cheerfulness, his chosen rôle as a prophet—to spread alarm and despondency among all those who believed in religion, family life, the prospect of progress, innocence, charity, diligence, altruism or any other illusion whatever. He put his own faith where Ivy put hers, in material goods and very little else.

Hence no doubt the happy ending of *The Way of All Flesh*, whereby the woes of Ernest Pontifex are cancelled at a stroke on his coming suddenly into a suitably large fortune. The book, in some ways so like her own, perhaps showed Ivy what might be done with the past, if once one were sufficiently distanced from it; but here one treads on shaky ground, for Butler's novel belongs rather to the genre of satire or confessional than to imaginative fiction. Its characters are puppets deployed with a bland, judicious humour which is at once the measure of Butler's detachment from his childhood and the source of the book's controlled and savage power. His brilliance lies in extracting so much enjoyment, with so little bitterness, from his mother as a comic creation and, more subtly, from his father whose ferocity would be tragic were it not so humorous in the person of poor, fretful, hapless, hopeless, red-handed Canon Pontifex. Their brutality is the more atrocious for being dispassionately recorded; and the absurd dénouement, when Ernest returns home a rich man to confound his father, is all of a piece with the insouciance of the whole. There could be no atonement, not even the slow deaths in agony of both parents, in proportion to Ernest's suffering. Butler's tone is as light as his tale is dark, and the one fiercely illumines what in the other is shadowy, grim and fearful.

Butler preferred not to delve too deeply into horrors, whether in himself or his tormentors, which Ivy spent the greater part of her life probing. Beneath these opposite reactions one may detect a similar strength of will and a strong, though perhaps a superficial similarity of pattern: a tragic early life violently demolished and followed by a steadfast, stoical refusal ever again to put oneself emotionally at risk. Both, before they reached maturity, had survived a prolonged crisis or series of crises from which both emerged exhausted but intact. Butler made meagre use of the independence which he had so dearly bought, constructing for himself a routine of extreme and self-protective dullness pursued in drab surroundings with frugal pleasures, few excursions and fewer friends. His life became a matter of husbanding resources thriftily preserved from a struggle which left him in some directions permanently maimed, and which had intimate connections with the persistent 'knot of ideas' explored by P. N. Furbank in Butler's writings: 'the virtue of luck, the morality of health, the duty to be born of good ancestry, the reverence due to money'.[35] Ivy adopted this programme so naturally that the resigned and level voice of reason in her books might at times be Butler speaking:

'Have you never been taught about poverty not being a thing to be ashamed of?'
'I have always been ashamed of it. I would save anyone in my power from it. I have done so in the one case I could . . . things like poverty and old age and death are shameful. We cannot help them; but that is the humiliation. To accept conditions that would not be your choice must be a disgrace.'[36]

One may see also, in the apparent narrowness and sheltered regularity of Ivy's life with Margaret, something of the invalid sensibility detected by Furbank in Butler's dealings with his friends: 'It is the tone of the convalescent, and of the habitual rather than the temporary convalescent . . . Butler's life should be seen as a sharp and heroic resistance to a nearly mortal illness followed by a restoration to an inevitably low and never quite secure state of health.'* Ivy, on her own slow recovery from physical and nervous prostration, saw no reason to dismantle the camouflage of dullness remarked on in the 'twenties and 'thirties by Margaret's friends, most of whom incautiously dismissed her as the nondescript companion who poured tea and seldom spoke. After the precarious existence of the last few years, Ivy must have been relieved and thankful for this comparative oblivion. 'Relief is the keenest form of joy' is a characteristically guarded saying from *Brothers and Sisters* which recurs, in almost identical words, more than forty years later in the last of her novels.37 But, though Ivy took much the same counter measures as Butler against unmanageable forces which threatened her with extinction, the resemblance goes no further. The difference lies in the degree of damage inflicted: self-imposed restrictions were essential to Butler's survival, dictating his scope as a writer as well as his plan for living, whereas for Ivy they seem to have been incidental, a convenient withdrawal which she exercized at will in her private life and which, far from inhibiting her work, enabled her to draw for the rest of her career on material stored at the deepest levels of consciousness.

As one turns the pages of her copy of the *Note-Books*, from the first terse confession to the last vigorous scrawl in the margin, one has the irresistible impression of watching her return to health and spirits. 'Then I got well, but I could do very little for some years, and then as my strength came back my mental strength came back too. But one did get very delayed,'38 said Ivy. The delay must have been almost over by the time she finished Butler's book. He had restored her brain, sharpened her humour, improved her morals, confirmed her dislike of religion and, perhaps most potent tonic of all, shown her cause to congratulate herself on a good riddance from family life. A writer who touches on the emotions as reluctantly as Butler can have had little to do with reconciling her to the death of her brother. But as she settled into the security provided by Margaret's companionship, she had at least the consolation that, having insured her feelings as far as possible against

* Dolores' experience in a dark hour suggests that Ivy well understood this state of mind long before Noel's death: 'She felt that her soul was dead. . . . She felt it was dead; and had a strange, dull gladness in feeling it; for that it might awaken was a petrifying thing.' (*Dolores*, pp.258–9.) I have relied heavily in the following on Furbank's *Samuel Butler*, which contains a brilliant analysis of Butler's intellectual and emotional evolution, and goes far towards explaining what seems to have been a parallel development in Ivy.

damage or loss, she would never again be so mercilessly exposed to either. A programme of security, tranquillity, inactivity had much to recommend it after the '14–'18 war. It is the programme invariably adopted in the novels of I. Compton-Burnett by people who have seen and felt as much as they can stand: 'We have seen some real life, Roberta, a thing I have always wanted to see. But now I don't want to see any more as long as I live.'[39]

Ivy had reached the stage favoured by Sophia Stace in *Brothers and Sisters* 'when people have had experience, and are not quite in the dark about things'—though, as Sophia's son points out, darkness is what they might well prefer if given the choice: 'Every shedding of light has been a shock to me so far'.[40] The war had completed a process begun, for a nature as susceptible to shock as Ivy's, almost before she could think at all. From now on she looked clearly at things obscurely sensed in the past, chief among them that love of power which Butler had taught her to recognize in a domestic setting and which Lowes Dickinson called 'the most disastrous, if not the most evil, of the human passions.'[41] Perhaps Dickinson himself contributed something to the scheme which must have been beginning to take shape at the back of Ivy's mind in the years when she visited him after the war. The two had much in common, besides their memories of Noel. Dickinson minded as acutely about the disasters which afflict states and nations as most people mind about personal disaster. He had recovered from despair but not from the misery induced by a calamity whose causes he could dissect but not remedy. He still hoped that people might somehow be persuaded to abandon the urge to power both collectively and individually—indeed he spent the rest of his life working through the League of Nations to that end. But he seems to have been by this time more or less resigned to the defeat of hope by experience; and one cannot help suspecting that there was something deeply congenial to Ivy in Dickinson's imperturbability. He was, as one of his friends remarked, 'the sort of person you felt you could tell anything to, and he wouldn't be horrified or surprised, and he would say, "Oh well, my dear, I think we must just consider what's the best thing to be done if you've really killed this man."'[42]

This sort of person was later to become a familiar figure in Ivy's novels. Murder leaves him or her as unruffled as jealousy, incest, adultery, greed, rage or any other explosion of the aggressive and acquisitive instincts. These are the cynics and sceptics in her books, what Butler called 'the sub-vicious', people clever enough to be kind but too intimately acquainted with their own vices to admit of anything but a despairing acceptance of viciousness in others. They are gentle, humorous, melancholy, intensely curious and profoundly ineffectual. Mortimer Lamb or Dudley Gaveston serve admirably to represent the type but almost every book contains one or more examples of people who stand aside from the central conflict between parent and child, tyrant and victim, watching what the one does to the other; who see the abuse of power and recognize that the powerful can no more prevent themselves from exploiting their position than the weak can avoid being crushed; and who, understanding the tyrants, feeling for their victims, are helpless to intervene between the two. Dickinson's definition of the Cambridge outlook, set down in 1930 when he was sadly aware of another approaching war, provides as succinct an analysis as one may hope to find of the role played by this dispassionate spectator in the novels of I. Compton-Burnett:

. . . there is, I think, a certain type, rare like all good things, which seems to be associated in some peculiar way with my alma mater. . . . It is a type unworldly without being saintly, unambitious without being inactive, warmhearted without being sentimental. Through good report and ill such men work on, following the light of truth as they see it; able to be sceptical without being paralysed; content to know what is knowable and to reserve judgement on what is not. The world could never be driven by such men, for the springs of action lie deep in ignorance and madness. But it is they who are the beacon in the tempest, and they are more, not less, needed now than ever before.[43]

Ivy had no need to look further than the passionate will transmitted down three generations in her own family to find the submerged violence Dickinson describes. It was to become the central subject matter of her novels. All the ingredients lay ready to her hand. From Butler, she had learnt where to look and how to interpret what she saw. From Cambridge, she had learnt both the charm and the weakness of a sceptical intelligence: brothers and sisters in her books, mournfully contemplating their own lack of power, constantly echo Noel's last words to Ivy: 'Oh! we *were* clever'. From her mother, and from traces of her mother which she found and perhaps feared in herself, she knew well enough the dangers threatening a person ruled by the emotions, and to what desperate lengths that person might be driven. At all events, she never again attempted to recreate the position of authority thrust on her in her last four years at Hove. From now on her interest in the way people prey on one another was confined to the strictly intellectual pleasures of observation, speculation and deduction. The daily doings of her circle provided abundant material for all three; and her friendship with Margaret restored her emotional balance to the point at which she could begin to scrutinize the present through the mirror of the past. 'First the one brother dying like that—and then the other brother dying—put a full stop,' said her sister Juliet. 'And then she went into a retrospect.'

APPENDICES

APPENDIX ONE
Burnetts and Comptons

SO MANY MISLEADING claims have been made for I. Compton-Burnett's family tree that it is perhaps worth summarizing what little factual evidence survives. The earliest Burnett transactions which I have succeeded in tracing are the marriages of Ivy's great-grandfather, Richard Burnett, at St Maurice's in 1803, and his presumed brother William at St Bartholomew Hyde, Winchester, in 1811. Richard came from Wherwell, William from Barton Stacey. The explanation of this discrepancy seems to be that Gavelacre Farm, which was rented by Burnetts between 1790 and 1835, lies at the meeting place of three parishes, the farmhouse itself being just within Longparish boundary on one bank of the Test and much of its land in Barton Stacey on the other side of the river, a few hundred yards upstream from Wherwell parish boundary. A family living at Gavelacre would have been free to take its choice between these three parishes.

Barton Stacey Churchwarden's Accounts record Burnetts paying rent on Gavelacre land, while a 'Sarah Burnett of Gavelacre' was married at Longparish in 1812 (perhaps the same Sarah Burnett who had witnessed the marriage of William Burnett of Barton Stacey to Anne Compton at Winchester the year before). A witness to this wedding was the John Burnett who rented Gavelacre land from 1811 until his death in 1835, and who must have been kinsman to Richard and William, possibly their eldest brother. There are no entries in Barton Stacey rate books between 1794 and 1811, but before that a William Burnett was tenant of Gavelacre. None of these Burnetts left wills. A search of the registers at Longparish, Barton Stacey, Wherwell and the neighbouring parishes (Whitchurch, Stockbridge, Upper Clatford and Chilbolton, as well as the voluminous records at Andover which contain a fair number of Burnetts) reveals nothing of interest[*] save that, between 1737 and 1759, Henry and Hannah Burnett brought nine children to be baptized at Longparish: a Richard, a William and a John were among this couple's six sons, any one of whom might have been father to Richard of Wherwell and William of Barton Stacey.

[*] The only Burnetts recorded at Wherwell are Ann, wife of James, buried in 1754 and —more promising—Harry, son of Richard and Mary, baptized in 1793 (Ivy's great-grandfather, Richard Burnett of Wherwell, was born in 1790); Barton Stacey has only two baptisms—John, bastard son of Ann Burnett, and the daughter of Isaac and Mary Burnett, travellers, both in 1795.

Their marked absence from Church of England records of birth, marriage and death almost certainly means that the Gavelacre Burnetts were nonconformist. There was a chapel at Wherwell from 1712 (Willis' *Dissenters' Meeting House Certificates*) but no records survive. The flourishing Independent Chapel four miles away at Andover, where 'Mr Burnet gave the charge' at the ordination of a new minister in 1739, records no other Burnetts among its congregation between 1730 and 1790 (when records cease for the next sixteen years)—but its members were Congregationalists, which may perhaps cast some light on why Ivy's two uncles (grandsons to Richard Burnett of Wherwell) later became Congregationalist ministers.

Richard and William become easier to trace after their marriages: William settled as a tenant farmer at Baybridge in the parish of Owslebury, Richard returned to Wherwell where his seven children were baptized between 1804 and 1815. He is not listed in the Wherwell Poor Book as a ratepayer, but from 1804 to 1816 he appears on Land Tax Assessments as a tenant of John Iremonger who was lord of the manor of Wherwell. Two notes on a disputed right-of-way in the parish register, dated 1805 and 1812, are signed by Richard Burnett as parish overseer and churchwarden to the vicar, Richard Iremonger (the squire's family, being patrons of the living, were often incumbents as well). Probably Richard Burnett had obtained this tenancy a year after his marriage on the strength of the loan from his father-in-law, John Compton,* who died in 1814 and whose will records that he had already lent £300 each to Richard and William Burnett; he left the interest in her lifetime to his widow and required her to bequeath the original capital sums to his sons-in-law—which she did, providing only that there should be enough money left after paying other legacies, and signing the will with her mark on 1 May 1814. She died the year after and it must have been a considerable relief to the Burnetts when the estate was sworn at £1500, a sum amply sufficient to provide for both daughters' inheritances. Richard seems to have left Wherwell round about this time and is next heard of in 1834, living thirty miles away at Alverstoke where four of his children married Wilsons in the parish church of St Mary.

These Wilsons do not seem to have been persons of consequence in Alverstoke. Their family left no wills (or not at any rate wills proved in the Archdeacons and Bishops and peculiar courts of the diocese of Winchester), no certain entries in the copious parish registers at Alverstoke and Gosport (apart from their marriages—which suggests that they too were nonconformist, since nonconformists at that time were commonly married, though not baptized or buried, by the Church of England), and no records in Land Tax

* The registers of St Bartholomew Hyde, Winchester, record the marriage of John Compton to Elizabeth Ellis in 1771, and the baptism of his son and three daughters— Catherine Maria, Ivy's great-grandmother, in March 1774, and Anne Hutchins, Ivy's great-great-aunt by blood and by marriage, in 1785.

Assessments (unless perhaps the 'J. Wilson' who had a small holding assessed at one shilling and eightpence in 1810 and 1820 might be identified with the 'James Wilson, farmer' who was Jesse's father).

I can find no trace of Richard Burnett's son Charles and his wife Sarah (née Wilson) in the first six years of their marriage; the 1841 census records that Charles Compton Burnett was then living at Hamptonworth, a hamlet in the eastern part of Redlynch, that his household included no servants, and that (since his three elder children, born in 1835, 1837 and 1839, were not born in Wiltshire) he had been there for at most two years. The birth of James Compton Burnett in 1840 is recorded in the Redlynch register and at Somerset House. Such information as I have on Charles' subsequent career comes chiefly from entries in local directories,* from which it is possible to piece together a complicated pattern of business relationships. Ivy's great uncle Richard Compton Burnett (who gave his occupation as 'labourer' on the birth certificate of his daughter Sarah in 1847) and his wife, Agnes the bonnet-maker, are found from 1847 at 3 West Street, Southampton, moving in 1853 to 5 Pembroke Square, and being joined in 1851 by Charles Compton Burnett, who describes himself as a shopkeeper at 74 French Street. Four years later Charles begins dealing in coal and corn and by 1859 there is a joint operation, Richard advertising as a coal carrier from Church Lane, French Street, and Charles as a coal dealer from Richard's old address in Pembroke Square, while a '— Burnett' has appeared selling coal at Millbrook. (One may suspect that this is Charles Compton, using the Pembroke Square address for business purposes.) In 1861 'Charles C. Burnett' is back as a coal dealer at 74 French Street and there is another Charles (possibly a nephew—it can hardly have been his eldest son, who obtained his first Congregational ministry at Sheerness the following year) dealing in coal at Pembroke Square. The situation is the same in 1862 but by 1865 Charles Compton has become a dairyman at Mousehole, Millbrook, and in 1869 has moved to Pinks Farm at Dibden, while a Charles Burnett is shown at Mousehole and a William Wilson Burnett deals in coal and corn at Millbrook.

By 1880 Charles Compton Burnett has disappeared for ever from the Hampshire directories. He seems to have moved to the Midlands to be near his son John, who lived at Bedford; his death certificate records that he was an annuitant when he died aged seventy-two of a diseased liver, 'A Feble Heart' and 'A Fainting Fit' on 21 August 1883, at Leighton Buzzard, being attended by his son John and leaving no will.

* Southampton Directories for 1803, 1811 (ed. Cunningham), 1836 (Fletcher), 1845, 1849 (Rayner), 1851, 1853, 1855, 1857 (Forbes), 1859 (Forbes), 1861 (Forbes), 1863, 1865, 1876 (Cox), 1878 (Cox), 1880 (Cox). Also Post Office Directory of Hampshire 1867 and 1875; Mercer and Crocker's General, Topographical and Historical Directory for Hampshire 1871, and William White's Directory of Hampshire 1878.

APPENDIX TWO

Helen Cam's key to Dolores

DR HELEN CAM (1885–1968) was not only a student at Holloway in Ivy's last two years but also a lecturer at the college from 1912 to 1921. She later became Vice-Principal of Girton and, in 1948, the first woman to hold a chair at Harvard; her reputation as an historian for scrupulous factual accuracy, and her knowledge of both senior and junior common rooms at Holloway, suggest that one could hardly ask for more reliable evidence. Her key, written at the back of a copy of Dolores which is signed at the front 'H. M. Cam 1912', runs as follows:

Miss Cliff   =   K. S. Block
  „   Butler   =   M. E. J. Taylor
  „   Dorrington =   M. Cunningham
  „   Greenlow   =   C. Frost
  „   Lemaître   =   M. Péchinet
  „   Adam   =   M. Hayes Robinson
Claverhouse? (looks only)   T. Seccombe
                     Visiting lecturer in history
                     1905—

A brief survey of the evidence suggests that 'actual life' supplied Ivy, at the start of her career, with characters who were not so much developed or made over as simply transferred direct from fact to fiction. Photographs in the archive at Holloway (mostly taken by Miss Frost, who was a keen amateur photographer) confirm that the six staff portraits in Dolores were faithfully copied from the models listed above; and the reader may like to compare the photograph following page 176 with the relevant passages from pages 97–100 of the novel, printed below together with biographical and other details:

The dispenser of the beverage is crossing the room with movements of easy briskness. She is a woman of forty, older at a glance; with a well-cut, dark-skinned face, iron-grey hair whose waving is conquered by its drawing to the knot in the neck, and dark eyes keen under thick, black brows. That is Miss Cliff, the lecturer in English literature.
[Miss Cliff's chief characteristics are her keen feminism and a 'half-philosophizing interest in her kind', both undoubtedly shared by Katharine Block who was Senior Staff Lecturer in English at Holloway, and who had

her fortieth birthday in Ivy's third year. Miss Block, known to her colleagues as 'our intellectual conscience', had joined the college in 1899 and left it only on her retirement twenty-seven years later: 'There was iron in her; she went through the bogus, the pretentious, the sentimental like a knife through cheese. . . . She worked hard herself and would tolerate no slackers, but she invested the routine of the business of teaching and learning with an aura of greatness.' (*R.H.C. College Letter*, December 1954). She also wrote the college song:

> Our College is well-founded,
> Foursquare a stately pile . . .
> Great women watched it growing,
> Just women, steadfast, wise;
> They set the roses blowing,
> They planted memories.
>
> The sacred torch of learning
> They in our halls did light;
> The right to keep it burning,
> They won for us in fight. . . .]

The companion to whom she is handing a cup—the lecturer in classics, Miss Butler,—and who takes it with a word in a vein of pleasantry, is a small, straight woman, a few years younger; whose parted hair leaves the forehead fully shown, and whose hazel eyes have humour in their rapid glancing.

[For a comparison between Miss Butler and Margaret Taylor, see pp. 155–6. Miss Taylor, who had come to Holloway from a lecturing post at Girton, retired in 1954 and died in 1964: 'She watched firmly over our morals and could be highly outspoken—a grand fighter for causes she approved of: Women in the Church, and Woman's Suffrage, and an equally fierce denouncer of things she disliked, such as bad grammar and slovenly speech.']*

'I remember the last time you made it,' said a genial, guttural voice at the side of Miss Butler—the voice of Miss Dorrington, the lecturer in German, and a strong illustration of the power of moral attractiveness over the physical opposite; which, in her case, depended on uncouth features, an eruptive skin, and general ungainliness.

[Miss Dorrington is given no particular characteristic beyond her geniality, which is several times employed in the novel to soothe other people's ruffled feelings. Marjorie Cunningham, head of the German department at Hollo-

* All the quotations marked with an asterisk come from Miss Delp's pamphlet, *Royal Holloway College 1908-1914*.

way from 1900 to 1906 (when she left to become Warden of Trinity Hall, Dublin), had also suffered from an unsightly skin disease. 'She was Irish . . . and she brought a breath of untrammelled gaiety into the SCR', wrote Miss Block in the *College Letter* for November 1941. 'She had a heart overflowing with loving kindness, and no one who sought her in trouble for advice or for comfort went unhelped away.']

A short, quaint-looking, middle-aged lady, with a pathetic manner which somehow was comical in its union with her calling of mathematical teacher, looked up with a slow smile.

[This is Miss Greenlow, whose 'comical pathos' is mentioned whenever she puts in an appearance. Catherine Frost was senior lecturer in mathematics at Holloway from 1887 to 1907, and the jubilee booklet, *Royal Holloway College 1887–1937*, refers on page 28 to 'Miss Frost, demurely concealing a bagful of mirth and mimicry. . . .']

A lady who was standing apart came forward to join in the talk. She was a Frenchwoman, over fifty, with a sallow, clever face, and sad brown eyes which lighted with her smile; who had led a difficult life in the land of her forced adoption, and lived with its daughters, feeling that she owed it no gratitude.

[This is Miss Lemaître, who is something of a wit—the most nearly frivolous member of Dolores' staff common room—and whose ironic levity is keenly resented by its sterner inmates. Marie Péchinet, head of the French department at Holloway from 1887 to 1909 (Pernel Strachey was her assistant in Ivy's day), was 'commonly called "Peck" and not without reason—her Gallic wit was *very* sure of aim. She once returned the essay of a rather cocksure first year scholar with: "Here is your essay, Miss So-and-so, I don't mark below delta minus."'* People who were not afraid of her found her enchanting ('just meeting her in the corridor or at her door allowed me to catch something of her sparkle')*; and both Miss Delp and the anonymous obituarist in the *College Letter* for July 1912 pay tribute to her stoicism in a life dogged by 'bad health' and 'disappointments'.]

The speaker was Miss Adam, the lecturer in history—younger than the others, and young for her youth; with her zeal for the world where she had her life, not untempered by a wistfulness on the world outside, and her faith in the creed of her nurture as untouched by any of the usual shattering forces, as by her special knowledge of its growth.

[Miss Adam is alternately petted and teased by her colleagues, who find something irresistibly fetching in her combination of youth and innocence with learning (and, when someone suggests that she may once have had a proposal, 'Miss Adam yielded without great unwillingness to the impulse to look conscious', p. 329). Margaret Hayes Robinson, head of the History department, had come to Holloway straight from taking a first at Oxford in 1898; she was a good ten years younger than any of the others except Miss Taylor, and the only one who married (an Oxford don in 1916). 'To work with her was not so much to become her pupil as to share an adventure: friendliness and democracy were the natural traditions of the history school she founded. . . . In that smaller Holloway of twenty to thirty years ago, many outside her own school knew her well, and to know her was to love her,' wrote Dr Cam in the *College Letter* when she died in 1930.]

[Thomas Seccombe's influence on Claverhouse is examined in the text on pp. 173–5; and it is perhaps not uninteresting to note that three of these comparatively crude copies in *Dolores* provided starting points for some rather more complex characters among the staff of Josephine Napier's school in *More Women Than Men*, where Miss Lemaître's neutral attitude to Miss Adam has grown into the highly charged relationship between Maria Rosetti and the young and charming newcomer from Oxford, Helen Keats; while traces of Miss Greenlow may still be seen in Miss Munday's subtle and secretive sense of humour.]

NOTES

BIBLIOGRAPHY

NOTES

In order not to annoy the reader with too many numbers, some of these notes are composite; anyone wishing to find the source of an unnumbered quotation should look under the nearest number given in the text.

Abbreviations used in the notes
The works of I. Compton-Burnett distinguished by initials, as P & M= *Pastors and Masters*, B & S=*Brothers and Sisters*, F & Fate=*A Father and his Fate*, F & Fortune=*A Family and a Fortune*, H & Head=*A House and its Head*, H & History=*A Heritage and its History*, etc.

Butler	*The Note-Books of Samuel Butler.*
Clarke	*Life and Work of James Compton Burnett, M.D.* by J. H. Clarke.
'A Conversation'	'A Conversation between I. Compton-Burnett and M. Jourdain', *Orion*, vol. 1.
Dick	*Ivy and Stevie* by Kay Dick.
DC	*Dover Chronicle.*
DE	*Dover Express.*
DT	*Dover Telegraph.*
50 Reasons	*Fifty Reasons for Being a Homoeopath* by James Compton Burnett.
Forster	*Goldsworthy Lowes Dickinson* by E. M. Forster.
HW	*Homoeopathic World.*
Mitchell NS	Julian Mitchell in the *New Statesman*, 5 September 1969.
Mowll	Compton Burnett papers in the possession of Mowll and Mowll of Dover.
Wortham	*Victorian Eton and Cambridge* by H. E. Wortham.

Chapter One

1 This and the previous quotation from Clarke, p.4.
2 The Earl of Dartmouth, quoted in *Bishop Burnet's History of His Own Times*, edited by His Son, Oxford, 1833, vol. 1, p.5 note.
3 See 'The Family Burnett of Leys' from the MSS. of the late George Burnett, LL.D, Lyon King of Arms, *Aberdeen University Studies No. 4*, Aberdeen, 1906, p.140.

4 Clarke, p.5; the next two quotations in this paragraph from *50 Reasons*, p.46, and Clarke, p.5.

5 *Ecce Medicus*, p.41. (Dr Burnett afterwards claimed to have been at Edinburgh University, where records show only a 'James Burnett' who matriculated in arts subjects 1865–6; Ivy's father is said to have hesitated at first between philology and medicine so, if this was our man, he must promptly have abandoned the arts in favour of medicine at Vienna, where he was duly awarded an honorary M.B.)

6 Miss Vera and Miss Juliet Compton-Burnett; further quotations about their family come from Ivy's sisters, unless otherwise attributed.

7 *50 Reasons*, p.38.

8 Clarke, p.8; the next quotation from *50 Reasons*, p.38.

9 *50 Reasons*, pp.32–5. (There is an excellent account of conditions in the Glasgow Medical School at this time in *Reminiscences of an Old Physician* by Robert Bell, John Murray, 1924.)

10 *50 Reasons*, p.158; the comparison with St Paul comes in *Tumours of the Breast*, p.15; the next two quotations in this paragraph from Clarke, p.44, and from Dr Bodman's 'Richard Hughes Memorial Lecture'.

11 Annual Report of the Chester Free Homoeopathic Dispensary, HW November 1882, *Diseases of the Veins*, p.61, and *Curability of Cataract*, p.177.

12 Dr Burnett sold 17 Hamilton Square in 1879 (Mowll). His earlier addresses from his marriage certificate, the birth certificates of his children and medical directories; information on the Thomas family from Miss Gwenda Haynes-Thomas; the advertisement from the *Homoeopathic Directory* for 1853 (Edward Thomas later moved both businesses from Bridge Street to Pepper Street).

13 Clarke, p.iii; the previous quotation from *Gout and Its Cure*, p.158.

14 *Diseases of the Liver*, p.33; the other case histories cited in this paragraph from *50 Reasons*, pp.220–6, *Curability of Cataract*, pp.2–14, *Diseases of the Skin*, p.17.

15 HW July 1880; the next two quotations from HW August 1880 and September 1879.

16 James Cuthbert Compton Burnett was born at 51 Hamilton Square on 17 July 1877, and died on 29 May 1879 at Moselle Villa, Lee Road, Lee of 'concussion of the brain 25 days'; the death was certified by his father. I can find no report of an inquest (or of any accident on 4 May) in the local papers, and Ivy's sisters have no recollection of this half-brother's existence.

17 HW January 1882 (Edward Thomas was a fully qualified member of the Pharmaceutical Association of Great Britain).

18 B & S p.4; Ivy's sisters confirm that this is an exact likeness of their mother.

19 See family tree. One of Rowland Rees' first cousins had married a Robert Blackie of Liverpool whose daughter Georgiana was married in 1871 to a Liverpool businessman named John Thomas Norman Thomas. I have found no connection between this John Thomas and Agnes Thomas' family in Chester; but in 1875 Georgiana's brother and sister, Robert and Esther Blackie, married their second cousins, Elizabeth and Charles Rees (sister and brother to Ivy's mother), and it was Robert Blackie who—acting presumably on advice from the Thomases in Liverpool—took Katharine up to London to see Dr Burnett.

20 *50 Reasons*, pp.153–6; Ivy's sisters confirm that their mother was 'the patient in question'.

21 *Dolores*, p.39.

22 M & F p.50.

23 Information from Miss Gwenda Haynes-Thomas (who had met her much older cousins, Olive and Daisy Compton-Burnett, on visits to her parents' home, and remembered hearing as a child the sad story of her Aunt Agnes: 'My mother used to say that all her brothers and sisters had been deeply fond of her and greatly mourned her').

24 *Vaccinosis*, preface dated March 1884 (this, like several of Dr Burnett's early books, was printed by Edward Thomas in Chester).

25 Mitchell NS.

26 See Kenneth Walker's *Martello Towers and the Defence of N. E. Essex in the Napoleonic War* for a detailed account of John Rees' activities at Clacton. Mr Walker assures me that 'Charles Rees' in this article is a misprint for 'John Rees', and I am greatly indebted to him for information about the marriage of Ivy's grandparents on 23 December 1813, at the parish church of Great Clacton where their eight children were baptized between 1814 and 1825; the ancient inhabitant who told Mr Walker about the coal business was born round about 1860.

27 Mitchell NS.

28 Believed by her Compton-Burnett grandchildren to have been named for a Huguenot ancestor, Sir Avery Sabine, which is perfectly possible since the name is common among Kentish families and seems to have come originally from Avery Sabine, *c.*1580–1648, a wealthy woollen-merchant and three times Mayor of Canterbury; a kinsman of his was Sir Avery Sabine, Bart., whose younger brother Phillip took as his second wife in the late seventeenth century Elizabeth Woodward of St Mary's, Dover (*Sabin(e): The History of an English Surname* by W. H. W. Sabine, London and New York, 1953). Sophia's father died in 1872, leaving £4000 among his surviving children and grandchildren.

29 B & S p.2.

30 Rule's *Recollections*, p.77; the next quotation in this paragraph is from *Wesleyan Local Preachers* by the author of 'Tyneside Celebrities' (W. D.

Lawson), Newcastle-upon-Tyne, 1874, p.297, which contains an enthusiastic account of contemporary mission work. Rowland Rees' conversion, his subsequent religious activity, his keen support of foreign missions and his address to the China Breakfast Meeting were reported throughout his life in the local press and summed up in the *Methodist Recorder*, 30 July 1878 and 14 August 1902, and the *Methodist Times*, 31 July 1902.

31   This and the next two quotations from an article, 'Mr Rowland Rees, J.P.', in a series on 'The Mayors of Dover' published *c.*1890 in a local paper (almost certainly the *Dover Express*) and kindly supplied by the Librarian of Dover Public Library.

32   DC 22 June 1850; for the development of this rearguard action see also DC 22 December 1849, 13 July 1850, 3 August 1850 and DT 14 June 1849, 4 August 1849.

33   DC 26 October 1851; the following quotations in this paragraph from DT 13 November 1858, DC 23 June 1860, DT 15 December 1860.

34   DC 10 August 1861; the next three quotations from DC 11 May and 16 March 1861, and the whole affair is reported blow by blow in both papers from March to mid-November (when Rowland Rees triumphantly settled his libel action out of court).

35   *The Life of Hugh Price Hughes*, p.78.

36   DC 18 February 1871.

37   She was the only daughter of Joseph Stace who died on 23 January 1877, leaving £20,000 to be divided equally between 'my dear daughter' and his three sons; her marriage settlement assigning the capital to her trustees in her lifetime was drawn up on 29 January 1879 (Mowll).

38   Mitchell NS.

39   DE 27 February 1885.

40   DE 18 January 1884; the previous quotation from DE 23 November 1883.

41   This and the next quotation from *The Life of Hugh Price Hughes*, pp.78–9; the *Spectator*'s comment is cited in Maldwyn Edwards' *Methodism and England*, p.150.

42   This and the next quotation from DE 5 June 1885 (Rowland Rees was asked to retire, and did so on 25 February 1885; a contemporary minute at the Harbour Board records that he felt himself entitled to £70 more than the £250 pension accorded him by his employers).

43   DE 11 January 1884 (further reports on 1 and 8 February); the next two quotations from HW January 1883 and *50 Reasons*, p.151.

44   HW January 1882.

Chapter Two

1   To Barbara Robinson.
2   'A Conversation', p.26.
3   Information from Maureen Beresford.
4   P & C p.108.
5   MWTM p.9.
6   P & C p.223.
7   This and the previous quotation from G & G pp.217 and 221–2.
8   *Further Extracts from the Notebooks of Samuel Butler*, edited by T. A. Bartholomew, Cape, 1934, p.112.
9   Dick, p.4.
10 *Delicate, Backward, Puny and Stunted Children*, pp.12–13; Ivy's sisters confirm that the family described here is Dr Burnett's own.
11 Mitchell NS.
12 B & S pp.12–13; there is a portrait of Minnie following page 64.
13 Joseph Smith, Master Draper, died on 7 October 1912 (leaving his house called 'Boscombe' and chattels—including 'my oil painting "Highland Cattle"' but excluding 'my presentation clock in oak case with bracket'—and the income from £17,737 to his second wife in her lifetime, with instructions that she provide a home for her stepdaughters, Ellen, Alice and Emily Smith, each of whom would come into an annuity of £150 on her death).
14 Mitchell NS.
15 Letter from Ivy to Barbara Robinson, 21 November 1964.
16 P & P pp.11–12.
17 This and the next quotation from Mitchell NS.
18 *Delicate, Backward, Puny and Stunted Children*, p.65; for Dr Burnett's advanced views on the health and punishment of children, *ibid*, pp.71, 43 and 151; for his views on vegetables, *Gout and Its Cure*, pp.135–6.
19 'Harrow, including Pinner' by Diane K. Bolton, *Victoria County History, Middlesex*, vol.iv; information on Dr Burnett's acquisition of property from Mowll.
20 *Pike's Directory of Brighton and Hove*, 1895.
21 Dick, p.5.
22 Simon Blow.
23 Letter from Elizabeth Taylor to Robert Liddell, undated, *c*.1964; the next two memories of Ivy's childhood come from Francis King and Julian Mitchell.
24 D & D p.85.
25 P & C p.37.

26   P & C p.45.
27   This and the next quotation from P & C p.269 and P & P p.54.
28   E & B p.37.
29   'A Conversation', p.28.
30   E & B p.39; the next three quotations from E & B pp.63, 191 and 196.
31   D & S p.159.
32   D & D p.116.
33   Dick, pp.2–3.
34   P & P p.13.
35   *The Daisy Chain*, pp.163–4; the next two quotations from *The One Too Many*, vol.1, pp.151 and 104.
36   *Delicate, Backward, Puny and Stunted Children*, pp.89–92. (The phrase 'and twelve of them make a dozen'—meaning that the things in question were adequate but no more—was such a favourite with Dr Burnett that it became a family joke.)
37   Dick, p.8.
38   P & P p.17.

Chapter Three

1   H & Head p.15.
2   Julian Mitchell (his notes), who also remembered Ivy's description of her Uncle George.
3   M & W p.6.
4   Contemporary cutting, supplied by Kenneth Walker, to whom I am indebted for this account of Robert Blackie's career; details of property transactions from Mowll; and the wills of Robert Blackie, Robert Blackie senior and James Compton Burnett.
5   M & W p.262.
6   This and the previous quotations about missionary work among Ivy's relations come from the section entitled 'Two Elect Ladies and a Nephew' in a pamphlet, 'Lest We Forget. The Record of Fifty Years' Work in the Clacton-on-Sea Circuit of the Wesleyan Methodist Church. 1875–1925' by the Rev. George C. Gould, Clacton, 1925.
7   *Dolores* p.72.
8   The Rev. John Brown's funeral oration for John Compton Burnett, reported in the *Bedfordshire Times*, 21 March 1901. ('. . . It is no mere figure of speech to say that he [Mr Burnett] gave his very heart and life to the village churches and the village pastors of this county. It is simply true to say that for them he laboured up to and beyond his strength.') For an account of religious life in Bedford at this time, see *Gathering Up the Theards* by Florence Ada Keynes (who was John Brown's daughter and

Maynard Keynes' mother), W. Heffer, Cambridge, 1950, *Bunyan Meeting Bedford 1650–1950* by H. G. Tibbut, Bedford, 1950, and *The Life of Mark Rutherford* by Himself (William Hale White), O.U.P., 1913.

9 'Touchstone' in 'Bedfordian's Diary', *Bedfordshire Times*, 29 March 1963.
10 F & Fortune p.18; see also pp.22, 287 *et passim*.
11 Dick p.3.
12 M & F p.21.
13 Butler, p.35 (Ivy's copy of the *Note-Books*, with her annotations, in the possession of Hester Marsden-Smedley).
14 D & S p.139.
15 B & S p.4; the following quotation about Ivy's mother from Dick, p.4.
16 B & S p.28; the previous quotation from P & C p.46.
17 M & M p.123; the following quotation from M & W p.264.
18 TWTW p.195; the next quotation from p.100.
19 TWTW p.77.
20 L & F p.70.
21 TWTW p.125; the previous quotation from p.19.
22 E & B p.42.
23 *Delicate, Backward, Puny and Stunted Children*, p.13 (see chapter two, note 10).
24 Mrs J. A. Elliott; the previous quotation from Dick, p.2.
25 P & P p.19.
26 *The Daisy Chain*, p.163; the previous quotation from *The One Too Many*, vol. 1, p.3.
27 Mrs Elliott.
28 TWTW p.85 (Miss Marathon teaches mathematics at Clemence's school, like Miss Marsland at Ivy's; Miss Laurence, like Miss Laura Cadwallader, is the classics mistress).
29 P & M pp.66–7.
30 This and the two previous quotations from Mr L. R. Conisbee's recollections of Bedford at the turn of the century, in correspondence with the author.
31 This and the two following quotations about Howard College from Miss Grace J. Fothergill, who was a pupil at the school 1898–1902; Ivy's anecdote about her cousin from Soame Jenyns.
32 TWTW p.99.
33 TWTW p.72; the next quotation from p.19.
34 *Period Piece*, p.72.
35 TWTW p.197.
36 L & F p.70.
37 TWTW p.115; the two previous quotations from pp.108 and 114.

Chapter Four

1   Clarke, p.55.
2   *50 Reasons*, p.281.
3   B & S p.4; the next quotation from p.121.
4   Dr Kraft, quoted by Clarke (p.68), who also reprints obituaries from *The Times* (5 April), the *Westminster Gazette* (14 April), the *Monthly Homoeopathic Review* (May), and his own from HW (May). The quotation from TWTW is on p.221.
5   *Diseases of the Spleen*, pp.59–60.
6   HW December 1880; the three previous quotations from *New Cure of Consumption*, first preface, *Ecce Medicus*, p.3, *Tumours of the Breast*, p.15, and *50 Reasons*, p.293.
7   HW Sept. 1879; the previous quotation from *50 Reasons*, p.75.
8   B & S p.30.
9   *Tumours of the Breast*, pp.84–6 (needless to say, the clergyman retired in disarray and the lady's tumour was with time duly cured).
10 M & F p.200.
11 *Tumours of the Breast*, p.147; the previous quotation from HW November 1883.
12 'Richard Hughes Memorial Lecture' by Frank Bodman (to whom I am greatly indebted for this account of homoeopathic internal politics).
13 Clarke's *Life of Dr. Skinner*, p.86; the next two quotations from HW May 1901 (unsigned editorial, but Clarke was then editor and the style is recognizably his) and Clarke, p.44.
14 *Cure of Consumption*, p.184; the next three quotations from *50 Reasons*, p.219, *On Neuralgia*, p. 139, and *Gout and Its Cure*, p.27.
15 *Ecce Medicus*, p. 52; the next quotation from Clarke, p.41.
16 *50 Reasons*, pp.3–4.
17 Prescribed in *Diseases of the Spleen*, pp.97 and 11; *50 Reasons*, pp.73 and 252–5; *Gout and Its Cure*, pp.41–8; and *Diseases of the Liver*, p.30.
18 Unsigned, but identified by Dr Bodman; the following quotation from Bodman's 'Memorial Lecture'.
19 *Dolores*, pp.9 and 10.
20 *Curability of Tumours*, p.163.
21 *50 Reasons*, p.24.
22 HW September 1879.
23 Information from Alison Waley; the previous quotations from B & S pp.4 and 26.
24 F & Fortune p.14; for Dr Burnett's similar sentiments, see Chapter One, p.24.

25 D & S p.202.
26 *Diseases of the Spleen*, pp.19–20.
27 *50 Reasons*, p.93; the next two quotations from Clarke, p.106, and HW
    December 1880.
28 *Cure of Consumption*, pp.141 and 92.
29 Clarke, p.6.
30 G & G pp.21 and 80; the next four quotations from G & G pp.27 and 81,
    D & S p.26.
31 D & S p.238; for Dr Burnett's identical sentiments, see chapter two,
    p.67.
32 *Cure of Consumption*, second preface.
33 F & Fortune p.182; the previous quotation from p.55.
34 Information from Lady Ashton.
35 B & S p.26; the previous quotation on p.25.
36 Arthur Waley said so to Barbara and Walter Robinson; Elliott Felkin
    told Raisley Moorsom.
37 B & S p.34.
38 Butler, p.26; the two previous quotations from Clarke, p.55.
39 *On Neuralgia*, p.167.
40 *On the Prevention of Hare-Lip*, p.7.

Chapter Five

 1 B & S p.145.
 2 MWTM p.104.
 3 M & S p.134.
 4 B & S p.138; quotations from B & S in this and the next two paragraphs
    all come from pp.137–49.
 5 E & B pp.194–5.
 6 D & S p.48.
 7 D & S p.43.
 8 P & C p.30.
 9 B & S p.153.
10 D & D p.79.
11 D & S pp.126–7; the next quotation from p.10.
12 P & C p.213.
13 E & B p.187.
14 'A Conversation', p.25; the next quotation on p.28.
15 B & S p.100.
16 B & S p.178.
17 L & F pp.16–17; the previous quotation from F & Fate p.31 (for Sophia
    Stace's looks, see chapter one, p.30).

18 F & Fate p.21.

19 F & Fate p.33; the next quotation from p.34.

20 *Dolores*, p.45.

21 L & F p.26.

22 P & C p.125.

23 Olive, according to her half-sisters, had 'a tyrannical nature' bravely borne by Miss Pope; but Mr Percy Compton-Burnett and his family, who first met their cousin ('Olive was a great dear') after the second war and visited her thereafter regularly until her death in 1963, take the opposite view.

24 M & W p.49.

25 Dr Frank Bodman (who, as Daisy Compton-Burnett's G.P. in the 1930s and as an authority on homoeopathic history well acquainted with her father's career, was admirably placed to draw comparisons between the two).

26 The Rev. Edward Hayward, of the C.M.S. Mission at Panyam, 1911–20, and examining chaplain to the Bishop of W. Equatorial Africa. (Mr Hayward remained a friend of Daisy Compton-Burnett to the end of her life, and I am much indebted to him for information about her career.)

27 H & Head p.18; Ivy's similar jokes about her half-sister recalled by Janet Beresford.

28 P & P p.48.

29 B & S p.2.

30 F & Fate p.153.

31 DC 1 November 1862; the next two quotations from DE 23 November 1883 and 27 March 1885.

32 F & Fate pp.185–6.

33 Arthur Waley told Francis King (and others seem to have heard the same thing from Ivy herself).

34 M & W p.193.

35 This affair reported in DC 11, 18 and 25 March 1871.

36 DT 7 February 1906.

37 This and the following quotation from M & W, p.170.

38 Information from Francis King and Janet Beresford.

39 'A Conversation', p.27.

40 *A History of Brighton College* compiled by G. P. Burstow and M. B. Whittaker, London, 1957, pp.70 and 75. (See also *Brighton College Register*, 1922, ed. by E. K. Milliken).

41 B & S p.145.

Chapter Six

1 Thomas Davison, later Archbishop of Canterbury, quoted by John H. Ellison in 'Early Days' from the anniversary pamphlet, 'Royal Holloway College 1887–1937'.

2 'Social Life at R.H.C. 1887–1937', an unpublished MS. in the archive at Holloway by Marion Pick, who was a year behind Ivy at college and who returned as a lecturer from 1911 to 1946 (when her departure was lamented in a masque with the refrain: 'Who now shall keep the ancestral altars green?/Miss Pick forsakes the Hollowegian scene'; 'R.H.C. has produced no more devoted a Hollowegian,' wrote the *College Letter* when she died in 1968). Quotations about Holloway not otherwise attributed in this chapter come from her 'Social Life', and from a talk given at the college on 21 June 1969, by Miss W. E. Delp, later issued as a pamphlet, 'Royal Holloway College 1908–1914'.

3 Joan Evans' *Prelude and Fugue*, p.114.

4 *Dolores*, p.109.

5 *Dolores*, p.110 (the same comparison had occurred to Miss Pick, and to Lilian M. Faithfull in her autobiography, *In The House of My Pilgrimage*, Chatto, 1924, p.93).

6 Information from Barbara and Walter Robinson.

7 *RHC College Letter*, 1904 (Pernel Strachey was assistant lecturer in French, and her sister Marjorie a student at the college from 1901 to 1904).

8 Information from Barbara and Walter Robinson.

9 Miss Mabel Eastaugh (E III was the third floor corridor in the eastern block of the building); see also chapter three, p.82, for the view of another contemporary who thought Ivy 'not at all popular', and who wishes to remain anonymous.

10 Daisy Elizabeth Harvey (b. 3 September 1883, daughter of George Harvey, metal merchant, of Eltham Road, Lewisham, educated at Lewisham Grammar School before being sent to spend a year at a pension in Brunswick and two more at Howard College) took her B.Sc. in 1906, after which the college records contain no further reference to her (nor is there any record at Somerset House of her marriage or death in the next four years). The only Daisy Elizabeth Harvey who might fit this bill among those I have succeeded in tracing became a schoolmistress in London, and later at the Merchant Taylors' School for girls, Great Crosby, near Liverpool, where she eventually started a school of her own and died on 4 July 1963, when her age was given as 77; Ivy's friend would have been 79 at the time, but possibly there was some mistake in the dates.

11 *Dolores*, p.115.
12 Identified by Helen Cam, see Appendix Two.
13 Mrs A. E. Rampal, a friend who often partnered Ivy at dinner (the article, not in any *College Letter* or other periodical preserved in the archive at Holloway, must have appeared in one of the students' own more ephemeral productions which I am unable to trace).
14 Walter Robinson.
15 'A Visit to Royal Holloway College' by Greta Hahn, *Our Magazine*, N. London Collegiate School for Girls, November 1892.
16 *Dictionary of National Biography 1941–50*.
17 *Dolores*, p.98; for Miss Cam's key see Appendix Two.
18 *The Tragic Drama of the Greeks* by A. E. Haigh, OUP, 1896, p.280 (Ivy's copy given to the author by Hester Marsden-Smedley).
19 'A Conversation', p.23.
20 Letter from Ivy to Oscar Browning, 30 December 1911.
21 P & P p.72.
22 A Founder's scholarship was not the highest award at Holloway: a resolution of the staff-meeting on 5 May 1904 proposed that 'the standard be such that the student might be expected to obtain at least a second class in Finals'. (The college produced one first in 1905, two in 1906 and eight—out of twenty-one honours degrees—in 1907.)
23 Mitchell NS.
24 *Beginning Again*, p.34.
25 *Lytton Strachey* by Michael Holroyd, vol.1, p.34.
26 Letter to O.B., 29 January 1909.
27 *Rupert Brooke* by Christopher Hassall, p.121. (Noel lived from 1908 to 1911 in Room 13, Staircase A, Wilkins Buildings—Hassall has 'Fellows Building' but this must be a misprint since Brooke, by his own account, lived 'on a landing opposite Oscar Browning'.)
28 Forster, p.29.
29 Wortham, p.284.
30 *Dolores*, p.97.
31 *Dolores*, p.151.
32 Information from Simon Blow.
33 M & W p.148.
34 *Dolores*, p.150; the next five quotations from pp.211, 168, 210, 207 and 157.
35 HW November 1883.
36 *Scenes of Clerical Life*, O.U.P. World's Classics, 1909, p.48; the previous quotation from *Dolores*, p.32.
37 *Dolores*, p.3; the next quotation from p.4.
38 *Scenes of Clerical Life*, p.53; the next two quotations from *Dolores*, pp.82 and 24.

39 *Dolores*, pp.40–43; the two previous quotations from pp.62 and 63.

40 *H & Head*, p.285.

41 *Dolores*, p.152; the next two quotations from pp.90 and 20.

42 *Dolores*, p.166; the next quotation from p.140.

43 *Dolores*, p.138.

44 *Review of Eng. Lit.*, October 1962; the next quotation from *Dolores*,
p.112.

45 *Dolores*, p.199.

46 George Furlong and Rex Britcher.

47 *Dolores*, p.164; the next three quotations from pp.207, 197 and 257.

48 *Robert Elsmere*, p.153.

49 E & B p.106.

50 Address to the Dover Youths Institute, DE 29 February 1884; the next
two quotations from D & S, p.17 and G & G, p.22.

51 Dick, p.7; the previous quotation from F & F, p.190.

52 In the possession of Mrs Marsden-Smedley (though Ivy inscribed her
book to 'Noël', her brother himself dropped the dots after he reached
King's).

53 A second letter, dated 11 August 1909, from Noel to O.B. acknowledges the return of Blackwood's letter (which has since disappeared)
and thanks him for writing to John Lane, but there is no relevant reply
filed under L in O.B.'s correspondence.

54 D & S p.170.

55 Letter to O.B., 12 August 1911.

56 This is one of three letters to Ivy preserved in Blackwood's business files
(the fact that her original application and subsequent replies have disappeared suggests that she dealt only with the firm's London office in
Paternoster Row, which was destroyed in 1940 when all documents
were lost); further information on sales from Blackwood's ledger.

57 'M.M.' in the *Daily Mail*, 3 March 1911; the next two quotations from
the *T.L.S.*, 2 March, and the *Bystander*, 12 April.

58 *Krapp's Last Tape*, Faber, 1959, p.17.

Chapter Seven

1 Mr Noel-Baker is not sure whether this was May Week 1911 or 1912,
but Juliet Compton-Burnett is convinced it was 1911 (Ivy had also spent
May Week 1910 with her mother in Cambridge, according to a letter
from Noel to O.B., 13 June 1910).

2 *Cambridge Review*, 1 November 1916; Noel's speeches at the Union
criticized in *ibid.*, 27 February and 4 June 1908.

3 Letter undated, probably late November 1915; quotations from Noel's

correspondence in this and the next chapter are from letters to Jack
Beresford unless otherwise attributed.

4　*Basileon*, no.11, June 1909; anon. review identified in the King's Library
copy as the work of O. L. Richmond. (Professor Richmond, who was an
undergraduate and Fellow of King's at roughly the same time as Noel,
has 'absolutely *no* recollection of him . . . it is extraordinary that I do not
remember that name among the many undergraduates I knew. It even
supplies a bit of negative evidence about him. He cannot have been at all
interested in music, since no musician escaped my net.') The following
quotation from Arthur Schloss comes from the same source; Mr Noel-
Baker (who was present at the 1909 dinner and remembers that Noel
was too) and Mr Haslam recall respectively the debagging of Dalton
and ducking of Birrell.

5　Wortham, p.179.
6　Forster, p.101; the two previous quotations from Dalton's *Call Back
Yesterday*, p.57, and Christopher Morris in *Portrait of Lowes Dickinson*,
BBC Radio programme produced by Maurice Brown, 19 January 1960.
7　Forster, p. 119; the previous quotation on p.228.
8　P & M p.31.
9　P & M p.25; identified by Leigh Farnell.
10　Information from Raisley Moorsom.
11　Forster, p.120.
12　P & M p.32; the previous quotation from p.31.
13　*Lytton Strachey* by Michael Holroyd, vol.1, p.200; the next two quotations from *ibid.* p.256 and *Sowing* by Leonard Woolf, p.160.
14　Forster, p.66.
15　Forster, p.31; the next four quotations from P & M p.25, Wortham
pp.230-1, and P & M p.109.
16　Lady Darling, quoted in *Portrait of Lowes Dickinson*, BBC Radio, 19
January 1960.
17　P & M p.48.
18　Forster, p.155.
19　'Charles Kingsley Webster' by S. T. Bindoff, PBA.
20　A typescript of the thesis is in the London Library, bequeathed by
Horace Mann who had married Noel's widow.
21　This and the previous quotation from Clapham's obituary of Noel,
Cambridge Review, 1 November 1916.
22　P & M p.101.
23　*A Bundle of Time* by Harriet Cohen, Faber, 1969, p.36.
24　B & S p.239.
25　Butler, p.29.
26　*Ivy Compton-Burnett* by Cicely Greig, p.105.
27　M & S p.12.

28 Butler, p.31.
29 D & S p.45.
30 *Ivy Compton-Burnett* by Cicely Greig, p.39.
31 B & S p.254.
32 MWTM p.55.
33 *Spectator*, 6 September 1969.
34 See *Beresford of Beresford: Eight Centuries of a Gentle Family* by the Rev.
E. A. Beresford, S. B. Beresford and the Rev. William Beresford
(privately printed, 1893), according to which Beresfords fought at
Crécy and Poitiers, at Agincourt and under the red rose for the Lan-
castrians.
35 *Cambridge Review*, 23 January 1908; the following quotation from Clapham, *Cambridge Review*, 1 November 1916.
36 *Goodbye To All That* by Robert Graves, p.288.
37 *Goldsworthy Lowes Dickinson* by Roger Fry and John T. Sheppard.
38 M & S p.193.
39 P & C p.75; the previous quotation from D & S pp.139–40.
40 B & S p.272.
41 Butler, p.31.

Chapter Eight

1 F & Fortune, p. 236.
2 *Testament of Youth* by Vera Brittain, p.200.
3 P & M, p.23.
4 Information from Kenneth Walker (Winifred's mother had been an
Amelia Elliott, granddaughter of a farmer named Daniels whose
family belonged to the same little farming community as the Sadlers
and Pudneys).
5 B & S p.254.
6 *Testament of Youth* by Vera Brittain, p. 143.
7 *The Big Push* by Brian Gardner, p.81; the previous quotation from *The
World Crisis* by Winston Churchill, Odhams, 1938, p.1070. See also the
Official History of the War. France and Belgium 1916, Macmillan, 1932,
vol.1, p.485. ('The VII Corps, before Gommecourt, having played its
part in the preparatory period by attracting an extra enemy division,
the assault "à fond" at that spot should have been countermanded by
G.H.Q. order.')
8 The prize was £10 in books, but what book or books Noel bought with
it I am unable to discover.
9 MWTM, p.211.
10 *Letters of the Earl of Oxford and Asquith to a Friend. 1915–1922*, p.7.

11   Captain T. C. Howitt had been a second lieutenant with Noel at the start of the war.

12   *Testament of Youth* by Vera Brittain, p.450; the next quotation from Dick, p.8.

13   *Tell England* by Ernest Raymond, Cassell, 7th ed. 1929, p.167.

14   E & B pp.43, 75 and 207; the next quotation from p.130.

15   To Robert Liddell.

16   D & D p.201.

17   Information from Barbara and Walter Robinson; the following quotation from *Delicate, Backwood, Puny and Stunted Children*, p.152. (Trine's works on thought power include *What all the World's a-seeking: or, the Vital Law of True Life, The Greatest Thing Ever Known, The Higher Powers of Mind and Spirit, This Mystical Life of Ours: a book of suggestive thoughts for each week through the year*, etc., all of which went through many editions in America and were reissued in London between 1897 and 1918.)

18   Death certificates of Katharine and Primrose Compton-Burnett; further information from Vera and Juliet Compton-Burnett, Janet Beresford, *The Times* and *Morning Post*, 29 and 31 December 1917, *Kilburn Times*, 4 January 1918. (The official record of the inquest, held at Marylebone on 29 December, was destroyed after fifteen years.)

19   TWTW p.62.

20   Butler, p.30.

21   Dick, p.22.

22   Mitchell NS.

23   Dick, p.7; there is an excellent account of this influenza epidemic in Ursula Bloom's *Youth at the Gate*, Hutchinson, London, 1959.

24   F & Fortune, p.265; the previous quotation from MWTM, p.157.

25   Information from Alison Waley; the next two quotations from Barbara and Walter Robinson, and from Sonia Orwell.

26   Information on Jourdain ancestors from *Ranging Memories* by Lt.-Col. H. F. N. Jourdain, Oxford, privately printed, 1934, pp.7ff. (the crusaders' exploits were commemorated in the family arms by an heraldic pun—two bars wavy—on the River Jordan).

27   *Ottoline. The Early Memoirs of Lady Ottoline Morrell* edited by Robert Gathorne-Hardy, Faber, London, 1963, p.113.

28   *The Odes of Horace* collected and arranged by M. Jourdain, Temple Classics, London, 1904. Further information on Margaret's career from Hester Marsden-Smedley and Raisley Moorsom, and from Margaret's diaries, account book and papers in the possession of Mrs Marsden-Smedley.

29   *Practically True* by Ernest Thesiger, p.1.

30   Butler, pp.22–3.

31 *Testament of Youth* by Vera Brittain, pp.470–1; the previous quotation from Clarke, p.109.

32 D & S pp.163–4; the next quotation from p.218.

33 E & B p.78.

34 *Samuel Butler* by H. Festing Jones, vol.2, p.412 (Ivy's liking for Butler is confirmed by Hester Marsden-Smedley, and I shall deal with its bearing on MWTM in my second volume).

35 *Samuel Butler* by P. N. Furbank, p.13.

36 MWTM p.19; the following quotation from Furbank's *Samuel Butler*, p.32.

37 B & S p.153 (in a cancelled passage from the MS. of L & F, chap. 2, Hermia Heriot says about leaving home: 'If relief is the strongest form of joy, this is an illustration of it').

38 Dick, p.7.

39 L & F MS. (the last five words are omitted in the published text, p.144).

40 B & S, p.28.

41 *The European Anarchy* by Goldsworthy Lowes Dickinson, Allen and Unwin, 1916, p.138.

42 Mrs. C. R. Ashbee in *Portrait of Lowes Dickinson*, BBC Radio, 19 January 1960.

43 Quoted in *Essays in Biography* by J. M. Keynes, Macmillan, 1933, pp.302–3.

SELECT BIBLIOGRAPHY

HPC = Homoeopathic Publishing Company
Only editions used are cited

BINDOFF, S. T., 'Charles Kingsley Webster. 1886–1961', *Proceedings of the British Academy*, vol. xlviii, O.U.P., London.

BODMAN, FRANK, 'Richard Hughes Memorial Lecture', *British Homoeopathic Journal*, vol. lix no. 4, October 1970.

BRITTAIN, VERA, *Testament of Youth*, Gollancz, London, 1933.

BROWNING, OSCAR, *Memories of Sixty Years*, John Lane, London, 1910.

CLARKE, J. H., *Life and Work of James Compton Burnett, M.D.*, HPC, London, 1904. *The Life of Dr Skinner*, HPC, London, 1907.

COMPTON BURNETT, JAMES, *Cataract, Its Nature, Causes, Prevention and Cure*, HPC, London, 1889.

—— *The Change of Life in Women*, HPC, London, 1898.

—— *Curability of Cataract with Medicines*, HPC, London, 1880.

—— *Curability of Tumours by Medicines*, HPC, London, 1893.

—— *Delicate, Backward, Puny and Stunted Children*, HPC, London, 1895.

—— *Diseases of the Skin*, HPC, London, 1898 ed.

—— *Diseases of the Spleen*, James Epps, London, 1887.

—— *Ecce Medicus, or Hahnemann as a Physician*, HPC, London, 1881.

—— *Eight Years Experience in the New Cure of Consumption*, HPC, London, 1894.

—— *Enlarged Tonsils Cured by Medicines*, HPC, London, 1901.

—— *Fevers and Blood-Poisoning, and their Treatment*, James Epps, London, 1888.

—— *Fifty Reasons for Being a Homoeopath*, HPC, London, 1896 ed.

—— *Gold as a Remedy in Disease*, HPC, London, 1879.

—— *Gout and Its Cure*, James Epps, London, 1895.

—— *Greater Diseases of the Liver*, HPC, London, 1891.

—— *The Medicinal Treatment of Diseases of the Veins*, HPC, London, 1881.

—— *Natrum Muriaticum as Test of the Doctrine of Drug Dynamisation*, Gould, London, 1878.

—— *On Fistula and Its Radical Cure by Medicines*, James Epps, London, 1889.

—— *On Neuralgia: its causes and remedies*, HPC, London, 1894 ed.

—— *On the Prevention of Hare-Lip, Cleft Palate and Other Congenital Defects*, HPC, London 1880.

—— *Organ Diseases of Women*, HPC, London, 1896.

—— *Ringworm: its constitutional nature and cure*, HPC, London, 1892.

—— *Supersalinity of the Blood*, HPC, London, 1882.

—— *Tumours of the Breast*, James Epps, London, 1888.

—— *Vaccinosis and its Cure by Thuja*, HPC, London, 1884.

—— *Valvular Disease of the Heart from a New Standpoint*, Leath and Ross, London, 1885.

DALTON, HUGH, *Call Back Yesterday. Memoirs 1887–1931*, Muller, London, 1953.

DICK, KAY, *Ivy and Stevie*, Duckworth, London, 1971.

DELP, W. E., *Royal Holloway College 1908–1914*, text of a talk given at the college on 21 January 1969, privately printed.

EDWARDS, MALDWYN, *Methodism and England*, Epworth Press, London, 1943.

EVANS, JOAN, *Prelude and Fugue: An Autobiography*, Museum Press, London, 1964.

FORSTER, E. M., *Goldsworthy Lowes Dickinson*, Edward Arnold, London.

FRY, ROGER and SHEPPARD, JOHN T., *Goldsworthy Lowes Dickinson, 6 August 1862–3 August 1932*, privately printed, Cambridge, 1933.

FURBANK, P. N., *Samuel Butler*, C.U.P., London, 1948.

GARDNER, BRIAN, *The Big Push*, Cassell, London, 1961.

GRAVES, ROBERT, *Goodbye to All That*, Cape, London, 1929.

GREIG, CICELY, *Ivy Compton-Burnett. A Memoir*, Garnstone Press, London, 1972.

HUGHES, MISS, *The Life of Hugh Price Hughes*, by his daughter, Hodder and Stoughton, London, 1904.

HASSALL, CHRISTOPHER *Rupert Brooke*, Faber, London, 1964.

HOLROYD, MICHAEL, *Lytton Strachey*, vol. I. *The Unknown Years*, Heinemann, London, 1967.

JONES, HENRY FESTING, *Samuel Butler: A Memoir*, 2 vols., Macmillan, London, 1919.

JONES, HENRY FESTING (ed.), *The Note-Books of Samuel Butler*, A. C. Fifield, London, 1918.

LINTON, MRS LYNN, *The One Too Many*, 3 vols., Chatto, London, 1894.

MACCARTHY, DESMOND (ed.), *Letters of the Earl of Oxford and Asquith to a Friend, 1915–1922* (Hilda Harrisson), Geoffrey Bles, 1933.

MITCHELL, JULIAN, 'Ivy Compton-Burnett', *New Statesman*, 5 September 1969, London.

POWELL, MARGARET, *My Mother and I*, Michael Joseph, London, 1972.

RAVERAT, GWEN, *Period Piece*, Faber, London, 1952.

RULE, WILLIAM HARRIS, *Recollections of My Life and Work at Home and Abroad in Connection with the Wesleyan Methodist Conference*, London, 1886.

—— *Wesleyan Methodism in the British Army*, London, 1883.

SASSOON, SIEGFRIED, *Memoirs of an Infantry Officer*, Faber, London, 1930.

TREVELYAN, G. M. AND OTHERS, *John Harold Clapham. 1873–1946*, privately printed, Cambridge, 1949.

THESIGER, ERNEST, *Practically True*, Heinemann, London, 1927.

TRINE, RALPH WALDO, *In tune with the Infinite, or, fullness of peace, power and plenty*, G. Bell & Sons, London, 1900.

WALKER, KENNETH, 'Martello Towers and the Defence of N.E. Essex in the Napoleonic War', *Essex Review*, vol. xlvii, October 1938.

—— *The Story of Little Clacton—an Essex Village*, Little Clacton, 1959.

WARD, MRS HUMPHREY, *Robert Elsmere*, Smith, Elder, London, 1900.

WOOLF, LEONARD, *Sowing: An Autobiography of the Years 1880 to 1904*, Hogarth Press, London, 1960.

—— *Beginning Again: An Autobiography of the Years 1911 to 1918*, Hogarth Press, London, 1964.

WORTHAM, H. E., *Victorian Eton and Cambridge: being the Life and Times of Oscar Browning*, Arthur Barker, London, 1956 (2nd ed.).

YONGE, CHARLOTTE M., *The Daisy Chain*, Macmillan, 1911 ed.

—— *The Trial: More Links of the Daisy Chain*, Macmillan, 1911.

WORKS OF I. COMPTON-BURNETT

Dates in brackets are those of first editions

Dolores, Blackwood, 1971 (1911).

Pastors and Masters, Gollancz, 1967 (1925).

Brothers and Sisters, Gollancz, 1967 (1929).

Men and Wives, Eyre and Spottiswoode, 1948 (1931).

More Women Than Men, Eyre and Spottiswoode, 1948 (1933).

A House and Its Head, Heinemann, 1935.

Daughters and Sons, Gollancz, 1967 (1937).

A Family and a Fortune, Gollancz, 1939.

Parents and Children, Gollancz, 1941.

Elders and Betters, Gollancz, 1964 (1944).

Manservant and Maidservant, Gollancz, 1969 (1947).

Two Worlds and their Ways, Gollancz, 1964 (1949).

Darkness and Day, Gollancz, 1967 (1951).

The Present and the Past, Gollancz, 1967 (1953).

Mother and Son, Gollancz, 1967 (1955).

A Father and his Fate, Gollancz, 1969 (1957).

A Heritage and its History, Gollancz, 1960 (1959).

The Mighty and their Fall, Gollancz, 1961.

A God and his Gifts, Gollancz, 1963.

The Last and the First, Gollancz, 1971.

'A Conversation Between I. Compton-Burnett and M. Jourdain', *Orion: A Miscellany*, I, 1945.

'Interview with Miss Compton-Burnett', *Review of English Literature*, III, October 1962.

GENEALOGICAL TREE
INDEX

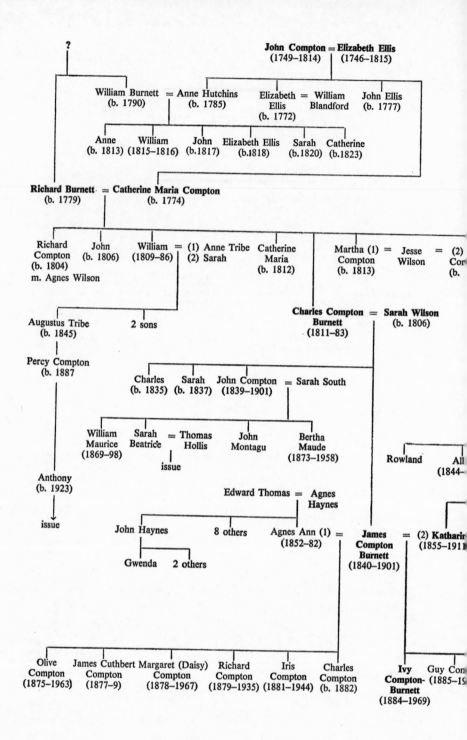

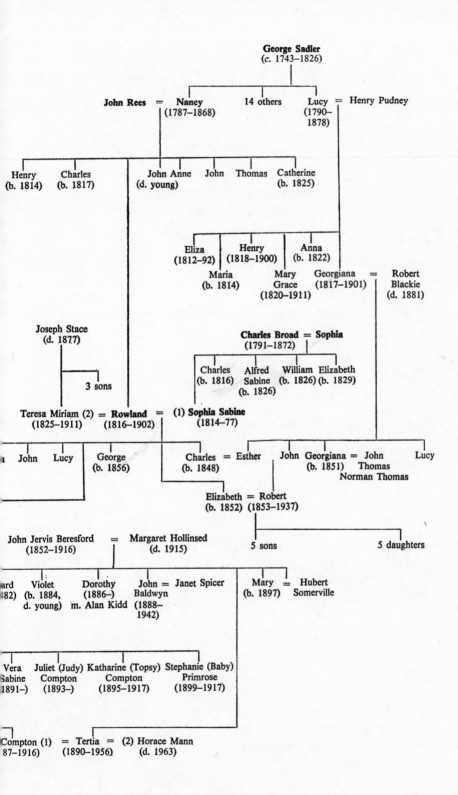

George Sadler
(*c.* 1743–1826)

John Rees = **Nancy**   14 others   Lucy = Henry Pudney
(1787–1868)   (1790–
                                  1878)

Henry   Charles   John Anne   John   Thomas   Catherine
(b. 1814)   (b. 1817)   (d. young)   (b. 1825)

Eliza   Henry   Anna
(1812–92)   (1818–1900)   (b. 1822)
    Maria   Mary   Georgiana   =   Robert
    (b. 1814)   Grace   (1817–1901)   Blackie
              (1820–1911)   (d. 1881)

Joseph Stace   **Charles Broad** = **Sophia**
(d. 1877)   (1791–1872)

                      Charles   Alfred   William   Elizabeth
       3 sons   (b. 1816)   Sabine   (b. 1826)   (b. 1829)
                              (b. 1826)

Teresa Miriam (2) = **Rowland** = (1) **Sophia Sabine**
(1825–1911)   (1816–1902)   (1814–77)

a   John   Lucy   George   Charles = Esther   John   Georgiana = John   Lucy
              (b. 1856)   (b. 1848)   (b. 1851)   Thomas
                                           Norman Thomas

                     Elizabeth = Robert
                     (b. 1852) (1853–1937)

John Jervis Beresford   =   Margaret Hollinsed   5 sons   5 daughters
(1852–1916)   (d. 1915)

ard   Violet   Dorothy   John = Janet Spicer   Mary   =   Hubert
82)   (b. 1884,   (1886–)   Baldwyn   (b. 1897)   Somerville
     d. young)   m. Alan Kidd   (1888–
                             1942)

Vera   Juliet (Judy)   Katharine (Topsy)   Stephanie (Baby)
Sabine   Compton   Compton   Primrose
1891–)   (1893–)   (1895–1917)   (1899–1917)

Compton (1)   =   Tertia   =   (2) Horace Mann
87–1916)   (1890–1956)   (d. 1963)

INDEX

by

SARAH MATTHEWS